KT-555-395

Fodor's 98

London

50p

The complete guide, thoroughly up-to-date

Packed with details that will make your trip

The must-see sights, off and on the beaten path

What to see, what to skip

Vacation itineraries, walking tours, day trips

Smart lodging and dining options

Essential local do's and taboos

Transportation tips

Key contacts, savvy travel advice

When to go, what to pack

Clear, accurate, easy-to-use maps

Background essay

Fodor's Travel Publications, Inc.
New York • Toronto • London • Sydney • Auckland
www.fodors.com/

Fodor's London

EDITOR: Robert I. C. Fisher

Author: Kate Sekules
Editorial Contributors: Robert Andrews, Jacqueline Brown, Audra Epstein, Jane Moss, Heidi Sarna, Ann Saunders, Helayne Schiff, M. T. Schwartzman, Dinah Spritzer, Brandy Whittingham
Editorial Production: Linda K. Schmidt
Maps: David Lindroth Inc., *cartographer*; Robert Blake, *map editor*
Design: Fabrizio La Rocca, *creative director*; Guido Caroti, *associate art director*; Jolie Novak, *photo editor*
Production/Manufacturing: Rebecca Zeiler
Cover Photograph: Richard T. Norwitz

Copyright

Special Sales

CONTENTS

Maps

ON THE ROAD WITH FODOR'S

WE'RE ALWAYS THRILLED to get letters from readers, especially one like this:

It took us an hour to decide what book to buy and we now know we picked the best one. Your book was wonderful, easy to follow, very accurate, and good on pointing out eating places, informal as well as formal. When we saw other people using your book, we would look at each other and smile.

Our editors and writers are deeply committed to making every Fodor's guide "the best one"—not only accurate but always charming, brimming with sound recommendations and solid ideas, right on the mark in describing restaurants and hotels, and full of fascinating facts that make you view what you've traveled to see in a rich new light.

About Our Writers

Our success in achieving our goals—and in helping to make your trip the best of all possible vacations—is a credit to the hard work of our extraordinary writers and editors.

Since **Kate Sekules** lives with a foot on either side of the Atlantic, her mission is getting the best of both worlds—and Fodor's is much the winner. Thanks for her knack for coming up with the *mots*—both *bon* and *juste*—her wit is much in demand: *Vogue, W, Harper's Bazaar, Travel & Leisure, The New Yorker,* and the *Time Out Guide to Eating and Drinking* are just some of the publications she writes for. Happily, she found enough time to do the lion's share of writing for this guidebook. Her idea of a smashing Saturday in old Londontown? The latest avant-garde art show at the Serpentine Gallery, dinner at Wódka, then a Baroque-period concert at Kenwood House.

A New York native, **Brandy Whittingham** is working on a doctoral dissertation on London's Victorian architecture. Stepping in as a helpmate for this edition, Brandy polished the periods on selected features, including the Close-Up, Great Itineraries, and What's Where sections. Her oft-told tale to first-time travelers: "W.S. Gilbert—of the celebrated Gilbert and Sullivan team—once wrote of a novice British Bobbie who lost his way in London's Soho and ended up wandering the streets for twenty years. Caution: the believe-or-not twists, turns, and windings of London's layout can outwit even an expert's sense of direction!"

Being a settler in London, says writer and editor **Jacqueline Brown,** is mainly different from being a true native in that one really tries to get the most out of what the city has to offer. After 20 years of living in the capital, her favorite targets are those culinary and cultural arenas which lie far beyond bully beef and Buckingham Palace. When she is not working as a freelance editor or helping to update the Gold Guide section of this book, Jacqueline can be found strolling the rolling parklands of a National Trust stately home in the countryside with her young family, hoping to pass on the spirit of adventure to them.

Robert I.C. Fisher—editor of *London '98,* art history buff, and Dickens diehard—says the true London can't be found on a map. It lies, rather, somewhere between the imagination and the 19th century. Even so, on a recent sojourn he managed to track down various Dickensian sites, such as Pip's rooms (in The Temple), Tiny Tim's home (on Bayham Street), and Fagin's Den (near Saffron Hill). The last time around, after a hard day's afternoon à la the Beatles, he added a newer sight to his historical researches: the famed album-cover zebra crossing (at Abbey Road).

New This Year

Just in time for the current London renaissance, this edition is loaded with new features, special close-ups, and expanded sections. Like an intricate painting, London takes careful study to fully appreciate its myriad wonders. To help you do that, we've more than doubled our handy London-at-a-glance section—What's Where now lets you in on the big picture, from its broad, rough strokes down to the tiniest details. We've also added terrific Great Itineraries that will lead you through the best of the city, taking into consideration how long you have to spend. Now that the London scene has been making headlines around the world, many of our chapters have greatly expanded scene-setting introductions. Also new are three sidebars, called Close-Ups, that throw the spotlight on a trio of high-interest subjects: Royalty Watching, Shakespeare's Globe Theatre, and the Beatles's London.

And this year, Fodor's joins Rand McNally, the world's largest commercial mapmaker to bring you a detailed color map of London. Just detach it along the perforation and drop it in your tote bag. To further help you navigate the neighborhoods, this edition now features a section called How to Get There, which lists the main bus and tube routes for each London district.

On the Web, check out Fodor's site (www.fodors.com/) for information on major destinations around the world and travel-savvy interactive features. The Web site also lists the 80-plus stations nationwide that carry the Fodor's Travel Show, a live call-in program that airs every weekend. Tune in to hear guests discuss their wonderful adventures—or call in to get answers for your most pressing travel questions.

How to Use This Book

Organization

Up front is the **Gold Guide,** an easy-to-use section divided alphabetically by topic. Under each listing you'll find tips and information that will help you accomplish what you need to in London. You'll also find addresses and telephone numbers of organizations and companies that offer destination-related services and detailed information and publications.

The first chapter in the guide, **Destination: London,** helps get you in the mood for your trip. In this section, you'll find several features: What's Where gets you oriented; New and Noteworthy cues you in on trends and happenings; Pleasures and Pastimes describes the activities and sights that really make London unique; Great Itineraries maps out exciting tours of the city; Fodor's Choice showcases our top picks; and Festivals and Seasonal Events alerts you to special events you'll want to seek out.

The **Exploring** chapter is subdivided by neighborhood; each subsection recommends a walking tour and then lists neighborhood sights alphabetically—which allows you to find your list of must-sees in a snap. The remaining chapters are arranged in alphabetical order by subject (dining, lodging, nightlife and the arts, outdoor activities and sports, shopping, and side trips).

At the end of the book you'll find **Portraits,** which includes an historical dateline and a wonderful essay about London's theaters.

Icons and Symbols

★   Our special recommendations
✕   Restaurant
🏠   Lodging establishment
🦆   Rubber duckie (good for kids)
☞   Sends you to another section of the guide for more information
✉   Address
☎   Telephone number
🕐   Opening and closing times
💰   Admission prices (those we give apply to adults; substantially reduced fees are almost always available for children, students, and senior citizens)

Numbers in white and black circles—②
and ❷, for example—that appear on the maps, in the margins, and within the tours correspond to one another.

Restaurant Reservations and Dress Codes

Reservations are always a good idea; we note only when they're essential or when they are not accepted. Book as far ahead as you can, and reconfirm when you get to town. Unless otherwise noted, the restaurants listed are open daily for lunch and dinner. We mention dress only when men are required to wear a jacket or a jacket and tie.

Credit Cards

The following abbreviations are used: **AE,** American Express; **DC,** Diners Club; **MC,** MasterCard; and **V,** Visa.

Please Write to Us

You can use this book in the confidence that all prices and opening times are based on information supplied to us at press time; Fodor's cannot accept responsibility for any errors. Time inevitably brings changes, so always confirm information when it matters—especially if you're making a detour to visit a specific place. In addition, when making reservations be sure to mention if you have a disability or are traveling with children, if you prefer a private bath or a certain type of bed, or if you have specific dietary needs or other concerns.

Were the restaurants we recommended as described? Did our hotel picks exceed your expectations? Did you find a museum we recommended a waste of time? If you have complaints, we'll look into them and revise our entries when the facts warrant it. If you've discovered a special place that we haven't included, we'll pass the information along to our correspondents and have them check it out. So send us your feedback, positive *and* negative: email us at editors@fodors.com (specifying the name of the book on the subject line) or write the London editor at Fodor's, 201 East 50th Street, New York, New York 10022. Have a wonderful trip!

Karen Cure
Editorial Director

Central London

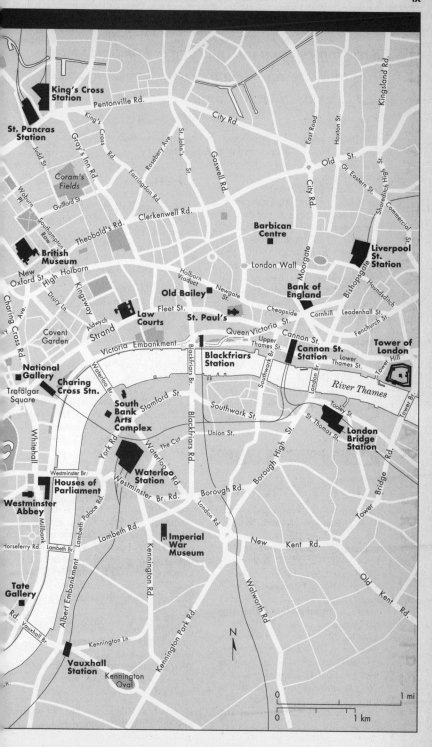

SMART TRAVEL TIPS A TO Z

Basic Information on Traveling in London, Savvy Tips to Make Your Trip a Breeze, and Companies and Organizations to Contact

Half the fun of traveling is looking forward to your trip—but when you look forward, don't just daydream. There are plans to be made, things to learn about, serious work to be done. The following travel tips will give you helpful pointers on many of the questions that arise when planning your trip. In addition, the organizations listed in this section will supplement the information in this guide book. For many travelers, the journey will begin at a Great Britain tourist office: the addresses and telephone numbers for main branches are listed below under the Visitor Information heading. The actual trip will begin when the plane touches down in London—and you start to panic about finding your way from the airport to the city! Don't fret—just consult the Airports & City Transfers section, directly below. Happy landings!

A

AIR TRAVEL

AIRPORTS & CITY TRANSFERS

International flights to London arrive at either **Heathrow Airport** (℡ 011–44–181/759–4321), 15 mi west of London, or at **Gatwick Airport** (℡ 011–44-12931/535–353), 27 mi south of the capital. Flying time is about 6½ hours from New York, 7½ hours from Chicago, and 10 hours from Los Angeles. Most flights from the United States go to Heathrow, which is divided into four terminals, with Terminals 3 and 4 handling transatlantic flights (British Airways uses Terminal 4). Gatwick is London's second gateway. It has grown from a European airport into an airport that serves 21 scheduled U.S. destinations. A third, new, state-of-the-art airport, **Stansted,** is to the east of the city. It handles mainly European and domestic traffic, although there is a scheduled service from New York. There are fast connections from

all the London airports into the capital.

➤ BETWEEN THE AIRPORT AND DOWN-TOWN: **Heathrow:** The quickest and least expensive route into London is via the **Piccadilly Line** of the **Underground** (London's subway system). Trains on the "Tube" run every four to eight minutes from all four terminals; the 40-minute trip costs £3.20 one-way and connects with London's extensive tube system.

London Transport (℡ 0171/222–1234) runs two bus services from the airport; each costs £6 one-way and £10 round-trip and travel time each direction is about one hour. The **Airbus A1** leaves for Victoria Station, with stops along Cromwell Road, at Earls Court, and at Hyde Park Corner, every 30 minutes 5:40 AM–8:30 PM. The **Airbus A2** leaves for King's Cross and Euston, with stops at Marble Arch, and Russell Square every 30 minutes 6 am–9:30 pm.

Gatwick: Fast, nonstop **Gatwick Express** trains leave for Victoria Station every 15 minutes 5:30 AM–9:45 PM; hourly 10 PM–5 AM. The 30-minute trip costs £8.90 one-way. An hourly local train also runs all night. Hourly bus services (5:20 AM to 10 PM) are provided by Green Line Coaches, including **Speedlink's Flightline 777** to Victoria Coach Station. This takes about 70 minutes and costs £7.50 one-way.

Stansted: London's newest airport, opened in 1991, serves mainly European destinations. The **Stansted Skytrain** to Liverpool Street Station runs every half hour and costs £10 one-way.

Cars and taxis drive into London on M4; the trip can take more than an hour, depending on traffic, from Heathrow. The taxi fare is about £25, plus tip. From Gatwick, the taxi fare is at least £35, plus tip; traffic can be very heavy.

MAJOR AIRLINE OR LOW-COST CARRIER?

Most people choose a flight based on price. Yet there are other issues to consider. Major airlines offer the greatest number of departures; smaller or regional carriers—including low-cost and no-frill airlines—usually have a more limited number of flights daily. Major airlines have frequent-flyer partners, which allow you to credit mileage earned on one airline to your account with another. Low-cost airlines offer a definite price advantage and fewer restrictions, such as advance-purchase requirements. Safety-wise, low-cost carriers as a group have a good history, but **check the safety record before booking** any low-cost carrier; call the Federal Aviation Administration's Consumer Hotline (☞ Airline Complaints, *below*).

➤ MAJOR AIRLINES: **American Airlines** (☎ 800/433–7300; in London, ☎ 0181/572–5555) to Heathrow, Gatwick. **British Airways** (☎ 800/247–9297; in London, ☎ 0345/222–111) to Heathrow, Gatwick. **Continental** (☎ 800/231–0856; in London ☎ 0800/776–464) to Gatwick. **Delta** (☎ 800/241–4141; in London, ☎ 0800/414–767); to Heathrow, Gatwick. **Northwest Airlines** (☎ 800/447–4747; in London, ☎ 0990/561–000) to Gatwick. **United** (☎ 800/241–6522; in London, ☎ 0181/990–9900) to Heathrow. **TWA** (☎ 800/892–4141; in London, ☎ 01293/439–0707) to Gatwick. **Virgin Atlantic** (☎ 800/862–8621; in London, ☎ 01293/747–747) to Heathrow, Gatwick.

British Airways (☎ 800/AIRWAYS) is the national flag carrier and offers mostly nonstop flights from 18 U.S. cities to Heathrow and Gatwick airports, along with flights to Manchester, Birmingham, and Glasgow. As the leading British carrier, it offers a myriad of add-on options, helping to bring down ticket costs. In addition, it has a vast program of discount airfare/hotel packages.

GET THE LOWEST FARE

The least-expensive airfares to London are priced for round-trip travel. Major airlines usually require that you **book far in advance and stay at least seven days** and no more than 30 to get the lowest fares. Ask about "ultrasaver" fares, which are the cheapest; they must be booked 90 days in advance and are nonrefundable. A little more expensive are "supersaver" fares, which require only a 30-day advance purchase. Remember that penalties for refunds or scheduling changes are stiffer for international tickets, usually about $150. International flights are also sensitive to the season: **plan to fly in the off season** for the cheapest fares. If your destination or home city has more than one gateway, **compare prices to and from different airports.** Also price flights scheduled for off-peak hours, which may be significantly less expensive.

DON'T STOP UNLESS YOU MUST

When you book, **look for nonstop flights** and **remember that "direct" flights stop at least once.** International flights on a country's flag carrier are almost always nonstop; U.S. airlines often fly direct. Try to **avoid connecting flights,** which require a change of plane. Two airlines may jointly operate a connecting flight, so ask if your airline operates every segment—you may find that your preferred carrier flies you only part of the way.

USE AN AGENT

Travel agents, especially those who specialize in finding the lowest fares (☞ Discounts & Deals, *below*), can be especially helpful when booking a plane ticket. When you're quoted a price, **ask your agent if the price is likely to get any lower.** Good agents know the seasonal fluctuations of airfares and can usually anticipate a sale or fare war. However, waiting can be risky: The fare could go *up* as seats become scarce, and you may wait so long that your preferred flight sells out. A wait-and-see strategy works best if your plans are flexible, but if you must arrive and depart on certain dates, don't delay.

CHECK WITH CONSOLIDATORS

Consolidators buy tickets for scheduled flights at reduced rates from the airlines then sell them at prices that beat the best fare available directly from the airlines, usually without advance restrictions. Sometimes you can even get your money back if you need to return the ticket. Carefully read the fine print detailing penalties for changes and cancellations, and **confirm your consolidator reservation with the airline.**

➤ CONSOLIDATORS: **United States Air Consolidators Association** (✉ 925 L St., Suite 220, Sacramento, CA 95814, ☎ 916/441–4166, FAX 916/441–3520).

CONSIDER A CHARTER

Charters usually have the lowest fares but are not dependable. Departures are infrequent and seldom on time, flights can be delayed for up to 48 hours or can be canceled for any reason up to 10 days before you're scheduled to leave. Itineraries and prices can change after you've booked your flight, so you must **be very careful to choose a legitimate charter carrier.** Don't commit to a charter operator that doesn't follow proper booking procedures. Be especially careful when buying a charter ticket. Read the fine print regarding refund policies. If you can't pay with a credit card, **make your check payable to a charter carrier's escrow account** (unless you're dealing with a travel agent, in which case his or her check should be made payable to the escrow account). The name of the bank should be in the charter contract.

AVOID GETTING BUMPED

Airlines routinely overbook planes, knowing that not everyone with a ticket will show up, but sometimes everyone does. When that happens, airlines ask for volunteers to give up their seats. In return these volunteers usually get a certificate for a free flight and are rebooked on the next flight out. If there are not enough volunteers the airline must choose who will be denied boarding. The first to get bumped are passengers who checked in late and those flying on discounted tickets, **so get to the gate and check in as early as possible,** especially during peak periods.

Always **bring a photo ID to the airport.** You may be asked to show it before you are allowed to check in.

ENJOY THE FLIGHT

For more legroom, **request an emergency-aisle seat**; don't, however, sit in the row in front of the emergency aisle or in front of a bulkhead, where seats may not recline.

If you don't like airline food, **ask for special meals when booking.** These can be vegetarian, low-cholesterol, or kosher, for example.

To avoid jet lag try to maintain a normal routine while traveling. At night **get some sleep.** By day **eat light meals, drink water (not alcohol), and move about the cabin** to stretch your legs.

Some carriers have prohibited smoking throughout their systems; others allow smoking only on certain routes or even certain departures from that route, so **contact your carrier regarding its smoking policy.**

B

BUS TRAVEL

In central London, buses are traditionally bright red double- and single-deckers, though there are now many privately owned buses of different colors. Not all buses run the full length of their route at all times; check with the driver or conductor. On some buses you pay the conductor after finding a seat, on others you pay the driver upon boarding. Bus stops are clearly indicated; the main stops have a red LT symbol on a plain white background. When the word "Request" is written across the sign, you must flag the bus down. Buses are a good way of seeing the town, but **don't take one if you are in a hurry.** Single fares start at 60p for short hops (90p in the central zone).

London is divided into six concentric zones for both bus and tube fares: the more zones you cross, the higher the fare. Regular single-journey or round-trip **One Day Travelcards** (£2.80–£3.80) allow unrestricted travel on bus and tube after 9:30 AM and all day on weekends and national holidays. **LT Cards** (£3.90–£6.50) do not have any restricted times of travel. **Visitor Travelcards** (£3.90) are the same as the One Day Travelcards, but with the bonus of a booklet of money-off vouchers to major attractions (these are also available in the United States, for three, four, and seven days; contact ✉ BritRail Travel International, 1500 Broadway, New York, NY 10036, ☎ 212/382–3737).

Traveling without a valid ticket makes you liable for an on-the-spot fine (£10 at press time), so always pay your fare before you travel. For more information, there are **LT Travel Information Centres** at the following tube stations: Euston, Hammersmith, King's Cross, Oxford Circus, Piccadilly Circus, St James's Park, Victoria, and Heathrow (in Terminals 1 and 2); open 6AM–12 AM, or call 0171/222–1234.

C

CAMERAS, CAMCORDERS, & COMPUTERS

Always **keep your film, tape, or computer disks out of the sun.** Carry an extra supply of batteries, and **be prepared to turn on your camera, camcorder, or laptop** to prove to security personnel that the device is real. Always **ask for hand inspection of film,** which becomes clouded after successive exposure to airport x-ray machines, and **keep videotapes and computer disks away from metal detectors.**

➤ PHOTO HELP: Kodak Information Center (☎ 800/242–2424). *Kodak Guide to Shooting Great Travel Pictures,* available in bookstores or from Fodor's Travel Publications (☎ 800/533–6478; $16.50 plus $4 shipping).

CUSTOMS

Before departing, **register your foreign-made camera or laptop with U.S. Customs** (☞ Customs & Duties, *below*). If your equipment is U.S.-made, call the consulate of the country you'll be visiting to find out whether the device should be registered with local customs upon arrival.

CAR RENTAL

When considering a rental car, it's worth noting that unless you are going to be traveling extensively outside London, a car in the city is often more of a liability than an asset. Remember that Britain drives on the left, and the rest of Europe on the right. Therefore, you may want to leave your rented car in Britain and pick up a left-side drive if you cross the Channel. (☞ Driving, *below*.)

Rates in London begin at $39 a day and $136 a week for an economy car with air conditioning, a manual transmission, and unlimited mileage. This does not include tax on car rentals, which is 17.5%.

➤ MAJOR AGENCIES: **Alamo** (☎ 800/879–2847 in Canada). **Budget** (☎ 800/522–9696 or 0800/272–2000 in the U.K.). **Dollar** (☎ 800/800–4000; 0990/565656 in the U.K., where it is known as Eurodollar). **Hertz** (☎ 800/654–3001, 800/263–0600 in Canada, 0345/555888 in the U.K.). **National InterRent** (☎ 800/227–3876; 0345/222525 in the U.K., where it is known as Europcar InterRent).

CUT COSTS

To get the best deal, **book through a travel agent who is willing to shop around.**

Also **ask your travel agent about a company's customer-service record.** How has it responded to late plane arrivals and vehicle mishaps? Are there often lines at the rental counter, and, if you're traveling during a holiday period, does a confirmed reservation guarantee you a car?

Be sure to **look into wholesalers,** companies that do not own fleets but rent in bulk from those that do and often offer better rates than traditional car-rental operations. Prices are best during off-peak periods. Rentals booked through wholesalers must be paid for before you leave the United States.

➤ RENTAL WHOLESALERS: **Auto Europe** (☎ 207/828–2525 or 800/223–5555). **Europe by Car** (☎ 212/581–3040 or 800/223–1516, FAX 212/246–1458). **DER Tours** (✉ Box 1606, Des Plaines, IL 60017, ☎ 800/782–2424, FAX 800/282–7474).

NEED INSURANCE?

When driving a rented car you are generally responsible for any damage to or loss of the vehicle. Before you rent, **see what coverage you already have** under the terms of your personal auto-insurance policy and credit cards.

Collision policies that car-rental companies sell for European rentals typically do not cover stolen vehicles. Before you buy additional coverage for theft, find out if your credit card or personal auto insurance will cover the loss.

BEWARE SURCHARGES

Before you pick up a car in one city and leave it in another, **ask about drop-off charges or one-way service fees,** which can be substantial. Note, too, that some rental agencies charge extra if you return the car before the time specified on your contract. To avoid a hefty refueling fee, **fill the tank just before you turn in the car,** but be aware that gas stations near the rental outlet may overcharge.

MEET THE REQUIREMENTS

In London your own driver's license is acceptable. An International Driver's Permit is a good idea; it's available from the American or Canadian automobile association, or, in the United Kingdom, from the Automobile Association or Royal Automobile Club.

THE CHANNEL TUNNEL

Short of flying, the "Chunnel" is the fastest way to cross the English Channel: 35 minutes from Folkestone to Calais, 60 minutes from motorway to motorway, or 3 hours from London's Waterloo Station to Paris's Gare du Nord.

➤ CAR TRANSPORT: **Le Shuttle** (☎ 800/388–3876 in the U.S., 0990/353535 in the U.K.).

➤ PASSENGER SERVICE: In the U.K., **Eurostar** (☎ 0345/881881), **InterCity Europe** (✉ Victoria Station, London, ☎ 0171/834–2345, 0171/828–0892 for credit-card bookings). In the U.S., **BritRail Travel** (☎ 800/677–8585), **Rail Europe** (☎ 800/942–4866).

CHILDREN & TRAVEL

CHILDREN IN LONDON

Be sure to plan ahead and **involve your youngsters** as you outline your trip. When packing, include things to keep them busy en route. On sightseeing days try to schedule activities of special interest to your children. If you are renting a car don't forget to **arrange for a car seat** when you reserve.

➤ LOCAL INFORMATION: **Kidsline** (☎ 0171/222–8070; open during school time only). **Visitorcall,** London

Tourist Board's dedicated lines: What's on for Children (☎ 0839 123404) and Places for Children to Go (☎ 0839 123424), both 50p per minute.

The **Children's Guide to London,** by Christopher Pick (✉ Cadogan Books, 16 Lower Marsh, London SE1 7RJ; £3.50), and **Kids' London,** by Elizabeth Holt and Molly Perham (✉ St. Martin's Press, 175 5th Ave., New York, NY 10010; $5.95), cover the subject. Up-to-date information is available in **Kids Out!** magazine, available at good newsstands during holiday seasons (£1.50). The information sheet, **Children's London** (available free from the London Tourist Board, Tourist Information Centre, Victoria Station Forecourt, London SW1V 1JT and other London TICs) gives a complete story.

➤ BABY-SITTING: **The Nanny Service** (✉ 9 Paddington St., London W1M 3LA, ☎ 0171/935–3515). **Nanny Connection** (✉ Stern House, 85 Gloucester Rd., London SW7 4SS, ☎ 0171/835–2277). **Universal Aunts** (✉ Box 304, London SW4 0NN).

HOTELS

Most hotels in London allow children under a certain age to stay in their parents' room at no extra charge, but others charge them as extra adults; be sure to **ask about the cutoff age for children's discounts.**

➤ BEST CHOICES: Hotels that are noticeably family- and child-friendly include **Forte Hotels** (☎ 0171/301–2000), **Basil Street Hotel** (✉ Basil St., Knightsbridge, London SW3 1AH, ☎ 0171/581–3311), and **Edward Lear** (✉ 30 Seymour St., London W1H 5WD, ☎ 0171/402–5401).

FLYING

As a general rule, infants under two not occupying a seat fly at greatly reduced fares and occasionally for free. If your children are two or older **ask about children's airfares.**

In general the adult baggage allowance applies to children paying half or more of the adult fare. When booking, **ask about carry-on allowances for those traveling with infants.** In general, for babies charged 10% of the adult fare you are allowed one carry-on bag and a collapsible stroller, which may have to be checked; you may be limited to less if the flight is full.

According to the FAA it's a good idea to use safety seats aloft for children weighing less than 40 pounds. Airlines, however, can set their own policies: U.S. carriers allow FAA-approved models but usually require that you buy a ticket, even if your child would otherwise ride free, since the seats must be strapped into regular seats. Airline rules vary regarding their use, so it's important to **check your airline's policy about using safety seats during takeoff and landing.** Safety seats cannot obstruct any of the other passengers in the row, so get an appropriate seat assignment as early as possible.

When making your reservation, **request children's meals or a free-standing bassinet** if you need them; the latter are available only to those seated at the bulkhead, where there's enough legroom. Remember, however, that bulkhead seats may not have their own overhead bins, and there's no storage space in front of you—a major inconvenience.

GROUP TRAVEL

If you're planning to take your kids on a tour, look for companies that specialize in family travel.

➤ FAMILY-FRIENDLY TOUR OPERATORS: **Grandtravel** (✉ 6900 Wisconsin Ave., Suite 706, Chevy Chase, MD 20815, ☎ 301/986–0790 or 800/247–7651) for people traveling with grandchildren ages 7–17. **Families Welcome!** (✉ 92 N. Main St., Ashland, OR 97520, ☎ 541/482–6121 or 800/ 326–0724, ℻ 541/482–0660).

Whenever possible, **pay with a major credit card** so you can cancel payment if there's a problem, provided that you can provide documentation. This is a good practice whether you're buying travel arrangements before your trip or shopping at your destination.

If you're doing business with a particular company for the first time, **contact your local Better Business Bureau and the attorney general's offices** in your state and the company's home state, as well. Have any complaints been filed?

Finally, if you're buying a package or tour, always **consider travel insurance that includes default coverage** (☞ Insurance, *above*).

➤ LOCAL BBBs: **Council of Better Business Bureaus** (✉ 4200 Wilson Blvd., Suite 800, Arlington, VA 22203, ☎ 703/276–0100, ℻ 703/525–8277).

When shopping, **keep receipts for all of your purchases.** Upon reentering the country, be ready to show customs officials what you've bought. If you feel a duty is incorrect, appeal the assessment. If you object to the way your clearance was handled, get the inspector's badge number. In either case, first ask to see a supervisor, then write to the port director at the address listed on your receipt. Send a copy of the receipt and other appropriate documentation. If you still don't get satisfaction you can take your case to customs headquarters in Washington.

ENTERING GREAT BRITAIN

There are two levels of duty-free allowance for travelers entering Great Britain: one for goods bought outside the EU, the other for goods bought in the EU (Belgium, Greece, the Netherlands, Denmark, Italy, Portugal, France, the Irish Republic, Spain, Germany, or Luxembourg).

In the first category, you may import duty-free: 200 cigarettes or 100 cigarillos or 50 cigars or 250 grams of tobacco; 2 liters of table wine and, in addition, (a) 1 liter of alcohol over 22% by volume (most spirits), (b) 2 liters of alcohol under 22% by volume (fortified or sparkling wine or liqueurs), or (c) 2 more liters of table wine; 50 milliliters of perfume; ¼ liter of toilet water; and other goods up to a value of £136, but not more than 50 liters of beer or 25 cigarette lighters.

In the second category, the EU has set guidelines for the import of certain goods. Following side trips entirely within the EU, you no longer need to go through customs on your return to the United Kingdom; however, if you exceed the guideline amounts, you may be required to prove that the goods are for your personal use only ("personal use" includes gifts). The guideline levels are: 800 cigarettes, 400 cigarillos, 200 cigars, and 1 kilogram of smoking tobacco, plus 10 liters of spirits, 20 liters of fortified wine, 90 liters of wine, and 110 liters of beer, plus goods to the value of £71. No animals or pets of any kind can be brought into the United Kingdom without a lengthy quarantine. The penalties are severe and are strictly enforced. Similarly, fresh meats, plants and vegetables, controlled drugs, and firearms and ammunition may not be brought into Great Britain.

You will face no customs formalities if you enter Scotland or Wales from any other part of the United Kingdom, though anyone coming from Northern Ireland should expect a security check.

ENTERING THE U.S.

You may bring home $400 worth of foreign goods duty-free if you've been out of the country for at least 48 hours and haven't already used the $400 allowance or any part of it in the past 30 days.

Travelers 21 and older may bring back 1 liter of alcohol duty-free. In addition, regardless of your age, you are allowed 200 cigarettes and 100 non-Cuban cigars. Antiques, which the U.S. Customs Service defines as objects more than 100 years old, enter duty-free, as do original works of art done entirely by hand, including paintings, drawings, and sculptures.

You may also send packages home duty-free: up to $200 worth of goods for personal use, with a limit of one parcel per addressee per day (and no alcohol or tobacco products or perfume worth more than $5); label the package PERSONAL USE, and attach a list of its contents and their retail value. Do not label the package UNSOLICITED GIFT, or your duty-free exemption will drop to $100. Mailed items do not affect your duty-free allowance on your return.

➤ INFORMATION: **U.S. Customs Service** (Inquiries, ✉ Box 7407, Wash-

ington, DC 20044, ☎ 202/927–6724; complaints, ✉ Commissioner's Office, 1301 Constitution Ave. NW, Washington, DC 20229; registration of equipment, ✉ Resource Management, 1301 Constitution Ave. NW, Washington DC, 20229, ☎ 202/927–0540).

ENTERING CANADA

If you've been out of Canada for at least seven days you may bring in C$500 worth of goods duty-free. If you've been away for fewer than seven days but more than 48 hours, the duty-free allowance drops to C$200; if your trip lasts 24–48 hours, the allowance is C$50. You may not pool allowances with family members. Goods claimed under the C$500 exemption may follow you by mail; those claimed under the lesser exemptions must accompany you.

Alcohol and tobacco products may be included in the seven-day and 48-hour exemptions but not in the 24-hour exemption. If you meet the age requirements of the province or territory through which you reenter Canada you may bring in, duty-free, 1.14 liters (40 imperial ounces) of wine or liquor or 24 12-ounce cans or bottles of beer or ale. If you are 16 or older you may bring in, duty-free, 200 cigarettes and 50 cigars; these items must accompany you.

You may send an unlimited number of gifts worth up to C$60 each duty-free to Canada. Label the package UNSOLICITED GIFT—VALUE UNDER $60. Alcohol and tobacco are excluded.

➤ INFORMATION: **Revenue Canada** (✉ 2265 St. Laurent Blvd. S, Ottawa, Ontario K1G 4K3, ☎ 613/993–0534, 800/461–9999 in Canada).

D

DISABILITIES & ACCESSIBILITY

ACCESS IN LONDON

➤ LOCAL RESOURCES: Contact **London Transport's Unit for Disabled Passengers** (✉ 172 Buckingham Palace Rd., London SW1W 9TN ☎ 0171/918–3312) for details on **Stationlink**, a wheelchair-accessible "midibus" service, as well as information on other access information. **Artsline** (☎ 0171/388–2227) provides information on the accessibility of arts events.

TIPS AND HINTS

When discussing accessibility with an operator or reservationist, ask hard questions. Are there any stairs, inside *or* out? Are there grab bars next to the toilet *and* in the shower/tub? How wide is the doorway to the room? To the bathroom? For the most extensive facilities meeting the latest legal specifications, **opt for newer accommodations,** which are more likely to have been designed with access in mind. Older buildings or ships may offer more limited facilities. Be sure to discuss your needs before booking.

➤ COMPLAINTS: **Disability Rights Section** (✉ U.S. Department of Justice, Box 66738, Washington, DC 20035–6738, ☎ 202/514–0301 or 800/514–0301, FAX 202/307–1198, TTY 202/514–0383 or 800/514–0383) for general complaints. **Aviation Consumer Protection Division** (☞ Air Travel, *above*) for airline-related problems. **Civil Rights Office** (✉ U.S. Department of Transportation, Departmental Office of Civil Rights, S-30, 400 7th St. SW, Room 10215, Washington, DC, 20590, ☎ 202/366–4648) for problems with surface transportation.

TRAVEL AGENCIES & TOUR OPERATORS

The Americans with Disabilities Act requires that travel firms serve the needs of all travelers. That said, you should note that some agencies and operators specialize in making travel arrangements for individuals and groups with disabilities.

➤ TRAVELERS WITH MOBILITY PROBLEMS: **Access Adventures** (✉ 206 Chestnut Ridge Rd., Rochester, NY 14624, ☎ 716/889–9096), run by a former physical-rehabilitation counselor. **Accessible Journeys** (✉ 35 W. Sellers Ave., Ridley Park, PA 19078, ☎ 610/521–0339 or 800/846–4537, FAX 610/521–6959), for escorted tours exclusively for travelers with mobility impairments. **Flying Wheels Travel** (✉ 143 W. Bridge St., Box 382, Owatonna, MN 55060, ☎ 507/451–5005 or 800/535–6790), a travel agency specializing in European cruises and tours. **Hinsdale Travel Service** (✉ 201 E. Ogden Ave., Suite 100, Hinsdale, IL 60521, ☎ 630/325–1335), a travel agency that benefits from the advice of wheelchair traveler Janice Perkins. **Wheelchair Journeys** (✉ 16979 Redmond Way, Redmond, WA 98052, ☎ 206/885–2210 or 800/313–4751), for general travel arrangements.

DISCOUNTS & DEALS

Be a smart shopper and **compare all your options before making a choice.** A plane ticket bought with a promotional coupon may not be cheaper than the least expensive fare from a discount ticket agency. For high-price travel purchases, such as packages or tours, keep in mind that what you get is just as important as what you save. Just because something is cheap doesn't mean it's a bargain.

LOOK IN YOUR WALLET

When you use your credit card to make travel purchases you may get free travel-accident insurance, collision-damage insurance, and medical or legal assistance, depending on the card and the bank that issued it. American Express, MasterCard, and Visa provide one or more of these services, so get a copy of your credit card's travel-benefits policy. If you are a member of the American Automobile Association (AAA) or an oil-company-sponsored road-assistance plan, always **ask hotel or car-rental reservationists about auto-club discounts.** Some clubs offer additional discounts on tours, cruises, or admission to attractions. And don't forget that auto-club membership entitles you to free maps and trip-planning services.

DIAL FOR DOLLARS

To save money, look into "1-800" discount reservations services, which use their buying power to get a better price on hotels, airline tickets, even car rentals. When booking a room, always **call the hotel's local toll-free number** (if one is available) rather than the central reservations number—you'll often get a better price. Always ask about special packages or corporate rates.

When shopping for the best deal on hotels and car rentals **look for guaranteed exchange rates,** which protect you against a falling dollar. With your rate locked in you won't pay more even if the price goes up in the local currency.

➤ AIRLINE TICKETS: ☎ 800/FLY–4–LESS.

➤ HOTEL ROOMS: **Hotels Plus** (☎ 800/235–0909). **Hotel Reservations Network (HRN)** (☎ 800/964–6835). **International Marketing & Travel Concepts (IMTC)** (☎ 800/790–4682).

SAVE ON COMBOS

Packages and guided tours can both save you money, but don't confuse the two. When you buy a package your travel remains independent, just as though you had planned and booked the trip yourself. Fly/drive packages, which combine airfare and car rental, are often a good deal. In cities, ask the local visitors bureau about hotel packages. These often include tickets to major museum exhibits and other special events.

JOIN A CLUB?

Many companies sell discounts in the form of travel clubs and coupon books, but these cost money. You must use participating advertisers to get a deal, and only after you recoup the initial membership cost or book price do you begin to save. If you plan to use the club or coupons frequently you may save considerably. Before signing up, find out what discounts you get for free.

➤ DISCOUNT CLUBS: **Entertainment Travel Editions** (✉ Box 1068, Trumbull, CT 06611, ☎ 800/445–4137; $28–$53, depending on destination). **Great American Traveler** (✉ Box 27965, Salt Lake City, UT 84127, ☎ 800/548–2812; $49.95 per year). **Moment's Notice Discount Travel Club** (✉ 7301 New Utrecht Ave., Brooklyn, NY 11204, ☎ 718/234–6295; $25 per year, single or family). **Privilege Card International** (✉ 201 E. Commerce St., Suite 198, Youngstown, OH 44503, ☎ 330/746–5211 or 800/236–9732; $74.95 per year). **Sears's Mature Outlook** (✉ Box 9390, Des Moines, IA 50306, ☎ 800/336–6330; $14.95 per year). **Travelers Advantage** (✉ CUC Travel Service, 3033 S. Parker Rd., Suite 1000, Aurora, CO 80014, ☎ 800/548–1116 or 800/648–4037; $49 per year, single or family). **Worldwide Discount Travel Club** (✉ 1674

Meridian Ave., Miami Beach, FL 33139, ☎ 305/534–2082; $50 per year family, $40 single).

DRIVING

The best advice on driving in London is: don't. Because the capital grew up as a series of villages, there never was a central plan for London's streets, and the result is a winding mass of chaos, aggravated by a passion for one-way streets.

If you must risk life and limb, however, note that the speed limit is 30 mph in the royal parks, as well as (theoretically) in all streets—unless you see the large 40 mph signs (and small repeater signs attached to lampposts) found only in the suburbs. Other basic rules: Pedestrians have right-of-way on "zebra" crossings (those black-and-white stripes that stretch across the street between two Belisha beacons—orange-flashing globe lights on posts). The curb on each side of the zebra crossing has zigzag markings. It is illegal to park within the zigzag area, or to pass another vehicle at a zebra crossing. At other crossings pedestrians must yield to traffic, but they do have right-of-way over traffic turning left at controlled crossings—if they have the nerve.

Traffic lights sometimes have arrow-style lights directing left or right turns; it is therefore important not to get into the turn lane if you mean to go straight ahead, so try to catch a glimpse of the road markings in time. The use of horns is prohibited between 11:30 PM and 7 AM.

You can park at night in 30-mph zones, provided you are within 25 yards of a lighted street lamp, but not within 15 yards of a road junction. To park on a bus route, you must show side (parking) lights, but you'll probably get a ticket anyway. On "Red Routes"—busy stretches with red lines painted in the gutter—you may not even stop to let a passenger out. During the day—and probably at all times—it is safest to believe that you can park nowhere except at a meter, in a garage, or where you are sure there are no lines or signs; otherwise, you run the risk of a towing cost of about £100, or a wheel clamp, which costs about the same, since you pay to have the clamp removed, plus the one or two tickets you'll have earned first. It is also illegal to park on the sidewalk.

LONDON DISTRICTS

Greater London is divided into 32 boroughs—33, counting the City of London, which has all the powers of a London borough. More useful for finding your way around, however, are the subdivisions of London into various postal districts. Throughout the guide we've listed the full postal code for places you're likely to be contacting by mail, although you'll find the first half of the code more important. The first one or two letters give the location: N=north, NW=northwest, etc. Don't expect the numbering to be logical, however. You won't, for example, find W2 next to W3.

E

ELECTRICITY

To use your U.S.-purchased electric-powered equipment, **bring a converter and adapter.** The electrical current in Great Britain is 220 volts, 50 cycles alternating current (AC); wall outlets take continental-type plugs, with two round prongs.

If your appliances are dual-voltage, you'll need only an adapter. Don't use 110-volt outlets, marked FOR SHAVERS ONLY, for high-wattage appliances such as blow-dryers. Most laptops operate equally well on 110 and 220 volts and so require only an adapter.

G

GAY & LESBIAN TRAVEL

➤ TOUR OPERATORS: **R.S.V.P. Travel Productions** (✉ 2800 University Ave. SE, Minneapolis, MN 55414, ☎ 612/379–4697 or 800/328–7787), for cruises and resort vacations for gays. **Hanns Ebensten Travel** (✉ 513 Fleming St., Key West, FL 33040, ☎ 305/294–8174), one of the oldest operators in the gay market.

➤ GAY- AND LESBIAN-FRIENDLY TRAVEL AGENCIES: **Advance Damron** (✉ 1 Greenway Plaza, Suite 800, Houston, TX 77046, ☎ 713/682–2002 or 800/695–0880, FAX 713/888–1010). **Club Travel** (✉ 8739 Santa Monica Blvd., West Hollywood, CA 90069, ☎ 310/358–2200 or 800/429–

8747). **Islanders/Kennedy Travel** (✉ 183 W. 10th St., New York, NY 10014, ☎ 212/242–3222 or 800/988–1181). **Now Voyager** (✉ 4406 18th St., San Francisco, CA 94114, ☎ 415/626–1169 or 800/255–6951). **Yellowbrick Road** (✉ 1500 W. Balmoral Ave., Chicago, IL 60640, ☎ 773/561–1800 or 800/642–2488). **Skylink Women's Travel** (✉ 3577 Moorland Ave., Santa Rosa, CA 95407, ☎ 707/585–8355 or 800/225–5759), serving lesbian travelers.

H

HEALTH

MEDICAL PLANS

No one plans to get sick while traveling, but it happens, so consider signing up with a medical-assistance company. Members get doctor referrals, emergency evacuation or repatriation, 24-hour telephone hot lines for medical consultation, cash for emergencies, and other personal and legal assistance. Coverage varies by plan, so **review the benefits carefully.**

➤ MEDICAL-ASSISTANCE COMPANIES: **International SOS Assistance** (✉ Box 11568, Philadelphia, PA 19116, ☎ 215/244–1500 or 800/523–8930; ✉ Box 466, pl. Bonaventure, Montréal, Québec H5A 1C1, ☎ 514/874–7674 or 800/363–0263; ✉ 7 Old Lodge Pl., St. Margarets, Twickenham TW1 1RQ, England, ☎ 0181/744–0033). **MEDEX Assistance Corporation** (✉ Box 5375, Timonium, MD 21094, ☎ 410/453–6300 or 800/537–2029). **Traveler's Emergency Network** (✉ 3100 Tower Blvd., Suite 1000B, Durham, NC 27707, ☎ 919/490–6055 or 800/275–4836, FAX 919/493–8262). **TravMed** (✉ Box 5375, Timonium, MD 21094, ☎ 410/453–6380 or 800/732–5309). **Worldwide Assistance Services** (✉ 1133 15th St. NW, Suite 400, Washington, DC 20005, ☎ 202/331–1609 or 800/821–2828, FAX 202/828–5896).

I

INSURANCE

Travel insurance is the best way to **protect yourself against financial loss.** The most useful policies are trip-cancellation-and-interruption, default, medical, and comprehensive insurance.

Without insurance you will lose all or most of your money if you cancel your trip, regardless of the reason. It's essential that you buy trip-cancellation-and-interruption insurance, particularly if your airline ticket, cruise, or package tour is nonrefundable and cannot be changed. When considering how much coverage you need, look for a policy that will cover the cost of your trip plus the nondiscounted price of a one-way airline ticket, should you need to return home early. Also **consider default or bankruptcy insurance,** which protects you against a supplier's failure to deliver.

Medicare generally does not cover health-care costs outside the United States, nor do many privately issued policies. If your own policy does not cover you outside the United States, consider buying supplemental medical coverage. **Remember that travel health insurance is different from a medical-assistance plan** (☞ Health, *above*).

Citizens of the United Kingdom can buy an annual travel-insurance policy valid for most vacations during the year in which it's purchased. If you are pregnant or have a preexisting medical condition, make sure you're covered.

If you have purchased an expensive vacation, particularly one that involves travel abroad, comprehensive insurance is a must. **Look for comprehensive policies that include trip-delay insurance,** which will protect you in the event that weather problems cause you to miss your flight, tour, or cruise. A few insurers sell waivers for preexisting medical conditions. Companies that offer both features include Access America, Carefree Travel, Travel Insured International, and Travel Guard (☞ *below*).

Always buy travel insurance directly from the insurance company; **if you buy it from a travel agency or tour operator that goes out of business you probably will not be covered for the agency or operator's default, a major risk. Before you make any purchase,** review your existing health and home-owner's policies **to find out whether they cover expenses incurred while traveling.**

➤ TRAVEL INSURERS: In the U.S., **Access America** (✉ 6600 W. Broad St., Richmond, VA 23230, ☎ 804/285–3300 or 800/284–8300), **Carefree Travel Insurance** (✉ Box 9366, 100 Garden City Plaza, Garden City, NY 11530, ☎ 516/294–0220 or 800/323–3149), **Near Travel Services** (✉ Box 1339, Calumet City, IL 60409, ☎ 708/868–6700 or 800/654–6700), **Travel Guard International** (✉ 1145 Clark St., Stevens Point, WI 54481, ☎ 715/345–0505 or 800/826–1300), **Travel Insured International** (✉ Box 280568, East Hartford, CT 06128–0568, ☎ 860/528–7663 or 800/243–3174), **Travelex Insurance Services** (✉ 11717 Burt St., Suite 202, Omaha, NE 68154-1500, ☎ 402/445–8637 or 800/228–9792, FAX 402/491–0016), **Wallach & Company** (✉ 107 W. Federal St., Box 480, Middleburg, VA 20118, ☎ 540/687–3166 or 800/237–6615). In Canada, **Mutual of Omaha** (✉ Travel Division, 500 University Ave., Toronto, Ontario M5G 1V8, ☎ 416/598–4083, 800/268–8825 in Canada). In the U.K., **Association of British Insurers** (✉ 51 Gresham St., London EC2V 7HQ, ☎ 0171/600–3333).

L

LODGING

APARTMENT AND HOUSE RENTALS

If you want a home base that's roomy enough for a family and comes with cooking facilities, **consider a furnished rental.** These can save you money, however some rentals are luxury properties, economical only when your party is large. Home-exchange directories list rentals (often second homes owned by prospective house swappers), and some services search for a house or apartment for you (even a castle if that's your fancy) and handle the paperwork. Some send an illustrated catalog; others send photographs only of specific properties, sometimes at a charge. Up-front registration fees may apply.

➤ RENTAL AGENTS: At **Home Abroad** (✉ 405 E. 56th St., Suite 6H, New York, NY 10022, ☎ 212/421–9165, FAX 212/752–1591). **Europa-**

Let/Tropical Inn-Let (⊠ 92 N. Main St., Ashland, OR 97520, ☎ 541/482–5806 or 800/462–4486, FAX 541/482–0660). **Hometours International** (⊠ Box 11503, Knoxville, TN 37939, ☎ 423/690–8484 or 800/367–4668). **Interhome** (⊠ 124 Little Falls Rd., Fairfield, NJ 07004, ☎ 201/882–6864, FAX 201/808–1742). **Property Rentals International** (⊠ 1008 Mansfield Crossing Rd., Richmond, VA 23236, ☎ 804/378–6054 or 800/220–3332, FAX 804/379–2073). **Rental Directories International** (⊠ 2044 Rittenhouse Sq., Philadelphia, PA 19103, ☎ 215/985–4001, FAX 215/985–0323). **Vacation Home Rentals Worldwide** (⊠ 235 Kensington Ave., Norwood, NJ 07648, ☎ 201/767–9393 or 800/633–3284, FAX 201/767–5510). **Villas and Apartments Abroad** (⊠ 420 Madison Ave., Suite 1003, New York, NY 10017, ☎ 212/759–1025 or 800/433–3020, FAX 212/755–8316).

HOME EXCHANGES

If you would like to exchange your home for someone else's, **join a home-exchange organization.**

➤ EXCHANGE CLUBS: **HomeLink International** (⊠ Box 650, Key West, FL 33041, ☎ 305/294–7766 or 800/638–3841, FAX 305/294–1148) charges $83 per year.

M

MAIL

Stamps may be bought from main or subpost offices (the latter are located in stores), from stamp machines outside post offices, and from many newsagents stores and newsstands. Mailboxes are known as post or letter boxes and are painted bright red; large tubular ones are set on the edge of sidewalks, while smaller boxes are set into post-office walls.

Postal rates are: airmail letters up to 10 grams to North America, 43p; postcards 37p, aerogrammes 36p. Letters within Britain are 26p for first class, 20p for second class. Always check rates in advance, however, as they are subject to change.

RECEIVING MAIL

If you're uncertain where you'll be staying, you can have mail sent to you c/o Poste Restante, The **London Main**

Post Office at Trafalgar Square (⊠ 24–28 William IV St., London WC2N 4DL), open Monday–Saturday 8:30–9. They will hold international mail for one month (☎ 0171/930–9580). You can also collect letters at **American Express** (⊠ 6 Haymarket, SW1Y 4BS, ☎ 0171/930–4411, or any other branch). The service is free to card-holders and traveler's check holders; all others pay a small fee.

MONEY

The units of currency in Great Britain are pound sterling (£) and pence (p): £50, £20, £10, and £5 bills; £1 (100p), 50p, 20p, 10p, 5p, 2p, and 1p coins. At press time, the exchange rate was about U.S. $1.65 and Canadian $2.35 to the pound sterling.

ATMS

Before leaving home, **make sure that your credit cards have been programmed for ATM use in London.** Note that Discover is accepted mostly in the United States. Local bank cards often do not work overseas or may access only your checking account; **ask your bank about a MasterCard/Cirrus or Visa debit card,** which works like a bank card but can be used at any ATM displaying a MasterCard/Cirrus or Visa logo. These cards, too, may tap only your checking account; check with your bank about their policy.

➤ ATM LOCATIONS: **Cirrus** (☎ 800/424–7787). A list of **Plus** locations is available at your local bank.

COSTS

A movie in the West End costs £5–£9.50 (less on Mondays and at matinees); a theater seat, from £6 to about £20, more for hit shows; admission to a museum or gallery, around £3 (though many are free and others request a "voluntary contribution"); coffee, £1–£2; a pint of light (lager) beer in a pub, £1.70–£2.20; whiskey, gin, vodka, and so forth, by the glass in a pub, £1.50 and up (the measure is smaller than in the United States); house wine by the glass in a pub or wine bar, around £2, in a restaurant, £3.50 or more; a Coke, around 60p; a ham sandwich from a sandwich bar in the West End, £2; a 1-mile taxi ride, £4; an average Underground or bus ride, £1.40, a longer one, £2.40.

Of course, London now ranks with Tokyo as one of the world's most expensive hotel capitals. Finding budget accommodations—especially during July and August—can be difficult; you should try to book well ahead if you are visiting during these months. Many London hotels offer special off-season (October–March) rates, however. Dining out at top-line restaurants can be prohibitively expensive, but there are new chains of French-Ital style café-brasseries, along with a large number of pubs and ethnic restaurants that offer excellent food at reasonable prices. Fast-food facilities of every nationality are widespread.

CURRENCY EXCHANGE

For the most favorable rates, **change money at banks.** Although fees charged for ATM transactions may be higher abroad than at home, Cirrus and Plus exchange rates are excellent, because they are based on wholesale rates offered only by major banks. You won't do as well at exchange booths in airports or rail and bus stations, in hotels, in restaurants, or in stores, although you may find their hours more convenient. To avoid lines at airport exchange booths, **get a small amount of local currency before you leave home.**

➤ EXCHANGE SERVICES: **Ruesch International** (☎ 800/424–2923 for locations). **Thomas Cook Currency Services** (☎ 800/287–7362 for telephone orders and locations).

TRAVELER'S CHECKS

Whether or not to buy traveler's checks depends on where you are headed. **Take cash if your trip includes rural areas** and small towns, traveler's checks to cities. If your checks are lost or stolen, they can usually be replaced within 24 hours. To ensure a speedy refund, buy your checks yourself (don't ask someone else to make the purchase). When making a claim for stolen or lost checks, the person who bought the checks should make the call.

P

PACKING FOR LONDON

London can be cool, damp, and overcast, even in summer. You'll need a heavy coat for winter and a lightweight coat or warm jacket for summer. Always **bring an umbrella and, if possible, a raincoat.** Pack as you would for an American city: coats and ties for expensive restaurants and nightspots, casual clothes elsewhere. Jeans are popular in London and are perfectly acceptable for sightseeing and informal dining. Tweeds and sport jackets are popular here with men. For women, ordinary street dress is acceptable everywhere. If you plan to stay in budget hotels, take your own soap. Many do not provide soap, and some give guests only one tiny bar per room.

Bring an extra pair of eyeglasses or contact lenses in your carry-on luggage, and if you have a health problem, **pack enough medication** to last the entire trip or have your doctor write you a prescription using the drug's generic name, because brand names vary from country to country. It's important that you **don't put prescription drugs or valuables in luggage to be checked:** it might go astray. To avoid problems with customs officials, carry medications in the original packaging. Also, don't forget the addresses of offices that handle refunds of lost traveler's checks.

LUGGAGE

In general, you are entitled to check two bags on flights within the United States and on international flights leaving the United States. A third piece may be brought on board, but it must fit easily under the seat in front of you or in the overhead compartment.

If you are flying between two foreign destinations, note that baggage allowances may be determined not by piece but by weight—generally 88 pounds (40 kilograms) in first class, 66 pounds (30 kilograms) in business class, and 44 pounds (20 kilograms) in economy. If your flight between two cities abroad *connects* with your transatlantic or transpacific flight, the piece method still applies.

Airline liability for baggage is limited to $1,250 per person on flights within the United States. On international flights it amounts to $9.07 per pound or $20 per kilogram for checked baggage (roughly $640 per 70-pound bag) and $400 per passenger for unchecked baggage. Insurance for losses exceeding these amounts can be bought from the airline at check-in for about $10 per $1,000 of coverage; note that this coverage excludes a rather extensive list of items, which is shown on your airline ticket.

Before departure, **itemize your bags' contents** and their worth, and label the bags with your name, address, and phone number. (If you use your home address, cover it so that potential thieves can't see it readily.) Inside each bag, **pack a copy of your itinerary.** At check-in, **make sure that each bag is correctly tagged** with the destination airport's three-letter code. If your bags arrive damaged or fail to arrive at all, file a written report with the airline before leaving the airport.

PASSPORTS & VISAS

Once your travel plans are confirmed, **check the expiration date of your passport.** It's also a good idea to **make photocopies of the data page**; leave one copy with someone at home and keep another with you, separated from your passport. If you lose your passport, promptly call the nearest embassy or consulate and the local police; having a copy of the data page can speed replacement.

U.S. CITIZENS

All U.S. citizens, even infants, need only a valid passport to enter Great Britain for stays of up to 90 days.

➤ INFORMATION: **Office of Passport Services** (☎ 202/647–0518).

CANADIANS

You need only a valid passport to enter Great Britain for stays of up to 90 days.

➤ INFORMATION: **Passport Office** (☎ 819/994–3500 or 800/567–6868).

S
SENIOR-CITIZEN TRAVEL

To qualify for age-related discounts, **mention your senior-citizen status up front** when booking hotel reservations (not when checking out) and before you're seated in restaurants (not when paying the bill). Note that discounts may be limited to certain menus, days, or hours. When renting a car, **ask about promotional car-rental discounts,** which can be cheaper than senior-citizen rates.

➤ EDUCATIONAL TRAVEL PROGRAMS: **Elderhostel** (✉ 75 Federal St., 3rd floor, Boston, MA 02110, ☎ 617/426–7788). **Overseas Adventure Travel** (✉ Grand Circle Corporation, 625 Mt. Auburn St., Cambridge, MA 02138, ☎ 617/876–0533 or 800/221–0814, FAX 617/876–0455).

SIGHTSEEING

BY BUS

Guided sightseeing tours offer passengers a good introduction to the city from double-decker buses, which are open-topped in summer. Tours run daily and depart from Haymarket, Baker Street, Grosvenor Gardens, Marble Arch, and Victoria. You may board or alight at any of about 21 stops to view the sights, and then get back on the next bus. Tickets (£10) may be bought from the driver. Agencies include **Evan Evans** (☎ 0181/332–2222), **Frames Rickards** (☎ 0171/837–3111), **The Original London Sightseeing Tour** (☎ 0181/877–1722), and **The Big Bus Company** (☎ 0181/944–7810). These tours include stops at places such as St. Paul's Cathedral and Westminster Abbey. Prices and pickup points vary according to the sights visited, but many pickup points are at major hotels. **Black Taxi Tour of London** is a personal tour by cab direct from your hotel (☎ 0171/289–4371).

BY CANAL

During summer, narrow boats and barges cruise London's two canals, the Grand Union and Regent's Canal; most vessels (they seat about 60) operate on the latter, which runs between Little Venice in the west (nearest tube: Warwick Avenue on the Bakerloo Line) and Camden Lock (about 200 yards north of Camden Town tube station). **Jason's Trip** (☎ 0171/286–3428) operates one-way and round-trip narrow-boat cruises on this route. During April to September, there are three cruises per day; in October, just two. Trips last 1½ hours (£5.50 round-trip). The **London Waterbus Company** (☎ 0171/482–2660) operates this route year round with a special stop at London Zoo (£9.80 one-way with combined zoo entrance): daily from April to October, then at weekends only, November to March (£4.50 round-trip). **Canal Cruises** (☎ 0171/485–4433) also offers three or four cruises daily from March to October (£4.60) on the *Jenny Wren* and all year on the cruising restaurant *My Fair Lady* (Tues.–Sat. dinner and entertainment, £26.95; Sun. lunch, £16.95).

BY FOOT

One of the best ways to get to know London is on foot, and there are many guided walking tours from which to choose. **Original London Walks** (☎ 0171/624–3978) has a very wide selection and takes great pride in the infectious enthusiasm of its guides. Other firms include **City Walks** (☎ 0171/700–6931) and **Streets of London** (☎ 0181/346–9255).

BY RIVER

All year round, but more frequently in April to October, boats cruise the Thames, offering a different view of the London skyline. Most leave from Westminster Pier, Charing Cross Pier, and Tower Pier. Downstream routes go to the Tower of London, Greenwich, and the Thames Barrier; upstream destinations include Kew, Richmond, and Hampton Court. Most of the launches seat between 100 and 250 passengers, have a public-address system, and provide a running commentary on passing points of interest. Depending upon the destination, river trips may last from one to four hours. For more information, call **Catamaran Cruisers** (from Westminster to Greenwich (☎ 0171/839–3572), or **Westminster Passenger Boat Services** (☎ 0171/930–4097; **City Cruises** for The Tower and the Thames Barrier(☎ 0171/928–9009) and **Thames Barrier Cruises** (☎ 0171/930–3373). A **Sail and Rail** ticket combines the modern wonders of Canary Wharf by Docklands Light Railway with a trip on the river. Tickets available year round from Westminster Pier or Tower Gateway (☎ 0171/363–9700)— ticket holders also get a 20% discount at the National Maritime Museum, Greenwich.

EXCURSIONS

London Regional Transport, Green Line, Evan Evans, and **Frames Rickards** all offer day excursions by bus to places within easy reach of London, such as Hampton Court, Oxford, Stratford, and Bath.

STUDENTS

To save money, **look into deals available through student-oriented travel agencies.** To qualify you'll need a bona fide student ID card. Members of international student groups are also eligible.

➤ STUDENT IDs AND SERVICES: **Council on International Educational Exchange** (✉ CIEE, 205 E. 42nd St., 14th floor, New York, NY 10017, ☎ 212/822–2600, ℻ 212/822–2699), for mail orders only, in the United States. **Travel Cuts** (✉ 187 College St., Toronto, Ontario M5T 1P7, ☎ 416/979–2406 or 800/667–2887) in Canada.

➤ HOSTELING: **Hostelling International—American Youth Hostels** (✉ 733 15th St. NW, Suite 840, Washington, DC 20005, ☎ 202/783–6161, ℻ 202/783–6171). **Hostelling International—Canada** (✉ 400-205 Catherine St., Ottawa, Ontario K2P 1C3, ☎ 613/237–7884, ℻ 613/237–7868). **Youth Hostel Association of England and Wales** (✉ Trevelyan House, 8 St. Stephen's Hill, St. Albans, Hertfordshire AL1 2DY, ☎ 01727/855215 or 01727/845047). Membership in the U.S., $25; in Canada, C$26.75; in the U.K., £9.30).

➤ STUDENT TOURS: **Contiki Holidays** (✉ 300 Plaza Alicante, Suite 900, Garden Grove, CA 92840, ☎ 714/740–0808 or 800/266–8454). **AESU Travel** (✉ 2 Hamill Rd., Suite 248, Baltimore, MD 21210-1807, ☎ 410/323–4416 or 800/638–7640, ℻ 410–323–4498).

T

TAXES

AIRPORT

As of November 1, 1997, all travelers departing the United Kingdom must now pay a £10 (within EU) or £10 (outside EU) Air Passenger Duty.

VAT

The British sales tax (VAT, Value Added Tax) is 17½%. The tax is almost always included in quoted prices in shops, hotels, and restaurants.

You can **get a VAT refund** by either the Retail Export or the more cumbersome Direct Export method. Most large stores provide these services, but only if you request them, and will handle the paperwork. For the Retail Export method, you must ask the store for Form VAT 407 (you must have identification—passports are best), to be given to customs at your last port of departure. (Lines at major airports can be long, so allow plenty of time.) The refund will be forwarded to you in about eight weeks, minus a small service charge, either in the form of a credit to your charge card or as a British check, which American banks usually charge you to convert. With the Direct Export method, the goods go directly to your home; you must have a Form VAT 407 certified by customs, police, or a notary public when you get home and then sent back to the store, which will refund your money. For inquiries, call the local Customs & Excise office listed in the telephone directory.

TAXIS

Those big black taxicabs are as much a part of the London streetscape as the red double-decker buses, yet many have been replaced by the new boxy, sharp-edged model, while the beauty of others is marred by the advertising they carry on their sides. Hotels and main tourist areas have cab stands (just take the first in line), but you can also **flag one down from the roadside.** If the yellow FOR HIRE sign on the top is lit, the taxi is available. Many cab drivers often cruise at night with their FOR HIRE signs unlit; this is to enable them to choose their passengers and avoid those they think might cause trouble. If you see an unlit, passengerless cab, hail it: You might be lucky.

FARES

Fares start at £1.40 and increase by units of 20p per 281 yards or 55.5 seconds until the fare exceeds £8.60. After that, it's 20p for each 188 yards or 37 seconds. A 60p surcharge is added on weekday nights 8–midnight and until 8 PM on Saturday. Over Christmas and New Year's Eve, it rises to £2. Fares are usually raised in

June of each year. Tips are extra, usually 10% to 15% per ride.

TELEPHONES

The country code for Great Britain is 44.

London has two area codes, 0171 for inner London and 0181 for outer London. You don't have to dial either if you are calling inside the same zone. Drop the 0 from the prefix and dial only 171 or 181 when calling from overseas.

There are three types of phones: those that accept (a) only coins, (b) only British Telephone (BT) phonecards, or (c) BT phonecards and credit cards.

The coin-operated phones are of the push-button variety; the workings of coin-operated telephones vary, but there are usually instructions in each unit. Most take 10p, 20p, 50p, and £1 coins. Insert the coins *before* dialing (minimum charge is 10p). If you hear a repeated single tone after dialing, the line is busy; a continual tone means the number is unobtainable (or that you have dialed the wrong—or no—prefix). The indicator panel shows you how much money is left; add more whenever you like. If there is no answer, replace the receiver and your money will be returned.

All calls are charged according to the time of day. Standard rate is weekdays 8 AM–6 PM; cheap rate is weekdays 6 PM–8 AM and all day on weekends. A local call before 6 PM costs 15p for three minutes; this doubles to 30p for the same from a payphone. A daytime call to the United States will cost 30p a minute, on a regular phone; £1.50 on a payphone (evenings, £1.30).

Card phones operate with special cards that you can buy from post offices or newsstands. They are ideal for longer calls, are composed of units of 10p, and come in values of £2, £4, £10, and more. To use a card phone, lift the receiver, insert your card, and dial the number. An indicator panel shows the number of units used. At the end of your call, the card will be returned. Where credit cards are taken, slide the card through, as indicated.

LONG-DISTANCE

Before you go, **find out the local access codes** for your destinations. AT&T, MCI, and Sprint long-distance services make calling home relatively convenient, but you may find the local access number blocked in many hotel rooms. First ask the hotel operator to connect you. If the hotel operator balks, ask for an international operator, or dial the international operator yourself. One way to improve your odds of getting connected to your long-distance carrier is to travel with more than one company's calling card (a hotel may block Sprint, for example, but not MCI). If all else fails, call your phone company collect in the United States or call from a pay phone in the hotel lobby.

➤ To Obtain Access Codes: **AT&T** USADirect (☎ 800/874–4000). **MCI** Call USA (☎ 800/444–4444). **Sprint** Express (☎ 800/793–1153).

For long-distance calls within Britain, dial the area code (which begins with 01), followed by the number. The area code prefix is only used when you are dialing from outside the city. In provincial areas, the dialing codes for nearby towns are often posted in the booth.

OPERATORS AND INFORMATION

For information anywhere in Britain, dial 192. For the operator, dial 100. For assistance with international calls, dial 155.

TIPPING

Many restaurants and large hotels (particularly those belonging to chains) will automatically add a 10%–15% service charge to your bill, so **always check in advance before you hand out any extra money.** You are, of course, welcome to tip on top of that for exceptional service. If you are dissatisfied with the service, however, refuse to pay the service charge, stating your reasons for doing so; you will be within your rights legally.

Do not tip movie or theater ushers, elevator operators, or bar staff in pubs—although you may buy them a drink if you're feeling generous. Washroom attendants may display a saucer, in which it's reasonable to leave 20p or so.

Here's a guide for other tipping situations: **Restaurants:** 10%–15% of the check for full meals if service is not already included; a small token if you're just having coffee or tea. **Taxis:** 10%–15%, or perhaps a little more for a short ride. **Porters:** 50p–£1 per bag. **Doormen:** £1 for hailing taxis or for carrying bags to check-in desk. **Bellhops:** £1 for carrying bags to rooms, £1 for room service. **Hairdressers:** 10%–15% of the bill, plus £1–£2 for the hair-washer.

TOUR OPERATORS

Buying a prepackaged tour or independent vacation can make your trip to London less expensive and more hassle-free. Because everything is prearranged you'll spend less time planning.

Operators that handle several hundred thousand travelers per year can use their purchasing power to give you a good price. Their high volume may also indicate financial stability. But some small companies provide more personalized service; because they tend to specialize, they may also be more knowledgeable about a given area.

A GOOD DEAL?

The more your package or tour includes, the better you can predict the ultimate cost of your vacation. Make sure you know exactly what is covered, and **beware of hidden costs.** Are taxes, tips, and service charges included? Transfers and baggage handling? Entertainment and excursions? These can add up.

If the package or tour you are considering is priced lower than in your wildest dreams, **be skeptical.** Also, **make sure your travel agent knows the accommodations** and other services. Ask about the hotel's location, room size, beds, and whether it has a pool, room service, or programs for children, if you care about these. Has your agent been there in person or sent others you can contact?

BUYER BEWARE

Each year consumers are stranded or lose their money when tour operators—even very large ones with excellent reputations—go out of business. So **check out the operator.** Find out how long the company has been in business, and ask several agents about its reputation. **Don't book unless the firm has a consumer-protection program.**

Members of the National Tour Association and United States Tour Operators Association are required to set aside funds to cover your payments and travel arrangements in case the company defaults. Nonmembers may carry insurance instead. Look for the details, and for the name of an underwriter with a solid reputation, in the operator's brochure. Note: When it comes to tour operators, **don't trust escrow accounts.** Although there are laws governing charter-flight operators, no governmental body prevents tour operators from raiding the till. For more information, *see* Consumer Protection, *above.*

➤ TOUR-OPERATOR RECOMMENDA-TIONS: **National Tour Association** (✉ NTA, 546 E. Main St., Lexington, KY 40508, ☎ 606/226–4444 or 800/ 755–8687). **United States Tour Operators Association** (✉ USTOA, 342 Madison Ave., New York, NY 10173, ☎ 212/599–6599).

USING AN AGENT

Travel agents are excellent resources. When shopping for an agent, however, you should **collect brochures from several sources;** some agents' suggestions may be skewed by promotional relationships with tour and package firms that reward them for volume sales. If you have a special interest, **find an agent with expertise in that area.** Don't rely solely on your agent, who may be unaware of small-niche operators. Note that some special-interest travel companies only sell directly to the public and that some large operators only accept bookings made through travel agents.

SINGLE TRAVELERS

Prices for packages and tours are usually quoted per person, based on two sharing a room. If traveling solo, you may be required to pay the full double-occupancy rate. Some operators eliminate this surcharge if you agree to be matched with a roommate of the same sex, even if one is not found by departure time.

GROUP TOURS

Among companies that sell tours to London, the following are nationally known, have a proven reputation, and offer plenty of options. The classifications used below represent different price categories, and you'll probably encounter these terms when talking to a travel agent or tour operator. The key difference is usually in accommodations, which run from budget to better, and better-yet to best.

➤ SUPER-DELUXE: **Abercrombie & Kent** (✉ 1520 Kensington Rd., Oak Brook, IL 60521-2141, ☎ 630/954–2944 or 800/323–7308, FAX 630/ 954–3324). **Travcoa** (✉ Box 2630, 2350 S.E. Bristol St., Newport Beach, CA 92660, ☎ 714/476–2800 or 800/992–2003, FAX 714/476–2538).

➤ DELUXE: **Globus** (✉ 5301 S. Federal Circle, Littleton, CO 80123-2980, ☎ 303/797–2800 or 800/ 221–0090, FAX 303/347–2080). **Maupintour** (✉ 1515 St. Andrews Dr., Lawrence, KS 66047, ☎ 913/ 843–1211 or 800/255–4266, FAX 913/843–8351). **Tauck Tours** (✉ Box 5027, 276 Post Rd. W, Westport, CT 06881-5027, ☎ 203/226–6911 or 800/468–2825, FAX 203/221–6828).

➤ FIRST-CLASS: **Brendan Tours** (✉ 15137 Califa St., Van Nuys, CA 91411, ☎ 818/785–9696 or 800/ 421–8446, FAX 818/902–9876). **British Airways Holidays** (☎ 800/ 247–9297). **Caravan Tours** (✉ 401 N. Michigan Ave., Chicago, IL 60611, ☎ 312/321–9800 or 800/ 227–2826, FAX 312/321–9845). **CIE Tours** (✉ 108 Ridgedale Ave., Morristown, NJ 07960, ☎ 201/ 292–3438 or 800/243–8687). Collette Tours (✉ 162 Middle St., Pawtucket, RI 02860, ☎ 401/728–3805 or 800/832–4656, FAX 401/728–1380). **Gadabout Tours** (✉ 700 E. Tahquitz Canyon Way, Palm Springs, CA 92262–6767, ☎ 619/325–5556). **Insight International Tours** (✉ 745 Atlantic Ave., #720, Boston, MA 02111, ☎ 617/ 482–2000 or 800/582–8380, FAX 617/482–2884 or 800/622–5015). **Trafalgar Tours** (✉ 11 E. 26th St., New York, NY 10010, ☎ 212/689–8977 or 800/854–0103, FAX 800/457–6644).

➤ BUDGET: **Cosmos** (☞ Globus, *above*). **Trafalgar** (☞ *above*).

PACKAGES

Like group tours, independent vacation packages are available from major tour operators and airlines. The companies listed below offer vacation packages in a broad price range.

➤ AIR/HOTEL: **American Airlines Fly AAway Vacations** (☎ 800/321–2121). **British Airways Holidays** (☞ *above*). **Celtic International Tours** (✉ 1860 Western Ave., Albany, NY 12203, ☎ 518/463–5511 or 800/833–4373). **Continental Vacations** (☎ 800/634–5555). **Delta Dream Vacations** (☎ 800/872–7786). **DER Tours** (✉ 11933 Wilshire Blvd., Los Angeles, CA 90025, ☎ 310/479–4140 or 800/937–1235). **United Vacations** (☎ 800/328–6877).

Also contact **Budget WorldClass Drive** (☎ 800/527–0700, 0800/181181 in the U.K.) for self-drive itineraries.

THEME TRIPS

Travel Contacts (✉ Box 173, Camberley, England GU15 1YE, ☎ 011/44/1/27667–7217, FAX 011/44/1/2766–3477), which represents 150 tour operators, can satisfy just about any special interest in London. **Great British Vacations** (✉ 4800 S.W. Griffith Dr., #125, Beaverton, OR 97005, ☎ 503/643–8080 or 800/452–8434).

➤ ANTIQUES: **Travel Keys Tours** (✉ Box 162266, Sacramento, CA 95816, ☎ 916/452–5200).

➤ COOKING SCHOOLS: **Le Cordon Bleu** (✉ 404 Airport Executive Pk., Nanuet, NY 10954, ☎ 800/457–2433 in U.S.).

➤ HOMES AND GARDENS: **Coopersmith's England** (✉ Box 900, Inverness, CA 94937, ☎ 415/669–1914, FAX 415/669–1942). **Expo Garden Tours** (✉ 70 Great Oak, Redding, CT 06896, ☎ 203/938–0410 or 800/448–2685, FAX 203/938–0427).

➤ PERFORMING ARTS: **Dailey-Thorp Travel** (✉ 330 W. 58th St., #610, New York, NY 10019-1817, ☎ 212/307–1555 or 800/998–4677, FAX 212/974–1420). **Keith Prowse Tours** (✉ 234 W. 44th St., #1000, New York, NY 10036, ☎ 212/398–1430 or 800/669–8687, FAX 212/302–4251).

➤ TENNIS: **Championship Tennis Tours** (✉ 7350 E. Stetson Dr., #106, Scottsdale, AZ 85251, ☎ 602/990–8760 or 800/468–3664, FAX 602/990–8744). **Sportstours** (✉ 2301 Collins Ave., #A1540, Miami Beach, FL 33139, ☎ 800/879–8647, FAX 305/535–0008). **Steve Furgal's International Tennis Tours** (✉ 11828 Rancho Bernardo Rd., #123-305, San Diego, CA 92128, ☎ 619/675–3555 or 800/258–3664).

U

UNDERGROUND TRAVEL

Known colloquially as "the Tube," London's extensive Underground system is by far the most widely used form of city transportation. As many travelers learn, using its easily marked routes, crystal-clear signage, and extensive connections, it's a delight to travel on. Trains run both beneath and aboveground out into the suburbs, and all stations are clearly marked with the London Underground circular symbol. (In Britain, the word "subway" means "pedestrian underpass.") Trains are all one class; smoking is *not* allowed on board or in the stations.

There are 10 basic lines—all named. The East London line, which runs from Shoreditch and Whitechapel south to New Cross, is due to re-open after major reconstruction in summer 1997. One of the newest is the Docklands Light Railway, which runs from Stratford in east London and from Bank and Tower Gateway to Island Gardens across the river from Greenwich (which connects under the river by a foot tunnel, although there are plans afoot to connect under the river as part of the millennium developments). Spring 1998 should see the opening of the Jubilee line extension from Green Park all the way east to Stratford. The not-yet-built Metro Express, which will run from Haringey to Wimbledon underneath Soho and Fulham, may start appearing on maps, too—it's the light green line. The Central, District, Northern, Metropolitan, and Piccadilly lines all have branches, so **be sure to note which branch is needed for your particular destination.** Electronic platform signs tell you the final stop and route of the next train, and some signs conveniently indicate how many minutes you'll have to wait for the train to arrive.

FARES

For both buses and tube fares, London is divided into six concentric zones; the fare goes up the farther out you travel. Ask at Underground ticket counters for the London Transport booklets that give details of all the various ticket options for the tube. Traveling without a valid ticket makes you liable for an on-the-spot fine (£10 at press time), so always pay your fare before you embark.

For one trip between any two stations, you can buy an ordinary single (one-way ticket) for travel anytime on the day of issue; if you're coming back on the same route the same day, an ordinary return (round-trip ticket) costs twice the single fare. Singles vary in price from 90p to £3.20—expensive if you're making several journeys in a day. There are several passes good for both the tube and the bus; ☞ Important Contacts A to Z, *above*.

HOURS

From Monday to Saturday, trains begin running just after 5 AM; the last services leave central London between midnight and 12:30 AM. On Sundays, trains start two hours later and finish about an hour earlier. Frequency of trains depends on the route and the time of day, but normally you should not have to wait more than 10 minutes in central areas.

INFORMATION

A pocket map of the entire tube network is available free from most Underground ticket counters. There is a large map on the wall of each platform.

There are LT (London Transport) Travel Information Centres at the following tube stations: Euston, Hammersmith, King's Cross, Oxford Circus, Piccadilly Circus, St James's Park, Victoria, and Heathrow (in Terminals 1 and 2); open 6–12 AM. For information on all London tube and bus times, fares, and so on, dial 0171/222–1234 (24 hours). For travelers with disabilities, get the free leaflet, "Access to the Underground," ☎ 0171/918–3312.

PASSES

Several **Travelcards** for tube and bus travel are available at tube and rail stations, as well as some newsstands. These allow unrestricted travel on the tube, most buses, and British Rail trains in the Greater London zones and are valid weekdays after 9:30 AM, weekends, and all public holidays. They cannot be used on airbuses, night buses, or for certain special services. A **One Day Travelcard** (£3–£3.90); **Weekend Travelcards,** for the two days of the weekend and on any two consecutive days during public holidays (£4.50). **Family Travelcards**: one-day ticket for two adults with one to four children (£5.80 with one child, extra children cost 50p each)—adults do not have to be related to the children or even to each other! The **Carnet** is a book of 10 single tickets valid for central Zone 1 (£10) to use any time over a year. The **Visitor's Travelcard** may be bought in the United States and Canada for three, four, and seven days' travel; it is the same as the LT Card and has a booklet of discount vouchers to London attractions. In the United States, the Visitor's Travelcard costs $25, $32, and $49, respectively; in Canada, C$29, C$36, and C$55, respectively. Apply to travel agents or, in the United States, to BritRail Travel International (✉ 1500 Broadway, New York, NY 10036, ☎ 212/382–3737).

U.S. GOVERNMENT

The U.S. government can be an excellent source of inexpensive travel information. When planning your trip, **find out what government materials are available.**

➤ ADVISORIES: **U.S. Department of State American Citizens Services Office** (✉ Room 4811, Washington, DC 20520); enclose a self-addressed, stamped envelope. Interactive hot line (☎ 202/647–5225, FAX 202/647–3000). Computer bulletin board (☎ 202/647–9225).

V

VISITOR INFORMATION

➤ IN THE U.S. Contact the **British Tourist Authority** (BTA) in the United

States (⌧ 551 5th Ave., 7th Floor, New York, NY 10176, ☎ 212/986–2200 or 800/462–2748; ⌧ 625 N. Michigan Ave., Suite 1510, Chicago, IL 60611 (personal callers only); ⌧ 620 Cranberry Place, Roswell, GA 30076 (no personal callers), ☎ 404/594–8818); ⌧ Columbus Center, 1 Alhambra Plaza, Suite 1465, Coral Gables FL 33134 (personal callers only); in Canada (⌧ 111 Avenue Rd., 4th floor, Toronto, Ontario M5R 3J8, ☎ 416/925–6326), and in the United Kingdom (⌧ Thames Tower, Black's Rd., London W6 9EL, ☎ 0181/846–9000).

➤ IN LONDON: Go in person to the **London Tourist Information Centre** at Victoria Station Forecourt for general information, in summer, Monday–Saturday 8–7 and Sunday 8–5, winter, Monday–Saturday 8–6 and Sunday 8:30–4, or to the **British Travel Centre** (⌧ 12 Regent St., SW1Y 4PQ) for travel, hotel, and entertainment information weekdays 9–6:30, weekends 10–4 (Sat. May–Sept., 9–5).

➤ BY PHONE: The London Tourist Board's **Visitorcall** (☎ 0839/123456) phone guide to London gives information about events, theater, museums, transport, shopping, and restaurants. A three-month events calendar (☎ 0839/401279) and an annual version (☎ 0839/401278) are available by fax (set fax machine to polling mode, or press start/receive after the tone). Visitorcall charges are 39p–49p per minute, depending on the time of the call.

W
WHEN TO GO

The heaviest tourist season in Britain runs from mid-April to mid-October,

with another peak around Christmas—though the tide never really ebbs. The spring is the time to see the countryside and the royal London parks and gardens at their freshest; early summer to catch the roses and full garden splendor; the fall for near-ideal exploring conditions. The British take their vacations mainly in July and August, and the resorts are crowded. London in summer, however, though full of visitors, is also full of interesting things to see and do. But be warned: Air-conditioning is rarely found in places other than department stores, modern restaurants, hotels and cinemas in London, and in a hot summer you'll swelter. The winter can be rather dismal and is frequently wet and usually cold, but all the theaters, concerts, and exhibitions go full speed.

CLIMATE

London's weather has always been contrary, and in recent years it has become positively erratic, with hot summers and mild winters proving that the greenhouse effect is running rampant over Britain. It is virtually impossible to forecast what the pattern might be, but you can be fairly certain that it will not be what you expect! The main feature of the British weather is that it is generally mild—with some savage exceptions, especially in summer. It is also fairly damp—though even that has been changing in recent years, with recurring periods of drought. What follows are the average daily maximum and minimum temperatures for London.

➤ FORECASTS: **Weather Channel Connection** (☎ 900/932–8437), 95¢ per minute from a Touch-Tone phone.

Climate in London

LONDON

Jan.	43F	6C	May	62F	17C	Sept.	65F	19C
	36	2		47	8		52	11
Feb.	44F	7C	June	69F	20C	Oct.	58F	14C
	36	2		53	12		46	8
Mar.	50F	10C	July	71F	22C	Nov.	50F	10C
	38	3		56	14		42	5
Apr.	56F	13C	Aug.	71F	21C	Dec.	45F	7C
	42	6		56	13		38	4

1 Destination: London

THE CITY OF VILLAGES

LONDON IS AN ENORMOUS CITY—600 square miles—on a tiny island, hosting about 7 million Londoners, ⅙ of the entire population of England, Scotland, and Wales; but it has never felt big to me. It is fashioned on a different scale from other capital cities, as if, given the English penchant for modesty and understatement, it felt embarrassed by its size. Each of the 32 boroughs that comprise the whole has its own attitude, and most are subdivided into yet smaller enclaves exhibiting yet more particular behaviors, so that there is really no such person as a generic Londoner. Stay here long enough, and Professor Higgins's feat of deducing Eliza Dolittle's very street of birth from the shape of her vowels will seem like nothing special. It's a cliché, but London really is a city of villages.

I have lived in several of these, and am fluent in the language of a few others, but my village, Holland Park, is the one I know best, and it illustrates as well as any how London is changing. Holland Park is small—just a few streets surrounding the former grounds of Holland House, a Jacobean mansion whose remains (it was bombed during World War II) now house a restaurant, a gallery, an open-air theater, and a youth hostel. North of the park, Holland Park Avenue metamorphoses into the windy local high street, Notting Hill Gate, then into bleak Bayswater Road, abutted on its right by Kensington Gardens and Hyde Park before breaking, where the main London gallows once stood, into irritating, commercial Oxford Street. But here, for a few West Eleven moments (postal-district terminology you'd do well to master, to help with navigation), it is a broad, plane tree–lined boulevard, strung with vast white-stuccoed late-Victorian houses and looking an awful lot like Paris.

In our sophisticated age, the European ambience of Holland Park Avenue has been seized upon by niche-marketeers, and we now have two French patisseries, three international newsstands, a BMW showroom, and a candlelighted Provençale restaurant within a couple of blocks. The history racket is doing similar things all over town, history being what London has to sell now that it no longer cuts much ice in the world economy. It would be sentimental to prefer the avenue's old hardware store and late-night family grocer (open till 9!) to the fancy Continental shops that have replaced them—London's got to move with the times, after all.

Both good and bad come with the new territory. The Pakistani family who used to take turns minding the grocery store bought the block a decade later. Those Patels are now a well-known London dynasty, with most of the capital's newsstands in their empire—a satisfying reversal of roles from the British Raj days. Meanwhile, homeless Londoners (the number is about 100,000, and rising) work the overpriced yuppie supermarket threshold selling their magazine, *The Big Issue,* for a profit of 25p per guilty conscience. As one of the many villages built during Victoria's reign, Holland Park is a neighborhood unaccustomed to urban blight. But much of London has weathered several centuries of coping with the indigent population.

That's one of the best things about the city: Everything has been seen before, and history is forever poking its nose in. Whatever you're doing, you're doing it on top of a past layered like striated rock. You can see the cross sections clearly sometimes, as in the City, where lumps of Roman wall nest in the postmodern blocks of the street helpfully named London Wall. Walk toward the Thames to Cheapside, which you can tell was the medieval marketplace if you know the meaning of "ceap" ("to barter"), and there's the little Norman church of St. Mary-le-Bow, rebuilt by Wren and then again after the Blitz, but still ringing the Bow Bells. Then look to your right, and you'll be gobsmacked by the dome of St. Paul's. Of course, all you really wanted was to find a place for lunch—nearly impossible on a weekend in this office wasteland.

Instead of going weak-kneed at the sights, Londoners are apt to complain about such privations, while pretending simultaneously that no other city in the United

Kingdom exists. Edinburghers and Liverpudlians can complain till Big Ben tolls 13, but Londoners continue to pull rank with a complacency that amuses and infuriates visitors in about equal measure. London definitely *used* to be important. The vein of water running through its center has always linked the city with the sea, and it once gave British mariners a head start in the race to mine the world's riches and bring them home. The river proved convenient for building not only palaces (at Westminster, Whitehall, Hampton Court, Richmond, Greenwich) but an empire, too.

The empire dissolved, but the first Thames bridge is still there, in almost the same spot that the emperor Claudius picked in AD 43, and although the current drab concrete incarnation dates only from 1972, it's still called London Bridge. The Tudor one was much better—something I learned before I was 10 from visits to the Museum of London, which used to be located nearby in Kensington Palace. I liked the old bridge because of the row of decapitated heads stuck on poles above the gatehouse, which you could see on the model. It added a frisson to history, which more recent exhibitions, like the amazingly popular London Dungeon, have rather cynically packaged.

The old London Bridge lasted 600 years. Lined with shops and houses, it presided over a string of fairs *on* the Thames, when winters were colder and the water froze thick. Nowadays we rarely see a snowfall, though we'll talk endlessly about its possibility. We are genuinely obsessed by the weather, because we have so much of it, though most of it is damp. Snow varies the scenery, stops any tube train with an overground route, makes kids of everyone with a makeshift toboggan and access to a park (99% of the population), and fosters a community spirit normally proscribed by the city's geography and its citizens' cool. Winters were colder as recently as the '60s, when waiting for the crust to thicken enough to skate on the Round Pond in Kensington Gardens—now good only for model-boat sailors and duck feeders—was only a matter of time.

The corollary to our temperate winter, though, is a fresh confidence in summer sufficient to support herds of sidewalk tables. Holland Park Avenue no longer has the monopoly on Parisian ambience. All over town, an epidemic of Continental-style café chains serving croissants and *salade frisée* has devoured the traditional tobacco-stained pubs serving warm bitter and bags of pork scratchings. Most of the remaining pubs have turned into faux-Edwardian parlors with coffee machines and etchings or, more recently, wood-floored bars serving flavored vodkas and Tuscan food. The change has been going on for about a decade, and it suits London, as does its momentous discovery that restaurants are allowed to serve good food in smart surroundings and not charge the earth.

London is increasingly a European city, as if England were no longer stranded alone in the sea. In fact, ever since airplanes superseded ships, this island race has been undergoing an identity crisis, which reached its apogee in the '70s when Prime Minister Edward Heath sailed us irrevocably into the Common Market. Occasionally Britain still holds out against some European Community legislation or other, attempting to reassert differences that are following executions at the Tower and British Colonial supremacy into history. But however much the social climate changes, London is built on a firm foundation. Until the ravens desert the Tower of London—which is when, they say, the kingdom will fall—we have Westminster Abbey, and St. Paul's and the Houses of Parliament, the Georgian squares and grand Victorian houses, the green miles of parks, the river, the museums and galleries and theaters, and 32 boroughs of villages to keep us going.

–Kate Sekules

NEW AND NOTEWORTHY

Everyone's talking about swinging-again London. *Vanity Fair* recently proclaimed it "the coolest, hottest city in the world," and *Newsweek* announced last year that Britain's capital is the *only* place to be. Shops are multiplying, hotels opening and being renovated—with 3,000 new beds currently coming online. Even fashion designers are making waves: Two natives, John Galliano and Alexander McQueen, recently conquered Paris by taking over the houses of Dior and Givenchy. Cool Britannia! Cash is being poured from the National Lottery piggybank into public buildings, ready for Europe's most hysterical millennium party. Even Shakespeare is ready for the year 2000. After decades of planning and years of construction, the **Globe Theatre**—that long-missing Exhibit A of Shakespearean England, the venue for which the Bard wrote *Hamlet, King Lear,* and *Macbeth,* among other peerless dramas—has been reconstructed, just 200 yards from where the original playhouse stood. On June 12, 1997, it officially opened with a performance of "Triumphes and Mirth" in the presence of Her actual Majesty. The widespread interest in the Globe has been enormous: it's not every day that the world gains another top (think Eiffel Tower, Colosseum) tourist icon.

There's enormous interest, too, in the city's dining scene. London has fallen in love with its tummy and there's been a **restaurant boom** of seismic proportions. Every "quality" paper—and there's more newsprint than coastline in England—devotes several pages a week to restaurant reviews, recipes, food news and general gastroporn, with celebrities (like Andrew Lloyd Webber, Michael Winner, and novelist Will Self), roped in to rate eateries, and chefs (like Gary Rhodes, Antony Worral-Thompson, and Rowley Leigh), given superstar status on TV. What it all means to you, the visitor, is, naturally, a great many more choices, though the hot competition among the hundreds of new restaurants for the handful of good staff means there's been no improvement in the standard of service—in fact, quite the opposite. If you don't expect your waiter to introduce him or herself, smile, notice your frantic semaphoring, know anything about the dishes or apologize for whatever goes amiss, you'll be quite happy. This is only a slight exaggeration of the service situation, something which Sir Terence Conran's (and partners') new restaurant school, with its cut-rate practice dining room, **The Apprentice,** near Tower Bridge is trying to remedy. Conran is largely responsible for the tenacious trend toward gigantic halls of eating, the biggest being his Mezzo, at 700 seats, and the next biggest, his yet-to-open-at-press-time spot, **The Bluebird.**

Our listings, now as ever, strike a balance between the new-and-trendy and the old-and-reliable, and include places where you can just get well fed without having to perform in some dining-as-theater routine. The new places are so numerous we can't keep up with them all: some Stop Press places not included in our Dining chapter include **Zafferano, Fables, Maison Novelli, Quo Vadis, Mirabelle,** and **Searcy's** (in the Barbican Centre). That will do for now. Just read the papers for the latest batch, or log onto the London Tourist Board's restaurant website at **http://www.londondining.co.uk/london/dining/.** And watch for the sushi invasion, which is hitting now, more than a decade after cresting in New York City.

Restaurants aren't the only new things. Among the latest openings are several adjuncts to the best-loved tourist sights. At the Royal Palaces, for instance, don't miss the Tower of London's next trick (after the rehousing of the Crown Jewels), **Crowns and Diamonds**—a bunch of naked crown frames with a pile of loose gems, all very valuable and historic. At Kensington Palace, the **Ceremonial Dress Collection** should be back on display by now, and the State Apartments are newly restored too. Hampton Court now hosts a **Tudor Christmas,** with all sorts of fanfare, including dancing the Farandole through the palace to the sound of sackbut and bagpipe, plus performances by jesters, stiltwalkers, and jugglers. Don't visit **Kew Palace,** though; it's being refurbished through spring 1999. Another thing not to see is the historic, symbolic, but (some have said) boring-to-behold Stone of Scone, which has been removed from its resting place beneath a series of royal posteriors under the Coronation Chair in Westminster Abbey, and been returned home to Scotland's Edinburgh Castle.

In the museums, there are new galleries or displays at the Victoria and Albert, National Portrait, London, Natural History, Horniman, and even at the British. At the British Museum, the **HSBC Money Gallery** has opened, the better to display countless coins and recount the 4,000-year history of counting cash. The Museum of London has unveiled the **London Now** gallery, which is as it sounds, and also a thing called the **Catwalk** which has computer-aided bits and pieces to take the visitor through the capital's story (the name and running motif are inspired by that icon of London's mythic past, Dick Whittington's cat). At the V&A, there are the new **Silver Galleries,** with more than 1,500 English silver things dating from 1300 to 1800. Its famed **Raphael Gallery** has been restored, and they're working on new **British Art and Design Galleries** and an expanded **Boilerhouse,** for contemporary design purposes, and to act as an educational, cultural center. The National Portrait Gallery has a new toy, the Piers Gough–designed **Victorian and Early 20th Century Galleries.** Last and largest, the Natural History Museum has come through with the biggest project since it opened in 1881, the **Earth Galleries,** which examine earthly phenomena, like volcanoes, tornadoes, deserts and so on, and then take you out into space and onto other planets. For budding Einsteins, this is sure to ignite a Jurassic spark.

Less edifyingly, there's been a lot of new whiz-bang virtual-simulated computer-driven wizardry installed at the Piccadilly Trocadero, which has been rechristened the "Adrenaline Zone," and stars **Segaworld.** The **Legoland** Theme Park is up and running out in Windsor, and the new **London Aquarium** in the former County Hall opposite the Houses of Parliament should be holding water by the time you read this.

This year, you might have more luck finding sharks than opera in central London, as both major opera companies were almost going to wind up homeless. The world-renowned **Royal Opera** finalized its relocation plans at press time, with its eviction date (to allow for major refurbishment of the Covent Garden Opera House) imminent. For the 1997–98 season, the opera will present full opera productions at the Barbican Theatre, the Shaftesbury Theater, and Royal Albert Hall and concert versions at Royal Festival Hall, Barbican Hall, and Royal Albert Hall. The **Royal Ballet** will take up residence in the Labatt's Apollo Theatre in Hammersmith and Royal Festival Hall. For the 1998–99 season, most productions should be concentrated in the newly refurbished Sadler's Wells Theatre. The English National Opera—or **ENO,** as it is called—had decided just at press time to abandon the Coliseum, its home since 1968. Possible sites for a new house,

funded by the Lottery, include several places along the South Bank; King's Cross, near the new **British Library** (another long-delayed stop-start project); and the sadly disused yet magisterial Battersea Power Station.

Out in the East End, the 15th-century **Eltham Palace** has been restored and opened by British Heritage. If you head to the wide open spaces of Hampstead, you can catch the fantastic, small, but perfectly formed Erno Goldfinger house at **2 Willow Road,** which is the National Trust's first Modern Movement acquisition, or head in the other direction, for Twickenham, and the new **Museum of Rugby,** where you can learn all about the national sport that's like football played without padding. In yet another direction—south—**Crystal Palace** is going to become a massive entertainment complex, big enough to merit the trek, but not expected to be completed until late 1998.

Back in town, two riverside developments will soon be joined by many more in readiness for that 1999 celebration. Already there is the **OXO Tower,** which is a real must-see, and, on a tinier scale, the *Golden Hinde,* a faithful copy of the galleon in which Sir Francis Drake circumnavigated the globe, now resting in her final berth after a 23-year voyage. The estimable Coin Street Community Builders, who restored the Tower, want to *float* a swimming pool *in* the river—a **Thames Lido**—and Lambeth Council has permission to erect a—gasp!—towering **Ferris wheel** nearby, at the Aquarium. Presently, there'll be an undulating glass canopy over the South Bank Centre, and the **Millennium Dome** ("the largest structure in the world with a diameter of over 300 metres"). Nearby there'll be the new **Tate Gallery** at Bankside, the all-complete Shakespeare's Globe Theatre, and goodness knows what else. The Tate, by the way, celebrated its centenary in 1997, and opened itself Sunday mornings as a birthday gift (now daily 10–5:50).

In hotel land, things are heating up too—all those *Newsweek* readers flocking to the new hot city have to sleep somewhere. Look in our listings for the lovely **Covent Garden,** the sweet all-suite **Leonard,** and the **Hempel,** the supermodel of London hostelries. Apart, that is, from the **Metropolitan**—yet to open at press time—which may turn out to be *the* glamor palace, the hip hangout for modernists, the sellout of the lot, especially since it has managed to secrete the chic London **Nobu** eaterie inside.

Last but not least: In April 1997, No. Ten Downing Street welcomed a new occupant—dashing Tony Blair, who led his Labor Party to a precedent-breaking victory over the Tories. Hopes are high that the new prime minister will rev Britain's national economy up to London's booming levels. Finally, make a note of the British Tourist Authority's newish U.S. 800-number: ☎ 800–462–2748.

WHAT'S WHERE

Nine out of ten tourists visiting London return home feeling there is no other place like it. It is easy to understand why. London is actually a city whose celebrated sites and distinct neighborhoods each has its own character, lore, and rhythm. There is the heraldic splendor of Westminster, the chic of artistic Chelsea, the architectural elegance of Belgravia and Mayfair, the cosmopolitan charm of Soho, and the East End, home-base of the Cockney—to name just a few. With these myriad options, it's no wonder many visitors, especially first-time travelers, see London as a giant patchwork quilt thickly studded with must-see sights. The number of choices is awesome, and takes some thinking through. So, for those with what feel like a million questions, the following tell-all digest introduces each London neighborhood step by step. Happily, the city's expansive tube and bus systems bring far-flung sights within easy reach of each other. Keep in mind, however, that London's contrasts can best be savored by strolling from one district to another.

First pick a starting point. Most travelers choose Piccadilly Circus, which the British think of as "the hub of the universe." Keeping your wits about you—the Circus is a swirl of traffic, rather fetchingly surrounded by grand Edwardian-era buildings—face in the direction of the area of central London you want to explore, and start moving. To the north runs Regent Street, curving up one side of ritzy, mostly residential Mayfair. To the south is Lower Regent Street, leading toward Whitehall, the parks, and the palaces. To the east are Shaftesbury Avenue and Leicester Square, for theaters and Soho; to the west is Piccadilly itself, heading out to Hyde Park and Knightsbridge. This is also a great place to board a double-decker sightseeing bus—offering a perfect two-hour introduction to "The Flower of Cities All." Just remember to wrap a tartan muffler around your neck—atop these buses it's *always* windy.

Westminster and Royal London

No matter how you first approach London—historically, geographically, emotionally—all things start at Westminster, one of the truly ancient centers of the city. One hesitates to try to list historical highlights, because *everything* is a highlight. There is as much history in these few acres as there is in many complete cities. To view the 1,000 rooms of the Houses of Parliament would require at least a week—but an hour is all that's needed to enjoy the best show staged for free in the world's most renowned ego chamber, the House of Commons. Then there is Westminster Abbey, crammed with memorials and monuments to the great, the famous, and the totally forgotten (visitors should not allow their search for noted names to blind them to the spectacular Gothic splendor surrounding them). Whitehall is both an avenue and the heartbeat of the British government; here is the prime minister's official residence, No. 10 Downing Street and the Horse Guards, where two mounted sentries of the Queen's Life Guard provide London's most frequently taken-up photo op. Whitehall leads to Trafalgar Square—camera-happy tourists love its milling pigeons, and art aficionados love the Leonardos and Rubenses of the incomparable National Gallery (art treasures of a more modern ilk lie in the Tate Gallery). From the grand Admiralty Arch, the Mall leads straight to Buckingham Palace, as unprepossessing on the outside as it is sumptuous inside (as the summer tours now let you see). Naturally, in a district which regularly witnesses the pomp and pageantry of royal occasions, the streets are wide and the vistas are long. With beautifully kept St. James's Park at its center, the Westminster area exudes a feeling of timeless dignity and offers frequent glimpses of pinnacles and towers over treetops and, of course, the deep tones of Big Ben counting off the quarter-hours.

Belgravia

Just a short carriage ride from Buckingham Palace is the most splendidly aristocratic enclave to be found in London: Belgravia—this is *Upstairs, Downstairs,* Eaton Square territory. One of the city's grand-dame neighborhoods, Belgravia was built in the mid-1800s; today, untouched by neon, it basks in an authentic vintage patina. Comparisons to a stage set designed by Cecil Beaton after visiting Ascot would not be amiss: Here you will see block after block of grand, porticoed mansions, many currently serving as embassies, all painted Wedgwood-china white (to signify they remain the property of the Dukes of Westminster). Pedigree-proud locations include Belgrave Square, Grosvenor Crescent, and Belgrave Place, but also check out the chic alleyways, called "mews" from the time when they housed Milord's horse and carriage (nowadays dukes live in these former stables while the oil-rich occupy the houses). Although Belgravia remains exclusively residential, and therefore off the usual tourist path, no other spot in London will make you feel so much like warbling "On the Street Where You Live," just as Freddy Eynsford-Hill sang to Eliza in *My Fair Lady.*

Bloomsbury

The self-centered free-thinking set that made the name of Bloomsbury world-famous have left hardly a trace, but this remains the heart of learned, literary London. The University of London is here; so are the Law Courts, and "Mankind's Attic"—the British Museum, home of the Elgin Marbles, the Rosetta Stone, and the Magna Carta. Until the British Library moves to its new venue at St. Pancras, a greater number of books can probably be found in Bloomsbury than in all the rest of London. Virginia Woolf and T.S. Eliot would be pleased to note that some of London's most beautiful domestic architecture, elegant houses that would have been familiar to Dr. Johnson, still line the area's prim squares. A must for most visitors will be No. 48 Doughty Street, Charles Dickens's House—still standing is the tall upright clerk's desk where he worked on *Oliver Twist.*

Bloomsbury is really part of Holborn, the core of Legal London. Stroll through the quiet courts, leafy gardens, and magnificent halls that comprise the Inns of Court, the finest group of historic buildings in the city in an almost unspoiled setting—the closest thing to the spirit of Oxford London has to offer. In Holborn, you'll also find several of London's fascinating "time-machines": Sir John Soane's Museum, a mansion that whisks you back to the mid 1800s, and the Victorian-era Pollock's Toy Museum—so delightful an experience it merits a visit with or without children.

Chelsea

Chelsea has always beckoned to free-thinkers and fashion-fringers—from Sir Thomas More to Isadora Duncan (she couldn't find a place to stay her first night, so she decamped to the graveyard at Chelsea Old Church, which natives *still* insist is a lovely place to stay). Major sights include Christopher Wren's magisterial Royal Hospital—now the site of the famous Chelsea Flower Show—and lovely Cheyne Walk, where Henry James and Dante Gabriel Rossetti once lived. Now an extremely expensive place to live (through parted curtains you may glimpse rooms of exquisite taste, which here in Chelsea is entirely as it should be), the area on Saturdays continues to draw an army of trendaholics to the King's Road, whose boutiques gave birth to the paisleyed '60s and the pink-headed-punk '70s.

The City

Known as "The Square Mile," the City is to London as Wall Street is to Manhattan. And as the site of the Celtic settlement the Romans called Londinium, this is the oldest part of London. Unfortunately, thanks to blocks of high-rise apartments and steel skyscrapers, it now looks like the newest part. Yet within and around the capital-c City are some of London's most memorable attractions—St. Paul's Cathedral, the Tower of London, the storybook Tower Bridge, and the Royal Shakespeare Company (at the Barbican Centre). Charles and Diana tied the knot at St. Paul's, but they could have found equally beautiful options here, including St. Bride's (its distinctive multitiered spire gave rise to today's wedding cakes), St. Giles-without-Cripplegate, and St. Mary-le-Bow. At the east border of the City is the legendary

Tower of London, where the young Princes of the Bloody Tower, and Sir Thomas More and Anne Boleyn all met untimely ends. Considered England's most perfectly preserved medieval fortress, it boasts London's earliest church, a charming Tudoresque village, and the Crown Jewels (polished every February by Garrard, the royal jewelers). Here, too, nest Larry, Hardy, George, Hugin, Mumia, and Rhys—the six Tower Ravens. Legend has it if they fly away, England will fall—but have no fear, their wings are clipped.

Covent Garden

In not much more than a decade, Covent Garden—which lies just to the east of Soho—has gone from a down-at-heels district to one of the busiest, most raffishly enjoyable parts of the city. Continental-style open-air cafés create a very un-English atmosphere. Warehouses, once cavernous and grim, now accommodate fashion boutiques and a huge variety of shops favored by the trendoisie. A network of narrow streets, arcades, and pedestrian malls, the area is dominated by the Piazza—scene of a food market in the 1830s, then a flower market in the 1870s—today the indoor/outdoor complex overflows with clothing shops and crafts stalls. The London Transport Museum and the famed Royal Opera House (undergoing extensive renovations at press time) are conveniently nearby. Eliza "My Fair Lady" Dolittle wasn't the only one singing in the neighborhood.

The East End

In the East End, you'll find sights and sounds that are as much a part of the real London as a November fog. Although its 19th-century slums—immortalized by Charles Dickens and the evocative etchings of Gustave Doré—are a relic of the past, the area still possesses a haunting beauty, and a warm spirit of humor and friendliness. Here you'll find, on Sundays, the 20th-century version of a medieval fair, called Petticoat Lane, and other fascinating sights including the Geffrye Museum—an overlooked venue of wonderful historic interiors—Hawksmoor's Christ Church, and The Blind Beggar, the Victorian den of iniquity where Salvation Army founder William Booth was moved to preach his first sermon. Off the main thoroughfare, tap into the true pulse of East End life by

exploring the lanes and alleys that still comprise one of the world's most fascinating melting-pots. If you can fit it in, take one of the evening walking tours that trace the footsteps of the infamous Jack the Ripper; at night, these mean streets still seem shrouded in a Dickensian aura.

Greenwich

A quick 8-mi jaunt down the Thames will bring you past the National Maritime Museum and the *Cutty Sark* to Greenwich's Old Royal Observatory, where if time stood still, all the world's timepieces would be off. When you tire of straddling the hemispheres at the Greenwich Meridan, take a stroll through the acres of parkland that cover the area or, on weekends, the weekend crafts and antiques markets. Must-sees also include Sir Christopher Wren's Royal Naval College and Inigo Jones's Queen House, both of which scale architectural heights. The pretty streets of Greenwich Village house numerous bookstores and antiques shops. The journey to Greenwich is most appealing if you approach by river, affording as it does fine views of the Tower of London (a guaranteed spine-chiller), the Royal Naval College, and the Queen's House. This also gives you a superb opportunity to do what Londoners have loved doing ever since there was a London: watch the river traffic glide by.

Hampstead

One of the great glories of England is the English village, and on the northern outskirts of London you'll find one of the most fetching: Hampstead. Today, its flower-spangled Georgian houses, its picturesque tidiness, and its expensive French delicatessens attract personages from the arts and wealthy entrepreneurs. For sheer pleasure, exploring Hampstead is hard to top, as an amble along Church Walk—possibly the finest (and certainly the prettiest) row of 18th-century houses in London—will prove. Connoisseurs of old and new will want to check out London's most beautiful painting by Vermeer, on view at Kenwood House (its park hosts grand concerts and fireworks in the summer), and the latest cutting-edge art at the Saatchi Collection. Here, too, are the Freud Museum and the Keats House; why not visit the garden where the poet penned his immortal "Ode to a Nightingale," then go bird-watching in the 800-plus emerald-green acres of Hampstead Heath. Toward dusk,

Victoriana buffs might head for Highgate Cemetery—its Gothic mausolea have been featured in many a Dracula film. In the nearby neighborhood of St. John's Wood, Beatles-lovers will want to visit Abbey Road to snap the famed road crossing outside the studios where John, Paul, George, and Ringo recorded nearly all of their music.

Hyde Park, Kensington Gardens

When in need of elbow room, Londoners head for their green "lungs"—Hyde Park and Kensington Gardens. Viewed by natives as their own private backyards, they form an open swathe across central London; together with St. James's Park, Green Park, and Buckingham Palace Gardens, they make up almost 600 beauty-filled acres that offer a taste of serene remoteness from the great city. The handsome trees and quiet walks found in these spots will refresh you as thoroughly as, centuries ago, these grounds refreshed Henry VIII after a hard day's shenanigans. In the Regency era, splendid horseflesh and equipages were the grand attraction; today, the soapbox orators (most oratorical on Sunday mornings) at Hyde Park Corner remain grand entertainment. Sooner or later, however, everyone heads to the Long Water in Kensington Gardens, for one of London's most beloved sights: the Peter Pan statue (J.M. Barrie had the sprite living on a nearby island). Then circumnavigate the Round Pond, or swim in the Serpentine, or try to catch a glimpse of the Household Cavalry on Rotten Row.

Knightsbridge and Kensington

This is Princess Di's official neighborhood—Kensington Palace is her current address, while the surrounding neighborhood gave rise to the "Sloane Rangers," a quintessential-London gilded youth of which Diana is a prime example. Within the district's cavalcade of streets lined with decorous houses are tucked-away corners—small squares that would not be out of place in a dozy cathedral town; delightful pubs nestled away in back lanes; and antiques shops, their windows aglow with the luminous colors of oil paintings. Not surprisingly, the capital's snazziest department stores are also here, Harrods and Harvey Nichols (the latter being Chic London's center of gravity). With unlikely self-discipline, however, head first for the area's main attraction—the great museum complex of South Kensington. Raphael and Constable canvases, Ossie Clark couture, and William Morris chairs all beckon at the Victoria and Albert Museum, a grand pile whose forte is the decorative arts and whose predominant audience is an especially decorative crowd. Next to the V&A come three museums devoted to science, including the Natural History Museum (kids will head for its Creepie Crawlies exhibit first). Most delightful are two historic homes: Leighton House, Lord Leighton's stunning Persian extravaganza, and the Linley Sambourne House, whose elegant Edwardian interiors were featured in *A Room with a View*. Regroup at Kensington Palace—its state rooms are open to view—than repair to its Orangery for a pot of Earl Grey.

Notting Hill and Holland Park

These are two of London's most fashionable, coveted residential areas. Notting Hill, around Portobello Road, is a trend-setting square mile of multi-ethnicity, galleries, small exciting shops, and see-and-be-seen-in restaurants. The style-watching media dub the natives—by and large, musicians, novelists, and fashion plates—Notting Hillbillies. If Notting Hill is for the young, neighboring Holland Park is entirely the opposite—its leafy streets are full of expensive white stucco Victorians that lead to bucolic Holland Park itself.

Regent's Park

Helping to frame the northern border of the city, Regent's Park is home to the much-loved Zoo, the much-loved rose-bedecked Queen Mary's Gardens, and the much-loved Regent's Park Open-Air Theatre. A walk around the perimeter of the park is a must for devotees of Classical architecture; the payoff is a view of John Nash's Terraces, a grandiose series of white-stucco terraced houses, built around 1810. The People of Quality for whom these stately buildings were intended demanded London homes as nearly as possible resembling their grand country estates, and Nash magnificently obliged. In summer, be sure to take in Queen Mary's Gardens. Next, head over to the theater for a picture-perfect performance of *A Midsummer Night's Dream*. Year-round, the park is a favorite spot for mothers with strollers, joggers, and hand-holding senior citizens enjoying the fresh air. Watch out for those airborne objects—softballs, footballs, and cricket balls.

St. James's and Mayfair

St. James's and Mayfair form the core of the West End, the city's smartest and most desirable central area—St. James's to the south of Piccadilly and north of the Mall, Mayfair to the north of Piccadilly and south of Oxford Street. Neither are stuffed with must-sees, though there is no shortage of history and gorgeous architecture, but they *are* custom-built for window shopping, expansive strolling, and getting a peak into the lifestyles of London's rich and famous—18th-*and*-20th-century versions. Although many will say Mayfair is only a state of mind, the heart of Mayfair has shifted from the 19th-century's Park Lane to beautiful Carlos Place and Mount Row. The shops of New and Old Bond Streets lure the wealthy; even if you bid on a letter at Sotheby's signed by one of the Brönte sisters, or stop in at Graff's for a weighty diamond, the window shopping is next best to the real thing and is free. Mayfair is primarily residential, so its homes are off limits except for two satisfyingly grand houses: Apsley House, the Duke of Wellington's home, built by Robert Adam in 1771, and once known as No. 1, London, and, on gorgeous Manchester Square, the Wallace Collection, situated in a palatial town house filled with Old Masters and fine French furniture. The district of St. James's—named after the centuries-old palace that lies at its center—remains the ultimate enclave of the old-fashioned gentleman's London. Here you'll find Pall Mall, with its many noted clubs, including the Reform Club—where Jules Verne's Phileas Fogg wagered he could go around the world in 80 days—and Jermyn Street, where you can follow in the Duke of Windsor's sartorial footsteps by purchasing a half-dozen shirts made at Turnbull & Asser.

Soho and Theatreland

Once the setting for London's red-light district, Soho these days is more stylish than seedy, and is now home to film and record bigwigs (Sir Paul McCartney's offices are here). The area is not especially rich architecturally, but it has an intriguing atmo-

sphere. Built up around quaint Soho Square, the density of Continental residents means some of London's best restaurants—whether pricey Italian, budget Chinese, or the latest opening—are in the vicinity. Nearby is Carnaby Street, still hoping to stage a revival of swinging '60s psychedelic fashion. Shaftesbury Avenue cuts through the southern part of Soho; this is Theatreland—home to almost 50 West End theaters, and a stand-in for Mecca for those who love Shakespeare, Maggie Smith, and *Oliver!* To the south of Theatreland lies Leicester Square, London's answer to Times Square, and Charing Cross Road, the bibliophile's dream.

The South Bank

You won't say "How very British" in this section of town across the Thames from London Bridge, which was totally rebuilt after the bombs of World War II flattened the remains of medieval Southwark. However, if William Shakespeare returned today, he would be delighted to find a complete reconstruction of his Globe Theatre, which was inaugurated in 1996, not far from where the original closed in 1642. In fact, this side of the Thames—walk along the riverside embankment for great views of the city—has become a perch for diehard culture vultures: The Design Museum is here, and the gigantic Bankside Power Station building (hard by the Globe) is being readied to become the new Tate Gallery. Also here is the South Bank Arts Complex—the country's chief arts center, with its important Museum of the Moving Image, Royal National Theatre, and Royal Festival Hall and London's newest culinary hot spot, the Oxo Tower Restaurant and Brasserie. And who could resist The London Dungeon—a waxwork extravaganza full of scenes featuring plenty of blood-'n'-guts and medieval dismemberments—where "a perfectly horrible experience" is guaranteed.

The Thames Upstream

London has been Britain's power center for centuries, so it is only natural that many visitable places associated with royalty and the ruling establishment—among them, Chiswick, Kew Gardens, Osterley Park, Richmond, and Putney—should be found close to the capital. The link between London and these idyllic retreats is Father Thames—who offers a river cruise as a particularly nice way to escape the city on a sweltering summer day. These palaces and country houses are enveloped with serenity and beautiful rolling greenery, which explains the astronomical prices that some of the local real estate commands. Stroll around and get lost in a daydream breathing the rural air or find your way out of the famous maze at Hampton Court Palace, England's version of Versailles.

PLEASURES AND PASTIMES

Food, Glorious Food: The Delights of Dining

London now ranks—and longtime absentees must suspend disbelief here—among the world's top dining scenes. A new generation of chefs has precipitated a fresh approach to food preparation, which you could call "London-style" though most refer to it as "Modern British." Everyone seems to have an opinion about it, and newspapers and magazines now devote columns if not pages to food and restaurant reviews. Everyone reads them and everyone dines out to the point where London has become a significant foodies' town.

Today, almost everything on the culinary front has changed. The old standards have been given a nouvelle spin—although roast suckling pig topped with strawberry papaya and served on a bed of chili noodles may not be everyone's cup of tea. The nouvelle push has taken the starch—literally—out of many of the city's menus, and this new energy is even finding a vogue for old standbys like angels-on-horseback (crisp bacon wrapped around oysters). It probably won't be long before some of-the-moment hot spot unveils a trendy variation on the nursery-rhyme pie, with four-and-twenty rock stars popping out in place of black birds to sing for the king. As for where to find such marvelous new dining experiences, check out the Dining chapter in this book.

There will be times, however, when you'll be sitting in your charming room watching the rain streaming down the Georgian sash windowpane, surrounded by his-

tory, hungry as a horse, and looking for a dinner bargain. What do you do? A Londoner with nouse (British for savvy) goes for the nearest Tandoori house—this Indian food goes beyond a cliché into national-dish territory. The dining chapter doesn't list many curry places; discover your own and be guided by your budget. Londoners have now enlarged their purview to encompass most of the world; in the space of two weeks, diners can cover as much tongue-tingling ground as in a two-week package tour of exotic, far-flung places.

In fact, so many people are eating Ethnic that the indigenous caff (the British diner)—which offers such grab-and-gulp goodies as fish-and-chips, chip butties (Wonder Bread with margarine and fries), or chips and ketchup—have become less ubiquitous in central London than good sandwich bars. Today, such native delicacies as the cockles, winkles, and smoked eels found in the Cockney stalls of the East End appear as just one more exotic cuisine in the pantheon.

Cheers!: The Pub Experience

Londoners could no more live without their "local" than they could forgo dinner. The pub—or public house, to give it its full title—is ingrained in the British psyche as social center, bolt-hole, second home. Pub culture—revolving around pints, pool, darts, and sports—is still male-dominated; however, as a result of the gentrification trend that started in the late '80s by the major breweries (which own most pubs), transforming many ancient smoke- and spittle-stained dives into fantasy Edwardian drawing rooms, women have been entering their welcoming doors in increasing numbers. This decade, the trend has been toward The Bar, superficially identified by its cocktail list, creative paintwork, bare floorboards, and chrome fittings. The social function is the same: these are English pubs, but not as we formerly knew them.

When doing a London pub crawl, you must remember one thing: Arcane licensing laws forbid the serving of alcohol after 11 PM (10:30 on Sunday; there are different rules for restaurants)—a circumstance you see in action at 10 minutes to 11, when the "last orders" bell signals a stampede to the bar. After many decades, however, some relaxation of these unpopular laws are in evidence with weekend "extensions" being granted, especially in Soho, plus a slew of clubs/bars/pubs that get around it by charging a moderate cover after 11 PM.

The Performing Arts: From the Boards to the Bard

One of the main reasons for so many people wanting to visit London is its enviable reputation in the performing arts. There is a strength and fluidity about the performing arts in the metropolis which makes them very difficult to pin down. An actor planing Lear wich the Royal Shakespeare Company one day could quite possibly appear in a television farce the next; an opera that has played to the small exclusive audience at Glyndebourne in the English countryside might reappear the next week at the Royal Albert Hall, delighting millions through radio. In music and drama, opera and ballet, there are endless opportunities for visitors to enjoy themselves to the hilt.

THEATER➤ Shakespeare, of course, supplies the backbone to the theatrical life of the city. There can hardly have been a day since the one on which the Bard breathed his last, when one of his plays, in some shape or form, was not being performed. On the London stage, they have survived being turned into musicals (from Purcell to Rock), they have made the reputations of generations of famous actors (and broken not a few), they have seen women playing Hamlet and men playing Rosalind. Every so often, the theatergoing public is sorely tempted to forbid the production of *Hamlet,* with so many versions being staged. But then something like the magnificent new reconstruction of Shakespeare's Globe comes about, and promises to show the play in a whole new light. If the Bard of Bards remains the headliner at Stratford-upon-Barbican, the London theater scene is amazingly varied. From a West End *Oliver!* revival to an East End feminist staging of *Ben-Hur,* London remains a theatergoer's town.

If you're a theater junkie, and want to put together a West End package, the *Complete Guide to London's West End Theatres* has seating plans and booking information for all of the houses. It costs £9.95 from the Society of London Theatres (✉ Bedford Chambers, The Piazza, Covent Garden, London WC2 E8HQ, ☎ 0171/836–0971).

MUSIC➤ London is home to four world-class orchestras. The London Symphony Orchestra is in residence at the Barbican Centre, while the London Philharmonic lives at the Royal Festival Hall—one of the finest concert halls in Europe. Between the Barbican and South Bank, there are concert performances almost every night of the year. The Barbican also presents chamber music concerts in partnership with such celebrated orchestras as the City of London Sinfonia. The Royal Albert Hall during the Promenade Concert season—July to September—is a don't-miss pleasure. Also look for the lunchtime concerts held throughout the city in either smaller concert halls, arts-center foyers, or churches; they usually cost under £5 or are free. St. John's, Smith Square, and St. Martin-in-the-Fields are the major venues for these, and they also present evening concerts.

BALLET AND OPERA➤ For decades, London's leading troupes, the Royal Opera and the Royal Ballet, have shared grnadiose quarters at the Royal Opera House in Covent Garden—a fact that rather cut down on the number of opera and ballet performances which could be mounted in a season. Even with a backstage renovation done several years ago, there was still a great pressure on rehearsal and dressing room space. Now change is finally here: the grand Opera House has been closed for a major two-year renovation, and the resident companies are scurrying for other venues. When the red-and-gold curtain finally does go back up at "the Garden," however, only opera may been seen there: Plans are in the offing for a completely new venue for the ballet.

Best Foot Forward: Walking Through London

London is a great walking city because so many of its real treasures are untouted details: tiny alleyways barely visible on the map; garden squares; churchyards; shop windows; sudden vistas of skyline or park. However, it is big, VERY BIG. And often rather damp. With the obvious precautions of comfortable, weatherproof shoes and an umbrella, this least expensive of tourist activities might well become your favorite pastime.

GREAT ITINERARIES

In a city with as many richly stocked museums and marvels as London, visitors risk seeing half of everything and all of nothing. One could easily spend two solid weeks exploring the many layers of the city, but if time is limited you'll need to plan carefully. The following suggested itineraries can help insure an exciting and efficiently mapped-out visit. See Chapter 2 for complete information about individual sights and detailed neighborhood walking tours.

If You Have 1 Day

Touring the largest city in England in the space of a single day sounds like an impossible goal, but it can actually—almost—be done in the span of one sunrise to sunset. Think London 101. Begin at postcard-London, the **Houses of Parliament,** best viewed from Westminster Bridge. If you're lucky, you'll hear **Big Ben** chiming, a sound still likened to the heartbeat of the commonwealth by a sentimental few. Move on to centuries-old **Westminster Abbey**—if and when Prince Charles becomes king, this is where his coronation will be staged—then tube it from the Westminster stop to Charing Cross (if you want to catch a glimpse of Her Majesty's two mounted sentries at Horse Guards Parade, bus it up Whitehall) to arrive at **Trafalgar Square** for your photo op with Nelson's Column and hundreds of pigeons. Take in the treasures of the **National Gallery,** which ranks right up there with the collections of the Louvre and the Uffizi; history buffs might opt instead for a flip-book-fast tour of the adjacent **National Portrait Gallery.** Break for lunch in the **Brasserie** of the National Gallery, then take a short taxi trip over to a **sight dear to your heart**: for connoisseurs, this might be the Wallace Collection or Tate Gallery; for time-travelers, Apsley House, which is the home of the Duke of Wellington or Sir John Soane's Museum; for those with pre-teens in tow, the London Dungeon or Madame Tussaud's. For a mid-afternoon session, choose between two royal monuments. First choice: Heading west

from Trafalgar Square, taxi through the impressive Admiralty Arch down **the Mall** to what there is reason to believe is the world's most photographed building, **Buckingham Palace.** During summer weeks, when the state rooms are open to the public, you can ogle their full pomp. **Theatreland** awaits palace-trekkers with a hit West End musical—a refreshing finale to the day. Second choice: Eastward (take the tube to the Tower Hill stop) lies the **Tower of London,** home to the Beefeaters, the Crown Jewels, and the six resident ravens who nest on high. At dusk, after leaving the Tower, head across the way to the East End for a guaranteed spine-chiller, a Jack the Ripper guided walking tour. Of course, if you have more than one day to spend, many of these sights would merit an extended visit—an entire afternoon, for example, could easily be spent at the National Gallery, the Tower, or Parliament.

If You Have 3 Days

A breakneck first day in London has been outlined above. On your second day you can slow down a bit. Begin at the beginning of mankind's search for enlightenment and art: Tour the **British Museum,** home of such wonders as the Rosetta Stone, the Elgin Marbles, and the Lindow Man. If the idea of traipsing through "mankind's attic" doesn't grab you—the number of Londoners who have never been to the British Museum is vast—head for **Sir John Soane's Museum,** the quirky, 19th-century (but unexpectedly modern) home of the architect of the Bank of England headquarters. Here in Bloomsbury other treats beckon: **Pollock's Toy Museum,** the **Charles Dickens House,** and, on Gordon Square, former address of Virginia Woolf and Lytton Strachey, the **Percival David Foundation of Chinese Art.** For an early lunch, take the tube from Russell Square to Leicester Square in Soho, for dim sum in Chinatown. Next, for a dose of magisterial grandeur, hop back on the tube to arrive at the St. Paul's stop and **St. Paul's Cathedral.** Walk off lunch by strolling south through Blackfriars—a quaint district full of crooked streets, historic courtyards, and minuscule cul-de-sacs—to the Thames river. After downing a refreshing pint at the **Black Friar** (possibly London's most spectacular 19th-century pub), cross Blackfriars bridge to Southwark's riverside embankment for a splendid view of St. Paul's dome. Keep an eye out for **Cardinal's Cap Alley**—here is the adorable house Sir Christopher Wren, architect of St. Paul's, built so he could easily check on the cathedral's construction. Take the time to drink in this scene, held to be **one of the most enchanting views in all London.** A stone's throw away is the rebuilt **Shakespeare's Globe Theatre**; if you're not catching an open-air performance (held only in warmweather months), tour the adjoining museum. Keep heading eastward along the river, cross Southwark Bridge, then take the tube from the Mansion House stop to **Covent Garden.** Dine at one of the area's chic restaurants, then watch the colorfully costumed street performers called buskers, take in some jazz at Ronnie Scott's in Soho, or run down an evening recital at one of London's historic churches.

Start your third day with Buckingham Palace's **Changing of the Guard,** held April through July at 11:30 daily, August through March at the same hour on alternate days. Warm up for this ceremony by viewing a selection of Her Majesty's treasures in the **Queen's Gallery** and the nearby **Royal Mews.** If the state rooms of the palace are closed to viewing when you're in town, head through Green Park to **Apsley House,** the 19th-century mansion of the Duke of Wellington and check out its memorably palatial interiors. Wander up Park Lane into **Mayfair,** one of London's ritziest neighborhoods, and stroll past Grosvenor Square and Oxford Street to Manchester Square and the **Wallace Collection,** whose gilded interiors are stuffed with 18th-century art. For a pub break, visit the **Devonshire Arms,** a Henry Higgins's–parlour look-alike on Duke Street, a few blocks south of the Wallace. (Londonfact: the Beatles used to chow down here.) For serious retail therapy, return south, then east to scout three great shopping destinations: **Bond Street** for world-class glitz, **Regent Street** for savvy sophistication, and **Carnaby Street** for some Rocker-style street gear. For an evening highlight, book a performance of the **Royal Shakespeare Company** at the Barbican Centre.

If You Have 7 Days
Each section of London provides distinct clues to the city's past. In your first three days, you've made a start on piecing together the story of this great, crowded, endlessly fascinating city. Now you're ready

to build on that foundation. Kick off day four at the South Kensington museums. This is a district planned by the Victorians to induce gallery gout and museum feet: The **Victoria and Albert,** the **Natural History Museum,** and the **Science Museum** are all here. Art lovers will want to explore the first first, while budding Einsteins will run for either of the latter. All three cultural palaces could easily consume an entire day, so you'll need to pick one to do it justice. Then head over to Knightsbridge to either mercantile-and-fashion giants **Harrods** or **Harvey Nichols** (whose Fifth Floor eatery is favored by Princess Di). Move on to **Kensington Gardens,** where almost everyone throws a kiss to the famous statue of **Peter Pan,** and to **Kensington Palace,** Princess Di's home, where the state rooms are open to view year-round. For a perfect late afternoon pot of tea, check out the palace's elegant Orangerie. For modern art buffs, the **Serpentine Gallery** should be the next stop. Along the way, let yourself venture into the many winding lanes and narrow courts in the area, and smell the roses in all those lovely well-kept squares.

Day five dawns at **The City**—London's ancient core. Built up around St. Paul's, the area has numerous attractions, including **Dr. Johnson's House,** the **Old Bailey,** the **Museum of London,** and several Christopher Wren churches. The nearby East End beckons with its **Petticoat Lane** sprawling market (open weekends); the **Geffrye Museum,** a must for decorative arts lovers; and the **Spitalfields** restoration. After lunch at the Whitechapel Gallery Café, serious folk will want to head west on the tube to Holborn (Chancery Lane, Temple stops) to visit the historic **Inns of Court** and **The Temple,** the historic foundations of Legal London. Farther along lies that storybook icon, **Tower Bridge,** which you must cross to reach the South Bank, where the **London Dungeon** awaits—this medieval waxworks show is devoted to the more gory aspects of British history (and there were plenty of them!).

On day six, leave the city behind for pleasures along the Thames: Choose either to visit **Greenwich,** or the storied palace and gardens of **Hampton Court.** Or else opt to head for the outskirts of northern London and the relentlessly picturesque village of **Hampstead,** where you'll find **Kenwood**—a noble Robert Adam house—as well as the **homes of Keats and Freud,** and the bustling **Camden Lock** market. (Nearby, in swank St. John's Wood, is **Abbey Road,** beloved address to Beatlemaniacs.) Just south of Hampstead is **Regent's Park,** surrounded by Nash's Terraces—a must for Regency-era buffs and admirers of splendid urban creations.

Begin your last day by taking the tube to the Knightsbridge stop and heading south for an early morning stroll through **Belgravia**; few tourists venture here but it's London at its most *Upstairs, Downstairs.* Head over to the endless cavalcade of glitzy emporiums of **Sloane Street** and **Sloane Square** and join the likes of Princess Di for some world-class shopping. **Chelsea,** along King's Road, is where much of London comes to shop and stroll. After viewing Wren's historic **Royal Hospital,** relax over lunch at a King's Road pub, move on to **Cheyne Walk,** where leading 19th-century artists lived, then bus over to Millbank to take in the **Tate Gallery**'s incomparable collection of British paintings. As dusk settles, head over to the **South Bank Arts Complex,** where you might finish up your visit with a play in the Olivier Theatre or a concert in the Queen Elizabeth Hall. Don't fret if the performances are entirely booked: by now you've learned that London can be the most wonderful free show in the world.

FODOR'S CHOICE

No two people will agree on what makes a perfect vacation, but it's fun and helpful to know what others think. Here's a compendium drawn from the must-see lists of hundreds of tourists. We hope you'll have a chance to experience some of these great memories-in-the-making yourself while visiting London. For detailed information about entries, refer to the appropriate chapters within this guidebook.

Long Live the Queen!

★ **Changing of the Guard.** Adding a dash of color to the gloomiest of London days, this ceremony is mounted (daily, depending on the season) at both Whitehall and Buckingham Palace. The Life Guards—all scarlet tunics and silvergilt helmets—ride on horseback to Whitehall from Hyde Park, while, outside Buck House, the Guard of Color marches as the band plays (they have been known to cut loose to Billy Joel when Her Majesty is away).

★ **The Mall.** Look down this grand thoroughfare to Buckingham Palace from underneath Admiralty Arch and you'll see what the Queen sees during all those royal ceremonies.

★ **Trooping the Colour.** Marking the Queen's birthday in June (like Paddington Bear, she has two—the real one is in April), this is the capital's most spectacular military occasion, with bands playing, flags fluttering, and massed ranks of soldiers in scarlet coats and immense "busbies."

Quintessential London

★ **The Houses of Parliament at sunset.** Cross the Thames to Jubilee Gardens to see this view of London at its storybook best. The headliner is Big Ben, which looks almost as magical as when Walt Disney used it as a perch for Peter and the children in *Peter Pan.*

★ **Sunday afternoon at Speakers' Corner, Hyde Park.** A space especially reserved for anyone with anything to say that they *must* say publicly makes for great entertainment. Speakers seem to be most oratorical on Sunday afternoons.

★ **St. Paul's Cathedral Thames-side.** The most thrilling vantage point to take in St. Paul's is at Cardinal Cap's Alley, across the Thames on the southern embankment, right by Shakespeare's Globe. Here, you'll find the architect Christopher Wren's elegant little house (built so he could monitor progress on his masterpiece, directly across the river).

★ **An Afternoon Performance at Shakespeare's Globe.** As with a flick of a Wellsian time machine, this new, spectacular, open-to-the-skies reconstruction of Shakespeare's beloved "wooden O" magically transports you back to Elizabethan London. In 16th-century fashion, audience participation is welcome: Jump in and hiss Iago—you'll have plenty of company.

★ **Tower Bridge at Night.** A dramatically floodlighted Tower Bridge confronts you as you come out of the Design Museum on a winter's night. By day, have your Nikon ready to frame the nearby Tower of London between the splendid Victorian-style guard railings of the bridge.

Fascinating Walks

Beatles' Magical Mystery Tour. If you're one of the 63 million people who tuned into Ed Sullivan that Sunday night, chances are you'll want to take this wonderful stroll down Memory Lane offered by Original London Walks. Stops include the London Palladium, No. 3 Savile Row—the Fab Four's London headquarters—and Abbey Road.

A Belgravia Promenade. Far from the madding crowd, Belgravia represents all that is gracious in London living. A vision out of a Regency-period engraving, Belgrave Place is one of the most moneyed addresses in town and adorned with elegant mansions and picturesque mews; today, the lords and dukes have moved out of the former and into the latter.

In and Around Hampstead Heath. Just like John Le Carré, you can climb the rolling hills of Hampstead Heath, from Hampstead Village to Kenwood, perhaps in time for a summer concert.

Jack the Ripper Walk. *Cor Blimey Guv'nor, Jack the Ripper woz ere!* Several organizations offer tours of "Jack's London"—the East End and its grisly settings for the Whitechapel murders. Unforgettable!

London Splendor

Apsley House. Known as No. 1 London, this was the august residence of the Duke of Wellington, fabled conqueror of Napoleon. The house's centerpiece, the Waterloo Gallery, is one of the grandest rooms in Europe.

Linley Sambourne House. A little masterpiece of Victoriana, this former residence of Punch cartoonish Linley Sambourne is unusually charming. Steep yourself in its atmosphere and let the years roll back.

Sir John Soane's Museum. Eccentric architect of the Bank of England, Sir John left his house to the nation on condition nothing be changed; the result is a phantasmagoria of colors, unusual perspectives, and artifacts from many centuries.

Spencer House. The London house to end all London houses, this glamorous 18th-century Palladian pile was built by Princess Diana's ancestors. Now restored to all its glory by Lord Rothschild, it proves the 18th-century Spencers were also no slouch in the flash department.

Wallace Collection. The serene 18th-century mansion, Hertford House, which houses this sumptuous collection is as much a part of the appeal as its rich array of porcelain, paintings, furniture, and sculpture. Top treats here are Frans Hals's *Laughing Cavalier,* Fragonard's *The Swing,* and Thomas Sully's *Queen Victoria,* which is hung in a 19th-century rouge-pink salon, which must be the prettiest room in London.

Magnificent Museums

British Museum. Yes, Virginia, those are the Elgin Marbles. Curiosity seekers could move into this grand pile and never tire of all that it has to offer, from the Rosetta Stone to the Mildenhall Treasure. The pick-of-the-peak, of course, are the beautiful Elgin Marbles from ancient Greece.

Tate Gallery. The greatest glories of English painting are here, from Elizabethan portraits to the most avant avant-garde works. Everyone's favorite: Sir John Everett Millais' Pre-Raphaelite vision of *Ophelia.*

National Gallery. Leonardos, Rubenses, and Rembrandts wallpaper the rooms here—an incomparably rich treasure trove of Old Masters. It's an awe-inspiring experience to see some of the most beloved works of art in the world, such as Jan van Eyck's *Arnofini Marriage,* in the flesh.

Top Hotels

Claridge's. The same fine qualities that attracted the King of Morocco, among many others, to this world-renowned Mayfair hotel are sure to make you feel right at home too. ££££

Covent Garden Hotel. Discerning travelers now call this the most stylish hotel in London. ££££

The Dorchester. It's a true accomplishment that so much gold leaf and marble, linens and brocades have managed the effect of sophisticated intimacy in this hotel that has all of Hyde Park as its front garden. ££££

The Savoy. Secure a river suite at this historic, late-Victorian hotel overlooking the Thames, and you'll get one of the best stays—and views—in London. ££££

The Beaufort. It's fair to use this set of Victorian houses, run by a wonderfully friendly all-female staff, as a home away from home, especially if you live practically next door at Harrods. £££

★**The Franklin.** Everything is romantic here from the quiet garden to tea in the lounge to the sweet smell of the Floris toiletries that you'll find in your room. £££

★**The Pelham.** Designed to capture the essence of English country housedom, Tim and Kit Kemp's boutique hotel offers the comforting feel of a tranquil country retreat with all the advantages of being in the center of South Kensington. £££

★**Basil Street.** So many people return to this Knightsbridge hotel that there is a standard discount for repeat guests—what more need be said. ££

★**The Commodore.** Secreted in a quiet square behind Bayswater Road, this family-run hotel has some great value duplex-style rooms. ££

★**The Vicarage.** Friendly and homey, this Kensington B&B has kept high standards for years. £

Great Restaurants and Pubs

★**La Tante Claire.** Pierre Kaufman is probably London's best chef. The decor is light and sophisticated, the service impeccable, the French wine list impressive, but the food is the point. Walk your meal off afterward along the nearby Thames embankment. ££££

★**Le Caprice.** This glamorous place has stood the test of time—the food is great, the ambience even better. It has no business being so good, because the other reason everyone comes here is that everyone else does, which leads to the best people-watching in town. £££

★**Quaglino's.** This isn't the biggest, but it is still the best of Sir Terence Conran's London hot spots. Now past its fifth birthday, "Quags" is *the* out-of-towners' post-theater or celebration destination, while Londoners like its late hours. £££

★**Rules.** Come, escape from the 20th century. London's answer to Maxim's in Paris, this enjoys an incomparably beautiful setting, one that has welcomed everyone from Dickens to the Duke of Windsor. The food is good but the decor is truly delicious. £££

★**Wódka.** Laid back and stylish, this serves London's only modern Polish food. Order from the separate menu a carafe of the purest vodka in London (and watch the check inflate). ££

★**The Black Friar.** You can't miss it—it's the only wedge-shaped, ornate building with a statue of a friar on the front as you step out of Blackfriars tube station! Inside is one of London's most splendiferous pubs—all colored marbles, inlaid mother-of-pearl, and stained glass, with painted friars, devils, and fairies all about. The pub grub is minimal but the pints and the fetching locals are great. £

★**Geales.** Fish and chips as you always imagined it. The decor is stark but the fish will have been swimming just hours beforehand. £

★**George Inn.** London at its Time-Machine best, this inn sits in a courtyard where Shakespeare's plays were performed. The present building dates from the 17th century, and is London's last remaining galleried inn. Dickens was a regular—the inn is even featured in *Little Dorrit*. £

FESTIVALS AND SEASONAL EVENTS

Top seasonal events in and around London include the Chelsea Flower Show in May, Derby Day at Epsom Racecourse, Wimbledon Lawn Tennis Championships and Henley Regatta in June, and a new innovation, the London Arts Season, which combines many events in theater, art, and music with good deals on hotels and meals out. There is a complete list of ticket agencies in *Britain Events,* available in person only from the **British Travel Centre.** ⊠ *12 Regent St. Tube: Piccadilly Circus.*

Feb.–Mar.➤ **London Arts Season** showcases the city's extensive arts scene, with bargain-price tickets and special events. ⊠ *British Travel Centre, 12 Regent St., SW1Y 4PQ,* ☎ *0171/839–6181 (Arts Season only).*

SPRING

Mar. 19–29 and Sept. 10–20➤ **Chelsea Antiques Fair,** a twice-yearly fair with wide range of pre-1830 pieces for sale. ⊠ *Old Town Hall, King's Rd., Chelsea SW3 4PW,* ☎ *01444/482–514.*

Mar. 11–Apr. 5➤ **Daily Mail Ideal Home Exhibition** is a consumer show of new products and ideas for the home. ⊠ *Earl's Court Exhibition Centre, Warwick Rd., London SW5 9TA,* ☎ *01895/677–677.*

Mar.➤ **Camden Jazz Festival** is 10 days of concerts sponsored by the Borough of Camden. For information, call ☎ 0171/860–5866.

Mid-Apr.➤ **London Marathon,** a New York–style marathon through London's streets. Runners from 68 countries start in Greenwich and Blackheath 9–9:30 AM, then run via Docklands and Canary Wharf, the Tower of London and Parliament Square to finish in the Mall.

May 25–31➤ **British Antique Dealers' Association Fair,** the newest of the major fairs, is large and

prestigious, with many affordable pieces. ⊠ *Duke of York's Headquarters, King's Rd., Chelsea SW3,* ☎ *0171/589–6108.*

Mid-May➤ **Royal Windsor Horse Show,** a major show-jumping event attended by some members of the Royal Family. ⊠ *Show Box Office, 4 Grove Parade, Buxton, Derbyshire SK17 6AJ,* ☎ *01298/72272.*

May 21–22➤ **Chelsea Flower Show,** Britain's major flower show, covers 22 acres. ⊠ *Royal Hospital Rd., Chelsea SW3,* ☎ *0171/630–7422.*

SUMMER

Late May–Late Aug.➤ **Glyndebourne Festival Opera** is a unique opportunity to see international stars in a bucolic setting and in a brand-new theater. Tickets go fast and early. ⊠ *Glyndebourne Festival Opera, Lewes, Sussex BN8 5UU,* ☎ *01273/812–321.*

Early June➤ **Beating Retreat by the Guards Massed Bands,** when more than 500 musicians parade at Horse Guards, Whitehall. ⊠ *Tickets from Household Division Fund, Block 8, Wellington Barracks, Birdcage Walk, London SW1E 6HQ,* ☎ *0171/414–3253.*

Early June➤ **Derby Day** is the best-known event in the horse-racing calendar. ⊠ *Information from United Racecourses Ltd.,*

WINTER

Mid-Dec.➤ **Olympia International Show Jumping Championships,** international equestrian competition in Olympia's Grand Hall. For information, call ☎ 0171/370–8209.

Jan. 1➤ **The London Parade** is a good ole U.S.-style extravaganza complete with cheerleaders, floats, and marching bands, led by the Lord Mayor of Westminster. It starts on the south side of Westminster Bridge at 12:30, finishing in Berkeley Square around 3 PM. No tickets required.

Jan. 9–18➤ **43rd London International Boat Show,** the largest boat show in Europe. ⊠ *Earl's Court Exhibition Centre, Warwick Rd., London SW5 9TA,* ☎ *01784/473377.*

Racecourse Paddock, Epsom, Surrey KT18 5NJ, ☎ 013727/26311.

MID-JUNE➤ **Trooping the Colour,** Queen Elizabeth's colorful official birthday parade, is held at Horse Guards, Whitehall, usually on the second or third Saturday of June. Write for tickets *only* between January 1 and February 28, enclosing a self-addressed stamped envelope. ✉ *Ticket Office, Headquarters, Household Division, Horse Guards, London SW1A 2AX,* ☎ 0171/414–2497.

JUNE 11–20➤ **The Grosvenor House Antiques Fair** is one of the most prestigious antiques fairs in Britain. ✉ *Grosvenor House Hotel, Park La., London W1A 3AA,* ☎ 0171/499–6363.

JUNE 22–JULY 5➤ **Wimbledon Lawn Tennis Championships,** held at the All England Lawn Tennis and Croquet Club in Wimbledon. Write early to enter the lottery for tickets for Centre and Number One courts; tickets for outside courts available daily at the gate. ✉ *Church Rd., Wimbledon, London SW19 5AE,* ☎ 0181/946–2244.

JULY 1–5➤ **Henley Royal Regatta,** an international rowing event and top social occasion, at Henley-upon-Thames, Oxfordshire. For information, call ☎ 01491/572–153.

MID-JULY–MID-SEPT.➤ **Henry Wood Promenade Concerts,** a marvelous series of concerts at the Royal Albert Hall. ✉ *Box Office, Royal Albert Hall, Kensington Gore SW7 2AP,* ☎ 0171/589–8212.

JULY 21–AUG. 2➤ **The Royal Tournament** features military displays and pageantry by the Royal Navy, the Royal Marines, the Army, and the Royal Air Force. ✉ *Earl's Court Exhibition Centre, Warwick Rd., London SW5 9TA,* ☎ 0171/370–8226.

AUTUMN

EARLY NOV.➤ **London to Brighton Veteran Car Run,** a run from Hyde Park in London to Brighton in East Sussex. No tickets required. For information, call ☎ 01753/681–736.

EARLY NOV.➤ **Lord Mayor's Procession and Show.** At the lord mayor's inauguration, a procession takes place from the Guildhall in the City to the Royal Courts of Justice. No tickets required. For information, call ☎ 0171/606–3030.

2 Exploring London

If London contained only its landmarks it would still rank as one of the world's top destinations. But England's capital is much more. It is a bevy of British bobbies, an ocean of black umbrellas, and an unconquered continuance of more than 2,000 years of history. The city beckons with great museums, green parks, and history-steeped houses. Visit Princess Di's Kensington Palace, delight in Pollock's Victorian toy museum, then get Beatle-ized by visiting Abbey Road. You'll find London is a Dickens of a place.

Updated by
Kate Sekules

LONDON IS AN ANCIENT CITY and its history greets you at every corner. To gain a sense of its continuity, stand on Waterloo Bridge at sunset. To the east, the great globe of St. Paul's Cathedral glows golden in the dying sunlight as it has since the 17th century, still majestic amid the towers of glass and steel that hem it in. To the west stand the mock-medieval ramparts of Westminster, home to the "Mother of Parliaments," which has met here or hereabouts since the 1250s. And past them both snakes the swift, dark Thames, as it flowed past the first Roman settlement nearly 2,000 years ago.

For much of its history, innumerable epigrams and observations have been coined about London by her enthusiasts and detractors. The great 18th-century author and wit, Samuel Johnson, said that a man who is tired of London is tired of life. Oliver Wendell Holmes said, "No person can be said to know London. The most that anyone can claim is that he knows something of it." In all likelihood a more appropriate tribute paid to London would note that the capital of Great Britain is—simply stated—one of the most interesting places on earth. There is no other place like it in its agglomeration of architectural sins and sudden intervention of almost rural sights, in its medley of styles, in its mixture of the green loveliness of parks and the modern gleam of neon. Thankfully, the old London of Queen Anne and Georgian architecture can still be discovered, as in a palimpsest parchment, under the hasty routine of later architecture.

Discovering it takes a bit of work, however. Modern-day London still largely reflects its medieval layout, a willfully difficult tangle of streets. This swirl of spaghetti will be totally confusing to anyone brought up on the rigidity of a grid system. Even Londoners get lost in their own city, and all own at least one dog-eared copy of the indispensable A–Z street-finder (they come under different names). But London's bewildering street pattern will be a plus for the visitor who wants to experience its indefinable historic atmosphere. London is a walking city and will repay every moment you spend exploring on foot. The visitor to London who wants to penetrate beyond the crust of popular knowledge about this city is well advised not only to pay visits to St. Paul's Cathedral and to the Tower, but also to set aside some of his or her limited time for wandering. Walk in the city's back streets and mews, around Park Lane and Kensington. Pass up Buckingham Palace for the more truly authentic Kensington Palace (Princess Di's abode). Take in the National Gallery, but don't forget London's "Time Machine" museums, such as the 19th-century homes of Linley Sambourne and Sir John Soane. For out-and-out glamour, pay a call on the palatial Wallace Collection and Apsley House, the former abode of the Duke of Wellington. Abandon the city's identikit shopping streets to discover unique shopping emporia, such as that Victorian-era wonderland, Pollock's Toys. In such ways can you best visualize the shape or, rather, the various shapes of Old London, a curious city that engulfed its own past for the sake of modernity but still lives and breathes the breath of history.

Don't let the tag of "typical tourist" stop you from enjoying the pageantry of the British Royal Family, one of the greatest free shows in the world. Line up for the Changing of the Guard and poke into the Royal Mews for a look at the Coronation Coach. Pomp reaches its zenith in mid-June when the Queen celebrates her official birthday with a parade called Trooping the Colour. Royalty watching is by no means restricted to fascinated foreigners. You only have to open the tabloid

Central London Exploring *(Boxes Refer to Detail Maps)*

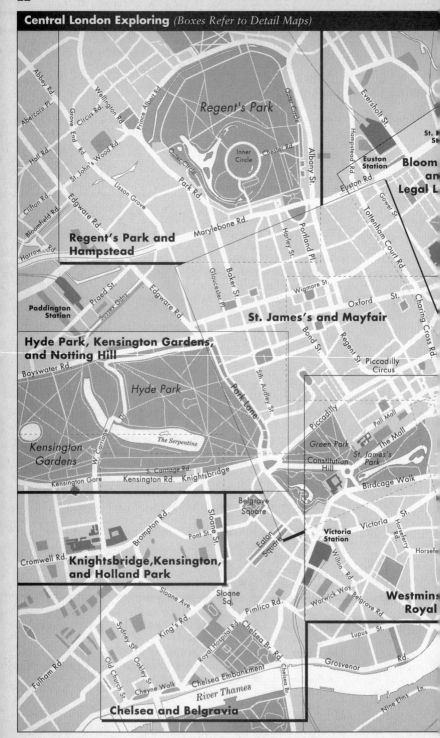

Regent's Park

Inner Circle

Outer Circle

Inner Circle

Chester Rd.

Albany St.

Prince Albert Rd.

Wellington Rd.

Circus Rd.

Grove End Rd.

St. John's Wood Rd.

Lisson Grove

Park Rd.

Abbey Rd.

Abercorn Pl.

Hall Rd.

Clifton Rd.

Bloomfield Rd.

Harrow Rd.

Edgware Rd.

Eversholt St.

Hampstead Rd.

Euston Rd.

Euston Station

Gower St.

Tottenham Court Rd.

St. ...
S...

Bloom...
an...
Legal L...

Marylebone Rd.

Harley St.

Portland Pl.

Regent's Park and Hampstead

Praed St.

Sussex Gdns.

Edgware Rd.

Paddington Station

Gloucester Pl.

Baker St.

Wigmore St.

Oxford St.

Charing Cross Rd.

St. James's and Mayfair

Hyde Park, Kensington Gardens, and Notting Hill

Bayswater Rd.

Hyde Park

The Serpentine

Bond St.

Regent St.

Park Lane

Sth. Audley St.

Piccadilly Circus

Piccadilly

Pall Mall

Green Park

Constitution Hill

The Mall

St. James's Park

Birdcage Walk

Kensington Gardens

W. Carriage Dr.

S. Carriage Rd.

Kensington Gore

Kensington Rd. Knightsbridge

Belgrave Square

Victoria St.

Horseferry ...

Victoria Station

Horsefe...

Brompton Rd.

Sloane St.

Pont St.

Eaton Square

Cromwell Rd.

Knightsbridge, Kensington, and Holland Park

Wilton Rd.

Warwick Way

Belgrave Rd.

Westmins...
Royal...

Sloane Ave.

Sloane Sq.

Pimlico Rd.

Lupus St.

Grosvenor Rd.

Sydney St.

King's Rd.

Old Church St.

Oakley St.

Royal Hospital Rd.

Chelsea Br. Rd.

Fulham Rd.

Cheyne Walk

Chelsea Embankment

Chelsea Br.

River Thames

Nine Elms Ln.

Chelsea and Belgravia

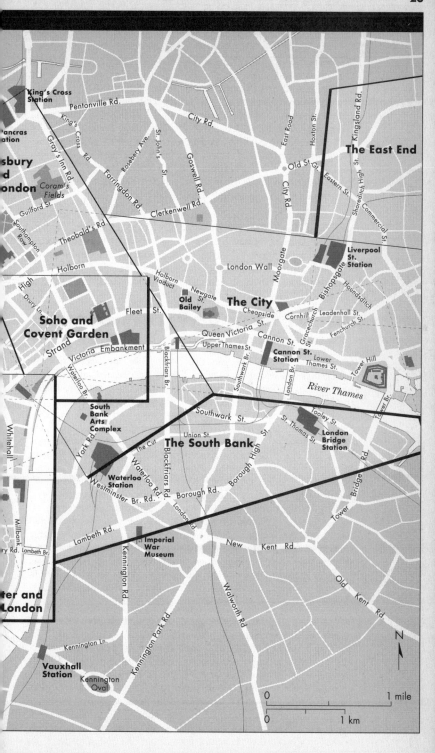

King's Cross Station

Pentonville Rd.

King's Cross Rd.

City Rd.

Pancras Station

sbury d ondon

Gray's Inn Rd.

Rosebery Ave.

St. John's St.

Goswell Rd.

East Road

Hoxton St.

Kingsland Rd.

The East End

Old St.

City Rd.

Farringdon Rd.

Coram's Fields

Guilford St.

Southampton Row

Theobald's Rd.

Clerkenwell Rd.

Old St.

Gt. Eastern St.

Shoreditch High St.

Commercial St.

Holborn

High

Drury Ln.

Holborn Viaduct

Newgate St.

London Wall

Moorgate

Liverpool St. Station

Bishopsgate

Houndsditch

Soho and Covent Garden

Fleet St.

Old Bailey

The City

Cheapside

Cornhill

Leadenhall St.

Fenchurch St.

Gracechurch St.

Strand

Victoria Embankment

Queen Victoria St.

Cannon St.

Upper Thames St.

Cannon St. Station

Lower Thames St.

Tower Hill

Blackfriars Br.

London Br.

River Thames

Tower Br.

Waterloo Br.

York Rd.

South Bank Arts Complex

Southwark St.

St. Thomas St.

Tooley St.

London Bridge Station

The Cut

Union St.

The South Bank

Borough High St.

Whitehall

Waterloo Rd.

Blackfriars Rd.

Waterloo Station

Westminster Br. Rd.

Borough Rd.

London Rd.

Borough High St.

Tower Bridge Rd.

Lambeth Rd.

Imperial War Museum

New Kent Rd.

ter and London

Millbank

ry Rd.

Lambeth Br.

Kennington Rd.

Kennington Park Rd.

Walworth Rd.

Old Kent Rd.

Kennington Ln.

Vauxhall Station

Kennington Oval

N

0   1 mile

0   1 km

newspapers to read reports of lurid rumors and family spats. Why not strike up a friendship with a native by discussing the latest installment of "Dallas at the Palace"?

Any vibrant metropolis changes, and crowded, noisy, frequently dirty London is no exception. New skyscrapers now puncture the city's skyline, gleaming and modern in a way that is difficult to accept in this stronghold of conservatism. The black taxi is being supplanted by a sleeker model and by versions of the old one in red, white, gold, and other colors. But all is not under threat. The British bobby is alive and well. The tall, red, double-decker buses still lumber from stop to stop, though their aesthetic match at street level, the glossy red telephone booths, are slowly disappearing. And, of course, teatime is still a hallowed part of the day, with, if you search hard enough, toasted crumpets in winter still honeycombed with sweet butter.

The London you'll discover will surely include some of our enthusiastic recommendations, but be prepared to be taken by surprise. The best that a great city has to offer often comes to you in unexpected ways. Armed with energy and curiosity, and all the practical information and helpful hints in the following pages, one thing remains certain: To quote Dr. Johnson again, you can find "in London all that life can afford."

WESTMINSTER AND ROYAL LONDON

This tour is London for Beginners. If you went no farther than these few acres, you would have seen many of the most famous sights, from the Houses of Parliament, Big Ben, Westminster Abbey, and Buckingham Palace, to two of the world's greatest art collections, housed in the National and the Tate galleries. You can truly call this area Royal London, as it is neatly bounded by the triangle of streets that make up the route that the Queen usually takes when journeying from Buckingham Palace to the Abbey or to the Houses of Parliament on state occasions. The three points on this royal triangle are Trafalgar Square, Westminster, and Buckingham Palace. If you have time to visit only one part of London, undoubtedly this should be it. There is as much history in these few acres as in many whole cities, as the statues of kings, queens, soldiers, and statesmen that stand guard at every corner attest—this is concentrated sightseeing, so pace yourself. The main drawback to sightseeing here is that half the world is doing it at the same time as you. So, even if you're tired after a long day on your feet, try to come back in the evening, when the crowds have dispersed, to drink in the serenity and grandeur at your leisure. You'll get to see it all in a brand new light, literally, as much of Royal London is spectacularly floodlit at night.

Westminster is by far the younger of the capital's two centers, post-dating the City by some 1,000 years. Edward the Confessor put it on the map when he packed up his court from its cramped City quarters and went west a couple of miles, founding the abbey church of Westminster—the minster west of the City—in 1050. Subsequent kings continued to hold court here until Henry VIII decamped to Whitehall Palace in 1512, leaving Westminster to the politicians. And here they are still, not in the palace, which burned almost to the ground in 1834, but in the Victorian mock-Gothic Houses of Parliament, whose 320-foot-high Clock Tower is as much a symbol of London as the Eiffel Tower is of Paris.

Numbers in the text correspond to numbers in the margin and on the Westminster and Royal London map.

A Good Walk

Trafalgar Square ① is the obvious place to start for several reasons. It is the geographical center of London and home to many political demonstrations, a raucous New Year's Eve party, and the highest concentration of bus stops and pigeons in the capital. After taking in the instantly identifiable **Nelson's Column** ② in the middle (read about the area on a plaque marking its 150th anniversary), head for the **National Gallery** ③, on the north side—this is Britain's greatest trove of masterpieces (everyone's favorite here is Jan van Eyck's *Arnolfini Marriage*). Detour around the corner to see the **National Portrait Gallery** ④—a veritable parade of the famous, often in unexpected guise, that can be very rewarding to anyone interested in what makes the British tick. East of the National Gallery, still on Trafalgar Square, see the much-loved church of **St. Martin-in-the-Fields** ⑤, then, stepping through grand **Admiralty Arch** ⑥ down on the southwest corner, enter the royal pink road, **the Mall**, with St. James's Park. On your right is the **Institute of Contemporary Arts** ⑦, known as the ICA and housed in the great Regency architect John Nash's **Carlton House Terrace** ⑧. At the foot of the Mall is one of London's most famous sights, **Buckingham Palace** ⑨, home, of course, to the monarch of the land, and punctuated by the ornate, white marble **Queen Victoria Memorial** ⑩. Turning left and left again, almost doubling back on yourself, follow the southern perimeter of St. James's Park around Birdcage Walk, passing the **Queen's Gallery** ⑪— a trove of Her Majesty's best Old Master paintings—and the HQ of the Queen's Guard, the **Wellington Barracks** ⑫ on your right, and, in turn, the hulking **Home Office** and **Queen Anne's Gate** ⑬. Cross Horse Guard's Road at the eastern edge of the Park, walk down Great George Street, with **St. Margaret's Church** ⑭ on your right, and across **Parliament Square,** to come to another of the great sights of London, the incomparably august **Houses of Parliament** ⑮—a mock-medieval extravaganza, down to the last detail (neo-Gothic umbrella stands), designed by two celebrated Victorian-era architects—built along the Thames, and including the famous Clock Tower, known the world over as Big Ben. Try to stick around for the sonorous chiming of the bell: For millions of citizens of the British empire, the sound of Big Ben's chimes is a mystic link with the heart and soul of the commonwealth. A clockwise turn around the Square brings you to yet another major landmark, breathtaking **Westminster Abbey** ⑯. Complete the circuit and head north up Whitehall, passing the **Cabinet War Rooms** ⑰, where you'll see a simple monolith in the middle of the street—the **Cenotaph,** designed by Edwin Lutyens in 1920 in commemoration of the 1918 Armistice. The gated alley on your left is **Downing Street** ⑱, where England's modest "White House" stands at No. 10. Soon after that you pass **Horse Guards Parade** ⑲, setting for the Queen's birthday celebration, Trooping the Colour, with the perfect classical Inigo Jones **Banqueting House** ⑳, scene of Charles I's execution, opposite. It's well worth it to backtrack a little ways down Whitehall, down Abington Street, to Millbank and the **Tate Gallery** ㉑—the most famous museum of British art.

TIMING

You could achieve this walk of roughly 3 mi in just over an hour, but you could equally spend a week's vacation on this route alone. Allow as much time as you can for the two great museums—the National Gallery requires at *least* two hours; the National Portrait Gallery can be whizzed round in less than one. Westminster Abbey can take half a day—especially in summer, when lines are long, both to get in and to get around. In summer, you can get inside Buckingham Palace too, a half day's operation increased to a whole day if you see the Royal

Mews, and the Queen's Gallery, or the Guards' Museum. If the Changing of the Guard is a priority, make sure you time this walk right.

HOW TO GET THERE

This is an easy neighborhood to access, especially if you start at Trafalgar Square, where many buses stop. The central neighborhood tube stop, Charing Cross (on the Jubilee, Northern, and Bakerloo lines), exits at the beginning of Northumberland Avenue, on the southeast corner. Practically all buses stop around here, including the Nos. 3, 6, 9, 12, 13, 15, 23, 24, 29, 53, 88, 94, and 139. Alternative tube stations are St. James's Park (on the District and Circle lines)—which is the best for Buckingham Palace—or the next stop, Westminster, which deposits you right by the Bridge, in the shadow of Big Ben.

Sights to See

❻ Admiralty Arch. Situated on the southwest corner of Trafalgar Square, the arch was designed in 1910 by Sir Aston Webb as part of a ceremonial route to Buckingham Palace and named after the adjacent Royal Navy headquarters. As you pass under the enormous triple archway—though not through the central arch, opened only for state occasions—the atmosphere changes along with the color of the road, for you are exiting frenetic Trafalgar Square and entering The Mall (rhymes with "shall"), which derives its name from a croquetlike 17th-century sport, and which leads to the Palace.

⑳ Banqueting House. This is all that remains today of the Tudor Palace of Whitehall, which was (according to one foreign visitor) "ill-built, and nothing but a heap of houses." Due for a grand remodeling, James I commissioned Inigo Jones (1573–1652), one of England's great architects, to do the job. Influenced by Andrea Palladio's work during a sojourn in Tuscany, Jones brought Palladian sophistication and purity back with him to London. The graceful and disciplined classical style of Banqueting House must have stunned its early occupants. James I's son, Charles I, enhanced the interior by employing the Flemish painter Peter Paul Rubens to glorify his father all over the ceiling. As it turned out, these allegorical paintings, depicting a wise monarch being received into heaven, were the last thing Charles saw before he was beheaded by Cromwell's Parliamentarians outside in 1649. But his son, Charles II, was able to celebrate the restoration of the monarchy in this same setting 20 years later. ⊠ *Whitehall,* ☎ *0171/930–4179.* ☞ *£3.* ☉ *Mon.–Sat. 10–5; closed on short notice for banquets, so call first. Tube: Westminster.*

❾ Buckingham Palace. Supreme among the symbols of London, indeed of Britain generally, and of the Royal Family, Buckingham Palace tops many must-see lists—although the building itself is no masterpiece and has housed the monarch only since Victoria moved here from Kensington Palace at her accession in 1837. Its great gray bulk sums up the imperious splendor of so much of the city: stately, magnificent, and ponderous. When Victoria moved in, the place was a mess. George IV, at *his* accession in 1820, had fancied the idea of moving to Buckingham House, his parents' former home, and had employed John Nash, as usual, to remodel it. The government authorized only "repair and improvement"; Nash, that tireless spendthrift, overspent his budget by about half a million pounds. George died, Nash was dismissed, and Edward Blore finished the building, adding the now familiar east front (facing the Mall). Victoria arrived to faulty drains and sticky doors and windows, but they did not mar her affection for the place, nor that of her son, Edward VII. The Portland stone facade dates only from 1913 (it, too, was part of the Aston Webb scheme), and the interior was renovated and redecorated only after it sustained World War II bomb dam-

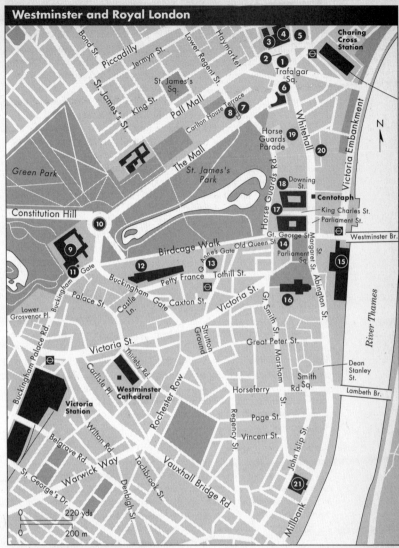

Westminster and Royal London

age. Indeed, compared to other great London residences, this is very much a johnny-come-lately affair.

The palace contains some 600 rooms, including the State Ballroom and, of course, the Throne Room. You'll find pomp and circumstance here, but little else. These state rooms are where much of the business of royalty is played out—investitures, state banquets, receptions, lunch parties for the famous, and so on. The royal apartments are in the north wing; when the queen is in, the royal standard is raised. Until fairly recently all the quarters were off limits to the public, but a 1992 fire at Windsor Castle created an urgent need for cash. And so the state rooms are now on show from August to early October, a time when the royal family is away. (Visitors can now even pre-book their tour reservations by credit card by phone.) Without an invitation to one of the queen's garden parties, however, you won't see much of the magnificent 45-acre grounds. Note that Her Majesty's finest Old Master paintings and drawings are not on view here but at the **Queen's Gallery** (☞ *below*), near the south side of the palace. ⊠ *Buckingham Palace Rd.,* ☎ *0171/839–1377, 0171/321–2233 credit-card reservation line (AE, MC, V).* ☞ *£8.50.* ☉ *Early Aug.–early Oct. (confirm dates, which are subject to queen's mandate), daily 9:30–4. Tube: St. James's Park, Victoria.*

⑰ Cabinet War Rooms. In back of the hulking **Foreign Office** (which was built in the 1860s by Sir Giles Gilbert Scott, better known for such fantastical Gothic Revival buildings as the House of Commons), this is an essential visit for World War II buffs. During air raids the War Cabinet met in this warren of 17 bomb-proof chambers. The Cabinet Room is still arranged as if a meeting were about to convene; in the Map Room, the Allied campaign is charted; the Prime Minister's Room holds the desk from which Churchill made his morale-boosting broadcasts; and the Telephone Room has his hot line to FDR. ⊠ *Clive Steps, King Charles St.,* ☎ *0171/930–6961.* ☞ *£4.20.* ☉ *Daily 10–5:15. Tube: Westminster.*

❽ Carlton House Terrace. This is a glorious example of Regency architect John Nash's genius. Between 1812 and 1830, under the patronage of George IV (Prince Regent until George III's death in 1820), Nash was responsible for a series of West End developments, of which these white-stucco facades and massive Corinthian columns may be the most imposing. It was a smart address, needless to say, and one that prime ministers Gladstone (1856) and Palmerston (1857–75) enjoyed. Today Carlton House Terrace is home to the Royal College of Pathologists, the Royal Society, the Turf Club, and, at No. 12, the **Institute of Contemporary Arts** (☞ *below*) better known as the ICA. *Tube: Charing Cross.*

⑱ Downing Street. Looking like an unassuming alley, but barred by iron gates at both its Whitehall and Horse Guards Road approaches, this is where **10 Downing Street,** London's modest version of the White House stands. Only three houses remain of the terrace built circa 1680 by Sir George Downing, who spent enough of his youth in America to graduate from Harvard—the second man ever to do so. **No. 11** is the residence of the chancellor of the exchequer (secretary of the treasury), **No. 12** the party whips' office. No. 10 has officially housed the prime minister since 1732. (The gates were former prime minister Margaret Thatcher's brainstorm.) Just south of Downing Street, in the middle of Whitehall, you'll see the **Cenotaph,** a stark white monolith designed in 1920 by Edward Lutyens to commemorate the 1918 armistice. On Remembrance Day (the Sunday nearest November 11) it is strewn with blood-red poppies to honor the dead of both world wars, with the first

ROYALTY WATCHING

YOU'VE SEEN BIG BEN, the Tower, and Westminster Abbey. But somehow you feel something is missing: a close encounter with Britain's most famous attraction—Her actual Majesty. Yes, you've toured Buckingham Palace, but the Windsors are notorious for never standing at a window (the London *Times* once suggested that the palace mount a full-scale mechanical procession of royal figures to parade in and out of the palace, on the hour, in cuckoo-clock fashion), and the odds are that you won't be bumping into Elizabeth II on the tube. But at a surprisingly wide variety of royal events, you can catch a glimpse of her, along with many other Windsor personages. Fairs and fetes, polo matches and horse races, first nights and banquets galore—her date book is crammed with events and, on one of them—who knows?—you might even meet her on a royal walkabout.

The Queen, in fact, attends 400 functions a year and if you want to know what she and the rest of the RF are doing on any given date, turn to the *Court Circular* printed in the major London dailies. You might catch Prince Charles launching a ship, Princess Margaret attending a film premiere, or the Queen ribbon-cutting at a hospital (it will be harder to catch Her No Longer Royal Highness The Princess of Wails—as some London papers now call her—because Princess Diana's court calendar has been drastically reduced). But most visitors want to see the Royals in all their dazzling pomp and circumstance. For this, the best bet is the second Saturday in June, when the Trooping the Colour is usually held to celebrate the Queen's official birthday. This spectacular parade begins when she leaves Buckingham Palace in her carriage and rides down the Mall to arrive at Horse Guards Parade at 11 AM exactly. (Well, occasionally the clock has been timed to strike as she arrives and not vice versa!) If you wish to obtain one of the 7,000 seats (no more than two per request, distributed by ballot), enclose a letter and stamped, self-addressed envelope or International Reply Coupon to Ticket Office, Headquarters, Household Division, Horse Guards, London SW1A 2AX, ☎ 0171/414–2497 (send January to Feb. 28). Of course, you can also just line up along the Mall with your binoculars!

Perhaps the nicest time to see the Queen is during Royal Ascot, held at the race track near Windsor Castle—just a short train ride out of London—usually during the third week of June (Tuesday to Friday). After several races, the Queen invariably walks down to the paddock on a special path, greeting race goers as she proceeds. Americans wishing a seat in the Royal Enclosure (fashion note: the big party hats come out on Ladies Day, normally the Thursday of the meet) should apply to the American Embassy, 24 Grosvenor Square, London W1, before the end of March. If you're lucky enough to meet the Queen (contrary to her stodgy public persona, she's actually a great wit), just remember to address her as "Your Majesty."

wreath laid by the queen. (Wherever you are on that day, you'll be inveigled to buy a plastic poppy to support veterans' charities.)

⑲ Horse Guards Parade. This large square faces Horse Guards Road, opposite St. James's Park, at one end, and Whitehall at the other. Once the tilt-yard of Whitehall Palace, where jousting tournaments were held, it is now notable mainly for the annual Trooping the Colour ceremony, in which the queen takes the Royal Salute, her official birthday gift, on the second Saturday in June. (Like Paddington Bear, the queen has two birthdays; her real one is on April 21.) There is pageantry galore, with marching bands and the occasional guardsman fainting clean away in his weighty busby, and throngs of onlookers. The ceremony is televised and also broadcast on Radio 4. Visitors may also attend the queenless rehearsals on the preceding two Saturdays. At the Whitehall facade of Horse Guards, two mounted sentries known as the Queen's Life Guard provide what may be London's most frequently exercised photo opportunity. They change, quietly, at 11 AM Monday–Saturday, 10 on Sunday. On a site reaching from here to the Thames and from Trafalgar to Parliament squares once stood Whitehall Palace, established by Henry VIII, who married two of his six wives (Anne Boleyn and Jane Seymour) and breathed his last here. The sheer scale of the 2,000-room labyrinth in red Tudor brick must have been breathtaking, but we won't dwell on it, as it burned to the ground in 1698, thanks to a fire started by a Dutch laundress whose name has not made it to posterity.

★ ⑮ Houses of Parliament. Postcard London come to life, the Houses of Parliament are, arguably, the city's most famous and photogenic sight, with the Clock Tower—which everyone mistakenly calls Big Ben—keeping watch on the corner and Westminster Abbey ahead of you across Parliament Square, in which stand statues of everyone from Richard the Lionhearted to Abraham Lincoln. The most romantic view of the complex is from the opposite, south side of the river, a vista especially dramatic at night when the storybook spires, pinnacles, and towers of the great building are floodlit green and gold—a fairy tale vision only missing the presence of Peter Pan and Wendy on their way to Never-Never Land.

The Palace of Westminster, as the complex is still properly called, was established by Edward the Confessor during the 11th century, when he moved his court here from the City, and has served as the seat of English administrative power ever since. In 1512, Henry VIII abandoned it for Whitehall. It ceased to be an official royal residence after 1547: At the Reformation, the Royal Chapel was secularized and became the first meeting place of the Commons. The Lords settled in the White Chamber. These, along with everything but the **Jewel Tower** and **Westminster Hall**, were destroyed in 1834 when "the sticks"—the arcane abacus beneath the Lords' Chamber on which the court had kept its accounts until 1826—were incinerated and the fire got out of hand.

The same cellar had seen an earlier attempt to raze the palace: the infamous Gunpowder Plot of November 5, 1605, perpetrated by the Catholic convert Guy Fawkes and his fellow conspirators. If you are in London in late October or early November, you may see children with dressed-up teddy bears demanding a "penny for the guy!" They do it because, to this day, November 5 is Guy Fawkes Day (a.k.a. Bonfire Night), when fireworks bought with the pennies accompany pyres of these makeshift effigies of Guy Fawkes.

After the 1834 fire, architects were invited to submit plans for new Houses of Parliament in the grandiose "Gothic or Elizabethan style." Charles Barry's were selected from among 97 entries, partly because

Barry had invited the architect and designer Augustus Pugin to add the requisite neo-Gothic curlicues to his own Renaissance-influenced style. As you can see, it was a happy collaboration, with Barry's classical proportions offset by Pugin's ornamental flourishes—although the latter were toned down by Gilbert Scott when he rebuilt the bomb-damaged House of Commons after World War II.

The two towers were Pugin's work. The **Clock Tower,** now virtually the symbol of London, was completed in 1858 after long delays due to bickering over the clock's design. (Barry designed the faces himself in the end.) It contains the 13-ton bell that chimes the hour (and the quarter) known as Big Ben. Some say Ben was "Big Ben" Caunt, heavyweight champ; others, Sir Benjamin Hall, the far-from-slim Westminster building works commissioner. At the other end is the 336-foot-high **Victoria Tower,** newly a-gleam from its recent restoration and cleaning. The rest of the complex was scrubbed down some years ago; the revelation of the honey stone under the dowdy, smog-blackened facades, which seemed almost symbolic at the time, cheered London up no end.

There are two Houses, the Lords and the Commons. The former consists of more than 1,000 peers (nowadays there are more "life peers," with recently bestowed titles, than aristocrats); the latter is made up of 650 elected Members of Parliament (MPs). The party with the most MPs forms the government, its leader becoming Prime Minister; other parties form the Opposition. Since 1642, when Charles I tried to have five MPs arrested, no monarch has been allowed into the House of Commons. The State Opening of Parliament in November consequently takes place in the House of Lords, after a ritual inspection of the cellars in case a modern Guy Fawkes lurks.

Visitors aren't allowed many places in the Houses of Parliament, though the Visitors' Galleries of the House of Commons do afford a view of the best free show in London staged in the world's most renowned ego chamber. The opposing banks of green leather benches seat only 346 MPs—not that this is much of a problem, since absentees far outnumber the diligent. When MPs vote, they exit by the "Aye" or the "No" corridor, thus being counted by the party "whips" (yes, it is a fox-hunting term); when they speak, it is not directly to each other but through the Speaker, who also decides who will get the floor each day. Elaborate procedures notwithstanding, debate is often drowned out by the amazingly raucous and immature jeers and insults familiar to TV viewers since 1989, when cameras were first allowed into the House of Commons.

Other public areas of the 1,100-room labyrinth are rather magnificently got up in high neo-Gothic style and punctuated with stirring frescoes commissioned by Prince Albert. You pass these en route to the Visitors Galleries—if, that is, you are patient enough to wait in line for hours (the Lords line is shorter) or have applied in advance through your embassy. ⊠ *St. Stephen's Entrance, St. Margaret St., SW1,* ☎ *0171/219–3000.* 🎟 *Free.* 🕑 *Commons Mon.–Thurs. 2:30–10, Fri. 9:30–3; Lords Mon.–Thurs. 2:30–10. Closed Easter wk, July–Oct., and 3 wks at Christmas. Tube: Westminster.*

❼ **Institute of Contemporary Arts (ICA).** Behind its incongruous white-stucco facade, at No. 12 Carlton House Terrace, the ICA has provided a stage for the avant-garde in performance, theater, dance, visual art, and music since it was established in 1947. There are two cinemas, an underused library of video artists' works, a bookshop, a café and a bar, and a team of adventurous curators. ⊠ *The Mall,* ☎ *0171/930–3647.*

📠 *1-day membership £1.50, additional charge for entry to specific events.* ⊙ *Daily noon–9:30, later for some events. Tube: Charing Cross.*

The **ICAfé** is windowless but brightly spotlighted, with a self-service counter offering good hot dishes, salads, quiches, and desserts. The bar upstairs, which serves baguette sandwiches, has a picture window overlooking the Mall. Both are packed before popular performances and are subject to the £1.50 one-day membership fee.

The Mall. This street was laid out around 1660 for the game of *pell mell* that also gave Pall Mall its name, and it quickly became the place to be seen. Samuel Pepys, Jonathan Swift, and Alexander Pope all wrote about it, and it continued as the beau monde's social playground into the early 19th century, long after the game it was built for had gone out of vogue. Something of the former style survives on those summer days when the queen is throwing a Buckingham Palace garden party: hundreds of her subjects throng The Mall, from the grand and titled to the humble and hardworking, all of whom have donned hat and frock to take afternoon tea with the monarch—or somewhere near her—on the lawns of Buck House. The old Mall still runs alongside the graceful, pink, 115-foot-wide avenue that replaced it in 1904 for just such occasions.

★ ❸ **National Gallery.** Jan van Eyck's *Arnolfini Marriage,* Leonardo da Vinci's *Madonna of the Rocks,* Velázquez's *"Rokeby Venus,"* Constable's *Hay Wain* . . . you get the picture. There are about 2,200 other paintings in this museum—many of them instantly recognizable and among the most treasured works of art anywhere. The museum's low, gray, colonnaded neo-classical facade fills the north side of Trafalgar Square. The institution was founded in 1824, when George IV and a connoisseur named Sir George Beaumont persuaded a reluctant government to spend £57,000 on part of the recently deceased philanthropist John Julius Angerstein's collection. These 38 paintings, including works by Raphael, Rembrandt, Titian, and Rubens, were augmented by 16 of Sir George's own and exhibited in Angerstein's Pall Mall residence until 1838, when William Wilkin's building was completed. By the end of the century, enthusiastic directors and generous patrons had turned the National Gallery into one of the world's foremost collections, with works from painters of the Italian Renaissance and earlier, from the Flemish and Dutch masters, the Spanish school, and of course the English tradition, including Hogarth, Gainsborough, Stubbs, and Constable.

In 1991, following years of wrangling and the rehanging of the entire collection, the Sainsbury Wing was opened. It had been financed by the eponymous British grocery dynasty to house the early Renaissance collection, and designed—eventually—by the American architect Robert Venturi after previous plans were abandoned. (Prince Charles hadn't liked these modernist designs. "A monstrous carbuncle on the face of a much-loved friend" was his infamous comment.)

The collection is really too overwhelming to absorb in a single viewing. It is wise to acquaint yourself with the layout—easy to negotiate compared with other European galleries—and plot a route in advance. The **Micro Gallery,** a computer information center in the Sainsbury Wing, might be the place to start. You can access in-depth information on any work here, choose your favorites, and print out a free personal tour map that marks the paintings you most want to see. Careful, though—you could spend hours in here scrolling through this colorful if pixelized history of art.

What follows is a list of 10 of the most familiar, to jog your memory, whet your appetite, and offer a starting point for your own exploration. The first five are in the Sainsbury Wing. In chronological order: (1) **van Eyck** (c. 1395–1441), *The Arnolfini Marriage.* A solemn couple holds hands, the fish-eye mirror behind them mysteriously illuminating what can't be seen from the front. (2) **Uccello** (1397–1475), *The Battle of San Romano.* In a work commissioned by the Medici family, the Florentine commander on a rearing white warhorse leads armored knights into battle with the Sienese. (3) **Bellini** (c.1430–1516), *The Doge Leonardo Loredan.* The artist captured the Venetian doge's beatific expression (and snail-shell "buttons") at the beginning of his 20 years in office. (4) **Botticelli** (1445–1510), *Venus and Mars.* Mars sleeps, exhausted by the love goddess, oblivious to the lance wielded by mischievous putti and the buzzing of wasps. (5) **Leonardo da Vinci** (1452–1519), *The Virgin and Child.* This haunting black chalk cartoon is partly famous for having been attacked at gunpoint, and now gets extra protection behind glass and screens. (6) **Caravaggio** (1573–1610), *The Supper at Emmaus.* A cinematically lighted, freshly resurrected Christ blesses bread in an astonishingly domestic vision from the master of chiaroscuro. (7) **Velázquez** (1599–1660), *The Toilet of Venus.* "The Rokeby Venus," named for her previous home in Yorkshire, has the most famously beautiful back in any gallery. She's the only surviving female nude by Velázquez. (8) **Constable** (1776–1837), *The Hay Wain.* Rendered overfamiliar by too many birthday cards, this is the definitive image of golden-age rural England. (9) **Turner** (1775–1851), *The Fighting Téméraire.* Most of the collection's other Turners were moved to the Tate Gallery (☞ *below*); the final voyage of the great French battleship into a livid, hazy sunset stayed here. (10) **Seurat** (1859–1891), *Bathers at Asnières.* This static summer day's idyll is one of the pointillist extraordinaire's best-known works.

Glaring omissions from the above include some of the most popular pictures in the gallery by Piero della Francesca, Titian, Holbein, Bosch, Brueghel, Rembrandt, Vermeer, Rubens, Canaletto, Claude, Tiepolo, Gainsborough, Ingres, Monet, Renoir, and Van Gogh. You can't miss the two most spectacular works on view—due to their mammoth size—Sebastiano del Piombo's *Sermon on the Mount* and Stubbs's stunning *Whistlejacket.* ✉ *Trafalgar Sq.,* ☎ *0171/839–3321, 0171/839–3526, or 0171/389–1773.* 🎫 *Free, charge for special exhibitions.* ◷ *Mon.–Sat. 10–6, Sun. 2–6; June–Aug., Wed. until 8; 1-hr guided tour starts at Sainsbury Wing weekdays at 11:30 and 2:30, Sat. 2 and 3:30. Tube: Charing Cross.*

NEED A BREAK?   The **Brasserie** in the Sainsbury Wing of the National Gallery offers a fashionable lunch—mussels, gravlax, charcuterie, salads, a hot special—plus baguette sandwiches, pastries, tea, coffee, and wine, in a sophisticated, spacious room on the second floor.

★ ➍ **National Portrait Gallery.** An idiosyncratic collection that presents a potted history of Britain through its people, past and present. As an art collection it is eccentric, as the subject, not the artist, is the point, and there are notable works (a Holbein portrait of Henry VIII, Stubbs and Hockney self-portraits) mixed up with photographs, busts, caricatures, and amateur paintings. (The miniature of Jane Austen by her sister Cassandra, for instance, is the only likeness we have of the great novelist.) Many of the faces are obscure and will be just as unknown to English visitors, because the portraits outlasted their sitters' fame. But the annotation is comprehensive, the layout is easy to negotiate, being chronological, with the oldest at the top, and there is a new, separate research center for those who get hooked on particular personages. Don't miss the new Victorian and early 20th-Century Portrait Galleries, nor the photography gallery. ✉ *St. Martin's Pl., WC2,* ☎ *0171/306–0055.* ✉ *Free.* ⊘ *Weekdays 10–5, Sat. 10–6, Sun. 2–6. Tube: Charing Cross, Leicester Square.*

❷ Nelson's Column. The famous column is the 145-foot-high granite perch from which E. H. Baily's 1843 statue of Admiral Lord Horatio Nelson, one of England's favorite heroes, keeps watch; three bas-reliefs depicting his victories at Cape St. Vincent, the Battle of the Nile, and Copenhagen (and a fourth, his death at Trafalgar itself in 1805) sit around the base—all four were cast from cannons he captured. The four majestic lions, designed by the Victorian painter Sir Edwin Landseer, were added in 1867. The calling cards of generations of picturesque pigeons have been a corrosive problem for the statue; this may have been finally solved by the statue's new gel coating.

❸ Queen Anne's Gate. Standing south of Birdcage Walk, by St. James's Park, are these two pretty 18th-century closes, once separate but now linked by a statue of the last Stuart monarch. (Another statue of Anne, beside St. Paul's, inspired the doggerel "Brandy Nan, Brandy Nan, you're left in the lurch,/Your face to the gin shop, your back to the church,"—proving that her attempts to disguise her habitual tipple in a teapot fooled nobody.) Also here is the Henry Moore bronze *Mother and Child.*

❿ Queen Victoria Memorial. You can't overlook this if you're near Buckingham Palace, which it faces from the traffic island at the west end of the Mall. The monument was conceived by Sir Aston Webb as the nucleus of his ceremonial route down The Mall to the Palace, and executed by the sculptor Thomas Brock, who was knighted on the spot when it was revealed to the world in 1911. Many wonder why he was, since the thing is Victoriana incarnate: The frumpy queen glares down the Mall, with golden-winged Victory overhead and her siblings Truth, Justice, and Charity, plus Manufacture, Progress-and-Peace, War-and-Shipbuilding, and so on—in Osbert Sitwell's words, "tons of allegorical females . . . with whole litters of their cretinous children"— surrounding her. Climbing it is not encouraged, even though it's the best vantage point for viewing the daily **Changing of the Guard,** which, with all the pomp and ceremony monarchists and children adore, remains one of London's best free shows. ✉ *Guard leaves Wellington Barracks 11 AM, arrives Buckingham Palace 11:30.* ⊘ *Apr.–July, daily; Aug.–Mar., every other day. Tube: St. James's Park, Victoria.*

⓫ Queen's Gallery. This is the former chapel at the south side of Buckingham Palace, which has been open to visitors since 1962. On display here are paintings from Her Majesty's collection—the country's largest by far—including works by Vermeer, Leonardo, Rubens, Rembrandt, Canaletto . . . and Queen Victoria, though by no means all at the same time. Sign-of-the-times note: Now that she is a taxpayer, HRH's artwork, along with all her other possessions (for example, Buckingham Palace), are officially part of a business known as Royal Collection Enterprises. ✉ *Buckingham Palace Rd.,* ☎ *0171/799–2331.* ✉ *£3.50, combined ticket for Queen's Gallery and Royal Mews £6.50.* ⊘ *Tues.–Sat. 10–5, Sun. 2–5. Closed Dec. 24–Mar. 4. Tube: St. James's Park, Victoria.*

☞ Royal Mews. Designed by John Nash, these stand nearly next door to the Queen's Gallery, close to Buckingham Palace. Mewses were originally falcons' quarters (the name comes from their "mewing," or feather shedding), but horses gradually eclipsed birds of prey. Now some of the magnificent royal beasts live here alongside the fabulous bejeweled, glass and golden coaches they draw on state occasions. The place is unmissable children's entertainment. ⊠ *Buckingham Palace Rd.,* ☎ *0171/799–2331.* ☎ *£3.50, combined ticket for Queen's Gallery and Royal Mews £6.* ☉ *Oct.–Mar., Wed. noon–4; Apr.–Oct., Tues.–Thurs. noon–4. Closed Mar. 25–29, Oct. 1–5, Dec. 23–Jan. 5. Tube: St. James's Park, Victoria.*

St. James's Park. London's smallest, most ornamental park, and the oldest of its royal ones. Henry VIII drained a marsh that festered here next to the lepers' hospital that St. James's Palace replaced, and bred his deer on the newly dry land. Later kings tinkered with it further, James I installing an aviary and zoo (complete with crocodiles); Charles I laying out formal gardens, which he then had to traverse to his execution at the Banqueting House (☞ *above*) in 1649; and Charles II employing André Lenôtre, Louis XIV's Versailles landscaper, to remodel it completely with avenues, fruit orchards, and a canal. Its present shape more or less reflects what John Nash designed under George IV, turning the canal into a graceful lake (which was cemented in at a depth of 4 feet in 1855, so don't even think of swimming) and generally naturalizing the gardens.

More than 30 species of birds—including flamingos, pelicans, geese, ducks, and swans (which belong to the queen)—now congregate on Duck Island at the east end of the lake, attracting ornithologists at dawn. Later on summer days the deck chairs (which you must pay to use) are crammed with office workers lunching while being serenaded by music from the bandstands. The best time to stroll the leafy walkways, though, is after dark, with Westminster Abbey and the Houses of Parliament rising above the floodlit lake, and peace reigning.

⓮ **St. Margaret's Church.** Dwarfed by its northern neighbor, Westminster Abbey, this church was founded during the 12th century and rebuilt between 1486 and 1523. St. Margaret's is the parish church of the Houses of Parliament and much sought after for weddings; Samuel Pepys married here in 1655, Winston Churchill in 1908. The east Crucifixion window celebrates another union, the marriage of Prince Arthur and Catherine of Aragon. Unfortunately, it arrived so late that Arthur was dead and Catherine had married his brother, Henry VIII. Sir Walter Raleigh is among the notables buried here, only without his head, which had been removed at Old Palace Yard, Westminster, and kept by his wife, who was said to be fond of asking visitors, "Have you met Sir Walter?" as she produced it from a velvet bag.

❺ **St. Martin-in-the-Fields.** One of Britain's best-loved churches, this was completed in 1726; James Gibbs's classical temple-with-spire design became a familiar pattern for churches in early Colonial America. Though it seems dwarfed by the surrounding structures of Trafalgar Square, the spire is actually slightly taller than Nelson's Column, which it overlooks. It is a welcome sight for the homeless, who have sought soup and shelter here since 1914. The church is also a haven for music lovers; the internationally known Academy of St. Martin-in-the-Fields was founded here, and a popular program of lunchtime (free) and evening concerts continues today. The church's fusty interior has a wonderful atmosphere for music making—but the wooden benches can make it hard to give your undivided attention to the music. St. Martin's is often called the royal parish church, partly because Charles II was christened here—not because his mistress, Nell Gwyn, lies under the stones, alongside William Hogarth, Thomas Chippendale (the cabinetmaker), and Jack Sheppard, the notorious highwayman. Also in the crypt is the **London Brass-Rubbing Centre,** where you can make your own souvenir knight from replica tomb brasses, with metallic waxes, paper, and instructions provided, and the **St. Martin's Gallery** showing contemporary work. There is also a crafts market in the courtyard behind the church. ⊠ *St. Martin-in-the-Fields, Trafalgar Sq.,* ☎ *0171/930–0089, 0171/839–8362 credit-card bookings for evening concerts.* ✆ *Brass rubbing from £1.* ☉ *Church daily 8–8; crypt Mon.–Sat. 10–8, Sun. noon–6. Tube: Charing Cross, Leicester Square.*

NEED A
BREAK?

St. Martin's **Café-in-the-Crypt** serves full meals, sandwiches, snacks, and even a glass of wine, Monday–Saturday 10–8; noon–6 on Sunday.

Smith Square. An elegant enclave of perfectly preserved early 18th-century town houses which still looks like the London of Dr. Johnson. The address is much sought after by MPs, especially of the Tory persuasion; No. 32 is the Conservative Party Headquarters. The Baroque church of **St. John's**, **Smith Square**, completed around 1720, dominates charmingly. It is well known to Londoners as a chamber-music venue; its popular lunchtime concerts are often broadcast on the radio.

NEED A
BREAK?

In the crypt of St. John's is **The Footstool**—about the only place to find refreshment around here. It has an interesting and reasonably priced lunchtime menu and also serves evening meals on concert nights.

★ ㉑ **Tate Gallery.** By the river, on traffic-laden Millbank, the Tate Gallery of Modern British Art, to give it its full title, opened in 1897, funded by the sugar magnate Sir Henry Tate. "Modern" is slightly misleading, as one of the three collections here consists of British art from 1545 to the present, including works by William Hogarth, Thomas Gainsborough, Sir Joshua Reynolds, and George Stubbs from the 18th century, and by John Constable, William Blake (a mind-blowing collection of his visionary works), and the pre-Raphaelite painters from the 19th century. Also from the 19th century is the second of the Tate's collections, the Turner Bequest, consisting of J. M. W. Turner's personal collection; he left it to the nation on condition that the works be displayed together. The James Stirling–designed **Clore Gallery** (to the right of the main gallery) has fulfilled his wish since 1987, and should not be missed.

The Tate's modern collection is international and so vast that it is never all on display at once. The current director, Nicholas Serota, instigated the strategy of annual rehanging, which goes some way toward solving the problem of the gallery's embarrassment of riches, but also means that a favorite work may not be on view, although the most famous and popular works are on permanent display. Come the year 2000, the Tate's space issue will be resolved with the opening of a new gallery, opposite St. Paul's, in the former Bankside Power Station, currently undergoing a £100 million transformation to the plans of Swiss architects, Herzog & de Meuron. Even now, though, you can see work by an abundance of late 19th- and 20th-century artists, and a good deal more besides. Your tour will deal you multiple shocks of recognition (Rodin's *The Kiss*, Lichtenstein's *Whaam!*), and you can rent a "Tateinform" hand-held audio guide, with commentaries by curators, experts, and some of the artists themselves, to enhance the picture. Here's a short list of names: Matisse, Picasso, Braque, Léger, Kandinsky, Mondrian, Dalí, Bacon, de Kooning, Pollock, Rothko, Moore, Hepworth, Warhol, Freud, Hockney. ⊠ *Millbank,* ☎ *0171/821–1313 or 0171/821–7128.* ✆ *Free, special exhibitions £3–£7.* ☉ *Mon.–Sat. 10–5:50, Sun. 2–5:50.*

❶ Trafalgar Square. This is the center of London, by dint of a plaque on the corner of the Strand and Charing Cross Road from which distances on U.K. signposts are measured. It is the home of **the National Gallery** (☞ *above*) and of one of London's most distinctive landmarks, **Nelson's Column** (☞ *above*); also of many a political demonstration, a raucous New Year's party, and the highest concentration of bus stops and pigeons in the capital. In short, it is London's most famous square.

Long ago the site housed the Royal Mews, where Edward I (1239–1307) kept his royal hawks and lodged his falconers. (Not the numberless Edward the Confessor of Westminster Abbey fame, who died in 1066, this one was known as "Longshanks" and died of dysentery in 1307.) Later, all the kings' horses were stabled here, in increasingly smart quarters, until 1830, when John Nash had the buildings torn down as part of his Charing Cross Improvement Scheme—which he did not live to complete. The baton was passed to Sir Charles Barry, architect of the Houses of Parliament, and in 1840 the Square was paved, with the fountains added five years later. (Sir Edwin Lutyens remodeled them in 1939, and they were further enhanced with cavorting sea creatures after World War II.)

There's a pathetic history attached to the **equestrian statue of Charles I,** which stands near Whitehall on the southern slope of the Square (on a pedestal *possibly* designed by Sir Christopher Wren and *possibly* carved by Grinling Gibbons). After Charles's High Treasurer ordered it (from Hubert le Sueur), the Puritan Oliver Cromwell tumbled Charles from the throne and commissioned a scrap dealer with the appropriate name of Rivett to melt the king down. Rivett made a fortune peddling knickknacks wrought, he claimed, from its metal, only to produce the statue miraculously unscathed after the restoration of the monarchy—and to make more cash reselling it to the authorities. In 1767 Charles II had it placed where it stands today, near the spot where his father was executed in 1649.

Today, street performers enhance the square's intermittent atmosphere of celebration, which is strongest in December, first when the lights on the gigantic Christmas tree (an annual gift from Norway to thank the British for harboring their royal family during World War II) are turned on, and then—less festively, when thousands see in the New Year.

⓬ Wellington Barracks. These are the headquarters of the Guards Division, the queen's five regiments of elite foot guards (Grenadier, Coldstream, Scots, Irish, and Welsh) who protect the sovereign and patrol her palace dressed in tunics of gold-purled scarlet and tall fur "busby" helmets of Canadian brown bearskin. (The two items together cost more than £4,000.) If you want to learn more about the guards, you can visit the **Guards Museum;** the entrance is next to the Guards Chapel. ✉ *Wellington Barracks, Birdcage Walk,* ☎ *0171/930–4466, Ext. 3430.* ▥ *£2.* ☉ *Sat.–Thurs. 10–4. Tube: St. James's Park.*

★ ⓰ **Westminster Abbey.** Announced by the teeming human contents of herds off tour buses, off the south side of Parliament Square, this is where nearly all of England's monarchs were crowned, amid vast pomp and circumstance; most are buried here, too. As the most ancient of London's great churches, the place is crammed with spectacular medieval architecture. Other than the mysterious gloom of the vast interior, the first thing to strike most people is the fantastic proliferation of statues, tombs, and commemorative tablets: In parts, the building seems more like a stonemason's yard than a place of worship. But it is in its latter capacity that this landmark truly comes into its own: Although attending a service is not something to undertake purely for sightsee-

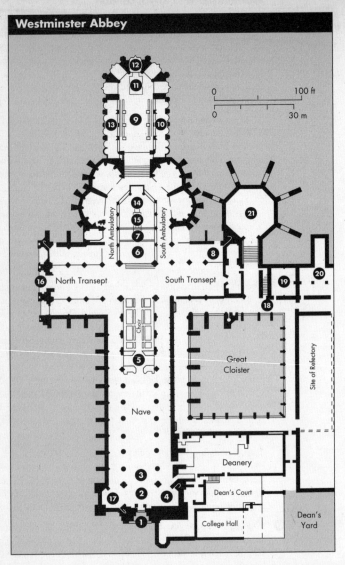

Westminster Abbey

ing reasons, it provides a glimpse of the abbey in its full majesty, accompanied by music from the Westminster choristers and the organ that Henry Purcell once played. During a service, you won't be bothered by the frequent and jarring loudspeaker announcements made during peak hours, requesting "a minute of silence" from the teeming masses. Note that some parts are closed on Sunday except to worshipers.

The origins of Westminster Abbey are uncertain. The first church on the site may have been built as early as the 7th century by the Saxon King Sebert (who may be buried here, alongside his queen and sister); a Benedictine abbey was established during the 10th century. There were certainly preexisting foundations when Edward the Confessor was crowned in 1040, moved his palace to Westminster, and began building a church. Only traces have been found of that incarnation, which was consecrated eight days before Edward's death in 1065. (It appears in the Bayeaux Tapestry.) Edward's canonization in 1139 gave a succession of kings added incentive to shower the Abbey with attention and improvements. Henry III, full of ideas from his travels in France, pulled it down and started again with Amiens and Rheims in mind. In fact it was the master mason Henry de Reyns ("of Rheims") who, between 1245 and 1254, put up the transepts, north front, and rose windows, as well as part of the cloisters and Chapter House; and it was his master plan that, funded by Richard II, was resumed 100 years later. Henry V (reigned 1413–1422) and Henry VII (1485–1509) were the chief succeeding benefactors. The Abbey was eventually completed in 1532. After that, Sir Christopher Wren had a hand in shaping the place; his West Towers were completed in 1745, 22 years after his death. The most riotous elements of the interior were, similarly, much later affairs.

The Nave is your first sight on entering; you need to look up to gain a perspective on the truly awe-inspiring scale of the church, because the eye-level view is obscured by the 19th- (and part 13th-) century choir screen, past which point admission is charged. Before paying, look at the poignant **Tomb of the Unknown Warrior,** an anonymous World War I martyr who lies buried here in memory of the soldiers fallen in both world wars. Nearby is one of the very few tributes to a foreigner, a plaque to Franklin D. Roosevelt.

There is only one way around the Abbey, and as there will almost certainly be a crocodile of shuffling visitors at your heels, you'll need to be alert to catch the highlights. Pass through the Choir, with its mid–19th-century choir stalls, into the North Transept. Look up to your right to see the painted-glass Rose Window, the largest of its kind; left for the first of the extravagant 18th-century monuments in the North Transept chapels. You then proceed into the **Henry VII Chapel,** passing the huge white marble tomb of Elizabeth I, buried with her half-sister, "Bloody" Mary I; then the tomb of Henry VII with his queen, Elizabeth of York, by the Renaissance master Torrigiano (otherwise known for having been banished from Florence after breaking Michelangelo's nose). All around are magnificent sculptures of saints, philosophers, and kings, with wild mermaids and monsters carved on the choir stall misericords (undersides), and exquisite fan vaulting above—one of the miracles of Western architecture.

Next you enter the **Chapel of Edward the Confessor,** where beside the royal saint's shrine stands the **Coronation Chair,** which has been briefly graced by nearly every regal posterior. Edward I ordered it around 1300; it used to shelter the Stone of Scone (pronounced *skoon*), upon which Scottish kings had been crowned since time began, but this precious relic returned in 1996 to Scotland's Edinburgh Castle for good.

The tombs and monuments for which Westminster Abbey is probably best loved began to appear at an accelerated rate starting in the 18th century. One earlier occupant, though, was Geoffrey Chaucer, who in 1400 became the first poet to be buried in **Poets' Corner.** Most of the other honored writers have only their memorials here, not their bones: William Shakespeare and William Blake (who both had a long wait before the dean deemed them holy enough to be here at all), John Milton, Jane Austen, Samuel Taylor Coleridge, William Wordsworth, Charles Dickens. All of Ben Jonson is here, though—buried upright in accord with his modest demand for a two-foot-by-two-foot grave site. ("O rare Ben Jonson," reads his epitaph, in a modest pun on the Latin *orare,* "to pray for.") Sir Isaac Newton, James Watt, and Michael Faraday are among the scientists with memorials. There is only one painter: Godfrey Kneller, whose dying words were "By God, I will not be buried in Westminster."

After the elbow battle you are guaranteed in Poets' Corner, you exit the Abbey by a door from the South Transept. Outside the west front is an archway leading into the quiet green **Dean's Yard** and the entrance to the **Cloisters,** where monks once strolled in contemplation. You may do the same, and catch a fine view of the massive flying buttresses above in the process. You may also, for a modest fee, take an impression from one of the tomb brasses in the **Brass-Rubbing Centre** (☎ 0171/222–2085). Also here is the entrance to Westminster School, formerly a monastic college, now one of Britain's finest public (which means the exact opposite) schools; Christopher Wren and Ben Jonson number among the old boys. The **Chapter House,** a stunning octagonal room supported by a central column and adorned with 14th-century frescoes, is where the King's Council and, after that, an early version of the Commons met between 1257 and 1547. In the **Undercroft,** which survives from Edward the Confessor's original church, note the deliciously macabre effigies made from the death masks and actual clothing of Elizabeth I, Charles II, and Admiral Lord Nelson (complete with eye patch), among others. Finally, the **Pyx Chamber** next door contains the Abbey's treasure, just as it used to when it became the royal strongroom during the 13th century. ⊠ *Broad Sanctuary,* ☎ *0171/222–5152.* ☞ *Nave free, Royal Chapels and Poets' Corner £4.* ☉ *Mon., Tues., Thurs., and Fri. 9–4; Wed. 9–7:45; Sat. 9–2 and 3:45–5; Sun. all day for services only. Closed weekdays to visitors during services. Tube: Westminster. Undercroft, Pyx Chamber, Chapter House, and Treasury,* ☎ *0171/222–5152.* ☞ *£2.50 for all 4.* ☉ *Daily 10:30–4. Tube: Westminster.*

Westminster Cathedral. This massive cathedral is hard to miss—once you are almost upon it, that is. It's set back from the left side of the street in a 21-year-old paved square that has fallen on hard times. Westminster Council, the local authority, would like to turn it into the Piazza San Marco of London, but until funding is found, it remains the windy haunt of homeless people and pigeons.

The cathedral is the seat of the Cardinal of Westminster, head of the Roman Catholic Church in Britain; consequently it is London's principal Roman Catholic church. The asymmetrical redbrick Byzantine hulk, dating only from 1903, is banded with stripes of Portland stone and abutted by a 273-foot-high campanile at the northwest corner, which you can scale by elevator. Faced with the daunting proximity of the heavenly Westminster Abbey, the architect, John Francis Bentley, flew in the face of fashion by rejecting neo-Gothic in favor of the Byzantine idiom, which still provides maximum contrast today—not only with the great church, but with just about all of London.

The interior is partly unfinished but worth seeing for its atmosphere of broody mystery; for its walls, covered in mosaic of a hundred different marbles from all over the world; and for a majestic nave—the widest in England—distinguished by a series of Eric Gill reliefs depicting the Stations of the Cross. ⊠ *Ashley Pl.,* ☎ *0171/834–7452.* ☞ *Tower £2.* ☉ *Cathedral daily, tower Apr.–Sept., daily.*

ST. JAMES'S AND MAYFAIR

St. James's and Mayfair form the very core of London's West End, the city's smartest central area. No textbook sights here; rather, these neighborhoods epitomize so much of the flavor that is peculiarly London's—the sense of being in a great, rich, (once) powerful city is almost palpable as you wander along its posh and polished streets. Here is the highest concentration of grand hotels, department stores, exclusive shops, glamorous restaurants, commercial art galleries, auction houses, swanky offices—all accoutrement that give this area an unmistakable air of wealth and leisure, even on busy days.

A late-17th-century ghost in the streets of contemporary St. James's would not need to bother walking through walls, because practically none have moved since he knew them. Its boundaries, clockwise from the north, are Piccadilly, Haymarket, The Mall, and Green Park: a neat rectangle, with a protruding spur satisfyingly located at Cockspur Street. The rectangle used to describe "gentlemen's London," where Sir was outfitted head and foot (but not in between, since the tailors were, and still are, north of Piccadilly in Savile Row) before repairing to his club. In fact, this has been a fashionable part of town from the first, largely by dint of the eponymous palace, St. James's, which was a royal residence—if not *the* palace—from the time of Henry VIII until the beginning of the Victorian era. In 1996, St. James's once again became a truly royal residence, as Prince Charles took up quarters here, shortly after leaving the Kensington Palace digs he once shared with his wife.

Mayfair, like St. James's, is precisely delineated—a trapezoid contained by Oxford Street and Piccadilly on the north and south, Regent Street and Park Lane on the east and west. Within its boundaries are streets both broad and narrow, but mostly unusually straight and grid-like for London, making it fairly easy to negotiate.

Numbers in the text correspond to numbers in the margin and on the St. James's and Mayfair map.

A Good Walk

Look at any street map and you'll quickly see what a random pattern the streets of St. James's and Mayfair make. The easiest approach seems to be the serendipitous one—follow your instincts and see where they take you. Here, however, is a tour that incorporates all the highlights. Starting in Trafalgar Square, you'll find Cockspur Street off the southwest corner; follow it to the foot of **Haymarket.** On your right is London's oldest shopping arcade, the splendid Regency Royal Opera Arcade, which John Nash finished in 1818. Now you come to **Pall Mall** ①, a showcase of 18th- and 19th-century patrician architecture, and home to such famous gentlemen's retreats as the Reform Club, halfway along on the right, from which Phileas Fogg set out to go Around the World. At the end of Pall Mall, you collide with the small Tudor brick **St. James's Palace** ②. Continue along Cleveland Row by the side of the palace to spy on York House, home of the duke and duchess of Kent, then turn left into Stable Yard Road to Lancaster House, built for the Duke of York in the 1820s but more notable as the venue for the 1978 conference that led to the end of white rule in Rhodesia/Zimbabwe; and Clarence House, designed by John Nash and built in 1825 for the Duke of Clarence (who became William IV) and which is now home to the Queen Mother. Now, head north up on St. James's Street to St. James's Place, where, if you turn left, you can spot, at No. 27, one of London's most spectacular 18th-century mansions, **Spencer House** ③, home of Princess Diana's ancestors; the interior can be viewed on tours given on Sundays only through the year (except August and January).

Cross back over St. James's Street to King Street—No. 8 is Christie's, the fine-art auctioneers who got £25 million for Van Gogh's *Sunflowers*; Duke Street on the left harbors further exclusive fine art salons—but straight ahead is **St. James's Square** ④, one of London's oldest, and home of the London Library. Leave the square by Duke of York Street to the north, and turn left on **Jermyn Street** ⑤, the world center of gentlemen's-paraphernalia shops. Set back from the street is the lovely **St. James's Church** ⑥. A right on Duke Street brings you to Piccadilly. Turn right again, and you'll pass the exclusive department store that supplies the queen's groceries, Fortnum and Mason, on the right, and the **Royal Academy of Arts** ⑦ opposite, with famous **Piccadilly Circus** ⑧ ahead. Turn around—**Wellington Arch** ⑨ and **Apsley House** ⑩, the gloriously opulent mansion the Duke of Wellington once called home, are ahead in the distance. Cross the street and head north up the shopping mecca of **Bond Street** ⑪, with **Burlington Arcade** ⑫ to the right. You could detour by turning right before you reach Oxford Street into Burlington Gardens, where you'll find the **Museum of Mankind** ⑬, or go into Brook Street (the composer Handel lived at No. 25), which leads to Hanover Square. Turning right down St. George Street brings you to the porticos of St. George's Church, where Percy Bysshe Shelley and George Eliot, among others, had their weddings. A right turn after the church down Mill Street brings you into the tailors' mecca of Savile Row, the fashionable center for bespoke suits and coats since the mid-19th century— No. 3 is Mecca for Beatlemaniacs: the former headquarters of Apple Corps and the place of John, Paul, George, and Ringo's legendary rooftop concert (the building now houses a financial institution and is not open to the public). From Savile Row, head westward over on Grosvenor Street to Duke Street: slightly to the south, you'll find one of Mayfair's beauty spots—Carlos Place (site of the Connaught) and neighboring Mount Row, both adorned with some veddy, veddy elegant residences. Shop-till-you-droppers can then head north to Oxford Street (**Selfridges** ⑭ and **Marks & Spencer** are here), while history buffs will want to detour to **Marble Arch** ⑮ and art lovers to beautiful Manchester Square for a must-see: the magnificent **Wallace Collection** ⑯.

TIMING

Although this walk doesn't cover an enormous distance, you'll probably do a lot of doubling back and detouring down beckoning alleys— and into interesting shops. If you want to do more than window-shop, we suggest most emphatically a weekday jaunt, starting in the morning, so you get time for visits to the Royal Academy and the Wallace Collection, or perhaps the Museum of Mankind and some of the commercial art galleries in and around Cork Street. The walk alone should take under two hours. Add at least an hour for the RA, depending on the exhibition, another two for the Wallace Collection, and one to two for the Museum of Mankind. Any of those could easily consume an afternoon, if you have one to spare. Shopping could take all week.

HOW TO GET THERE

You could start walking around this area from Trafalgar Square (☞ Westminster and Royal London, *above*), or get the Piccadilly or Bakerloo Line to the Piccadilly Circus tube stop, the Piccadilly to the Hyde Park Corner stop, or the Central Line to any of the stops along Oxford Street— Marble Arch, Bond Street (also Jubilee Line), Oxford Circus (also Victoria and Bakerloo lines), or Tottenham Court Road (also Northern Line). The Green Park stop on the Piccadilly, Victoria, or Jubilee lines is also central to many of this neighborhood's sights. The best buses are the Nos. 8, 9, 14, 19, 22, and 38 along Piccadilly, especially the 8, which loops around via New Bond Street to Oxford Street, and skims the eastern border of Green Park down Grosvenor Place.

Sights to See

★ ⑩ **Apsley House.** Once known, quite simply, as No. 1, London, this was long celebrated as the best address in town. Built by Robert Adam in the 1770s and later refaced and extended, this was where the Duke of Wellington lived from the 1820s until his death in 1852. As the Wellington Museum, it has been kept as the Iron Duke liked it, his uniforms and weapons, his porcelain and plate, and his extensive art collection, partially looted during military campaigns, displayed heroically. Unmissable, in every sense, is the gigantic Canova statue of a nude (but fig-leafed) Napoléon Bonaparte, Wellington's archenemy. Here, too, is the Waterloo Gallery, a state dining room that is a veritable orgy of opulence. Apsley House got iron shutters in 1830 after rioters, protesting the Duke's opposition (he was briefly Prime Minister) to the Reform Bill, broke the windows. Yes, the British loved him for defeating Napoléon, but mocked him with the name "Iron Duke"—referring not to his military prowess, but to those shutters. ✉ *149 Piccadilly,* ☎ *0171/499–5676.* ✑ *£3.* ☉ *Tues.–Sun. 11–5.*

Berkeley Square. As anyone who's heard the song knows, the word is pronounced to rhyme with "starkly." Not many of its original mid-18th-century houses are left, but look at Nos. 42–46 (especially No. 44, which the architectural historian Sir Nikolaus Pevsner thought London's finest terraced house) and Nos. 49–52 to get some idea of why it was once London's top address—not that it's in the least humble now. Snob nightclub Anabels is one current resident.

⑪ Bond Street. This world-class shopping haunt is divided into northern "New" (1710) and southern "Old" (1690) halves. New Bond Street boasts **Sotheby's,** the world-famous auction house, at No. 35, but there are other opportunities to flirt with financial ruin on Old Bond Street: the mirror-lined Chanel store, the vainglorious marble acres of Gianni Versace and the boutique of his more sophisticated compatriot Gucci, plus Tiffany's British outpost and art dealers Colnaghi, Léger, Thos. Agnew, and Marlborough Fine Arts. **Cork Street,** which parallels the top half of Old Bond Street, is where London's top dealers in contemporary art have their galleries—you're welcome to browse, but dress appropriately.

British Telecom Tower. The unlovely 620-foot glass pencil was imposed on London by the Post Office in 1965 (everyone still calls it the Post Office Tower) to field satellite phone calls and beam radio and TV signals around. It has a habit of popping up on the skyline from the most surprising locations, though since a terrorist bomb went off upstairs in 1975, its great view from its topmost lookout has been off-limits.

⑫ Burlington Arcade. Perhaps the finest of Mayfair's enchanting covered shopping alleys is the second-oldest in London, built in 1819. It's still patrolled by top-hatted beadles, who prevent you from singing, running, or carrying open umbrellas or large parcels (to say nothing of lifting English fancy-goods from the mahogany-fronted shops).

Faraday's Laboratory. In the basement of the Royal Institution is a reconstruction of the laboratory where the physicist Michael Faraday discovered electromagnetic induction in 1831—with echoes of Frankenstein. ✉ *21 Albermarle St.,* ☎ *0171/409–2992.* ✑ *£1.* ☉ *Weekdays 1–4.*

Grosvenor Square. Pronounced "Grove-na," this square was laid out in 1725–31 and is as desirable an address today as it was then. Americans certainly thought so—from John Adams, the second president, who as ambassador lived at No. 38, to Dwight D. Eisenhower, whose wartime headquarters was at No. 20. Now the ugly '50s block of the U.S. Embassy occupies the entire west side, and a British memorial to Franklin D. Roosevelt stands in the center. The little brick chapel used by Eisenhower's men during World War II, the 1730 Grosvenor Chapel, stands a couple of blocks south of the square on South Audley Street, with the entrance to pretty St. George's Gardens to its left. Across the gardens is the headquarters of the English Jesuits, and society-wedding favorite, the mid-19th-century Church of the Immaculate Conception, known as Farm Street because that is the name of the street on which it stands.

St. James's and Mayfair

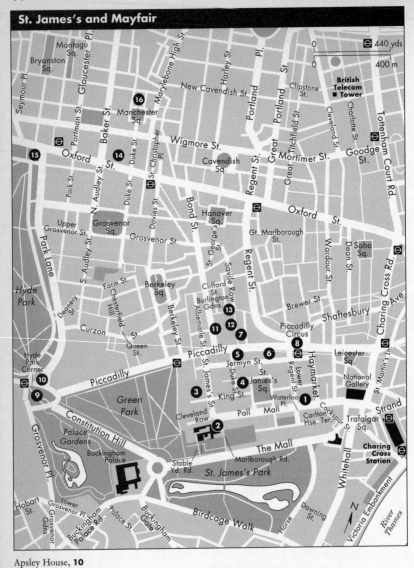

Apsley House, **10**
Bond Street, **11**
Burlington Arcade, **12**
Jermyn Street, **5**
Marble Arch, **15**
Museum of
Mankind, **13**
Pall Mall, **1**
Piccadilly Circus, **8**
Royal Academy of
Arts, **7**
St. James's Church, **6**
St. James's Palace, **2**
St. James's Square, **4**
Selfridges, **14**
Spencer House, **3**
Wallace Collection, **16**
Wellington Arch, **9**

Heinz Gallery. The gallery of the Royal Institute of British Architects has a changing program of exhibitions, and interesting, often cutting-edge, evening lectures. ⊠ *21 Portman Sq.,* ☎ *0171/580–5533.* ⌖ *Free.* ☉ *Weekdays during exhibitions 11–5, Sat. 10–1. Closed Aug. Tube: Bond Street.*

⑤ Jermyn Street. This is where the gentleman purchases his masculine paraphernalia. He buys his shaving sundries and hip flask from Geo. F. Trumper, briar pipe from Astley's, scent from Floris (for women too—both the Prince of Wales and his mother smell of Floris) or Czech & Speake, shirts from Turnbull & Asser, deerstalker and panama from Bates the Hatter, and his cheeses from Paxton & Whitfield (founded in 1740 and a legend among dairies). Shop your way east along Jermyn Street, and you're practically in Piccadilly Circus.

⑮ Marble Arch. The name denotes both the traffic whirlpool where Bayswater Road segues into Oxford Street and John Nash's 1827 arch, which moved here from Buckingham Palace in 1851. Search the sidewalk by the arch to find the stone plaque that marks (roughly) the place where the Tyburn Tree stood for four centuries, until 1783. This was London's central gallows, a huge wooden structure with hanging accommodations for 21. Hanging days were holidays, the spectacle supposedly functioning as a crime deterrent to the hoi polloi. It didn't work, though. Oranges, gingerbread, and gin were sold, alongside ballads and "personal favors," to vast, rowdy crowds, and the condemned, dressed in finery for his special moment, was treated more as hero than as villain. Cross over (or under—there are signs to help in the labyrinth) to the northeastern corner of Hyde Park to ☞ Speakers' Corner.

⑬ Museum of Mankind. More than overspill from the British Museum, with the best bits of the ethnographic collection, this museum is housed in a masterpiece of Victorian architecture and contains amazing artifacts from nonwestern civilizations. Long-running, imaginatively curated exhibitions are held on the first floor. When the long-awaited new British Library is up and running, the Department of Ethnography will be kicked back to the British Museum, so take advantage now. ⊠ *6 Burlington Gardens,* ☎ *0171/437–2224.* ⌖ *Free.* ☉ *Mon.–Sat. 10–5, Sun. 2:30–6. Tube: Tottenham Court Rd.*

NEED A BREAK? The suitably themed **Café de Colombia** is usually as peaceful as the Museum of Mankind it inhabits—unless you collide with a school visit. Salads and pastries, Colombian coffee, and wine and beer are on the lunch menu.

---

① Pall Mall. Like its near-namesake, *the* Mall, Pall Mall rhymes with "shall" and derives its name from the cross between croquet and golf that the Italians, who invented it, called *pallo a maglio,* and the French, who made it chic, called *palle-maille.* In England it was taken up with enthusiasm by James I, who called it "pell mell" and passed it down the royal line, until Charles II had a new road laid out for it in 1661. Needless to say, Catherine Street, as Pall Mall was officially named (after Charles's queen, Catherine of Braganza), was *very* fashionable. No. 79 must have been one of its livelier addresses, since Charles's gregarious mistress, Nell Gwyn, lived there. The king gave her the house when she complained about being a mere leaseholder, protesting that she had "always conveyed free under the Crown" (as it were); it remains, to this day, the only privately owned bit of Pall Mall's south side. Stroll slowly, the better to appreciate the creamy facades and perfect proportions along this showcase of 18th- and 19th-century British architecture.

Notable examples are two James Barry–designed buildings, the **Travellers' Club** and the **Reform Club,** both representatives of the upper-class gentleman's retreat that made St. James's the clubland of London. The Reform is the most famous club of all, thanks partly to Jules Verne's Phileas Fogg, who accepted the around-the-world-in-80-days bet in its smoking room, and was thus soon qualified to join the Travellers'. And—hallelujah—women can join the Reform. The RAC Club (for Royal Automobile Club, but it's never known as that), with its marble swimming pool, and the Oxford and Cambridge Club complete the Pall Mall quota; there are other, even older, establishments—Brooks's, the Carlton, Boodles, and White's (founded in 1736, the oldest of all)—in St. James's Street around the corner, alongside *the* gentlemen's bespoke (custom) shoemaker, Lobb's, and *the* hatter, James Lock.

⑧ Piccadilly Circus. The name got stuck during the early 17th century, when a humble tailor on the Strand named Robert Baker sold an awful lot of picadils—a collar ruff all the rage in courtly circles—and built a house with the proceeds. Snobs dubbed his new-money mansion Piccadilly Hall, and the name stuck. As for "Circus," that refers not to the menagerie of backpackers and camera-clickers clustered around the steps of **Eros,** but to the circular junction of five major roads.

Eros, London's favorite statue and symbol of the *Evening Standard* newspaper, is not in fact the Greek god of erotic love at all but the angel of Christian charity, commissioned in 1893 from the young sculptor Alfred Gilbert as a memorial to the philanthropic Earl of Shaftesbury (the angel's bow and arrow are a sweet allusion to the earl's name). It cost Gilbert £7,000 to cast the statue he called his "missile of kindness" in the novel medium of aluminum, and because he was paid only £3,000, he promptly went bankrupt and fled the country. (Don't worry—he was knighted in the end.) Eros has lately done his best to bankrupt Westminster Council, too, owing to some urgent leg surgery and a new coat of protective microcrystalline synthetic wax. Outside of Eros, there's not much to see in this sometime hub of London beyond a bank of neon advertisements, a very large branch of Tower Records, the tawdry Trocadero Centre (video arcades, food courts, chain stores, the Guinness World of Records), and a perpetual traffic jam.

Portland Place. The elegant throughway to Regent's Park was London's widest street during the 1780s when the brothers Robert and James Adam designed it. The first sight to greet you here, drawing the eye around the awkward corner, is the curvaceous portico and pointy Gothic spire of **All Souls Church,** one part of Nash's Regent Street plan that remains. It is now the venue for innumerable concerts and Anglican services broadcast to the nation by the British Broadcasting Corporation. The 1931 block of **Broadcasting House** next door is home to the BBC's five radio stations. It curves too, if less beautifully, and features an Eric Gill sculpture of Shakespeare's Ariel (aerial—get it?) over the entrance, from which the playful sculptor was obliged to excise a portion of phallus lest it offend public decency—which the modified model did in any case.

Queen's Chapel. Designed by Inigo Jones not for the queen of the realm, but for the Infanta of Castille when she was betrothed to Charles I in 1623. This was actually the first classical church in England, and attending a service is the only way you can get to delight in it. Behind it is **Marlborough House,** designed by Wren in 1709 for the duchess of Marlborough, who asked for something "strong plain and convenient," and so it was—she remained here until she died in 1744.

Regent Street. This curvaceous thoroughfare was conceived by John Nash and his patron, the Prince Regent—the future George IV—as a kind of ultra-catwalk from the prince's palace, Carlton House, to Regent's Park (then called Marylebone Park). The section between Piccadilly and Oxford Street was to be called the Quadrant and lined with colonnaded purveyors of "articles of fashion and taste," in a big P.R. exercise to improve London's image as the provincial cousin of smarter European capitals. The scheme was never fully implemented, and what there was fell into such disrepair that, early this century, Aston Webb (of the Mall route) collaborated on the redesign you see today. It is still a major shopping street. Hamleys, the gigantic toy emporium, is fun; and since 1875 there has been Liberty, which originally imported silks from the East, then diversified to other Asian goods, and is now best known for its "Liberty print" cottons, its jewelry department, and—still—its high-class Asian imports. The stained-glass–lighted mock-Tudor interior, with beams made from battleships, is worth a look.

❼ Royal Academy of Arts. Burlington House was built in the Palladian style for the Earl of Burlington around 1720, and is one of the few surviving mansions from that period. Two sides of the courtyard are occupied by learned societies: the Geological Society, Chemistry Society, Society of Antiquaries, and the Royal Astronomical Society, but at the top is its chief occupant, the Royal Academy of Arts, which mounts major art exhibitions, usually years in the planning. Unfortunately, its own fabled collection has been dispersed to other museums, notably the Tate and the National Gallery; the latter got the prize—the *Taddeo Tondo* (a sculpted disk) by Michelangelo of the Madonna and Child. Temporary exhibitions at the academy are in the Sackler Galleries (opened in 1991 and designed by another academician, Sir Norman Foster). Every June, the RA mounts the **Summer Exhibition,** a mishmash of sculpture and painting, with about 1,000 things crammed into every cranny. Art-weary now? Try the shop; it's one of the best museum stores in town. The White Card is accepted. ⊠ *Burlington House, Piccadilly,* ☎ *0171/439–7438 or 0171/439– 4996.* 🎫 *Admission varies according to exhibition.* ☺ *Daily 10–6. Tube: Piccadilly Circus.*

❻ St. James's Church. Recessed from the street behind a courtyard filled, most days, with a crafts market, and completed in 1684, this was the last of Sir Christopher Wren's London churches, and his own favorite. It contains one of Grinling Gibbons's finest works, an ornate limewood reredos (the screen behind the altar). A 1940 bomb scored a direct hit here, but the church was completely restored, albeit with a fiberglass spire. It's a lively place, offering all manner of lecture series—many on incongruously New Age themes—and concerts, mostly Baroque, as well as a brass-rubbing center.

NEED A BREAK?	**The Wren** at St. James's, attached to the church, has not the faintest whiff of godliness, as the cake display proves. Hot dishes at lunchtime are vegetarian, very good, and very inexpensive. There are tables outside in spring and summer.

❷ St. James's Palace. With its solitary sentry posted at the gate, this is a surprisingly small palace of Tudor brick. Matters to ponder as you look (you can't go in): It was named after a hospital for women lepers, which stood here during the 11th century; Henry VIII had it built; foreign ambassadors to Britain are still accredited to the Court of St. James's even though it has rarely been a primary royal residence; the present queen made her first speech here; and it's now the current address of Prince Charles (his front door actually debouches right onto the street, but he always uses a back entrance).

❹ St. James's Square. One of London's oldest and leafiest squares was also the most snobbish address of all when it was laid out around 1670, with 14 resident dukes and earls installed by 1720. Since 1841, No. 14—one of the several 18th-century residences spared by World War II bombs—has housed the **London Library,** which, with its million or so volumes, is the best private humanities library in the land. You can go in and read the famous authors' complaints in the comments book—but not the famous authors' books, unless you join, at £100 a year.

❶ Selfridges. With its row of massive Ionic columns, this huge store was opened three years after Harry Gordon Selfridge came to London from Chicago in 1906. Now British-run, Selfridges rivals Harrods (☞ Knightsbridge, Kensington, and Holland Park, *below*) in size and stock, and is finally rivaling its glamour, too, since investing in major face-lift operations. It stands toward the Marble Arch end of Oxford street, close by the flagship branch of everyone's favorite chain store, **Marks and Spencer** (usually known by its pet names M&S or Marks & Sparks)—supplier of England's underwear, purveyor of woollies (sweaters, that is), producer of dishes passed off as homemade at dinner parties. This place has by far the highest turnover of stock of any shop in the land, so expect crowds at all times.

Shepherd Market. Though it looks like a quaint and villagelike tangle of streetlets, this was anything *but* quaint when Edward Shepherd laid it out in 1735 on the site of the orgiastic, fortnight-long May Fair (which gave the whole district its name). Now there are sandwich bars, pubs and restaurants, boutiques and nightclubs, and a (fading) red-light reputation in the narrow lanes.

Speakers' Corner. This corner harbors a late-20th-century public spectacle. Here, on Sunday afternoons, anyone is welcome to mount a soapbox and declaim upon any topic. It's an irresistible showcase of eccentricity, though sadly diminished since the death in 1994 of the "Protein Man," who thought meat, cheese, and peanuts led to uncontrollable acts of passion that would destroy Western civilization. The pamphlets he sold for four decades down Oxford Street are now collector's items.

★ ❸ Spencer House. Ancestral abode of the Spencers—the family who gave us Princess Diana—this great mansion is perhaps the finest example of 18th-century elegance, on a domestic scale, left in London. Superlatively restored by Lord Rothschild, the house was built in 1766 for the first Earl Spencer, heir to the first Duchess of Marlborough. A gorgeous Doric facade, complete with pediment adorned with classical statues, announces at once Earl Spencer's passion for the Grand Tour and the classical antiquities of the past. Inside, James "Athenian" Stuart decorated the gilded State Rooms, including the Painted Room, the first completely Neo-Classical room in Europe. The most ostentatious part of the house (and the Spencers—as witness the $70,000 diamonded shoe-buckles the first countess proudly wore—could be given to ostentation) is the florid bow-window of the Drawing Room: covered with stucco palm trees, it conjures up both ancient Palmyra and modern Miami Beach. ✉ *27 St. James's Pl.,* ☎ *0171/499–8620.* ☞ *£6.* ☾ *Guided tour Sun. 10:45 AM–4:45 (tickets on sale Sun. at 10:30). Closed Aug. and Jan. Tube: Green Park.*

★ ❶ Wallace Collection. Assembled by four generations of Marquesses of Hertford and given to the nation by the widow of Sir Richard Wallace, bastard son of the fourth, this collection of art and artifacts is important, exciting, undervisited—and free. As at the Frick Collection in New York, the setting here, Hertford House, is part of the show—a fine late-18th-century mansion, built for the Duke of Manchester, and completely renovated during the late 1970s.

The first marquess was a patron of Sir Joshua Reynolds, the second bought Hertford House, the third—a flamboyant socialite—favored Sèvres porcelain and 17th-century Dutch painting; but it was the eccentric fourth marquess who, from his self-imposed exile in Paris, really built the collection, snapping up Bouchers, Fragonards, Watteaus, and Lancrets for a song (the French Revolution having rendered them dangerously unfashionable), augmenting these with furniture and sculpture, and sending his son Richard out to do the deals. With 30 years of practice behind him, Richard Wallace continued acquiring treasures after his father's death, scouring Italy for majolica and Renaissance gold, then moving most of it to London. Look for Rembrandt's portrait of his son, the Rubens landscape, the Van Dycks and Canalettos, the French rooms, and of course the porcelain. The highlight is Fragonard's *The Swing,* which conjures up the 18th century's let-them-eat-cake *frivolité* better than any other painting around. Don't forget to say hello to Frans Hals's *Laughing Cavalier* in the Big Gallery. ✉ *Hertford House, Manchester Sq.,* ☎ *0171/935–0687.* ☏ *Free.* ☾ *Mon.–Sat. 10–5, Sun. 2–5.*

Waterloo Place. This is a long rectangle off Pall Mall, punctuated by the Duke of York memorial column atop the Duke of York Steps, and littered with statues, among them Florence Nightingale, the "Lady with the Lamp" nurse-heroine of the Crimean War; Captain R. F. Scott, who led a disastrous Antarctic expedition in 1911–12 and is here frozen in a bronze by his wife; Edward VII, mounted; George VI; and, as usual, Victoria, here in terra-cotta.

Flanking Waterloo Place looking onto Pall Mall are two of the gentlemen's clubs for which St. James's came to be known as Clubland: the **Athenaeum** and the former United Service Club, now the **Institute of Directors.** The latter was built by John Nash in 1827–8 but was given a face-lift by Decimus Burton 30 years later to match it up with the Athenaeum across the way, which he had designed. It's fitting that you gaze on the Athenaeum first, since it was—and is—the most elite of all the societies. (It called itself "The Society" until 1830 just to rub it in.) Most prime ministers and cabinet ministers, archbishops, and bishops have belonged; the founder, John Wilson Croker (the first to call the British right-wingers "Conservatives"), decreed it the club for artists and writers, and so literary types (Sir Arthur Conan Doyle, Rudyard Kipling, J. M. Barrie—the posh ones) have graced its lists, too. Women are barred. Most clubs will tolerate female guests these days, but few admit women members, and anyway, even if your anatomy is correct it's almost impossible to become a member unless you have the connections—which, of course, is the whole point.

❾ **Wellington Arch.** It is marooned on the central island of Hyde Park Corner—the cyclist's nightmare at the extreme west end of Piccadilly—so you need to descend the pedestrian underpasses, following the signs, to reach the arch itself. This 1828 Decimus Burton triumphal gateway almost wound up at the back door of Buckingham Palace, but here it stands instead, empty now of London's smallest police station, which occupied its cramped insides until 1992.

SOHO AND COVENT GARDEN

A quadrilateral described by Regent Street, Coventry/Cranbourn streets, Charing Cross Road, and the eastern half of Oxford Street encloses

Soho, the most fun part of the West End. This appellation, unlike the New York neighborhood's similar one, is not an elision of anything, but a blast from the past—derived (as far as we know) from the shouts of "So-ho!" that royal huntsmen in Whitehall Palace's parklands were once heard to cry. One of Charles II's illegitimate sons, the Duke of Monmouth, was an early resident, his dubious pedigree setting the tone for the future: For many years Soho was London's strip show/peep show/clip joint/sex shop/brothel center. The mid-'80s brought legislation that granted expensive licenses to a few such establishments and closed down the rest; most prostitution had already been ousted by the 1959 Street Offences Act. Only a cosmetic smear of red-light activity remains now, plus a shop called "Condomania" and one or two purveyors of couture fetishwear for trendy club-goers.

These clubs, which cluster around the Soho grid, are the diametric opposite of the St. James's gentlemen's museums—they cater to youth, change soundtrack every month, and post tyrannical fashion police at the door. Another breed of Soho club is the strictly members-only media haunts (the Groucho, the Soho House, Fred's, Brown's, Black's), salons for carefully segregated strata of high-income hipster. The same crowd populates the astonishing selection of restaurants, but then so does the rest of London and all its visitors—because Soho is gourmet country.

It was after the First World War, when London households relinquished their resident cooks en masse, that Soho's gastronomic reputation was established. It had been a cosmopolitan area since the first immigrant wave of French Huguenots arrived in the 1680s. More French came fleeing the revolution during the late 18th century, then the Paris Commune of 1870, followed by Germans, Russians, Poles, Greeks, and (especially) Italians and, much later, Chinese. Pedestrianized Gerrard Street, south of Shaftsbury Avenue, is the hub of London's compact Chinatown, which boasts restaurants, dim sum houses, Chinese supermarkets, and annual February New Year's celebrations, plus a brace of scarlet pagoda-style archways and a pair of phone booths with pictogram dialing instructions.

The former Covent Garden Market became the Piazza in 1980, and it still functions as the center of a neighborhood—one that has always been alluded to as "colorful." It was originally the "convent garden" belonging to the Abbey of St. Peter at Westminster (later Westminster Abbey). The land was given to the first Earl of Bedford by the Crown after the Dissolution of the Monasteries in 1536. The Earls—later promoted to Dukes—of Bedford held on to the place right up until 1918, when the eleventh Duke managed to offload what had by then become a liability. In between, the area enclosed by Long Acre, St. Martin's Lane, Drury Lane, and assorted streets north of the Strand had gone from the height of fashion (until the nobs moved west to brand-new St. James's) to a period of arty-literary bohemia during the 18th century, followed by an era of vice and mayhem, to once more become vegetable provisioner to London when the market building went up in the 1830s, followed by the Flower Market in 1870 (Eliza Dolittle's alma mater in Shaw's *Pygmalion* and Lerner and Loewe's musical version, *My Fair Lady*).

Still, it was no Mayfair, what with 1,000-odd market porters spending their 40-shillings-a-week in the alehouses, brothels, and gambling dens that had never quite disappeared. By the time the Covent Garden Estate Company took over the running of the market from the 11th Duke, it seemed as if seediness had set in for good, and when the fruit-and-veg trade moved out to the bigger, better Nine Elms Market in Vauxhall in 1974, it left behind a decrepit wasteland. But this is one of London's success stories: Now the (sadly defunct) Greater London Council stepped in with a dream of a rehabilitation plan—not unlike the one that was tried, though less successfully, in the Parisian equivalent, Les Halles. By 1980, the transformation was complete.

Numbers in the text correspond to numbers in the margin and on the Soho and Covent Garden map.

A Good Walk

Soho, being small, is easy to explore, though it's also easy to mistake one narrow, crowded street for another, and even Londoners go astray here. Enter from the northwest corner, Oxford Circus, and head south for about 200 yards down Regent Street, turn left into Great Marlborough Street, and head to the top of **Carnaby Street** ①. Turn right off Broadwick Street into Berwick (pronounced "Berrick") Street, famed as central London's best fruit and vegetable market. Then step through tiny Walker's Court (ignoring the notorious hookers' bulletin board), cross Brewer Street, named for two extinct 18th-century breweries, and you'll have arrived at Soho's hip hangout, Old Compton Street. From here, Wardour, Dean (home of the **French House** ② and St. Anne's Church), Frith, and Greek streets lead north, all of them bursting with restaurants and clubs. Either of the latter two lead north to **Soho Square** ③, but head one block south instead, to Shaftesbury Avenue, heart of theaterland, across which you'll find Chinatown's main drag, Gerrard Street. Below Gerrard Street is **Leicester Square** ④, and running along its west side is Charing Cross Road, the bibliophile's dream. You'll find some of the best of the specialist bookshops in little Cecil Court, running east just before Trafalgar Square.

The easiest way to find the **Covent Garden Piazza** ⑤ and market building is to walk down Cranbourn Street, next to Leicester Square tube, then down Long Acre, and turn right at James Street. Here, and around here, are **St. Paul's** ⑥—the actors' church—the **London Transport Museum** ⑦ and the **Theatre Museum** ⑧ as well as plenty of shops and cafés. (If your aim is to shop, **Neal Street,** Floral Street, the streets around Seven Dials, and the Thomas Neale's mall all repay exploration.) From Seven Dials, veer 45 degrees south into Mercer Street, turning right on Long Acre, then left into Garrick Street, past the **Garrick Club** ⑨, left into Rose Street, and right into Floral Street. At the other end you'll emerge onto Bow Street, right next to the **Royal Opera House** ⑩ and the **Magistrates' Court** ⑪. Continuing on, and turning left into Russell Street, you reach Drury Lane, and the **Theatre Royal** ⑫.

At the end of Drury Lane is the Aldwych, a great big croissant of a potential traffic accident, with a central island on which stand three hulking monoliths: India House, Melbourne House, and the handsome 1935 neo-classical Bush House, headquarters of the BBC World Service. Stranded (oops) on traffic islands to the west, are the 1717 St. Mary-le-Strand, James Gibbs's (of St. Martin-in-the-Fields fame; ☞ Westminster and Royal London, *above*) first public building, inspired by the Baroque churches of Rome, and Wren's St. Clement Danes (with a tower appended by Gibbs), whose 10 bells peal the tune of the nursery rhyme "Oranges and lemons,/Say the bells of St. Clements . . ." even though the bells in the rhyme belong to St. Clements, Eastcheap. Inside is a book listing 1,900 American airmen who were killed during World War II. Heading west, perhaps stopping at the **Courtauld Institute Galleries** ⑬, walk the ¾-mi traffic-clogged **Strand** to the southern end, where you take Villiers Street down to the Thames. See the **York Watergate** ⑭ and **Cleopatra's Needle** ⑮ by Victoria Embankment Gardens, cross the gardens northwest to the **Adelphi** ⑯, circumnavigating the Strand by sticking to the embankment walk, and you'll soon reach Waterloo Bridge, where (weather permitting) you can catch some of London's most glamorous views, toward both the City and Westminster around the Thames bend.

TIMING

The distance covered here is around 5 mi, if you include the lengthy walk down the Strand, and riverside stroll back. Skip that, and it's barely a couple of miles, but you will almost certainly get lost, because the streets in both Covent Garden and Soho are winding and chaotic, and not logically disposed. Although getting lost is half the fun, it does make it hard to predict how long this walk will take. You can whiz round both neighborhoods in an hour, but if the area appeals at all, you'll want all day—for shopping, lunch, the Theatre and Transport museums, and the Courtauld Galleries. One way to do it is to start at Leicester Square at 2 PM, when the Half Price Theatre Booth opens, pick up tickets for later, and then walk, shop, and eat in between.

HOW TO GET THERE

A popular way to get to Soho is to hop on the Northern Line to Tottenham Court Road, and walk south down Charing Cross Road, then west along Old Compton Street into the district proper, or eastward, by turning left at Shaftsbury Avenue, over to the Covent Garden area. The Covent Garden tube stop is on the Piccadilly Line; Leicester Square—the nearest tube to Soho—on the Northern Line. The best Soho buses are the Nos. 14, 19, 24, 29, 38, or 176 to Charing Cross Road/Shaftsbury Avenue; for Covent Garden, get those listed above, or the ones that stop along the Strand: Nos. 1, 4, 11, 15, 23, 26, 68, 76, 91, 168, 171, and 188.

Sights to See

⑯   **Adelphi.** A regal riverfront row of houses that was the work of London's Scottish architects—all four of them. John, Robert, James, and William Adam, being brothers, gave rise to the name, from the Greek *adelphoi,* meaning brothers. All the late-18th-century design stars were roped in to beautify the interiors, but the grandeur gradually eroded, and today very few of the 24 houses remain; 7 Adam Street is the best.

⑪   **Bow Street Magistrates' Court.** This was where the prototype of the modern police force first operated. Known as the Bow Street Runners (because they chased thieves on foot), they were the brainchild of the second Bow Street magistrate—none other than Henry Fielding, the author of *Tom Jones* and *Joseph Andrews.* The late-19th-century edifice on the site went up during one of the market improvement drives. It now houses three courts, including that of the Metropolitan Chief Magistrate, who hears all extradition applications.

❶   **Carnaby Street.** The '60s synonym for swinging London fell into a postparty depression, reemerging sometime during the '80s as the main drag of a public-relations invention called West Soho. Blank stares would greet anyone asking directions to such a place, but it is geographically logical, and the tangle of streets—Foubert's Place, Broadwick Street, Marshall Street—do cohere, at least, in type of merchandise (youth accessories, mostly, with a smattering of designer boutiques). Broadwick Street is also notable as the birthplace, at No. 74, in 1758, of the great visionary poet and painter William Blake. At age 26 he came back for a year to sell prints next door, at No. 72 (now an ugly tower block), and then remained a Soho resident in Poland Street.

⑮   **Cleopatra's Needle.** Off the triangular-handkerchief Victoria Embankment Gardens, where office sandwich-eaters and people who call it home coexist, is London's *very oldest thing,* predating its arbitrary

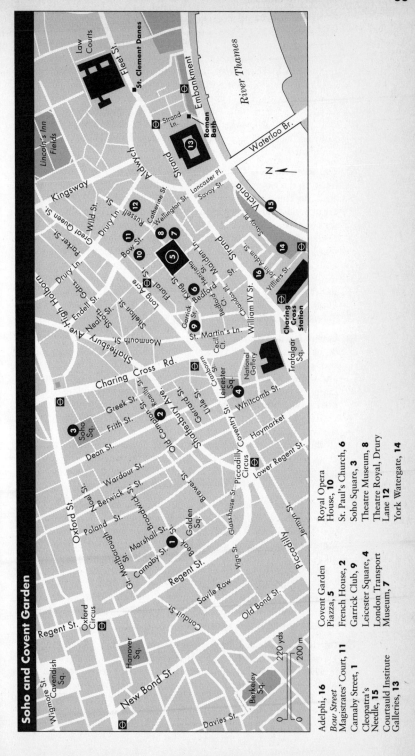

Soho and Covent Garden

namesake, and London itself, by centuries. The 60-foot pink granite obelisk was erected at Heliopolis, in Lower Egypt, in about 1475 BC, then moved to Alexandria, where in 1819 Mohammed Ali, the Turkish Viceroy of Egypt, rescued it from its fallen state and presented it to the British. The British, though grateful, had not the faintest idea how to get the 186-ton gift home, so they left it there for years until an expatriate English engineer contrived an iron pontoon to float it to London via Spain. Future archaeologists will find an 1878 "time capsule" underneath, containing the morning papers, several bibles, a railway timetable, some pins, a razor, and a dozen photos of Victorian pinup girls.

⑬　Courtauld Institute Galleries. One of London's most beloved art collections, the Courtauld, will be closed for a year beginning September 1997 for complete renovation. The Galleries are found in grand 18th-century classical Somerset House, alongside a vast compilation of civil servants (conjure up the red-tape-bestrewn Circumlocution Offices in Dickens's *Little Dorrit*) who still lurk inside. Founded in 1931 by the textile maven Samuel Courtauld, this is London's finest Impressionist and post-Impressionist collection, with bonus post-Renaissance works thrown in. Botticelli, Breughel, Tiepolo, and Rubens are represented, but the younger French painters (plus van Gogh) are the stars. ✉ *The Strand,* ☎ 0171/873–2526. ☞ *£4.* ☉ *Mon.–Sat. 10–6, Sun. 2–6. Tube: Temple, Embankment.*

❺　Covent Garden Piazza. The Piazza is what the restored 1840 market building around which Covent Garden pivots is known as. Inside, the shops are mostly higher-class clothing chains, plus a couple of cafés and some knickknack stores that are good for gifts. There's a superior crafts market on most days, too. If you turn right, you'll reach the indoor **Jubilee Market,** with stalls selling clothing, army surplus gear, more crafts, and more knickknacks. At yet another market off to the left (on the way back to the tube), the leather goods, antiques, and secondhand clothing stalls are a little more exciting. In summer it may seem that everyone you see around the Piazza (and the crowds are legion) is a fellow tourist, but there is still plenty of office life in the area, and Londoners continue to flock here.

❷　French House. A longstanding Gallic outpost, recognizable by the *tricolor* fluttering outside on Dean Street, this pub has been crammed with people ever since de Gaulle's Free French Forces rendezvoused here during World War II. Nowadays the crowd isn't French—it's Soho trendies and peculiar bohemians, some heading for the trendy restaurant upstairs. No pints of beer here, but you can get a decent *vin ordinaire* or a glass of pastis beneath the signed photos of French boxers. Opposite the French House is all that remains of once-famous **St. Anne's Church,** probably the work of Wren. A German bomb in 1940 spared only the tower, and the graveyard behind it, on Wardour Street.

❾　Garrick Club. Named for the 18th-century actor and theater manager David Garrick, this club is, because of its literary-theatrical bent, more louche than its St. James's brothers, and famous actors, from Sir Laurence Olivier down, have always been proud to join—along with Dickens, Thackeray, and Trollope, in their time. Find the **Lamb and Flag** down teeny Rose Street to the left. Dickens drank in this pub, better known in its 17th-century youth as the Bucket of Blood owing to the bare-knuckle boxing matches held upstairs. (You'll find that many London pubs claim Dickens as an habitué, and it's unclear whether they lie or the author was the city's premier sot.)

❹　Leicester Square. Pronounced "lester," not "lay-sess-ter," this square is showing no sign of its great age. Looking at the neon of the major movie houses, the fast-food outlets (plus a useful Häagen-Dazs café), and the disco entrances, you'd never guess it was laid out around 1630. By the 19th century it was already bustling and disreputable, and now it's usually one of the only places crowded after midnight— with suburban teenagers, Belgian backpackers, and London's swelling ranks of the homeless. That said, it is not a threatening place, and the liveliness can be quite cheering. In the middle is a statue of a sulking Shakespeare, clearly wishing he were somewhere else and perhaps remembering the days when the cinemas were live theaters—burlesque houses, but live all the same. Here, too, are figures of Hogarth, Reynolds, and Charlie Chaplin, and underneath is an invisible new £22 million electrical substation. One landmark certainly worth visiting is the **Society of London Theatre ticket kiosk,** on the southwest corner, which sells half-price tickets for many of that evening's performances (☞ Theater *in* Chapter 7). On the northeast corner, in Leicester Place, stands **Notre Dame de France,** with a wonderful mural by Jean Cocteau in one of its side chapels.

☺ ❼ **London Transport Museum.** Housed in the old Flower Market at the southeastern corner of the Covent Garden Piazza, this museum tells the story of mass transportation in the capital, and is much better than it sounds. It is particularly child-friendly, with lots of touch-screen interactive material, live actors in costume (including a Victorian horse-dung collector; though you should go early to see them), old rolling-stock, period smells and sounds, and best of all, a tube-driving simulator. There's also a café, and a shop selling the wonderful old London Transport posters, plus mugs, socks, bow ties, and so on, printed with that elegant London tube map, designed by Harry Beck in 1933 and still in use today. The White Card is accepted. ⊠ *Piazza,* ☏ 0171/379–6344. ▧ *£4.50.* ☉ *Daily 10–6. Tube: Covent Garden.*

Neal Street. One of Covent Garden's most intriguing shopping streets begins north of Long Acre catercorner to the tube station, and is closed to traffic halfway down. Here you can buy everything you never knew you needed—apricot tea, sitars, vintage aviators' jackets, silk kimonos, Alvar Aalto vases, halogen desk lamps, shoes with heel lower than toe, collapsible top hats, and so on. To the left off Neal Street, on Earlham Street, is Thomas Neal's—a new, upmarket, designerish clothing and housewares mall named after the founder (in 1693) of the star-shape cobbled junction of tiny streets just past there, called Seven Dials—a surprisingly residential enclave, with lots going on behind the tenement-style warehouse facades. Turning left into the next street off Neal Street, Shorts Gardens, you come to Neal's Yard (note the comical, water-operated wooden clock), originally just a whole-foods wholesaler, now an entire holistic village with therapy rooms, organic bakery and dairy, a great vegetarian café, and a medical herbalist's shop reminiscent of a medieval apothecary.

☺ **Rock Circus.** This shamelessly touristique offshoot of Madame Tussaud's waxworks (☞ Regent's Park and Hampstead, *below*) features animatronic and wax pop stars miming to their hits, or frozen in time, chronologically displayed to give the impression of a museum of popular music. Strictly for younger teens. ⊠ *London Pavilion, Piccadilly Circus,* ☏ 0171/734–8025. ▧ *£7.50.* ☉ *Sun., Mon., Wed., and Thurs. 11–9, Tues. noon–9; Fri. and Sat. 11–10. Tube: Piccadilly Circus.*

❿ **Royal Opera House.** Here, the Royal Ballet and Britain's finest opera company put on their grandest spectacles; here, Joan Sutherland once brought down the house as Lucia di Lammermoor and Rudolf Nureyev and Margot Fonteyn became the greatest ballet duo of all time. For such delights, seats can be top dollar—nearly £100—or just a 20th of that lordly amount. Whatever the price, it will be worth it if you love red-and-gold Victorian decor, which gives a very special feel to that hush that precedes the start of a performance. London's premier opera venue was designed in 1858 by E. M. Barry, son of Sir Charles, the House of Commons architect. This is actually the third theater on the site. The first opened in 1732 and burned down in 1808; the second opened a year later under the aegis of one John Anderson, only to succumb to fire in 1856 (Anderson, who had lost two theaters already, had an appalling record when it came to keeping the limelights apart from the curtains). Despite government subsidies, tickets for the Royal Opera remain pricey, though the expense is unlikely to lead to riots as it did in 1763, 1792, and 1809, when the cost of rebuilding inflated the price of admission. Nowadays, actually, you can see some of the glittering opera divas who perform here for free, when selected summer performances are relayed live to a giant screen in the Piazza. But then you would miss the opera house's bars, especially the Crush Bar, which add opulence to the pastime of people-watching during an intermission. Note, however, that the opera house will be undergoing extensive renovation work in the next few coming years, with resident troops finding temporary shelter elsewhere. Call for current updates. ✉ *Bow St.,* ☎ *0171/240–1066 or 0171/304–4000. Tube: Covent Garden.*

❻ St. Paul's Church. Find this across the Covent Garden Piazza, punctuated with street entertainers—those who have passed auditions for this most coveted of London's street venues. This 1633 work of the great Inigo Jones has always been known as "the actors' church" thanks to the several theaters in its parish, and well-known actors often read the lessons at services. Its portico was the setting for *Pygmalion*'s opening scene. The matching tall, terraced houses Jones designed to form a quadrangle with the church are long since history.

❸ Soho Square. Laid out about 1680, this square was fashionable during the 18th century. Only two of the original houses still stand, plus the 19th-century central garden. It's now a place of peace and offices (among them Paul McCartney's music publishers, and Bloomsbury Publishing). That isn't a tudor landmark in the center, but a picturesque Victorian gardener's hut, recently renovated.

NEED A BREAK?   Take any excuse you can think of to visit either of Soho's wonderful rival patisseries: **Maison Bertaux** (✉ 28 Greek St.) or **Pâtisserie Valerie** (✉ 44 Old Compton St.). Both serve divine gâteaux, milles-feuilles, croissants, éclairs, and more, the former in an upstairs salon, the latter in a darkish room behind the cake counters.

Strand. Here is one of London's oldest streets. It was already lined with mansions seven centuries ago, when it was a mere Thames-side bridle path. In 1706 Thomas Twining, the tea tycoon, moved his shop into No. 216 (it's still here); it was closely followed by a slew of coffeehouses, frequented by Boswell and Johnson, which persisted through most of that century. Remember Judy Garland doing Burlington Bertie in Chaplin drag, walking down the Strand with gloves in hand, in *A Star Is Born*? William Hargreaves's song was a popular number in the Strand music halls that put the street on the map afresh during the early 1900s. Now its presence on maps is about all that the characterless Strand has to recommend it.

�❽ Theatre Museum. This mostly below-ground museum aims to re-create the excitement of theater itself. There are usually programs in progress allowing children to get in a mess with makeup or have a giant dressing-up session. Permanent exhibits paint a history of the English stage from the 16th century to Mick Jagger's jumpsuit, with tens of thousands of theater playbills, and sections on such topics as Hamlet-through-the-ages and pantomime—the peculiar British theatrical tradition whereby men dress as ugly women (as distinct from RuPaul), and girls wear tights and play princes. There's a little theater in the bowels of the museum and a ticket desk for "real" theaters around town, plus an archive holding video recordings and audiotapes of significant British theatrical productions. ✉ *7 Russell St.,* ☎ *0171/836–7891.* 📠 *£3.50.* ☉ *Tues.–Sun. 11–7. Tube: Covent Garden.*

⑫ **Theatre Royal, Drury Lane.** This is London's best-known auditorium and almost its largest. Since World War II, its forte has been musicals (*Miss Saigon* is the current resident; past ones have included *The King and I, My Fair Lady, South Pacific, Hello, Dolly!,* and *A Chorus Line*)—though David Garrick, who managed it from 1747 to 1776, made its name by reviving the works of the by then obscure William Shakespeare. It enjoys all the romantic accessories of a London theater—a history of fires (it burned down three times, once in a Wren-built incarnation), rioting (in 1737, when a posse of footmen demanded free admission), attempted regicides (George II in 1716 and his grandson George III in 1800), and even sightings of the most famous phantom of theaterland, the Man in Grey (in the Circle, matinees). The entrance is on Catherine Street.

☺ **The Trocadero.** The nearest thing to a U.S. mall in London, this has shops and a food court, but it is best known for the amazing array of virtual reality machines and whiz-bang interactive rides—Virtual World, Emaginator, Funland, and the United Kingdom's first IMAX theater, and for Segaworld—seven floors based on Japan's Joypolis Park, with six rides starring the latest computer graphics, and everything cyber. This is where to go to placate kids who really wanted to go to Disneyworld. ✉ *13 Coventry St., tel. 0171/439–1791.* ☉ *Daily 10 AM–midnight.* 📠 *Trocadero free, Emaginator £3 per ride, Segaworld £12. Tube: Piccadilly Circus.*

⑭ **York Watergate.** Once the grand river entrance to York House, the Duke of Buckingham's mansion, this was built in 1625 and is about the oldest building extant around here, marking the place where the river used to flow before the road was built. A riverside road had seemed a good plan ever since Wren had come up with the idea after the Great Fire of 1666, but nobody got around to it until Sir Joseph Bazalgette set to work on the Victoria Embankment two centuries later. Bazalgette, incidentally, is better known for providing London with the sewer system still largely in use; he can be admired in effigy on the bronze bust right there by Hungerford Bridge.

Roman Bath. This curiosity is probably about a thousand years younger than Roman, but nobody is quite sure. To see it, you have to peer in the window at No. 5. Dickens may inadvertently have named it, in *David Copperfield,* though nobody seems quite sure of that, either.

BLOOMSBURY AND LEGAL LONDON

The character of an area of London can change visibly from one street to the next. Nowhere is this so clear as in the contrast between fun-loving Soho and intellectual Bloomsbury, a mere 100 yards to the northeast, or between arty, trendy Covent Garden and—on the other side of Kingsway—sober Holborn. Both Bloomsbury and Holborn are almost purely residential and should be seen by day. The first district is best known for its famous flowering of literary-arty bohemia during this century's first three decades, the Bloomsbury Group, and for the British Museum and the University of London, which dominate it now. The second sounds as exciting as, say, a center for accountancy or dentists, but don't be put off—filled with magnificently ancient buildings, it's more interesting and beautiful than you might suppose.

Let's get the Bloomsbury Group out of the way, since you can't visit them, and nothing exists to mark their territory beyond a sprinkling of Blue Plaques. (London has about 400 of these government-sponsored tablets commemorating persons who enhanced "human welfare or happiness" and have been dead for at least 20 years.) There's also a plaque in Bloomsbury Square, saying nothing about this elite clique of writers and artists except that they lived around here. The chief Bloomsburies were Virginia Woolf, E. M. Forster, Vanessa and Clive Bell, Duncan Grant, Dora Carrington, Roger Fry, John Maynard Keynes, and Lytton Strachey, with satellites including Rupert Brooke and Christopher Isherwood. They agreed with G. E. Moore's philosophical notion that "the pleasures of human intercourse and the enjoyment of beautiful objects . . . form the rational ultimate end of social progress." True to their beliefs, when they weren't producing beautiful objects the friends enjoyed much human intercourse, as has been exhaustively documented, not least in Virginia's own diaries. All you need do to find out more about them is read the Review supplements of the Sunday broadsheets, which are forever running Bloomsbury exposés as if they were fresh gossip.

More clearly visible than those literary salons is the time-warp territory of interlocking alleys, gardens and cobbled courts, town houses and halls where London's legal profession grew up. The Great Fire of 1666 razed most of the city but spared the buildings of legal London, and the whole neighborhood oozes history. What is best about the area is that it lacks the commercial veneer of other historic sites, mostly because it still is very much the center of London's legal profession. Barristers, berobed and bewigged, may add an anachronistic frisson to your sightseeing, but they're only on their way to work.

They are headed for one of the four "Inns of Court": Gray's Inn, Lincoln's Inn, Middle Temple, and Inner Temple. Those arcane names are simply explained. The inns were just that: lodging houses for the lawyers who, back in the 14th century, clustered together here so everyone knew where to find them, and presently took over the running of the inns themselves. The temples were built on land owned by the Knights Templar, a chivalric order founded during the First Crusade during the 11th century; their 12th-century Temple Church still stands here. Few barristers (British for trial lawyers) still live in the inns, but nearly all keep chambers (British for barristers' offices) here, and all are still obliged to eat a requisite number of meals in the hall of "their" inn during training—no dinner, no career. They take exams, too.

Numbers in the text correspond to numbers in the margin and on the Bloomsbury and Legal London map.

A Good Walk

From Russell Square tube, walk south down Southampton Row, and west on Great Russell Street, passing **Bloomsbury Square** on the left, en route to London's biggest and most important collection of antiquities, the **British Museum** ①. Leaving this via the back exit leads you to Montague Place, which you should cross to Malet Street, straight ahead, to reach the **University of London** ②. On the left after you pass the university buildings is the back of the Royal Academy of Dramatic

Art, or RADA (its entrance is on Gower Street), where at least half of the most stellar British thespians got their training, with **University College** ③ following at the top of Malet Place. For a delightful detour, head west over to Scala Street (just one block west from the Goodge Street Tube Stop, then one block north on Charlotte Street) to find the delightful Victorian-era wonders of **Pollock's Toy Museum** ④. Back around the university, head south down Gordon Street to reach Gordon Square. If you're interested in Asian art stop in at the **Percival David Foundation of Chinese Art** ⑤, otherwise continue south down busy Woburn Place, veering left down Guilford Street to reach Coram's Fields, home of the **Thomas Coram Foundation** ⑥, then turn left south of there on Guilford Place, then right to Doughty Street and the **Dickens House Museum** ⑦. Two streets west, parallel to Doughty Street, is pretty Lamb's Conduit Street (whose pretty pub, the Lamb, Dickens inevitably frequented), with Great Ormond Street, off it, where lies the **Hospital for Sick Children** ⑧.

At the bottom of Lamb's Conduit Street you reach Theobald's Road, where you enter the first of the Inns of Court, **Gray's Inn** ⑨, emerging from here onto High Holburn ("Hoe-bun")—heavy with traffic, as it (with the Strand) is the main route from the City to the West End and Westminster—and Hatton Garden, running north from Holburn Circus and still the center of London's diamond and jewelry trade. Pass another ghost of former trading, **Staple Inn** ⑩, and turn left down tiny Great Turnstile Row to reach **Lincoln's Inn** ⑪, where you pass the Hall and continue around the west side of New Square to Carey Street, which leads you round into Portugal Street. Here you'll find The Old Curiosity Shop, probably one of the rare places in London Dickens did *not* frequent. Recross to the north side of Lincoln's Inn Fields to **Sir John Soane's Museum** ⑫, or walk the other way on Carey Street to reach the **Royal Courts of Justice** ⑬, which run through to the Strand. Off to the left is Fleet Street and the 1610 **Prince Henry's Room** ⑭. Cross the Strand to **Temple** ⑮, and pass through the elaborate stone arch to Middle Temple Lane, which you follow past **Temple Church** ⑯ to the Thames.

TIMING

This is a substantial walk of 3 to 4 mi, and it has two distinct halves. The first half, around Bloomsbury, is not so interesting on the surface, but features a major highlight of London, the British Museum, where you could easily add 1 mi to your total, and certainly at least two hours. The Dickens House is also worth a stop. The second half, legal London, is a real walker's walk, with most of the highlights in the architecture and atmosphere of the buildings and streets. The exception is Sir John Soane's Museum, which will absorb an extra hour. The walk alone can be done comfortably in two hours, and is best on a sunny day.

HOW TO GET THERE

The best tube stops for the Inns of Court are Holborn on the Central and Piccadilly lines (surface and walk east up High Holburn, then south), or Chancery Lane on the Central Line. For the British Museum, Tottenham Court Road (Northern and Central lines) or Russell Square (Piccadilly line) are equidistant. The No. 7 is the best bus for the BM; For the Inns of Court, get Nos. 8, 17, 25, 45, 46, or 243 to High Holborn, or the 17, 19, 38, 45, 46, 55, or 243 to Theobalds Road.

Sights to See

Bloomsbury Square. This was laid out in 1660, making it the earliest of the Bloomsbury squares, although none of the original houses remain; what is most remarkable about it now is that you can always find a parking spot in the huge underground garage underneath. You'll find it by exiting the tube at Tottenham Court Road—a straight, very ugly street where London buys its electrical appliances, hi-fi equipment, and computer accessories—and taking Great Russell Street east.

★ ❶ **British Museum.** With a facade like a great temple, this celebrated treasure house—filled with plunder of incalculable value and beauty from around the globe—is housed in a ponderously dignified Greco-Victorian building that makes a suitably grand impression. This is only appropriate, for inside you'll find some of the greatest relics of humankind: the Elgin Marbles, the Rosetta Stone, the Magna Carta, the Ur Treasure—everything, it seems, but the Ark of the Covenant. The place is vast—there are 2½ mi of floor space inside, split into nearly 100 galleries—so arm yourself with a free floor plan directly as you go in or they'll have to send out search parties to rescue you.

The collection began in 1753, when Sir Hans Sloane, physician to Queen Anne and George II, bequeathed his personal collection of curiosities and antiquities to the nation, and then quickly grew, thanks to enthusiastic kleptomaniacs after the Napoleonic Wars—most notoriously the seventh Earl of Elgin, who lifted marbles from the Parthenon and Erechtheum while on a Greek vacation between 1801 and 1804. Although Lord Elgin did a great thing in saving the marbles for posterity, their continuing presence in the British Museum is a source of embarrassment to many British subjects, who believe the Greeks should now have their "Elgin Marbles" back, as, indeed, do the Greeks.

The enormous building, with its Classical Greek–style facade featuring figures representing the Progress of Civilization, was finished in 1847, the work of Sir Robert Smirke. Ascending the steps, you go straight into the main entrance hall (get your floor plan here). Wherever you go there are marvels, but certain objects and collections are more important, rarer, older, or downright unique, and because you may wish to include these in your wanderings, here follows a highly edited résumé (in order of encounter) of the BM's greatest hits:

Close to the entrance hall, in the south end of Room 25, is the **Rosetta Stone,** found in 1799, and carved in 196 BC with a decree of Ptolemy V in Egyptian hieroglyphics, demotic, and Greek. It was this multilingual inscription that provided the French Egyptologist Jean-François Champollion with the key to deciphering hieroglyphics.

Maybe the **Elgin Marbles** oughtn't to be here, but since they are—and they are, after all, among the most graceful and heartbreakingly beautiful sculptures on earth—you can find them in Room 8, west of the entrance. The best part is what remains of the Parthenon frieze that girdled the interior of Athena's temple on the Acropolis, carved around 440 BC. (The handless, footless Dionysus who used to recline along the east pediment is especially well known.) While you're in the west wing, you can see one of the Seven Wonders of the Ancient World—in fragment form, unfortunately—in Room 12: the **Mausoleum of Halicarnassus.** This 4th-century tomb of Mausolus, king of Caria, was the original "mausoleum."

Also close to the entrance, but east, in Rooms 30 and 31 in the part of the British Library open to the public, are two of the four existing copies of that prototype census and manual of early British law, King John's 1215 charter, the **Magna Carta,** as well as the spectacularly illuminated 7th-century **Lindisfarne Gospels,** the work of a monk called Eadfrith. Also on display are handwritten manuscripts by, among others, Jane Austen, William Wordsworth, and John Lennon.

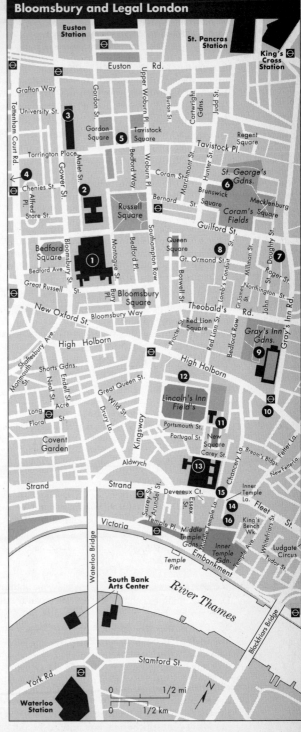

Bloomsbury and Legal London

Upstairs are some of the most perennially popular galleries, especially beloved by children: Rooms 60 and 61, where the **Egyptian Mummies** live. You'll find here the preserved corpses not only of humans but also of a menagerie of animal companions discovered alongside them.

Proceeding clockwise, you'll come to Room 40, above the main entrance, where the **Mildenhall Treasure** glitters. This haul of 4th-century Roman silver tableware was found beneath the sod of a Suffolk field in 1942. Next door, in Room 41, is the equally splendid **Sutton Hoo Treasure,** including swords and helmets, bowls and buckles, all encrusted with jewels—which was buried at sea with (they think) Redwald, King of the Angles, during the 7th century, excavated from a Suffolk field in 1938–39.

In Room 37 lies Pete Marsh, so named by the archaeologists who unearthed the **Lindow Man** from a Cheshire peat marsh. He was ritually slain, probably as a human sacrifice, during the 1st century, and lay perfectly pickled in his bog until 1984.

Since 1759, the **British Library** has also been on this site, but in an imminent turnabout in the world of English letters, the whole institution is in the process of being decanted into its new home in St. Pancras after years of delay. The year 1991 was the intended moving date for the innumerable (somewhere around 18 million, actually) volumes, but first the building wasn't finished, and the funding ran out, and then there were problems with the new stacks. The British Library is entitled to a free copy of every single book, periodical, newspaper, and map published in the United Kingdom—a gift of George II, along with his Royal Library—which translates into 2 mi of additional shelf space per year. Needless to say, room at the old library ran out long ago, and most of its books are not housed here. A Reader's Ticket for access to the library and entrance to the much-loved circular, copper-domed **Reading Room** is available only by written application, with proof of the serious intent of your research required. ⊠ *Great Russell St.,* ☎ *0171/636–1555 or 0171/580–1788.* 🎫 *Free, 1½-hr guided tour £6.* ◑ *Mon.–Sat. 10–5, Sun. 2:30–6; tour twice daily in winter, 4 times daily in summer (call for times). Tube: Tottenham Court Road, Holburn, Russell Square.*

NEED A BREAK? The museum's self-service **restaurant and café** gets very crowded but serves a reasonable selection of not overly mass-produced meals beneath a plaster cast of a part of the Parthenon frieze that Lord Elgin didn't remove. ◑ *Mon.–Sat. noon–4:15, Sun. 2:45–5:15; coffee shop Mon.–Sat. 10–3.*

---

❼ Dickens House Museum. This is the only one of the many London houses Dickens inhabited that's still standing, and would have had a real claim to his fame in any case, because he wrote *Oliver Twist* and *Nicholas Nickleby,* and finished *Pickwick Papers* here between 1837 and 1839. The house looks exactly as it would have in Dickens's day, complete with first editions, letters, and desk, plus a treat for Lionel Bart fans—his score of *Oliver!* ⊠ *48 Doughty St.,* ☎ *0171/405–2127.* 🎫 *£3.50.* ◑ *Mon.–Sat. 10–5. Tube: Russell Square.*

❾ Gray's Inn. Although the least architecturally interesting of the four Inns of Court and the one most damaged by German bombs during the '40s, this still has its romantic associations. In 1594, Shakespeare's *Comedy of Errors* was performed for the first time in its hall—which was lovingly restored after World War II and has a fine Elizabethan screen of carved oak. You must make advance arrangements to view Gray's Inn's hall, but you can stroll around the secluded and spacious gardens, first planted by Francis Bacon in 1606. You may visit only after applying in writing, in advance, to the librarian. ⌧ *Holborn,* ☎ *0171/405–8164.* ☉ *Chapel weekdays 10–4. Tube: Holburn, Temple.*

⑧ Hospital for Sick Children. The hospital was founded by Dr. Charles West, who, like Sir Thomas Coram a century before, was horrified at the inadequate provision made in London for the welfare of children–with some 21,000 dying every year. In 1929, Peter Pan, or rather his creator, Sir James Barrie, gave the hospital a new lease on life by donating the royalties from the play until 50 years after his death. (A special Act of Parliament enabled the gift to continue to the present day.) Latterly, the hospital—like many in London—has been in financial difficulties again, but a new generation of benefactors has saved the day for now, and Princess Diana came out of her self-imposed purdah early in 1994 to open a long-awaited new wing.

★ ⑪ Lincoln's Inn. There's plenty to see at one of the oldest, best preserved, and most comely of the Inns of Court—from the Chancery Lane Tudor brick gate house to the wide-open, tree-lined, atmospheric Lincoln's Inn Fields and the 15th-century Chapel remodeled by Inigo Jones in 1620. The wisteria-clad New Square, London's only complete 17th-century square, is not the newest part of the complex; the oldest-looking buildings are—the 1845 Hall and Library, which you must obtain the porter's permission to enter. Pass the Hall and continue around the west side of New Square, and you'll see an archway leading to Carey Street. You have just headed "straight for Queer Street." Since the bankruptcy courts used to stand here, you can divine what the old expression means. A guided tour is available. ⌧ *Chancery La.,* ☎ *0171/405–1393.* ☉ *Gardens and chapel weekdays 12:30–2:30; public may also attend Sun. service at 11:30 in chapel during legal terms. Tube: Chancery Lane.*

⑤ Percival David Foundation of Chinese Art. This collection, belonging to the University of London, is dominated by ceramics from the Sung to Qing dynasties—10th to 19th century, in other words. It's on **Gordon Square**, which Virginia Woolf, the Bells, John Maynard Keynes (all, severally, at No. 46), and Lytton Strachey (at No. 51) called home for a while. ⌧ *53 Gordon Sq.,* ☎ *0171/387–3909.* ▨ *Free.* ☉ *Weekdays 10:30–5 (sometimes closed 1–2 for lunch). Tube: Russell Square.*

✋ ④ Pollock's Toy Museum. This merits a visit whether you have children or not! A charming treasure trove of a small museum in a warren of rooms in an 18th-century town house, Pollock's is crammed with antique dolls, dolls' houses, and teddy bears. Best of all are the fabulous little toy theaters that Pollock made famous during the Victorian era: more than a few of England's most famous actors grew up playing with these cardboard delights. Even better: you can still buy reproductions of these cut-and-paste theater kits in the toy store on the premises. (Bring lots of money if you want to purchase some of the antique kits still for sale.) ⌧ *1 Scala St.,* ☎ *0171/636–3452.* ▨ *£2.* ☉ *Mon.–Sat. 10–5. Tube: Goodge St.*

⑭ Prince Henry's Room. This is the Jacobean half-timbered house built in 1610 to celebrate the investiture of Henry, James I's eldest son, as Prince of Wales, and marked with his coat of arms and a "PH" on the ceiling. It's an entrance to the lawyers' sanctum, Temple, where the Strand becomes Fleet Street, and you can go in to visit the small Samuel Pepys exhibition. ⌧ *17 Fleet St.,* ☎ *0171/936–2710.* ☉ *Mon.–Sat. 11–2. Tube: Temple.*

⑬ **Royal Courts of Justice.** Here is the vast Victorian Gothic pile containing the nation's principal Law Courts, with 1,000-odd rooms running off 3½ mi of corridor. And here are heard the most important civil law cases—that's everything from divorce to fraud, with libel in between—and you can sit in the viewing gallery to watch any trial you like, for a live version of *Court TV.* The more dramatic criminal cases are heard at the Old Bailey. Other sights to witness include the 238-foot-long main hall and the compact exhibition of judges' robes. ✉ *The Strand,* ☎ *0171/936–6000.* 🎫 *Free.* ⊙ *Weekdays 9–4:30. Closed Aug. and Sept. Tube: Temple.*

★ ⑫ **Sir John Soane's Museum.** Guaranteed to raise a smile from the most blasé and footsore tourist, this museum hardly deserves the burden of its dry name. Sir John, architect of the Bank of England, bequeathed his house to the nation on condition that nothing be changed. We owe him our thanks, because he obviously had enormous fun with his home, having had the means to finance great experiments in perspective and scale and to fill the space with some wonderful pieces. In the Picture Room, for instance, two of Hogarth's *Rake's Progress* series are among the paintings on panels that swing away to reveal secret gallery pockets with more paintings. Everywhere mirrors and colors play tricks with light and space, and split-level floors worthy of a fairground fun house disorient you. In a basement chamber sits the vast 1300 BC Sarcophagus of Seti I, lighted by a domed skylight two stories above. When Sir John acquired this priceless object for £2,000, he celebrated with a three-day party. ✉ *13 Lincoln's Inn Fields,* ☎ *0171/405–2107.* 🎫 *Free.* ⊙ *Tues.–Sat. 10–5. Tube: Holburn, Temple.*

⑩ **Staple Inn.** Despite its name, this is not an inn of court, but the former wool staple, where wool was weighed and traded and its merchants were lodged. It is central London's oldest surviving Elizabethan half-timbered building, and thanks to extensive restoration, with its overhanging upper stories, oriel windows, and black gables striping the white walls, looks the same as it must have in 1586 when it was brand-new.

⑮ **Temple.** The collective name for **Inner Temple** and **Middle Temple,** the entrance to Temple—the exact point of entry into the City—is marked by a young (1880) bronze griffin, the **Temple Bar Memorial.** He is the symbol of the City, having replaced (sadly) a Wren gateway. In the buildings opposite is an elaborate stone arch through which you pass into Middle Temple Lane, past a row of 17th-century timber-frame houses, and on into Fountain Court. This lane runs all the way to the Thames, more or less separating the two Temples, past the sloping lawns of Middle Temple Gardens, on the east border of which is the Elizabethan **Middle Temple Hall.** If it's open, don't miss that hammer-beam roof, among the finest in the land. ☎ *0171/353–4355.* ⊙ *Weekdays 10–noon and (when not in use) 3–4. Tube: Temple.*

⑯ **Temple Church.** Featuring "the Round"—a rare circular nave—this church was built by the Knights Templar during the 12th century. The Red Knights (so called after the red crosses they wore—you can see them in effigy around the nave) held their secret initiation rites in the crypt here. Having started poor, holy, and dedicated to the protection of pilgrims, they grew rich from showers of kingly gifts, until during the 14th century they were accused of heresy, blasphemy, and sodomy, thrown into the Tower, and stripped of their wealth. You might suppose the church to be thickly atmospheric, but Victorian and postwar restorers have tamed its air of antique mystery. Still, it's a very fine Gothic-Romanesque church, whose 1240 chancel ("the Oblong") has been accused of perfection. ⊠ *The Temple,* ☎ *0171/353–8462.* ☉ *Daily 10–4. Tube: Temple.*

❻ Thomas Coram Foundation. Captain Thomas Coram devoted half his life to setting up a sanctuary and hospital, which he called the Foundling Hospital, for London's street orphans. He was a remarkable man, a master mariner and shipbuilder, who, having played a major role in the colonization of Massachusetts, returned to London in 1732 to encounter sights he could not endure—babies and children "left to die on dung hills." Petitioning the lunching ladies of his day, and their lords, he raised the necessary funds to set up what became the most celebrated Good Cause around, thanks partly to the sparkling benefactors he attracted. Handel donated an organ to the chapel, which he played himself at fundraising performances of his *Messiah,* and the chapel in turn became *the* place to be seen worshiping on a Sunday. Coram's great friend William Hogarth was one of several famous hospital governors, and his portrait of the founder hangs alongside other works of art (including paintings by Reynolds and Gainsborough) and mementos in the museum, which now stands on the site of the hospital. The hospital was originally set in the 7-acre Coram's Fields, though it moved to Hertfordshire in 1926. Sadly, at press time, the museum was placed off-limits to the public—until the governors manage to find a fresh crop of volunteers to man the front of the house—indefinitely, in other words. ⊠ *40 Brunswick Sq.,* ☎ *0171/278–2424. Currently closed to visitors; Call to determine if museum has reopened. Tube: Russell Square.*

❸ University College. Set in a satisfyingly classical edifice designed by the architect of the National Gallery, William Wilkins, within the college portals is the **Slade School of Fine Art,** which did for many of Britain's artists what the nearby (on Gower Street) Royal Academy of Dramatic Art did for its actors. There is a fine collection of sculpture by one of the alumni, John Flaxman, on view inside. You can also see more Egyptology, if you didn't get enough at the neighboring British Museum (☞ *above*), in the **Petrie Museum** (accessed from Malet Place), which contains one of London's weirder treasures: the clothed skeleton of one of the university's founders, Jeremy Bentham, who bequeathed himself to the college.

❷ University of London. This relatively youthful institution grew out of the need for a nondenominational center for higher education (Oxford and Cambridge both demanded religious conformity to the Church of England). It was founded by Dissenters in 1826, with its first examinations held 12 years later. Jews and Roman Catholics were not the only people admitted for the first time to an English university—women were, too, though they had to wait 50 years (until 1878) to sit for a degree. The building you see here dates only from 1911. Previously this branch of academe had borrowed Somerset House (where the Courtauld Collection is now), Burlington House (now the Royal Academy), then Burlington House's extension (now the Museum of Mankind).

Wig and Pen Club. This—another of those St. James's–style affairs, this time for "men of justice, journalists, and businessmen of the City" (plus former U.S. presidents Nixon and Reagan)—has its home in the only Strand building to have survived the Great Fire of 1666. Its Legal Tours allow access to the gorgeous gardens of the Inner and Middle Temples, plus other secret sights, and include meals, refreshments, honorary membership for the day (even for women), and expert tour guides. ⊠ *229 Strand, WC2,* ☎ *0171/583–7255.* 🎫 *½-day Legal Tour £50, full day £70.50.*

THE CITY

You may have assumed you had entered the City of London when your plane touched down at Heathrow, but note that capital letter: the City of London is not the same as the city of London. The capital-C City is an autonomous district, separately governed since William the Conqueror started building the Tower of London, and despite its compact size, it remains the financial engine of Britain and one of the world's leading centers of trade. Temple Bar marks the western edge of the Square Mile, which does cover 677 acres (a square mile is 640), though not in a remotely straight-sided fashion. The curvy shape described by its boundaries—Smithfield in the north, Aldgate and Tower Hill in the east, and the Thames on the south—resembles nothing so much as an armadillo, with Temple Bar at snout level.

The City is London's most ancient part, although there is little remaining to remind you of that fact beyond a scattering of Roman stones. It was Aulus Plautius, Roman ruler of Britain under Claudius, who established the Romans' first stronghold on the Thames halfway through the 1st century AD. The name "Londinium," though, probably derives from the Celtic *Lyn-dun*, meaning "fortified town on the lake," which suggests far earlier settlement. Not much is known about the period between AD 410, when the Roman legions left, and the 6th century, when the Saxons arrived, but it was really after Edward the Confessor moved his court to Westminster in 1060 that the City gathered momentum. As Westminster took over the administrative role, the City was free to develop the commercial heart that still beats strong.

The Romans had already found Londinium's position handy for trade— the river being navigable yet far enough inland to allow for its defense— but it was the establishment of crafts guilds in the Middle Ages, followed in Tudor and Stuart times by the proliferation of great trading companies (the Honourable East India Company, founded in 1600, was the star), that really started the cash flowing. King John had confirmed the City's autonomy by charter in 1215, and its commerce and government fed off each other, the leaders of the former electing the leaders of the latter. This is still largely the case: The Corporation of London has control over the Square Mile and elects a Lord Mayor just as it did in the Middle Ages, when the famous folk hero Richard Whittington was four times (not thrice, as in *Dick Whittington,* the pantomime) voted in.

Three times the City has faced devastation—and that's not counting the "Black Monday" of 1992, when sterling crashed. The Great Fire of 1666 spared practically none of the labyrinthine medieval streets— a blessing in disguise, actually, because the Great Plague of the year before had wiped (or driven) out most of the population and left a terrible mess in the cramped, downright sordid houses. With the wind in the west, they said, you could smell London from Tilbury. The fire necessitated a total reconstruction, in which Sir Christopher Wren had a big hand, contributing not only his masterpiece, St. Paul's Cathedral, but 49 other parish churches.

The third wave of destruction, after the plague and the fire, was, of course, dealt by the German bombers of the Second World War, who showered the City with 57 days and nights of special attention, wreaking as much havoc as the Great Fire had managed. The ruins were rebuilt, but slowly, and with no overall plan, leaving the City a patchwork of the old and the new, the interesting and the flagrantly awful. The City's colorful past can be hard to visualize among today's gray reality, but there are clues. Wander through its maze of streets and you will come across ancient coats of arms and street names redolent of life in the Middle Ages: Ropemaker Street, Pudding Lane, Jewry Street, and Fish Street. Since a mere 8,000 or so people call the City home today, the financial center of Britain is deserted outside the working week, with most restaurants shuttered and streets forlorn and windswept. The City remains one of London's most schizophrenic sectors—a place where the past and future clash.

Numbers in the text correspond to numbers in the margin and on the City map.

A Good Walk

Begin at the gateway to the City—and we mean that literally. Until the 18th century there were eight such gates, all but one of which survives; the others exist in name only (Cripplegate, Ludgate, Bishopsgate, Moorgate, and so on). The surviving one is Temple Bar, a bronze griffin on the Strand opposite the Royal Courts of Justice, at which the sovereign has to ask the Lord Mayor's permission to enter the City. Walk east to **Fleet Street** and turn left on Bolt Court to Gough Square, and **Dr. Johnson's House** ①, passing **Ye Olde Cheshire Cheese** ② on Wine Office Courte en route back to Fleet Street and the journalists' church, **St. Bride's** ③. The end of Fleet Street is marked by the messy traffic intersection called Ludgate Circus, which you should cross to Ludgate Hill to reach **Old Bailey** ④, and the Central Criminal Courts.

Continuing along Ludgate Hill, you come to **St. Paul's Cathedral** ⑤, Wren's masterpiece. There's not much else to see around here, though plans are pending for the re-installation of Sir Christopher Wren's 1672 Temple Bar gateway close to its original site, which will serve as the City's western gateway. Instead, retrace your steps to Newgate Street, detouring up King Edward Street to the **National Postal Museum** ⑥, and to the road called Little Britain, where you'll see the archway to **St. Bartholomew's Church** ⑦ on the left, and will come to London's meat market, **Smithfield** ⑧ at the end. Cross Aldersgate Street and take the right fork to London Wall, named for the Roman rampart that stood along it. It's a dismal street, now dominated by postmodern architect Terry Farrell's late-'80s follies, but about halfway along you can see a section of 2nd- to 4th-century wall at St. Alphege Garden. There's another bit in an appropriate spot back at the start of London Wall, outside the **Museum of London** ⑨; and behind that is the important arts mecca of gray concrete, the **Barbican Centre** ⑩ and **St. Giles without Cripplegate** ⑪. You can walk all around there without touching the ground (well, ground level).

Back on London Wall, turn south into Coleman Street, then right onto Masons Avenue to reach Basinghall Street and the **Guildhall** ⑫, then follow Milk Street south to Cheapside ("chep" is Middle English), and on this street the bakers of Bread Street, the cobblers of Cordwainers Street, the goldsmiths of Goldsmith Street, and all their brothers gathered to sell their wares. Here is another symbolic center of London, the church of **St. Mary-le-Bow** ⑬. Walk to the east end of Cheapside, where seven roads meet, and you will be facing the **Bank of England** ⑭, behind which is the **London Stock Exchange** ⑮. Turn your back on the Bank, and there's the Lord Mayor's abode, **Mansion House** ⑯, with Wren's **St. Stephen Walbrook Church** ⑰ behind it, and the **Royal Exchange** ⑱ in between Threadneedle Street and Cornhill. Farther down Cornhill to Lime Street is **Lloyd's of London** ⑲.

Now head down Queen Victoria Street, where you'll pass the remains of the Roman **Temple of Mithras** ⑳, then, after a sharp left turn into

Cannon Street, you'll come upon **Monument** ㉑, Wren's memorial to the Great Fire of London. Just south of there is **London Bridge** ㉒. Turn left onto Lower Thames Street, for just under a mile's walk—passing Billingsgate, London's principal fish market for 900 years, until 1982, and the Custom House, built early in the last century—to the **Tower of London** ㉓, which may be the single most unmissable of London's sights. **Tower Bridge** ㉔ just outside it isn't bad either.

TIMING

This is a marathon. Unless you want to be walking all day, without a chance to do justice to London's most famous sights, the Tower of London and St. Paul's Cathedral—not to mention the Museum of London, Tower Bridge, and the Barbican Centre—you should consider splitting the walk into segments. Conversely, if you're not planning to go inside, this walk makes for a great day out, with lots of surprising vistas, river views, and history. The City is a wasteland on weekends and after dark, so choose your time. There's a certain romantic charm to the streets when they're deserted, but it's hard to find lunch.

HOW TO GET THERE

This is a big and confusing area, with, however, several tube stops that will deposit you within walking distance of most of the sights. These are: on the Central Line, the Bank and St. Paul's stops; on the District and Circle lines, the Monument, Cannon Street, and Mansion House stops (plus Blackfriars, which is a little off-center). The Moorgate and Barbican stops (Circle, Metropolitan, Hammersmith, and City lines) are the nearest to the theaters of the Barbican Centre, while the next stop west, Farringdon, is best for exploring Clerkenwell. Finally, the only sensible way to get to the Tower of London is via District and Circle lines to the Tower Hill stop. As for buses, Nos. 4, 8, 25, 56, or 172 deposit you centrally, by St. Paul's. For the Barbican Centre, Nos. 21, 43, 76, 133, 141, 172, 214, and 271 to Moorgate are best.

Sights to See

⓮ **Bank of England.** Known familiarly for the past couple of centuries as "The Old Lady of Threadneedle Street," after someone's parliamentary quip, the bank, which has been central to the British economy since 1694, manages the national debt and the foreign exchange reserves, issues banknotes, sets interest rates, looks after England's gold, and regulates its banking system. Sir John Soane designed the neo-classical hulk in 1788, wrapping it in windowless walls (which are all that survives of his building) to suggest a stability that the ailing economy of the post-Thatcher years tends to belie. The larger history of this economy, and the role that the Bank of England played in it, is traced in the Bank of England Museum. ⊠ *Bartholomew La.,* ☎ *0171/601-5545.* ◻ *Free.* ☉ *Easter–Sept., weekdays 10–5, Sun. 11–5; Oct.–Easter, weekdays 10–6. Tube: Bank, Monument.*

⓾ **Barbican Centre.** Home to the Royal Shakespeare Company and its two theaters, the London Symphony Orchestra and its auditorium, the Guildhall School of Music and Drama, a major gallery for touring exhibitions, two cinemas, a convention center, and apartments for a hapless two-thirds of the City's residents (most part-time), the Barbican is an enormous concrete maze Londoners love to hate. The name comes from a defensive fortification of the City, and defensive is what Barbican apologists (including architects Chamberlain, Powell, and Bon) became when the complex was finally revealed in 1982, after 20 years as a building site. There ensued an epidemic of jokes about getting lost forever in the Barbican bowels. A hasty rethinking of the contradictory signposts and nonsensical "levels" was performed, and navigatory yellow lines materialized, Oz-like, on the floors, but it didn't help

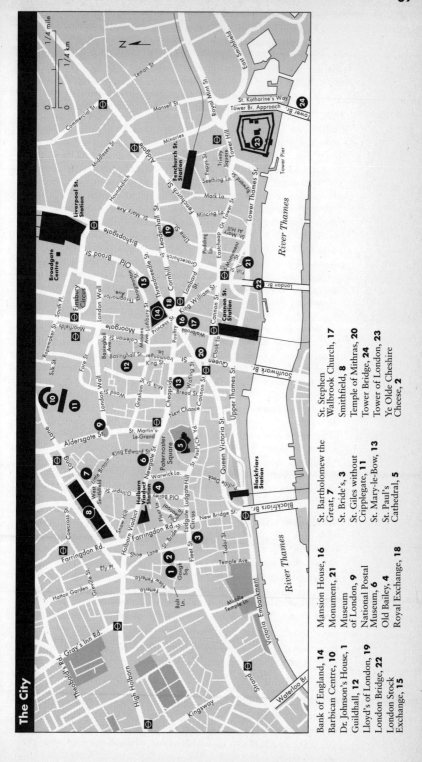

The City

Bank of England, **14**
Barbican Centre, **10**
Dr. Johnson's House, **1**
Guildhall, **12**
Lloyd's of London, **19**
London Bridge, **22**
London Stock
Exchange, **15**

Mansion House, **16**
Monument, **21**
Museum
of London, **9**
National Postal
Museum, **6**
Old Bailey, **4**
Royal Exchange, **18**

St. Bartholomew the
Great, **7**
St. Bride's, **3**
St. Giles without
Cripplegate, **11**
St. Mary-le-Bow, **13**
St. Paul's
Cathedral, **5**

St. Stephen
Walbrook Church, **17**
Smithfield, **8**
Temple of Mithras, **20**
Tower Bridge, **24**
Tower of London, **23**
Ye Olde Cheshire
Cheese, **2**

much—the Barbican remains difficult to navigate. Time has mellowed the elephant-gray concrete into a darker blotchy brownish-gray, and Londoners have come to accept, if not exactly love the place, because of its contents. Actors rate the theater acoustics especially high, and the steep bank of the seating makes for a good stage view. The visiting exhibitions are often worth a trek, as are the free ones in the foyer.

Negotiating the windy walkways of the deserted residential section, then descending in elusive elevators to the lower depths of the Centre (where the studio auditorium, the aptly named Pit, lives), spotting stray sculptures and water gardens, receiving electric shocks from the brass rails—all this has its perverse charm, but there is one unadulterated success in the Barbican, though unfortunately it's not often open to the public. Secreted on an upper floor is an enormous, lush conservatory in a towering glass palace, spacious enough for full-grown trees to flourish. The White Card is accepted. Tours are for a minimum of 10 people and must be booked in advance. ⊠ *Silk St.,* ☎ *0171/638–4141, 0171/628–0183 tour reservations, 0171/628–3351 RSC backstage tour.* ☒ *Barbican Centre free, gallery £4.50, conservatory 80p, tour £3.50.* ☉ *Barbican Centre Mon.–Sat. 9 AM–11 PM, Sun. noon–11 PM; gallery Mon.–Sat. 10–7:30, Sun. noon–7:30; conservatory weekends noon–5:30 when not in use for private function (call first). Tube: Moorgate, Barbican.*

NEED A BREAK? The Barbican Centre's **Waterside Café** has salads, sandwiches, and pastries; they're unremarkable but are served in a tranquil enclosed concrete (naturally) waterside terrace. Sometimes customers are serenaded by practice sessions of the Guildhall School of Music and Drama's orchestra next door.

Broadgate Centre. At the north end of Old Broad Street, hanging on the tails of the redeveloped Liverpool Street Station, is one of the City's more successful recent development projects. In contrast to the nearby Barbican, this collection of offices, shops, and restaurants received good notices as soon as it opened in 1987, especially for its circular courtyard surrounded by hanging gardens. The courtyard is iced over in winter to become London's only outdoor skating rink; it hosts bands and performers in summer.

❶ **Dr. Johnson's House.** This is where Samuel Johnson lived between 1746 and 1759, while in the worst of health, compiling his famous dictionary in the attic. Like Dickens, he lived all over town, but, like Dickens's House, this is the only one of Johnson's abodes remaining today. It is a shrine to the man possibly more attached to London than anyone else, ever, and includes a first edition of his dictionary among the Johnson-and-Boswell mementos. ⊠ *17 Gough Sq.,* ☎ *0171/353–3745.* ☒ *£3.* ☉ *May–Sept., Mon.–Sat. 11–5:30; Oct.–Apr., Mon.–Sat. 11–5. Tube: Chancery Lane, Temple.*

Fleet Street. This famous street follows the course of, and is named after, one of London's ghost rivers. The Fleet, so called by the Anglo-Saxons, spent most of its centuries above ground as an open sewer, offending local noses until banished below in 1766. It still flows underfoot, now a sanctioned section of London's sewer system. The street's sometime nickname, "Street of Shame," has nothing to do with the stench. It refers to the trade that made it famous: the press. Since the end of the 15th century, when Wynkyn de Worde set up England's first printing press here, and especially after 1702, when the first newspaper, the *Daily Courant,* moved in, followed by (literally) all the rest, "Fleet Street" has been synonymous with newspaper journalism. The papers themselves all moved out during the 1980s, but the British press is still collectively known as "Fleet Street." (Don't miss the black-glass-and-chrome Art Deco *Daily Mirror* building.)

⑫ Guildhall. The Corporation of London ceremonially elects and installs its Lord Mayor here in the symbolic nerve-center of the City, as it has done for 800 years. The Guildhall was built in 1411, and though it failed to avoid either the 1666 or 1940 flames, its core survived, with a new roof sensitively appended during the 1950s and further cosmetic embellishments added during the '70s. The fabulous hall is a psychedelic patchwork of coats of arms and banners of the City Livery Companies, which inherited the mantle of the medieval trade guilds, to which we actually owe the invention of the City in the first place. Actually, this honor really belongs to two giants, Gog and Magog, the pair of mythical beings who founded ancient Albion, and who glower upon the Prime Minister's annual November banquet from their west gallery grandstand in 9-foot-high painted limewood form.

The 1970s west wing houses the **Guildhall Library**—mainly City-related books and documents, plus a collection belonging to one of the Livery Companies, the Worshipful Company of Clockmakers, with more than 600 timepieces on show, including a skull-faced watch that belonged to Mary, Queen of Scots. ⊠ *Gresham St.,* ☎ *0171/606–3030.* 🎟 *Free.* ⊘ *Mon.–Sat. 10–5 (library closed Sat.). Tube: St. Paul's, Moorgate, Bank, Mansion House.*

⑲ Lloyd's of London. Richard Rogers's (of Paris Pompidou Centre fame) fantastical steel-and-glass medium-rise of six towers around a vast atrium, with his trademark inside-out ventilation shafts, stairwells, and gantries, may be the most exciting recent structure in London. The building is best seen at night, when cobalt and lime spotlights make it leap out of the deeply boring gray skyline as though it were Carmen Miranda at a wake.

The institution that commissioned this fabulous £163-million fun house has been trading in insurance for two centuries and is famous the world over for several reasons: (1) having started in a coffeehouse; (2) insuring Betty Grable's legs; (3) accepting no corporate responsibility for losses, which are carried by its investors; (4) having its "Names"—the rich people who underwrite Lloyd's losses; (5) seeming unassailable for a very long time . . .; (6) until 1990 when it lost £2.9 billion; (7) which caused the financial ruination, and worse, of many Names. Appropriately, the viewing galleries over the trading floor and the museum of Lloyd's history, containing the Lutine Bell, which heralds important announcements (one ring for bad news), remain closed to the public. ⊠ *1 Lime St.,* ☎ *0171/623–7100.*

㉒ London Bridge. Dating from only 1972, this bridge replaced the 1831 Sir John Rennie number that now graces Lake Havasu City, Arizona, the impulse purchase of someone at the McCulloch Oil Corporation, who (rumor has it) was under the impression that he'd bought the far more picturesque Tower Bridge. The version before that one, the first in stone and the most renowned of all, stood for 600 years after it was built in 1176, the focus of many a gathering thanks to the shops and houses crammed along its length, not to mention the boiled and tar-dipped heads of traitors that decorated its gate house after being removed in the Tower of London. Before *that* the Saxons had put up a wooden bridge; it collapsed in 1014, which was probably the origin of the refrain "London bridge is falling down." Nobody is sure of the exact location of the very earliest London Bridge—the Roman version around whose focus London grew—but it was certainly very close to the 100-foot-wide, three-span, pre-stressed concrete cantilever one that you see today.

⑮ **London Stock Exchange.** This institution was rendered practically useless a mere 14 years after this building opened (the third on its site), when the "Big Bang," the stock market crash of late 1986, put a stop to trading in equities on the floor. The London Traded Options Market persisted in one corner, which visitors could spy on from the Viewing Gallery, until security-consciousness following an IRA bomb in July 1990 closed *that* down. It was due to close anyway, because in February 1992 that last bastion of the jobbers and brokers of the stock exchange floor merged with the London International Financial Futures Exchange (LIFFE, pronounced "life"). Everyone packed their phones, and they all decamped to deal at **Cannon Bridge Station** (☎ 0171/623–0444) in nearby Cousin's Lane, leaving the dealing floor at the Stock Exchange echoing with red-suspender, stripe-shirt '80s phantoms. All you can visit here now is the reception desk, where a long-suffering security guard says you can't go in and somewhat tetchily hands over an information booklet. Tours of Cannon Bridge Station, however, are available by appointment.

⑯ **Mansion House.** With its mid-18th-century Palladian facade, this is the Lord Mayor's abode. Unfortunately, you won't see the colonnaded Egyptian Hall, or the cell where the suffragette Emmeline Pankhurst was held early in this century, or any of the state rooms where the mayor entertains his fellow dignitaries, because the building is closed to the public.

㉑ **Monument.** Commemorating the "dreadful visitation" of the Great Fire of 1666, this is the world's tallest isolated stone column. It is the work of Wren, who was asked to erect it "On or as neere unto the place where the said Fire soe unhappily began as conveniently may be." And so here it is—at 202 feet, exactly as tall as the distance it stands from Farriner's baking house in Pudding Lane, where the fire started. Above the viewing gallery (311 steps up—a better workout than any StairMaster) is a flaming bronze urn, and around it a cage for the prevention of suicide, which was a trend for a while during the 19th century. ⊠ *Monument St.,* ☎ *0171/626–2717.* ⌹ *£1.* ☉ *Apr.–Sept., weekdays 9–5:30, weekends 2–5:30; Oct.–Mar., Mon.–Sat. 9–3:30. Tube: Monument.*

🖐 ⑨ **Museum of London.** This museum, with its self-explanatory title, appropriately shelters a section of the 2nd- to 4th-century London wall, which you can view from a window inside, near to the Roman monumental arch the museum's archaeologists reconstructed a mere two decades ago. Anyone with the least interest in how this city evolved will adore this museum, especially said reconstructions and the dioramas—like one of the Great Fire (flickering flames! sound effects!), a 1940s air-raid shelter, a Georgian prison cell, and a Victorian street complete with fully stocked shops—as well as the Catwalk, which guides you interactively through the ages. There are plenty of treasures (the Cheapside Hoard of Jacobean jewelry shouldn't be missed), costumes, furniture, and domestic paraphernalia to flesh it all out, and galleries proceed chronologically for easy comprehension right up to the new "London Now" gallery. The White Card is accepted, and all tickets allow unlimited return visits for three months. ⊠ *London Wall,* ☎ *0171/600–3699.* ⌹ *£4, free 4:30–5:50.* ☉ *Tues.–Sat. 10–6, Sun. noon–6.*

⑥ **National Postal Museum.** An important landmark for philatelists, this was founded in 1965, but the collection is as old as the postal service itself, and is one of the world's best. ⊠ *King Edward Bldg., King Ed-*

ward St., ☎ *0171/239–5420.* 🖾 *Free.* ☉ *Mon.–Thurs. 9:30–4:30, Fri. 9:30–4. Tube: St. Paul's.*

❹ Old Bailey. This, the present-day **Central Criminal Court,** is where New-gate Prison stood from the 12th century right until the beginning of this one. Few survived for long in the version pulled down in 1770. Those who didn't starve were hanged, or pressed to death in the Press Yard, or they succumbed to the virulent gaol (the archaic British spelling of "jail") fever—any of which must have been preferable to a life in the stinking, subterranean, lightless Stone Hold, or to suffering the robberies, beatings, and general victimization endemic in what the novelist Henry Fielding called the "prototype of hell." The next model lasted only a couple of years before being torn down by raving mobs during the anti-Catholic Gordon Riots of 1780, to be replaced by the Newgate that Dickens visited several times (in between pubs) and de-scribed in several novels—Fagin ended up in the Condemned Hold here in *Oliver Twist,* from which he would have been taken to the public scaffold which replaced the Tyburn Tree (☞ *St. James's and Mayfair, above*) and stood outside the prison until 1868. The Central Criminal Court replaced Newgate in 1907. The most famous, and most inter-esting, feature of the solid Edwardian building is the gilded statue of blind Justice perched on top, scales in her left hand, sword in her right. Ask the doorman which current trial is likely to prove juicy, if you're that kind of ghoul—you may catch the conviction of the next Crippen or Christie (England's most notorious wife-murderers, both tried here). Cameras are not allowed in the court. Check the day's hearings on the sign outside. ☉ *Public Gallery weekdays 10–1 and 2–4 (line forms at Newgate St. entrance). Tube: Blackfriars.*

⑱ Royal Exchange. Inhabiting the isosceles triangle between Threadnee-dle Street and Cornhill, this is the third version to have stood here, but the first to have been blessed by Queen Victoria—at its 1844 opening. Sir William Tite designed the massive templelike building, its pediment featuring 17 limestone figures (Commerce, plus merchants) supported by eight sizable Corinthian columns, to house the then thriving futures market. This has now moved on, leaving the Royal Exchange, which you may no longer enter, as a monument to money.

❼ St. Bartholomew the Great. Reached via a perfect half-timbered gate house atop a 13th-century stone archway, this is one of London's old-est churches. Along with its namesake on the other side of the road, St. Bartholomew's Hospital, the Norman church was founded by Ra-here, Henry I's court jester. At the Dissolution of the Monasteries, Henry VIII had most of it torn down; the Romanesque choir loft is all that survives from the 12th century.

❸ St. Bride's. This, the first of Wren's city churches, did not escape wartime bomb damage, and was reconsecrated only in 1960 after a 17-year-long restoration. As St. Paul's (in Covent Garden) is the actor's church, so St. Bride's belongs to journalists, many of whom have been buried or memorialized here, as reading the wall plaques will tell you. Even before the press moved in, it was a popular place to take the final rest. By 1664 the crypts were so crowded that diarist Samuel Pepys had to bribe the grave digger to "justle together" some bodies to make room for his deceased brother. Now the crypts house a museum of the church's rich history, and a bit of Roman sidewalk. From afar, study its extraordinary steeple—its uniquely tiered shape gave rise, legend has it, to the traditional wedding cake. ✉ *Fleet St.,* ☎ *0171/353–1301.* 🖾 *Free.* ☉ *Mon.–Sat. 9–5, Sun. between services at 11 and 6:30. Tube: Chancery Lane.*

⑪ St. Giles Without Cripplegate. Standing south of the Barbican complex, this is one of the only City churches to have withstood the Great Fire, only to succumb to the Blitz bombs three centuries later. The tower and a few walls survived; the rest was rebuilt to the 16th-century plan during the 1950s, and now the little church struggles hopelessly for attention among the Barbican towers, whose parishioners it tends. Past parishioners include Oliver Cromwell, married here in 1620, and John Milton, buried here in 1674.

⑬ St. Mary-le-Bow. Wren's 1673 church has one of the most famous sets of bells around—a Londoner must be born within the sound of Bow bells to be a true cockney. The origin of that idea was probably the curfew rung on the Bow Bells during the 14th century, even though "cockney" only came to mean Londoner three centuries later, and then it was an insult.

NEED A BREAK?   The **Place Below** is literally below the church, in St. Mary-le-Bow's crypt, and gets packed with City workers weekday lunchtime—the self-service soup and quiche are particularly good. It's also open for breakfast, and Thursday and Friday evenings it features a posh and sophisticated vegetarian set dinner.

★ ⑤ **St. Paul's Cathedral.** The symbolic heart of London, St. Paul's will take your breath away. In fact, its dome—the world's third largest—will already be familiar, since you see it peeping through on the skyline from many an angle. The cathedral is, of course, Sir Christopher Wren's masterpiece, completed in 1710 after 35 years of building and much argument with the royal commission, then, much later, miraculously (mostly) spared by the World War II bombs. Wren had originally been commissioned to restore Old St. Paul's, the Norman cathedral that had replaced, in its turn, three earlier versions, but the Great Fire left so little of it behind that a new cathedral was deemed necessary.

Wren's first plan, known as the New Model, did not make it past the drawing board, while the second, known as the Great Model, got as far as the 20-foot oak rendering you can see here today before being rejected, too, whereupon Wren is said to have burst into tears. The third, however, known as the Warrant Design (because it received the royal warrant), was accepted, with the fortunate coda that the architect be allowed to make changes as he saw fit. Without that, there would be no dome, because the approved design had featured a steeple. Parliament felt that building was proceeding too slowly (in fact, 35 years is lightning speed, as cathedrals go) and withheld half of Wren's pay for the last 13 years of work. He was pushing 80 when Queen Anne finally coughed up the arrears.

When you enter and see the dome from the inside, you may find that it seems smaller than you expected. You aren't imagining things; it *is* smaller, and 60 feet lower, than the lead-covered outer dome. Between the inner and outer domes is a brick cone, which supports the familiar 850-ton lantern, surmounted by its golden ball and cross. Nobody can resist making a beeline for the dome, so we'll start beneath it, standing dead center, on top of Wren's memorial, which his son composed and had set into the pavement, and which reads succinctly: *Lector, si monumentum requiris, circumspice*—"Reader, if you seek his monument, look around you."

☙ Now climb the 259 spiral steps to the **Whispering Gallery**. This is the part of the cathedral with which you bribe children, who are fascinated by the acoustic phenomenon: Whisper something to the wall on one side, and a second later it transmits clearly to the other side, 107 feet

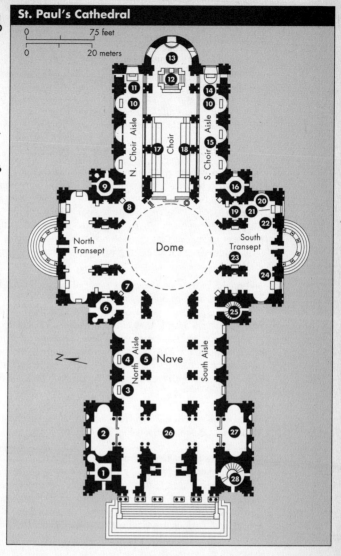

St. Paul's Cathedral

away. The only problem is identifying "your" whisper from the cacophony of everyone else's, since this is a popular game. Look down onto the Nave from here, and up to the frescoes of St. Paul by Sir James Thornhill (who nearly fell off while painting them), before ascending farther to the Stone Gallery, which encircles the outside of the dome and affords a spectacular panorama of London. Up again (careful—you will have tackled 627 steps altogether) and you reach the Golden Gallery, from which you can view the lantern through a circular opening called the oculus.

Back downstairs there are the inevitable monuments and memorials to see, though fewer than one might expect, because Wren didn't want his masterpiece cluttered up. The poet John Donne, who had been Dean of St. Paul's for his final 10 years (he died in 1631), lies in the south choir aisle; his is the only monument remaining from Old St. Paul's. The vivacious choir stall carvings nearby are the work of Grinling Gibbons, as is the organ, which Wren designed and Handel played. The painters Sir Joshua Reynolds and J. M. W. Turner are commemorated, as is George Washington. The American connection continues behind the high altar in the **American Memorial Chapel,** dedicated in 1958 to the 28,000 GIs stationed here who lost their lives in World War II.

A visit to the **crypt** brings you to Wren's tomb, the black marble sarcophagus containing Admiral Nelson (who was pickled in alcohol for his final voyage here from Trafalgar), and an equestrian statue of the Duke of Wellington on top of his grandiose tomb. ☎ *0171/248–2705. ☒ Cathedral, ambulatory (American Chapel), crypt, and treasury £3.50; galleries £3; combined ticket £6. ☉ Cathedral Mon.–Sat. 8:30–4:30 (closed occasionally for special services); ambulatory, crypt, and galleries Mon.–Sat. 9:30–4:15. Tube: St. Paul's.*

⓱ St. Stephen Walbrook Church. This is the parish church many think is Wren's best, by virtue of its practice dome, which predates the Big One at St. Paul's by some 30 years. Two inside sights warrant investigation: Henry Moore's 1987 central stone altar, which sits beneath the dome ("like a lump of Camembert," say critics), and, well, a telephone—an eloquent tribute to that genuine savior of souls, Rector Chad Varah, who founded the Samaritans, givers of phone help to the suicidal, here in 1953.

❽ Smithfield. Nowadays the vittles are dead in London's main meat market, but up to the middle of last century, it was livestock that was sold here, by human meatheads, who liked to get blind drunk and stampede their herds around the houses—"like a bull in a china shop," which is where that phrase comes from. This "smooth field" was already a market during the 12th century, but the building you see today, modeled on the Victorian Crystal Palace, was not opened until 1868. It remains a bloody and frantic place; if you wish to see it in all its glory, get here before 9 AM.

NEED A BREAK?   The **Fox and Anchor** (☒ 115 Charterhouse St.) serves beer alongside its famous Brobdingnagian mixed grills, from 6:30 AM.

⓴ Temple of Mithras. This minor place of pilgrimage in the Roman City was unearthed on a building site in 1954 and taken, at first, for an early Christian church. In fact, worshipers here favored Christ's chief rival during the 3rd and 4th centuries, Mithras, the Persian god of light. Mithraists aimed for all the big virtues, but still were not appreciated by early Christians, from whom their sculptures and treasures had to be concealed. These devotional objects are now on display back at the Museum of London, while here, on Queen Victoria Street, not far from the Bank of England, you can see the foundations of the temple itself.

☺ ★ **㉔ Tower Bridge.** Despite its venerable, nay medieval, appearance, this is a Victorian youngster that celebrated its centenary in June 1994. Constructed of steel, then clothed in Portland stone, it was deliberately styled in the Gothic persuasion to complement the Tower next door, and is famous for its enormous bascules—the "arms," which open to allow large ships through. Nowadays this rarely happens, but when river traffic was dense, the bascules were raised about five times a day.

The bridge's 100th-birthday gift was a new exhibition, one of London's most imaginative and fun. You are conducted back in time in the company of "Harry Stoner," an animatronic bridge construction worker worthy of Disneyland, to witness the birth of the Thames's last downstream bridge. History and engineering lessons are painlessly absorbed as you meet the ghost of the bridge's architect, Sir Horace Jones, see the bascules work, and wander the walkways with their grand upstream–downstream views annotated by interactive video displays.

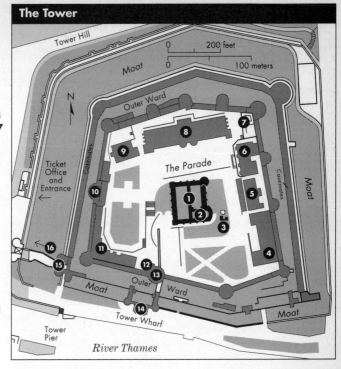

The Tower

Be sure to hang onto your ticket and follow the signs to the Engine Rooms for part two; here the original steam-driven hydraulic engines gleam, and a cute rococo theater is the setting for an Edwardian-style music-hall production of the bridge's story. ☎ 0171/403–3761. ✉ £5.50, combined ticket with Tower Hill Pageant (☞ below) £8.75. ☉ Apr.–Oct., daily 10–6:30; Nov.–Mar., daily 10–5:15 (last entry 1¼ hrs before closing). Tube: Tower Hill.

Tower Hill Pageant. London's first "dark-ride" museum, where automated cars take you past mock-ups of scenes from most periods of London's past, complete with "people," sound effects, and even smells. There's also an archaeological museum with finds from the Thames, set up by the Museum of London. ✉ Tower Hill Terr., ☎ 0171/709–0081. ✉ £6.95, combined ticket with Tower Bridge £8.75. ☉ Apr.–Oct., daily 9:30–5:30; Nov.–Mar., daily 9:30–4:30. Tube: Tower Hill.

★ ㉓ **Tower of London.** This has top billing on many tourist itineraries for good reason. Nowhere else does London's history come to life so vividly as in this mini-city of melodramatic towers stuffed to bursting with heraldry and treasure, the intimate details of lords and dukes and princes and sovereigns etched in the walls (literally in some places, as you'll see), and quite a few pints of royal blood spilled on the stones. Be warned that visitor traffic at the sight of sights is copious, meaning not only lines for the best bits, but a certain dilution of atmosphere, which can be disappointing if you've been fantasizing scenes from *Elizabeth and Essex*. At least you need no longer spend all day in line for the prize exhibit, the Crown Jewels, since they have been transplanted to a new home where moving walkways hasten progress at the busiest times.

The reason the Tower holds the royal gems is that it is still one of the royal palaces, although no monarch since Henry VIII has called it home. It has also housed the Royal Mint, the Public Records, the Royal

Menagerie, and the Royal Observatory, although its most renowned and titillating function has been, of course, as a jail and place of torture and execution.

A person was mighty privileged to be beheaded in the peace and seclusion of **Tower Green** instead of before the mob at Tower Hill. In fact, only seven people were ever important enough—among them Anne Boleyn and Catherine Howard, wives two and five of Henry VIII's six; Elizabeth I's friend Robert Devereux, Earl of Essex; and the nine-days queen, Lady Jane Grey, aged 17. Tower Green's other function was as a corpse dumping ground when the chapel just got too full. You can see the executioner's block, with its bathetic forehead-sized dent, and his axe—along with the equally famous rack, where victims were stretched, and the more obscure scavenger's daughter, which pressed a body nearly to death, plus assorted thumbscrews, iron maidens, and so forth—in the **Martin Tower,** which stands in the northeast corner.

Before we go any farther, you should know about the excellent free and fact-packed tours that depart every half hour or so from the Middle Tower. They are conducted by the 42 Yeoman Warders, better known as "Beefeaters"—ex-servicemen dressed in resplendent navy-and-red (scarlet-and-gold on special occasions) Tudor outfits. Beefeaters have been guarding the Tower since Henry VII appointed them in 1485. One of them, the Yeoman Ravenmaster, is responsible for making life comfortable for Larry, Hardy, George, Hugin, Mumia, and Rhys—the Tower Ravens. This used to be a delicate duty, since if they were to desert the Tower (goes the legend), the kingdom would fall. Today, the Tower takes no chances: the ravens' wings are clipped.

In prime position stands the oldest part of the Tower and the most conspicuous of its buildings, the **White Tower.** This central keep was begun in 1078 by William the Conqueror; by the time it was completed, in 1097, it was the tallest building in London, underlining the might of those victorious Normans. Henry III (1207–1272) had it whitewashed, which is where the name comes from, then used it to house his menagerie, including the polar bear the King of Norway had given him.

The spiral staircase—winding clockwise to help the right-handed swordsman defend it—is the only way up, and here you'll find the **Royal Armouries,** Britain's national museum of arms and armor, with about 40,000 pieces on display. One of the Tower's original functions was as arsenal, supplying armor and weapons to the kings and their armies. Henry VIII started the collection in earnest, founding a workshop at Greenwich as a kind of bespoke tailor of armor to the gentry, but the public didn't get to see it until the second half of the 17th century, during Charles II's reign—which makes the Tower Armouries Britain's oldest public museum.

Here you can see weapons and armor from Britain and the Continent, dating from Saxon and Viking times right up to our own. Among the highlights are four of those armors Henry VIII commissioned to fit his ever-increasing bulk, plus one for his horse. The medieval war horse was nothing without his *shaffron,* or head protector, and here you'll find a 500-year-old example, one of the oldest pieces of horse armor in the world. Don't miss the tiny armors on the third floor—one belonging to Henry's son (who survived in it to become Edward VI), and another just a bit more than 3 feet tall. In the **New Armouries,** added during the 17th century, are examples of almost every weapon made for the British soldier from the 17th to the 19th century.

Most of the interior of the White Tower has been much altered over the centuries, but the **Chapel of St. John,** downstairs from the armouries, is unadulterated 11th-century Norman—very rare, very simple, and very beautiful. Underneath it is a particularly nasty cell, "Little Ease," an ironic name, as the unfortunate inmate (Guy Fawkes was one of those brought here) couldn't stand, sit, or lie down—a replica is on view at the London Dungeon (☞ South Bank, *below*).

The other fortifications and buildings surrounding the White Tower date from the 11th to the 19th century. Starting from the main entrance, you can't miss the **moat.** Until the Duke of Wellington had it drained in 1843, this was a stinking, stagnant mush, obstinately resisting all attempts to flush it with water from the Thames. Now there's a little raven graveyard in the grassed-over channel, with touching memorials to some of the old birds (who are not known for their kind natures, by the way, and you risk a savage pecking if you try to befriend them).

Across the moat, the **Middle Tower** and the **Byward Tower** form the principal landward entrance, with **Traitors' Gate** a little farther on to the right. This London equivalent of Venice's Bridge of Sighs was where the boats delivered prisoners to their cells, and so it was where those condemned to death got their last look at the outside world. During the period when the Thames was London's chief thoroughfare, this was the main entrance to the Tower.

Immediately opposite Traitors' Gate is the former Garden Tower, better known since about 1570 as the **Bloody Tower.** Its name comes from one of the most famous unsolved murders in history, the saga of the "little princes in the Tower." In 1483 the boy king, Edward V, and his brother Richard were left here by their uncle, Richard of Gloucester, after the death of their father, Edward I. They were never seen again, Gloucester was crowned Richard III, and in 1674 two little skeletons were found under the stairs to St. John's Chapel. The obvious conclusions have always been drawn—and were, in fact, even before the skeletons were discovered.

Another famous inmate was Sir Walter Raleigh, who was kept here from 1603 to 1616. It wasn't such an ordeal, as you'll see when you visit his spacious rooms, where he kept two servants, had his wife and two sons live with him (the younger boy was christened in the Tower chapel), and amused himself by writing his *History of the World.* Unfortunately, he was less lucky on his second visit in 1618, which terminated in his execution at Whitehall.

Next to the Bloody Tower is the circular **Wakefield Tower,** which dates from the 13th century and once contained the king's private apartments. It was the scene of another royal murder in 1471, when Henry VI was killed in mid-prayer. Henry founded Eton College and King's College, Cambridge, and they haven't forgotten: Every May 21, envoys from both institutions mark the anniversary of his murder by laying white lilies on the site.

The shiniest, the most expensive, and absolutely the most famous exhibits here are, of course, the **Crown Jewels,** now housed in the **Duke of Wellington's Barracks.** In their new setting you get so close that you could lick the gems (if it weren't for the wafers of bulletproof glass), and they are enhanced by laser lighting, which hurts the eyes with sparkle. Before you meet them in person, you are given a high-definition-film preview along with a few scenes from Elizabeth's 1953 coronation.

It's a commonplace to call these baubles priceless, but it's impossible not to drop your jaw at the notion of their worth. They were, in fact, lifted once—by Colonel Thomas Blood, in 1671—though only as far as a nearby wharf. The colonel was given a royal pension instead of a beating, fueling speculation that Charles II, short of ready cash as usual, had had his hand in the escapade somewhere. These days security is as fiendish as you'd expect, since the jewels—even though they would be literally impossible for thieves to sell—are *so* priceless that they're not insured. However, they are polished every February by Garrard, the royal jewelers.

A brief résumé of the top jewels: Finest of all is the **Royal Sceptre,** containing the earth's largest cut diamond, the 530-carat Star of Africa. This is also known as Cullinan I, having been cut from the South African Cullinan, which weighed 20 ounces when dug up from a De Beers mine at the beginning of the century. Another chip off the block, Cullinan II, lives on the **Imperial Crown of State** that Prince Charles is due to wear at his coronation—the same one that Elizabeth II wore in her coronation procession; it had been made for Victoria's in 1838. Aside from its 2,800 diamonds, it features the Black Prince's ruby, which Henry V was supposed to have worn at Agincourt, and is actually an imposter— it's no ruby, it's a semiprecious spinel. The other most famous gem is the Koh-i-noor, or "Mountain of Light," which adorns the **Queen Mother's crown.** When Victoria was presented with this gift horse in 1850, she looked it in the mouth, found it lacking in glitteriness, and had it chopped down to almost half its weight.

An addendum to the major jewels in the Martin Tower is accurately called "Crowns and Diamonds." See naked crown frames—the coronation crown of George IV, George I's Imperial State Crown, Victoria's State Crown—surrounded by 12,500 loose diamonds on permanent loan from de Beers. It's a graphic illustration of how the royals once had to rent in the stones to adorn their headpiece on the big day.

The little chapel of **St. Peter ad Vincula** can be visited only as part of a Yeoman Warder tour. The third church on the site, it conceals the remains of some 2,000 people executed at the Tower, Anne Boleyn and Catherine Howard among them. Being traitors, they were not so much buried as dumped under the flagstones, but the genteel Victorians had the courtesy to rebury their bones during renovations.

One of the more evocative towers is **Beauchamp Tower,** built west of Tower Green by Edward I (1272–1307). It was soon designated as a jail for the higher class of miscreant, including Lady Jane Grey, who is thought to have added her Latin graffiti to the many inscriptions carved by prisoners that you can see here.

Just south of the Beauchamp Tower is an L-shape row of half-timbered Tudor houses, with the **Queen's House** at the center. Built for the governor of the Tower in 1530, this place saw the interrogation or incarceration of several of the more celebrated prisoners, including Anne Boleyn and the Gunpowder Plot conspirators. The Queen's House also played host to the Tower's last-ever prisoner, Rudolph Hess, the Nazi who parachuted into London in 1941 to seek asylum.

Don't forget to stroll along the battlements before you leave; from them, you get a wonderful overview of the whole Tower of London. ⊠ *H. M. Tower of London,* ☏ *0171/709–0765.* ▣ *£8.30, small additional charge for Fusiliers Museum.* ☽ *Mar.–Oct., Mon.–Sat. 9:30–6:30, Sun. 2–6; Nov.–Feb., Mon.–Sat. 9:30–5 (last admission may be sold as early as 4, depending on crowds). For tickets to Ceremony of the Keys (locking of main gates, nightly at 10), write well in advance to The Resident Governor and Keeper of the Jewel House, Queen's House, H. M. Tower of London, EC3. Give your name, the dates you wish to attend (including alternate dates), and number of people (up to 7) in your party, and enclose a self-addressed stamped envelope. Yeo-*

man Warder guides leave daily from Middle Tower, subject to weather and availability, at no charge (but a tip is always appreciated), about every 30 min until 3:30 in summer, 2:30 in winter. Tube: Tower Hill.

2 **Ye Olde Cheshire Cheese.** One of the many places in which that acerbic compiler of the first dictionary, Dr. Johnson drank (like Dickens, he is claimed by many a pub). This was, in fact, his "local," around the corner from his house. It retains a venerable open-fires-in-tiny-rooms charm when not too packed with tourists. Among 19th-century writers who followed Johnson's footsteps to the bar here were Mark Twain and, yes, Charles Dickens.

THE EAST END

Made famous by Dickens and infamous by Jack the Ripper, the East End remains one of London's most hauntingly evocative neighborhoods. There is a good argument for considering it the real London, since Eastenders are born "within the sound of Bow Bells," and are therefore cockneys through and through (not to mention models for the characters of England's favorite soap opera, *Eastenders*). The district began as separate villages—Whitechapel and Spitalfields, Shoreditch, Mile End, and Bethnal Green—melding together during the population boom of the 19th century, a boom that was shaped by French Huguenot and Jewish refugees, by poverty, and, in the past several decades, by a growing Bengali community. Whitechapel is where the Salvation Army was founded and the original Liberty Bell was forged, but, of course, what everyone remembers about it is that its Victorian slum streets were stalked by the most infamous serial killer of all, Jack the Ripper. Two centuries earlier, neighboring Spitalfields provided sanctuary for the French Huguenots. They had fled here after the Edict of Nantes (which had allowed them religious freedom in Catholic France) was revoked in 1685, and had found work in the nascent silk industry, many of them becoming prosperous master weavers. Prosperous is not really the word for the East End of today, but what the area lacks in tourist attractions it makes up for in history and urban romance of a sublime sort.

Numbers in the text correspond to numbers in the margin and on the East End map.

A Good Walk

The easiest way to reach Whitechapel High Street is via the District Line to Aldgate East tube. Turn left out of the tube station. Behind 90 Whitechapel High Street once stood George Yard Buildings, where Jack the Ripper's first victim, Martha Turner, was discovered in August 1888. Nowadays you'll find the **Whitechapel Gallery** ① instead. Continue east until you reach Fieldgate Street on the right, where you'll find the **Whitechapel Bell Foundry** ②, then, retracing your steps, turn right into Osborn Street, which soon becomes **Brick Lane** ③.

Brick Lane itself and the narrow streets running off it offer a paradigm of the East End's development. Its population has always been in flux, with some moving in to find refuge here as others were escaping its poverty. Just before the start of Brick Lane you can take a short detour (turn left, then right) to see the birthplace of one who did just that. Flower and Dean Street, past the ugly 1970s housing project on Thrawl Street and once the most disreputable street in London, was where Abe Sapperstein, founder of the *Harlem Globetrotters*, was born in 1908. On the west end of **Fournier Street** ④, see Nicholas Hawksmoor's masterpiece, **Christ Church, Spitalfields** ⑤, and some fine early Georgian houses, then follow Wilkes Street north of the church, where you'll find more 1720s Huguenot houses (one has been turned into the **Spitalfields**

Heritage Centre ⑥), and turn right into Princelet Street, once important to the Jewish settlers. Where No. 6 stands now, the first of several thriving Yiddish theaters opened in 1886, playing to packed houses until the following year, when a false fire alarm, rung during a January performance, ended with 17 people being crushed to death, and so demoralized the theater's actor-founder, Jacob Adler, that he moved his troupe to New York. Adler played a major role in founding that city's great Yiddish theater tradition—which, in turn, had a significant effect on Hollywood.

Now you reach Brick Lane again and the **Black Eagle Brewery** ⑦. Turn left at Hanbury Street, where, in 1888, behind a seedy lodging house at No. 29, Jack the Ripper left his third mutilated murderee, "Dark" Annie Chapman. A double murder followed, and then, after a month's lull, came the death on this street of Marie Kelly, the Ripper's last victim and his most revolting murder of all. He had been able to work indoors this time, and Kelly, a young widow, was found strewn all over the room, charred remains of her clothing in the fire grate. (Of course, Jack the Ripper's identity never has been discovered, although to this day theories are still bandied about.)

Now turn onto Lamb Street, and the two northern entrances to **Spitalfields Market** ⑧, or turn left on Commercial Street to Folgate Street, and **Dennis Sever's House** ⑨. (If you have kids, they might have fun—and learn something too—going to **Spitalfields City Farm** ⑩ a few blocks away.) Go back west through Folgate Street, to reach Shoreditch High Street, where you can catch Bus 22a, 22b, or 149 north to Kingsland Road, or get there across Bethnal Green Road, left, then right onto Club Row, **Arnold Circus** ⑪ and two streets north, **Columbia Road** ⑫. Cross Hackney Road and slip up Waterson Street—that's about a half-mile's walk. On Kingsland Road, you'll come to the row of early 18th-century almshouses which is the **Geffrye Museum** ⑬. Head east about 500 yards on Hackney Road (Cremer Street, south of the museum, gets you there) and you come to the **Hackney City Farm** ⑭. Going south down Warner Place (across Hackney Road opposite the farm entrance) you come to Old Bethnal Green Road, at the end of which a right turn brings you to the **Bethnal Green Museum of Childhood** ⑮.

Now you can catch either Bus 106 or 253 or walk south about a half mile down Cambridge Heath Road as far as the Mile End Road. Turning left, you'll pass several historical landmarks, which provide, let's be honest, more food for thought than thrills for the senses. On the north side of the street are the former **Trinity Almshouses** ⑯, with the statue of William Booth on the very spot where the first Salvation Army meetings were held. Behind you, on the northwest corner of Cambridge Heath Road is **The Blind Beggar** ⑰ pub, with the **Royal London Hospital** ⑱ a few yards to the left, and its Archives behind.

TIMING

This is a long walk, and not for everyone. The East End isn't picturesque, and the sights are anything but world famous. However, those who get pleasure from discovery and an adventurous route will enjoy these hidden corners. If you visit on a Sunday morning, the East End has a festive air: About half the neighborhood sprouts hundreds of market stalls (especially in and around Middlesex Street, Brick Lane, and Columbia Road). After shopping, you could go on to take brunch among cows and sheep on a farm, then play at being Georgians in a restored, candlelighted 18th-century town house. You would miss out on a few weekday-only sights, but—as a Victorian peep-show barker might say—yer pays yer money and yer takes yer choice. A weekday focus for your jaunt might well be the excellent Whitechapel Gallery, the Geffrye Museum, or the Bethnal Green Museum of Childhood, any of which will take an hour or two. Aside from visits, the walk alone is a three-hour marathon, done at a brisk pace. The suggested bus links might appeal, since the in-between parts aren't going to win tourism awards.

HOW TO GET THERE

The best tubes to start from are Whitechapel or Aldgate East on the District/Hammersmith and City lines, or Aldgate on the Metropolitan and Circle lines. Buses include Nos. 8, 22A, 22B, 26, 35, 47, 48, and 78. To continue up into the northern part of the area, around Shoreditch and Spitalfields, including the Geffrye Museum (get the 22A or B or the 67 for that), get Nos. 8, 22A, 22B, 26, 35, 47, 48, 55, 67, 78, and 243 to the junction of Shoreditch High Street and Bishopsgate.

Sights to See

⑪ Arnold Circus. A perfect circle of arts-and-crafts–style houses around a central raised bandstand, this is the core of the Boundary Estate—"model" housing built by Victorian philanthropists and do-gooders for the slum-dwelling locals, and completed as the century began. It's of special interest to architecture buffs.

⑮ Bethnal Green Museum of Childhood. This is the East End outpost of the Victoria and Albert Museum—in fact this entire iron, glass, and brown-brick building was transported here from South Kensington in 1875. Since then, believe it or not, its contents have grown into the biggest toy collection in the world. The central hall is a bit like the Geffrye Museum zapped into miniature: Here are doll's houses (some royal) of every period. Each genre of plaything has its own enclosure, so if teddy bears are your weakness, you need waste no time with the train sets. The museum's title is justified upstairs, in the recently opened, fascinating—and possibly unique—social-history-of-childhood galleries. Free art workshops are given for children over the age of 3. ⌑ *Cambridge Heath Rd.,* ☎ *0181/980–4315.* ⌑ *Free.* ☉ *Mon.–Thurs. and Sat. 10–5:50, Sun. 2:30–5:50; art workshop Sat. at 11 and 2. Tube: Bethnal Green.*

⑦ Black Eagle Brewery. This is the only one of the former East End breweries still standing. And a very handsome example of Georgian and 19th-century industrial architecture it is, too, along with its mirrored 1977 extension. It belonged to Truman, Hanbury, Buxton & Co., which in 1873 was the largest brewery in the world (the English always did like their bitter). The building now houses the East End Tourism Trust offices and the present Truman brewery's administration. You can't go in except to look at the old stables and vat house on the east side. Opposite, however, the old brewery canteen has been turned into the little **Brick Lane Music Hall,** a cute and shabby theater serving up an *echt* East End dinner (*latkes*—potato pancakes—are a feature on most menus) and an old-fashioned laugh-a-minute cabaret show. *Brewery:* ⌑ *91 Brick La. Music Hall:* ⌑ *152 Brick La.,* ☎ *0171/377–8787.* ⌑ *Dinner and show £20.* ☉ *Wed., Fri, and Sat. at 7:30. Tube: Aldgate East, Shoreditch.*

⑰ The Blind Beggar. The Victorian den of iniquity where Salvation Army founder William Booth preached his first sermon. Also, on the south side of the street stands a stone inscribed "Here William Booth commenced the work of the Salvation Army, July 1865," marking the position of the first Sally Army platform, while back by the pub, a statue of William Booth stands where the first meetings were held. Booth didn't supply the pub's main claim to fame, though. The Blind Beggar's real notoriety dates only from March 1966, when Ronnie Kray—one of

The East End

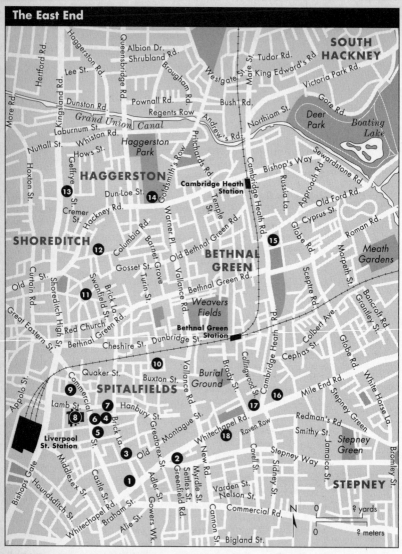

the Kray twins, the former gangster kings of London's East End underworld—shot dead rival "godfather" George Cornell in the saloon bar.

❸ Brick Lane. This street has, in its time, seen the manufacture of bricks (during the 16th century, when it was named), beer, and bagels, but nowadays it is the center of the East End's Bengali community. (You can still get the bagels, though, at No. 159, the 24-hour **Beigel Bake**.) All along here you'll see shops selling psychedelic saris and stacks of sticky Indian sweets, video stores renting Indian movies, and Bengali, Bangladeshi, and Pakistani restaurants, popular among Londoners for the most authentic and least expensive curries in town. On Sunday morning the entire street is packed with stalls in a companion market to the nearby Petticoat Lane.

❺ Christ Church, Spitalfields. This is the 1729 masterpiece of Wren's associate, Nicholas Hawksmoor. Hawksmoor built only six London churches; this one was commissioned as part of Parliament's 1711 "Fifty New Churches Act." The idea was to score points for the Church of England against such Nonconformists as the Protestant Huguenots. (It must have worked; in the churchyard, you can still see some of their gravestones, with epitaphs in French.) The Spitalfields district once flourished thanks to the silk-weaving trade of its emigré population, but as the silk industry declined (19th-century machinery had made hand weaving redundant), the church fell into disrepair and its gardens even acquired a reputation as a tramps' ground (and the sobriquet "Itchy Park"). By 1958 the structure was crumbling to bits and had to be closed. It was saved from demolition—but only just—and reopened in 1987, though restoration work won't be complete until 1998 or so. Until then, opening hours are restricted, but there are occasional evening concerts (and a music festival in June), and always a fine view of the colonnaded portico and tall spire from Brushfield Street to the west. ⊠ *Commercial St.,* ☎ *0171/377–0287.* 🎫 *Free, charge for concerts.* ☉ *Weekdays noon–2:30, Sun. services. Tube: Aldgate East.*

⑫ Columbia Road. On Sundays, this narrow street gets buried under forests of potted palms, azaleas, ivy, ficus, and freesia, tiger lilies, carnations, roses, and hosts of daffodils in London's main plant and flower market. Prices are ultra-low, and lots of the Victorian shop windows around the stalls are filled with wares—terra-cotta pots, vases, gardening tools, hats, and antiques. ☉ *Sun. 7–2. Tube: Old Street.*

❾ Dennis Sever's House. A Georgian terrace belonging to the eponymous performer/designer/scholar from Escondido, California, who has dedicated his life not only to the restoration of his house but also to raising the ghosts of a fictitious Jervis family who might have inhabited it over two centuries. Sever himself lives a replica of Georgian life, without electricity, but with a butler in full 18th-century livery to light the candles and lay the fires—for the Jervises. Three evenings a week he stages a performance, or a "time travel experience," of philosophical bent, trailing the Jervises through 10 rooms and five generations (from 1724 to 1919, to be precise), always missing them by moments. Sever's stunning house, sans Jervises, is also open one Sunday afternoon a month. Reservations are essential. ⊠ *18 Folgate St.,* ☎ *0171/247–4013.* 🎫 *£5 Sun., £30 evenings.* ☉ *1st Sun. of month 2–5, 3 performances per wk (days vary) 7:30–10:20. Tube: Liverpool Street.*

❹ Fournier Street. This contains fine examples of the neighborhood's characteristic Georgian terraced houses, many of them built by the richest of the early 18th-century Huguenot silk weavers (see the enlarged windows on the upper floors). Most of those along the north side of

Fournier Street have now been restored by conservationists, others still contain textile sweatshops—only now the workers are Bengali. On the Brick Lane corner is the **Jamme Masjid,** where local Muslims worship. *Umbra summus* ("We are shadows"), announces the inscription above the entrance, an apt epitaph for the successive communities that have had temporary claim on the building. Built in 1742 as a Huguenot chapel, it converted to Methodism in 1809, only to become the Spitalfields Great Synagogue when the Orthodox Machzikei Hadath sect bought it in 1897.

★ ⓱ **Geffrye Museum.** A small and perfectly formed museum that re-creates domestic English interiors of every period from Elizabethan through postwar '50s utility, all in sequence, so that you walk through time. The best thing about the Geffrye (named after the 17th-century Lord Mayor of London whose land this was) is that its rooms are not the grand parlors of the gentry one normally sees in historic houses but copies of real family homes, as if talented movie-set designers had been let loose instead of academic museum curators. There's also a walled, scented herb garden and a full program of accessible lectures, including regular "bring a room to life" talks. A new group of 20th-century rooms is in the offing. ⊠ *Kingsland Rd.,* ☏ *0171/739–9893.* ☑ *Free.* ⊙ *Tues.–Sat. 10–5, Sun. 2–5; period-room talks Sat. at 2 and 3:30. Tube: Liverpool Street, then Bus 2A, 22B, 67, 149, or 243.*

Ⓒ ⓲ **Hackney City Farm.** This one is smaller than the city farm at Spitalfields (☞ *below*), and so are its animals. Bees and butterflies are the stars here, along with the kinds of wildflowers they like, as well as an ecologically sound pond. If you're walking this route, drop in and buy a pot of London honey. ⊠ *1A Goldsmiths Row,* ☏ *0171/729–6381.* ☑ *Free.* ⊙ *Tues.–Sun. 10–4:30.*

OFF THE
BEATEN PATH

LONDON DOCKLANDS VISITORS CENTRE – This is the jumping-off place for exploring London's most rapidly changing neighborhood. Docklands has emerged from what only a decade ago was a wasteland—partly low-cost residential, partly working docks, partly nothing. Now it houses national newspaper offices, a brand-new riverside business community containing Britain's tallest building, sports facilities, and even a farm. Its boundaries are roughly defined by **Tower Bridge** and the **Design Museum** to the west and **London City Airport** and the **Royal Docks** to the east, though the area inside a loop of the Thames called the **Isle of Dogs** is of most interest. Here is **Canary Wharf,** which, with its 50-story Cesar Pelli **Tower** (⊠ 1 Canada Sq.), is the most notorious development project Britain has seen in years. Olympia & York, the Canadian developers, went bust; bomb scares closed the observation deck; the arts funding ran out; shops stayed unlet; jokes were made. But here are waterfront promenades and pubs, a new London piazza called **Cabot Square,** a large shopping mall, and even a concert hall. Take the high-tech **Docklands Light Railway** (DLR) to Crossharbour (change at Bank) and pick up a free map. An exhibition, information desk, and film introduce the area. ⊠ *3 Limeharbour, Isle of Dogs, E14,* ☏ *0171/512–1111.* ⊙ *Weekdays 9–6, weekends and holidays 10–4:30; bus tour of area departs Tues. at 2, Thurs. at 10:30, and Sun. at 11:30.*

⓳ **Royal London Hospital.** Founded in 1740, the early days of the Royal London were as nasty as its then-neighborhood near the Tower of London. Waste was carried out in buckets and dumped in the street; bedbugs and alcoholic nurses were problems, but according to hospital records, nobody died—they were "relieved." Anyone who lived but refused to give thanks to both the hospital committee and God went on a blacklist, to be banned from further treatment. In 1759, the hospital moved to a new building, the core of the one you see today. By then it had become the best hospital in London, and it was enhanced further by the addition of a small medical school in 1785, and then, 70 years later, an entire state-of-the-art medical college. Thomas John Barnado, who went on to found the famous Dr. Barnado's Homes for orphans, came to train here in 1866. Ten years later, with the opening of a new wing, the hospital became the largest in the United Kingdom, and now, though mostly rebuilt since World War II, it remains one of London's most capacious. Behind it, the **Royal London Hospital Archives** have displays of medical paraphernalia, objects, and documentation to illustrate the 250-year history of this East London institution. ⊠ *Crypt of St. Augustine with St. Philip's Church, Newark St.,* ☎ *0171/377–7000, Ext. 3364.* ⊠ *Free.* ⊙ *Weekdays 10–4:30. Tube: Whitechapel.*

👆 ⑩ **Spitalfields City Farm.** This is just what it sounds like—a sliver of rural England squashed between housing projects. It's one of about a dozen such places in London, which exist to educate city kids in country matters. Available are pony rides, local history tours by horse and cart, a Sunday brunch, summer barbecues—an altogether surreal experience. ⊠ *Pedley St.,* ☎ *0171/247–8762.* ⊠ *Free, horse and cart tour starting at £3.* ⊙ *Tues.–Sun. 9:30–5:30; Sun. brunch 11–3; barbecue June–Sept., Wed. at 7 (call to confirm); horse and cart tour Sun. at 11 and 2:30 (weather permitting). Tube: Shoreditch, Liverpool Street.*

⑥ **Spitalfields Heritage Centre.** This modest institution is dedicated to research into local immigrant communities and the preservation of the neighborhood's historic buildings. Huguenots rented the 1720 house—it still has their silk-weaving attic—but in 1870 the little **United Friends Synagogue** was grafted onto the back. You can still see its wooden ark, pulpit, seats, and boards listing benefactors, complete with Hebrew errors. London's third-oldest (purpose-built) synagogue sometimes houses exhibitions and presents videos about the Jewish East End; otherwise, the Heritage Centre remains rather erratic as a museum, since it is in the process of (underfunded) restoration. ⊠ *19 Princelet St.,* ☎ *0171/377–6901.* ⊠ *Free.* ⊙ *Normally open weekdays 10–5, but call first. Tube: Aldgate East.*

⑧ **Spitalfields Market.** There's been a market here since the mid-17th century, but the current version is overflowing with crafts and design shops and stalls, a sports hall, restaurants and bars, and different-purpose markets every day of the week. The nearer the weekend, the busier it all gets, culminating in the Sunday arts-and-crafts and greenmarket. The latest additions are an opera house and a swimming pool, and events are being staged all the time. ⊠ *65 Brushfield St.,* ☎ *0171/247–6590.* ⊠ *Free.* ⊙ *Daily 10–7; market stalls weekdays 11–2, weekends 9–4. Tube: Liverpool Street.*

⑯ **Trinity Almshouses.** This is just a redbrick student hostel, but it has interesting origins, having been built (possibly with Wren's help) in 1695 for "28 decayed Masters and Commanders of Ships or ye widows of such," bombed during World War II, and restored by London County Council. Behind, even better concealed, is the oldest Jewish cemetery in Britain, founded by the Sephardic community in 1657 after Cromwell allowed them back into the country. (If you would like to view the cemetery, call the United Synagogues Cemetery Maintenance Department, ☎ *0171/790–1445.*)

② **Whitechapel Bell Foundry.** It may be off the beaten track, but this working foundry was responsible for some of the world's better-known chimes. Before moving to this site in 1738, the foundry cast Westminster Abbey's bells (in the 1580s), but its biggest work, in every sense, was the 13-ton Big Ben, cast in 1858 by George Mears, and requiring 16 horses to transport it from here to Westminster. Its other important work was casting the original Liberty Bell (now in Philadelphia) in 1752, and both it and Big Ben can be seen in pictures, along with exhibits about bell-making, in a little museum in the shop. You can even buy a small table bell (for about £36) if they have them in stock, though the actual foundry is off-limits. ⊠ *34 Whitechapel Rd.,* ☎ *0171/247–2599.* ☞ *Free.* ☉ *Weekdays 8:30–5:30. Tube: Aldgate East.*

❶ **Whitechapel Gallery.** Housed in a spacious 1901 Art Nouveau building, this has an international reputation for its shows, which are often on the cutting edge of contemporary art. The American "action painter" Jackson Pollock exhibited here in the '50s, the pop artist Robert Rauschenberg in the '60s, and David Hockney had his first solo show here in the '70s. More recently the Tate Gallery visited the Whitechapel and bought the American Bill Viola's powerful video installation, the *Nantes Triptych,* which shows Viola submerged underwater, his wife giving birth on one side, his mother dying in a hospital on the other. Other exhibitions highlight the local community and culture, and there are programs of lectures, too. The Whitechapel Café serves remarkably inexpensive home-cooked whole-food hot meals, soups, and cakes. ⊠ *Whitechapel High St.,* ☎ *0171/377–0107.* ☞ *Free (fee for some exhibitions).* ☉ *Tues.–Sun. 11–5, Wed. 11–8. Tube: Aldgate East.*

OFF THE
BEATEN PATH

WILLIAM MORRIS GALLERY – An 18th-century house in northeast London where the artistic polymath William Morris (craftsman, painter, and writer) lived for eight years, this gallery contains many examples of his work and that of his fellow artisans in the Arts and Crafts Movement. ⊠ *Water House, Lloyd Park, Forest Rd.,* ☎ *0181/527-3782.* ☉ *Tues.–Sat. 10–1 and 2–5, 1st Sun. of each month 10–noon and 2–5. Tube: Walthamstow Central, then 15-min walk down Hoe St., turn left at Forest Rd.*

THE SOUTH BANK

London's oldest "suburb," **Southwark,** though just across the river from London Bridge, was conveniently outside the City walls and laws, and therefore was the ideal location for the taverns and cock-fighting arenas that served as after-hours entertainment in the Middle Ages. By Shakespeare's time it had become a veritable den of iniquity, famous above all for the "Southwark stews," or brothels, and for being very rough. The Globe Theatre, in which Shakespeare acted and held shares, was one of several established here after theaters were banished from the City in 1574 for encouraging truancy in young apprentices and being generally rowdy. The Globe was as likely to stage a few bouts of bear-baiting as the latest Shakespeare offering.

Southwark was heavily bombed during World War II, then neglected for a few decades while more central parts of London were repaired. The active ports had moved downstream by then anyway, so Southwark's 19th-century warehouses and winding alleys had little to recommend them to developers. This circumstance began to change when theater returned to the Bankside environs (Bankside being the street along the South Bank from Southwark to Blackfriars bridges) in the form of the national arts complex that opened downstream in 1976, but it took another decade or so for developers and local authorities to catch on to the potential farther east. Now the South Bank is turning into London's most happening new neighborhood, with Eighties and early Nineties renovations and innovations, like Gabriel's Wharf,

London Bridge City, Hay's Galleria, Butler's Wharf, and Shakespeare's Globe being joined by a second wave of new attractions, starring the OXO Tower and the London Aquarium. These will again be augmented in the lead-up to the millennium by the new Tate Gallery, a floating casino (probably), a giant Ferris wheel, and a new look for the South Bank Centre itself. That North London dig about needing a passport to cross the river is never heard now.

Numbers in the text correspond to numbers in the margin and on the South Bank map.

A Good Walk

Start scenically at the south end of Tower Bridge, finding the steps on the east (left) side, which descend to the start of a pedestrians-only street, Shad Thames. Now turn your back on the bridge and follow this quaint path between cliffs of the good-as-new warehouses, which are now **Butler's Wharf** ①, but were once the seedy, dingy, dangerous shadowlands where Dickens killed off evil Bill Sikes in *Oliver Twist*. See the foodies' center, the Gastrodrome, and the **Design Museum** ②, then just before you get back to Tower Bridge, turn away from the river, along Horsleydown Lane, follow Tooley Street, take the right turn at Morgan Lane to **HMS *Belfast*** ③, or continue to **Hay's Galleria** ④ with **St. Olave's House** ⑤, London Bridge, and the **London Dungeon** ⑥ beyond. Next, turn left into Joiner Street underneath the arches of London's first (1836) railway, then right onto St. Thomas Street, where you'll find the **Old St. Thomas's Operating Theatre** ⑦ and Herb Garret, with **Southwark Cathedral** ⑧ just across Borough High Street, and another of the South Bank's recent office developments, St. Mary Overie Dock down Cathedral Street. See the west wall, with rose window outline, of Winchester House, palace of the Bishops of Winchester until 1626 built into it, and take a tour of the little **Golden Hinde** ⑨, and the **Clink** ⑩ next door. Continue to the end of Clink Street onto Bankside, detouring left up Rose Alley, where in 1989 the remains of a famous Jacobean theater, the Rose Theatre, were unearthed, though because of office development surrounding the preserved foundations there's not much to see. The next little alley is New Globe Walk, where there is much to see: the reconstruction of that most famous of Jacobean theaters, **Shakespeare's Globe** ⑪. Next along Bankside is the 17th-century Cardinal's Wharf, where, as a plaque explains, Wren lived while St. Paul's Cathedral was being built, then Bankside Power Station, which is to become the new Tate Gallery by the year 2000, and **Bankside Gallery** ⑫.

Now you reach your fourth bridge on this walk, Blackfriars Bridge, which you pass beneath to join the street called Upper Ground, spending some time in the Coin Street Community Builders' fast-emerging neighborhood, which feature the **OXO Tower** ⑬ and **Gabriel's Wharf** ⑭. Farther along Upper Ground, you reach the South Bank Centre, with the **Royal National Theatre** ⑮ first, followed by the **Museum of the Moving Image (MOMI)** ⑯, the **Royal Festival Hall** ⑰, and the **Hayward Gallery** ⑱. You'll find distractions all over this section of the walk, especially in summer—secondhand bookstalls, entertainers, and a series of plaques annotating the buildings opposite. When you've passed the South Bank Centre, look across the river for the quintessential postcard vista of the Houses of Parliament which continues past Westminster Bridge to St. Thomas's Hospital. Jubilee Gardens is now razed in preparation for the 500-foot Ferris wheel that's coming in 1999. Next, you reach the former County Hall, which is now the **London Aquarium** ⑲ and farther along the river, beyond the **Florence Nightingale Museum** ⑳, **Lambeth Palace** ㉑ stands by Lambeth Bridge, with the **Museum**

of Garden History ㉒ in St. Mary's next door. Now if you take a detour to the right off Lambeth Road, you could be "doing the Lambeth Walk" down the street of the same name. A cockney tradition ever since the 17th century, when there was a spa here, the Sunday stroll was immortalized in a song from the 1937 musical *Me and My Girl,* which recently proved a hit all over again in the West End and on New York City's Broadway. A little farther east along Lambeth Road you reach the **Imperial War Museum** ㉓.

TIMING

On a fine day, this 2- to 3-mi walk makes a very scenic wander, since you're following the south bank of the great Thames nearly all the way. Fabulous views across to the north bank take you past St. Paul's and the Houses of Parliament, and you pass—under, over, or around—no fewer than seven bridges. It's bound to take far longer than a couple of hours, because the sightseeing is heavy. The Imperial War Museum, MOMI, Shakespeare's Globe, the Hayward Gallery, the Design Museum, and the Aquarium are major events, needing much more than an hour apiece (depending on your interests), while the London Dungeon doesn't take long, unless you have kids in tow–which is why you'd go in at all. The other museums on this route—the Clink, Garden History, Old Operating Theatre, Florence Nightingale, the South Bank Centre foyers, and the Bankside Gallery—are compact enough to squeeze together en route to your main event. And that's the nicest thing to do with this walk; have tickets waiting at the end. The National Theatres, the NFT, or Shakespeare's Globe can all oblige, but remember the theaters are dark on Sundays. Dinner or a riverside drink at the OXO Tower Brasserie, Café or Restaurant, the Gastrodrome restaurants or the People's Palace are another idea for a big finish. Public transportation is thin on the ground around this way, so pick a day when you're feeling energetic; there are no shortcuts once you're under way.

HOW TO GET THERE

The tube stop to use is Waterloo on the Northern and Bakerloo lines, though you could also go to the Embankment stop (same lines, plus District and Circle) or Charing Cross (same, plus Northern), and walk across the Charing Cross pedestrian bridge. Buses that take you into the rather confusing territory behind the South Bank Centre include Nos. 1, 68, 76, 168, 171, 176, 178, and 188. For farther downstream, near Shakespeare's Globe, get the 21, 35, 40, 47, or 133 to Tooley Street, or get the tube to Blackfriars and walk across that bridge (offering a particularly scenic walk), or to Mansion House, and walk across Southwark Bridge. The latter is the best way to the OXO Tower.

Sights to See

⓬ **Bankside Gallery.** In this modern building, two artistic societies—the Royal Society of Painter-Printmakers and the Royal Watercolour Society—have their headquarters. Together they mount exhibitions of current members' work, usually for sale, alongside artists' materials and books. Next door is **Bankside Power Station,** which is to become the new Tate Gallery by the year 2000. ✉ *48 Hopton St.,* ☎ *0171/928-7521.* 🎫 *£3.50.* ☉ *Tues.–Sat. 10–5, Sun. 1–5. Tube: Blackfriars, then walk across bridge.*

❶ **Butler's Wharf.** An '80s development that is maturing gracefully, full of deluxe loft-style warehouse conversions and swanky new blocks. People flock here thanks partly to London's saint of the stomach, Sir Terence Conran (also responsible for high-profile central London restaurants Bibendum, Mezzo, and Quaglino's). He has given it his "Gastrodrome" of four restaurants, a vintner's, a deli, a bakery, and who knows what else by now.

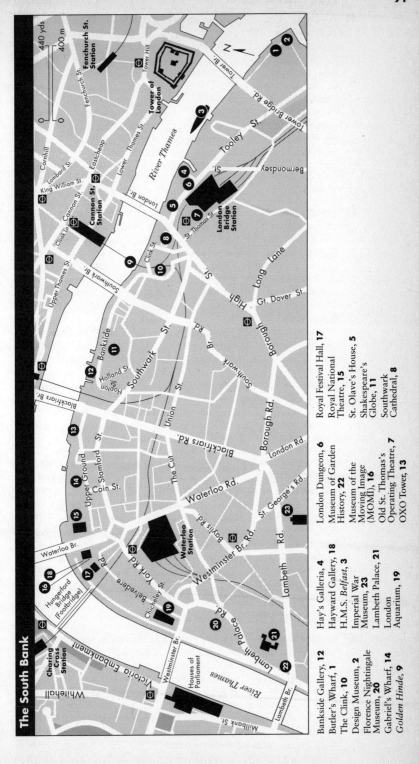

The South Bank

Bankside Gallery, **12**
Butler's Wharf, **1**
The Clink, **10**
Design Museum, **2**
Florence Nightingale
Museum, **20**
Gabriel's Wharf, **14**
Golden Hinde, **9**

Hay's Galleria, **4**
Hayward Gallery, **18**
H.M.S. *Belfast*, **3**
Imperial War
Museum, **23**
Lambeth Palace, **21**
London
Aquarium, **19**

London Dungeon, **6**
Museum of Garden
History, **22**
Museum of the
Moving Image
(MOMI), **16**
Old St. Thomas's
Operating Theatre, **7**
OXO Tower, **13**

Royal Festival Hall, **17**
Royal National
Theatre, **15**
St. Olave's House, **5**
Shakespeare's
Globe, **11**
Southwark
Cathedral, **8**

🔟 **The Clink.** Originally the prison attached to Winchester House, palace of the Bishops of Winchester until 1626, the name "the clink" still serves as a general term for jail. One of five Southwark prisons, it was the first to detain women, most of whom were "Winchester Geese"—another euphemism the bishops donated to the language, meaning prostitutes. The oldest profession was endemic in Southwark, especially around the bishops' area of jurisdiction, known as "The Liberty of the Clink." Their graces' sensible solution was to license prostitution rather than ban it, but a Winchester goose who flouted the rules ended up, of course, in the Clink. Now there is a museum tracing the history of prostitution in "the Liberty"—complete with an "R"–rated section— and showing what the Clink was like during its 16th-century prime. ✉ *1 Clink St.,* ☎ *0171/403–6515.* ᛒ *£3.50.* ⊘ *Daily 10–6. Tube: London Bridge.*

② **Design Museum.** The first museum in the world to elevate the everyday design we take for granted to the status of art exhibit, placing it in its social and cultural context, opened in 1989. On the top floor, the Collection traces the evolution of mass-produced goods, with showcases full of telephones and washing machines, plates and hi-fi equipment, computers and Coke bottles, and plenty of back-up material from ads to films. Alongside the Collection, the regularly revamped Review looks deeply into a particular aspect of the consumer durable. Special exhibitions are held downstairs on the first floor, and there's also a program of lectures and events, as well as the very good Blueprint Café with its own river terrace. ✉ *Butler's Wharf,* ☎ *0171/403–6933.* ᛒ *£4.75.* ⊘ *Daily 10:30–5:30. Tube: Tower Hill, then walk across river.*

OFF THE   **DULWICH PICTURE GALLERY –** A really distinguished and loveable small
BEATEN PATH   gallery with important works by Rembrandt, Van Dyck, Rubens, Poussin, and Gainsborough, among others. Anyone who fell in love with Sir John Soane's house (☞ Bloomsbury and Legal London, *above*) may wish to make the trek out here, since this gallery was designed by the same architect. If you do come all this way, you'll be happy to know that Dulwich Village itself is pleasant for wandering about in, and has handsome 18th-century houses strung out along its main street. Most of the land around here belongs to the local, famous school, the Dulwich College Estate, founded during the early 17th century by the actor Edward Alleyn, and this keeps strict control of modern development. This corner of southeast London's most famous resident, you might say, also kept strict control of modern development during the Eighties: it was Baroness Thatcher. Opposite the Gallery, Dulwich Park is a well-kept municipal park with a particularly fine display of rhododendrons in late May. ✉ *College Rd.,* ☎ *0181/693-8000.* ᛒ *£2, free Fri.* ⊘ *Tues.–Fri. 10-1 and 2-5, Sat. 11-5, Sun. 2-5. British Rail: Dulwich (from Victoria or London Bridge).*

⓴ **Florence Nightingale Museum.** Here you can learn all about the founder of the first school of nursing, that most famous of nursing reformers, "The Lady with the Lamp." See the reconstruction of the barracks ward at Scutari (Turkey), where she tended soldiers during the Crimean War (1854–56) and earned her nickname; here is also a Victorian East End slum cottage showing what she did to improve living conditions among the poor; and here is The Lamp. The museum is in **St. Thomas's Hospital,** which was built in 1868, to the specifications of Florence Nightingale. Most of it was bombed to bits in the Blitz, then rebuilt to become one of London's teaching hospitals. ✉ *2 Lambeth Palace Rd.,* ☎ *0171/620-0374.* ᛒ *£2.50.* ⊘ *Tues.–Sun. 10-4. Tube: Waterloo, or Westminster and walk over bridge.*

⑭ **Gabriel's Wharf.** A dinky marketplace of shops and cafés, where about 15 designers sell jewelry, ceramics, toys, etc., and where a three-month-long festival is held in summer. It's part of a (fairly) new development of an entirely different character from the surrounding business behemoths. Coin Street Community Builders, as the name suggests, is a nonprofit action group formed by local residents in the mid-'70s to create family housing and public spaces out of land that would otherwise have gone to commercial developers. You can see the human-scale homes and gardens they've already built since 1984, and adjacent Stamford Wharf, which is being converted into housing, performance spaces, crafts workshops, and restaurants. The nearby OXO building is London's favorite new place to hang out, featuring a restaurant-with-a-view, among other things.

NEED A BREAK? The second floor of the **OXO Tower** features a block-long café, full of colorful Arne Jacobson chairs and floor-to-ceiling river-view windows. It's a casual alternative to the swankier eighth-floor restaurant and brasserie.

❾ **Golden Hinde.** Sir Francis Drake circumnavigated the globe in this little galleon, or one just like it, anyway. This exact replica has now finished *its* 23-year round-the-world voyage—much of it spent along U.S. coasts both Pacific and Atlantic, and settled here to continue its educational purpose. ⊠ *St. Mary Overie Dock, Southwark,* ☎ *0171/403–0123.* ◷ *Daily 10–5. Tube: Mansion House.*

❹ **Hay's Galleria.** Hay's Wharf was built by Thomas Cubitt in 1857 on the spot where the port of London's oldest wharf had stood since 1651. It was known as "London's larder" on account of the edibles landed here until it wound down gradually, then closed in 1970. In 1987 it was reborn as this Covent Gardenesque parade of bars and restaurants, offices, and shops, all weatherproofed by an arched glass atrium roof supported by tall iron columns. The centerpiece is a fanciful kinetic sculpture by David Kemp, *The Navigators,* which looks like the skeleton of a pirate schooner crossed with a dragon and spouts water from various orifices. Inevitably, jugglers, string quartets, and crafts stalls abound. This courtyard hub of the developing London Bridge City needed all the help it could get in its early days, but it has settled in nicely now with its captive crowd of office workers from the adjacent new developments.

⑱ **Hayward Gallery.** This is one of the city's major art-exhibition spaces, its bias fixed firmly in this century. This stained and windowless bunker tucked behind the South Bank Centre concert halls has come in for the most flak of all the Thames-side buildings, enduring constant threats to flatten it and start again, but it's still here, topped by its multicolored neon tube sculpture, the most familiar feature on the South Bank skyline. ⊠ *South Bank Complex,* ☎ *0171/928–3144.* ⊠ *Admission varies according to exhibition.* ◷ *Thurs.–Mon. 10–6, Tues. and Wed. 10–8. Tube: Waterloo.*

❸ **HMS** *Belfast.* At 656 feet, this is one of the largest and most powerful cruisers the Royal Navy ever had. It played a role in the D-day landings off Normandy, left for the Far East after the war, and has been becalmed here since 1971. On board there's an outpost of the Imperial War Museum, which tells the Royal Navy's story from 1914 to the present and shows you what life on board a World War II battleship was like, from mess decks and bakery, punishment cells, and operations room to engine room and armaments. ⊠ *Morgan's La., Tooley St.,* ☎ *0171/407–6434.* ⊠ *£4.40.* ◷ *Mid-Mar.–Oct., daily 10–5:30; Nov.–mid-Mar., daily 10–4. Tube: London Bridge.*

OFF THE
BEATEN PATH

HORNIMAN MUSEUM – An educational museum of anthropology that manages to be fun too, set in 16 acres of gardens in south London with well-displayed ethnographic and natural history collections, a Music Gallery, and a colony of honey bees visibly at work in their glass-fronted hive. Other highlights are the aquarium stocked with endangered species and the new educationally oriented Centre for Understanding the Environment. ⊠ *100 London Rd., Forest Hill,* ☎ *0181/699–1872/2339.* ☜ *Free.* ⊙ *Mon.–Sat. 10:30–6, Sun. 2–6. British Rail: Forest Hill.*

㉓ Imperial War Museum. This national museum is housed in an elegant domed and colonnaded building, erected during the early 19th century to house the Bethlehem Hospital for the Insane, better known as the infamous Bedlam. By 1816, when the patients were moved here, they were no longer kept in cages to be taunted by tourists (see the final scene of Hogarth's *Rake's Progress* at Sir John Soane's Museum [☞ Bloomsbury and Legal London, *above*] for some sense of how horrific it was), since reformers—and George III's madness—had effected more humane confinement. Bedlam moved to Surrey in 1930.

Despite its title, this museum of 20th-century warfare does not glorify bloodshed but attempts to evoke what it was like to live through the two world wars. Of course, there is hardware for martial children—a Battle of Britain Spitfire, a German V2 rocket, tanks, guns, submarines—but there is an equal amount of war art (David Bomberg, Henry Moore, John Singer Sargent, Graham Sutherland, to name a few), poetry, photography, and documentary film footage. One very affecting exhibit is *The Blitz Experience,* which is what it sounds like—a 10-minute taste of an air raid in a street of acrid smoke with sirens blaring and searchlights glaring. More recent wars attended by British forces are thoughtfully commemorated, too, right up to the Gulf War of 1991. ⊠ *Lambeth Rd.,* ☎ *0171/416–5000.* ☜ *£4.50.* ⊙ *Daily 10–6. Tube: Lambeth North.*

㉑ Lambeth Palace. This has, for 800 years, been the London base of the Archbishop of Canterbury, top man in the Church of England. Much of the palace is hidden behind great walls, and even the Tudor gate house, visible from the street, is closed to the public, but you can stand here and absorb the historical vibrations echoing from such momentous events as the 1381 storming of the palace during the Peasants' Revolt against the poll tax (a modern version of which Thatcher recently reinstated, whereupon modern riots ensued, and the tax was sheepishly repealed), and the 1534 clash of wills when Thomas More refused to sign the Oath of Supremacy claiming Henry VIII (and not the pope) as leader of the English Church, for which he was sent to the Tower, and executed for treason the following year.

⑲ London Aquarium. Until recently, County Hall was the name of this curved, colonnaded neo-classical hulk, which took 46 years (1912–1958; two world wars interfered) to build, because it was home to London's local government, the Greater London Council (or GLC, which mutated out of the London County Council in 1965), until it disbanded in 1986. Since then the question of whether a new citywide governing body would enhance London has been a contentious issue. (It is the politicians who wrangle; most Londoners would like to have one.) Now, after a £25 million injection, a three-level aquarium has been installed, full of incongruous sharks and stingrays, educational exhibits and piscine sights previously unseen on these shores. No details about entrance charges were available at press time. Between here and the South Bank Centre is the former **Jubilee Gardens,** which is the site of the millennium Ferris wheel to be installed next year. Even without the 500-foot rotating elevation, views of the Houses of Parliament and Westminster Bridge are fine from here.

⑥ **The London Dungeon.** Here's the most gory, grisly, gruesome museum in town, where realistic waxwork people are subjected in graphic detail to all the historical horrors the Tower of London merely suggests. Tableaux depict famous bloody moments—like Anne Boleyn's decapitation, or the martyrdom of St. George—alongside the torture, murder, and ritual slaughter of more anonymous victims, all to a soundtrack of screaming, wailing, and agonized moaning. London's times of deepest terror—the Great Fire and the Great Plague—are brought to life, too, and so are its public hangings. And did you ever wonder what a disembowelment actually looks like? See it here. Children absolutely adore this place, which is among London's top tourist attractions; expect long lines. ✉ *28–34 Tooley St.,* ☎ *0171/403–0606.* ✉ *£7.95.* ✆ *Apr.–Sept., daily 10–5:30; Oct.–Mar., daily 10–4:30. Tube: London Bridge.*

㉒ **Museum of Garden History.** Housed in St. Mary's Church, next to Lambeth Palace, this museum was founded in 1977 (when the church was deconsecrated), by the Tradescant Trust. The Trust is named after John Tradescant (c. 1575–1638), botanist extraordinaire, who brought to these shores the lilac, larch, jasmine, and spiderwort, named Tradescantia in his honor. In the nave are changing horticultural exhibitions, supplemented by a reconstructed—or regrown—17th-century knot garden. Tradescant's tomb in the graveyard is carved with scenes from his worldwide plant-discovery tours and surrounded with the plants he discovered. Near it, William Bligh, captain of the *Bounty,* is buried, which suits the theme—the *Bounty* was on a breadfruit-gathering mission in 1787 when the crew mutinied. ✉ *Lambeth Palace Rd.,* ☎ *0171/261–1891.* ✆ *Donations welcome.* ✆ *Weekdays 11–3, Sun. 10:30–5. Closed mid–Dec.–early Mar. Tube: Waterloo.*

⑯ **Museum of the Moving Image (MOMI).** This popular museum is attached to the **National Film Theatre** (or NFT) underneath Waterloo Bridge, whose two movie theaters boast easily the best repertory programming in London, favoring rare, obscure, foreign, silent, forgotten, classic, noir, or short films over blockbusters. There's a third theater in MOMI, but if you reckon you'll just have a quick look around before you catch a movie here, think again. MOMI may be the most fun of all London's museums, and you will get stuck for a couple of hours minimum. The main feature is a history of cinema from 4,000-year-old Javanese shadow puppets to Spielbergian special effects, and very good the displays are, too, but the supporting program is even better, and it stars *you.* Actors dressed as John Wayne or Mae West, or usherettes, or chorus girls pluck you out of obscurity to read the TV news or audition for the chorus line or fly like Superman over the Thames. They also perform, mime, improvise, and generally bring celluloid to life, while all around, various screens show clips from such epoch-making giants as Hitchcock and Eisenstein, plus newsreels and ads. Techies can learn focus-pulling and satellite beaming; artists can try animation; eggheads can explore such ethical issues as censorship and documentary objectivity. Needless to say, this is always a big hit with kids. The White Card is accepted. ✉ *South Bank Centre,* ☎ *0171/401–2636.* ✆ *£5.95.* ✆ *Daily 10–6, last admission at 5. Tube: Waterloo.*

NEED A
BREAK?

The **NFT restaurant and cafeteria**—especially the big wooden tables outside—are popular for lunch or supper. You don't have to buy a membership.

❼ Old St. Thomas's Operating Theatre. All that remains of one of England's oldest hospitals, which stood here from the 12th century until the railway forced it to move in 1862, this was where women went under the knife. The theater was bricked up and forgotten for a century but has now been restored into an exhibition of early 19th-century medical practices: the operating table onto which the gagged and blindfolded patients were roped, the box of sawdust underneath for catching their blood, the knives, pliers, and handsaws the surgeons wielded, and—this was a theater in the round—the spectators' seats. Next door is a sweeter show: the **Herb Garret,** with displays of medicinal herbs used during the same period. ✉ *9A St. Thomas St.,* ☏ *0171/955–4791.* ▣ *£2.50.* ☼ *Tues.–Sun. 10–4. Closed Dec. 15–Jan. 5. Tube: London Bridge.*

⑬ OXO Tower. This might very well turn out to be the 21st century version of Big Ben—a wonderful Art Deco tower, dazzlingly adorned with a neon logo, overlooking the Thames. Long a London landmark to the cognoscenti, the OXO has graduated from its former incarnations as power generating station and warehouse into a vibrant community of artists' and designers' workshops, a pair of restaurants and cafés, as well as five floors of the best low-income housing in the city, via a £20 million plan by Coin Street Community Builders (the people behind Gabriel's Wharf; ☞ *above*). There's a rooftop viewing gallery for the latest river vista in town, and a Performance area on the ground (first) floor, which comes alive all summer long—as does the entire surrounding neighborhood. All the designer/makers have been selected by totally non-democratic methods, meaning that the work is of incredibly high standard. They all rely on you to disturb them any time they're open. Don't be shy—they really mean it; visitors are most welcome, whether buying, commissioning, or just browsing. The biggest draw remains the OXO Tower Restaurant—London's latest dining extravaganza (☞ Chapter 3). ✉ *Bargehouse St.,* ☏ *0171/401–3610.* ▣ *Free.* ☼ *Studios and shops Tues.–Sun. 11–6. Tube: Blackfriars or Waterloo.*

⑰ Royal Festival Hall. This is the largest auditorium of the South Bank Centre, with superb acoustics and a 3,000-plus capacity. It is the oldest of the riverside blocks, raised as the centerpiece of the 1951 Festival of Britain, a postwar morale-boosting exercise. The London Philharmonic resides here, symphony orchestras from the world over like to visit, and choral works, ballet, serious jazz and pop, and even film with live accompaniment are also staged. There is a multiplicity of foyers, with free rotating exhibitions, a good, independently run restaurant, the People's Palace, and a very good bookstore. The next building you come to also contains one medium and one small concert hall, the **Queen Elizabeth Hall** and the **Purcell Room,** respectively. Both offer predominantly classical recitals of international caliber, with due respect paid to 20th-century composers and the more established jazz and vocal artists.

⑮ Royal National Theatre. Londoners generally felt the same way about this low-slung, multilayered block the color of heavy storm clouds, designed by Sir Denys Lasdun, when it opened in 1976, that they would feel a decade later about the far nastier Barbican (☞ The City, *above*). But whatever its merits or demerits as a landscape feature (and architects have subsequently given it an overall thumbs-up, while rejecting the derogatory-sounding term "Brutalist"), the Royal National Theatre—still abbreviated colloquially to the preroyal warrant "NT"—has wonderful insides.

There are three auditoriums in the complex. The biggest one, the **Olivier,** is named after Sir Laurence, chairman of the first building commission and first artistic director of the National Theatre Company, formed in 1962. (In between the first proposal of a national theater for Britain and the 1949 formation of that building commission, an entire century passed.) The **Lyttleton** theater, unlike the Olivier, has a traditional proscenium arch, while the little **Cottesloe** mounts studio productions and new work in the round. Interspersed with the theaters are various levels of foyer, where exhibitions are shown, bars and restaurants are frequented, and free entertainment is provided, and the whole place is lively six days a week. The Royal National Theatre Company does not rest on its laurels. It attracts many of the nation's top actors (Anthony Hopkins, for one, does time here) in addition to launching future stars. Because it is a repertory company, you'll have several plays to choose from even if your London sojourn is short, but, tickets or not, have a wander round, and catch the buzz. ⊠ *South Bank,* ☎ *0171/928–2252 box office, 0171/633–0880 tour.* ▨ *Tour £3.50.* ☉ *1-hr tour of theater backstage Mon.–Sat. at 10:15, 12:30, and 5:30; foyer Mon.–Sat. 10 AM–11 PM. Tube: Waterloo.*

❺ St. Olave's House. In the former Hay's Wharf offices, this is an exciting black-and-white-and-gold-striped Art Deco block built in 1931 by H. S. Goodhart-Rendel and named after the church it replaced. The shiny square edifice has far more style than the newer buildings around it, and quite puts them to shame. At the end of Tooley Street (difficult to see how, but the name is a corruption of St. Olave's) stands the 1972 version of **London Bridge.**

★ ⑪ Shakespeare's Globe. The fruit largely of the American actor and film director Sam Wanamaker's last two decades. Until he died in 1993, he worked ceaselessly to raise funds for this ambitious project, so appalled had he been that England lacked a center for the study and worship of the Bard of Bards. In addition to an exact replica of Shakespeare's open-roofed Globe Playhouse (built in 1599; incinerated in 1613), using authentic Elizabethan materials and craft techniques—green oak timbers joined only with wooden pegs and mortise and tendon joints; plaster made of lime, sand, and goat's hair; and the first thatched roof in London since the Great Fire—he planned a second, indoor theater, which is being built to a design of the 17th-century architect Inigo Jones. The whole thing stands 200 yards from the original Globe on the appropriate site of the 17th-century Davies Amphitheatre, admittedly more a bull-baiting, prize fighting sort of venue than a temple to the legitimate stage, but at least Samuel Pepys immortalized it in his diaries. The Globe is a celebration of the great bard's life and work, an actual rebirth of his "Great Wooden O" (see *Henry V*), where his plays are presented in natural light (and sometimes rain), to 1,000 people on wooden benches in the "bays," plus 500 "groundlings," standing on a carpet of filbert shells and clinker, just as they did nearly four centuries ago. For any theater buff, this stunning project is unmissable. (For further information *see* the Close-Up section "Shakespeare Lives!") ⊠ *New Globe Walk, Bankside,* ☎ *0171/928–6406,* ℻ *0171/401–8261.* ▨ *Exhibition £5.* ☉ *Daily 10–5; call for performance schedule. Tube: Mansion House, then walk across Southwark Bridge, or Blackfriars, then walk across Blackfriars Bridge.*

❽ Southwark Cathedral. Pronounced "*suth*-uck," this is the second-oldest Gothic church in London, next to Westminster Abbey, with parts dating from the 12th century. Although it houses some remarkable memorials, not to mention a program of lunchtime concerts, it is little

SHAKESPEARE LIVES!

REBIRTH OF THE GLOBE THEATRE

AS IT IS SAID ABOUT THE one true church, Britain's theater is also founded on a rock—the enduring Shakespeare. Stratford-upon-Avon remains the primary shrine, but 1997 has welcomed the opening of the cathedral—London's new Globe Theatre. More than three centuries ago, the Puritans closed the first "Wooden O," for which venue Shakespeare wrote *Hamlet, King Lear, Julius Caesar,* among other peerless dramas. Now, 350 years later, the most famous playhouse in the world has been lovingly re-created, down to its Norfolk-reed roof. The theater has been reconstructed just 200 yards from its original site—ground as holy to Shakespeare's followers as Bayreuth's is to Wagnerophiles.

For sheer drama—literally—few things can top the memorable jolt of walking into the new Globe. Enter, and some Wellsian genie transports you back to Elizabethan England. Step past the entrance into a soaring 45-foot-high arena, made surprisingly intimate by three half-timbered galleries picturesquely encircling the stage. Ahead of you is the "pit," or orchestra level, filling up with 500 standees—or "groundlings," to use the historic term—massed in front of the high stage. Soaring overhead is a twin-gabled stage canopy—the "heavens"—framed by exquisitely painted *trompe l'oeil* marble columns and a "lords' gallery," all fretted with gilded bosses, painted planets, and celestial bodies. Above you is the lowering London sky, which may at any time provide an authentic midperformance drenching!

Of course, the new Globe is not a perfect time capsule. Occasionally, Juliet's wherefores will have to compete with the roar of jets. Ladies no longer proffer oranges or stools, and yesteryear's magpie hats have been superseded by Ray-bans and baseball caps. Some ground rules have also changed. Most performances begin in the afternoon and, while flood lighting will be used to illuminate the theater at dusk, there will be no spotlights to focus the action on stage. The audience, on view at all times, becomes as much a part of the theatrical proceedings as the actors onstage. Elizabethans made theatergoing almost as blood-and-thunder an experience as a football match of today. You've heard of the Super Bowl: view this as the Shakespeare Bowl—go ahead and boo Iago or hiss Macbeth; you'll have plenty of company.

The Globe Theatre is but one facet of the entire complex, which, when completed in 1999, will include the 300-seat Inigo Jones indoor theater (to be used year-round, unlike the open-air Globe, which will be open only from June to September), a restaurant, an education center (with wonderful classes and lectures year-round), a library and shop, and the largest Shakespearean exhibition in the world. The plan is to present four plays each season in a If-this-is-Tuesday-it-must-be-*Coriolanus* repertory. Happily, even when the Globe is not open for performances, a guided tour will always include its interior—a perfect opportunity to try out your "Friends, Romans, Countrymen!"

In case you want to see the world.

At American Express, we're here to make your journey a smooth one. So we have over 1,700 travel service locations in over 120 countries ready to help. What else would you expect from the world's largest travel agency?

do more

http://www.americanexpress.com/travel

Travel

In case you want to be welcomed there.

We're here to see that you're always welcomed at establishments everywhere. That's why millions of people carry the American Express® Card – for peace of mind, confidence, and security, around the world or just around the corner.

do more

Cards

And just in case.

We're here with American Express® Travelers Cheques and Cheques *for Two*.® They're the safest way to carry money on your vacation and the surest way to get a refund, practically anywhere, anytime.

Another way we help you...

do more

Travelers Cheques

visited. It was promoted to cathedral status only in 1905, before that having been the priory church of **St. Mary Overie** (as in "over the water"—on the South Bank). Look for the gaudily renovated 1408 tomb of the poet John Gower, friend of Chaucer, and for the Harvard Chapel. Another notable buried here is Edmund Shakespeare, brother of William.

CHELSEA AND BELGRAVIA

Chelsea is where J. M. W. Turner painted his sunsets, John Singer Sargent his society portraits, where Oscar Wilde wrote *The Importance of Being Earnest,* and Mary Quant created her first miniskirt. Today, Chelsea is a neighborhood as handsome as its real estate is costly. Strolling its streets you will often notice gigantic windows adorning otherwise ordinary houses. They are remnants of Chelsea's 19th-century bohemian days when they once served to light artists' studios; now, they are mostly used to hike property values a few notches higher. This is the place—especially the King's Road—that gave birth to Swinging '60s London, then to '70s punk youth culture. The '90s version of this colorful thoroughfare is not really the center of anything, but it's hard not to like walking it.

Chelsea's next-door neighborhood is aristocratic Belgravia, with King's Road and Knightsbridge its southern and northern borders, Sloane Street and Grosvenor Place its western and eastern ones, and vast Belgrave Square, home to many embassies, in the middle. Diagonally across the square, Belgrave Place will lead past grand mansions (all painted Wedgwood-white to denote they, as every other house in this district, are the property of England's richest landowners, the Dukes of Westminster) through to Eaton Square, the aptly chosen locale for the TV series, *Upstairs, Downstairs.* It is no accident that this whole neighborhood of wealth and splendor is grouped around the back of Buckingham Palace—many titled peers wished to live adjacent to the Court. Belgravia is relatively young: It was built between the 1820s and the 1850s by the builder-developer-entrepreneur Thomas Cubitt (who had as great an influence on the look of London in his day as Wren and Nash had in theirs), under the patronage of Lord Grosvenor, and was intended to rival Mayfair for spectacular snob value and expense. Today it still does.

Numbers in the text correspond to numbers in the margin and on the Chelsea and Belgravia map.

A Good Walk

Start at **Cheyne Walk** ①, stretching in both directions from Albert Bridge, going all the way west to see the statue of Thomas More, then doubling back for a left turn into Cheyne Row to reach **Carlyle's House** ②. Where the east end of Cheyne Walk runs into Royal Hospital Road, you'll find the **Chelsea Physic Garden** ③, while a right after the garden on Royal Hospital Road brings you to the **National Army Museum** ④. Royal Hospital Road takes its name from the institution next door to the museum, the magnificent **Royal Hospital** ⑤. A left turn from here up Franklin's Row and Cheltenham Terrace brings you to famous **King's Road** ⑥, which you could follow east until you reach the beginning of Belgravia: Sloane Square, named after Sir Hans Sloane, whose collection founded the British Museum (☞ Bloomsbury and Legal London, *above*), and who bought the manor of Chelsea in 1712. Cross the square more or less in a straight line, and follow Cliveden Place for a taste of Belgravia. The grand, white-stucco houses have changed not at all since the mid-19th century, and Eaton Square, which you'll soon come upon, remains such a desirable address that the rare event of one of its houses coming on the market makes all the property pages. Its most famous residents were fictional, of course, as the enduringly popular period soap, *Upstairs, Downstairs,* was set here. A left turn on **Belgrave Place** ⑦ brings you to Belgrave Square, dense with embassies, but the best thing to do around here is follow your nose. Other than Palladian-perfect mansions, chic alleys, and magnificent Georgian squares—in addition to Belgrave and Eaton, the smaller Lowndes, Cadogan, Trevor, Brompton, and Montpelier—there are no particular Belgravia sights.

TIMING

This may read like a short hop, but the walk above covers a good 2 to 3 mi. If you explore side streets, you could double the figure—and if you don't explore side streets, you'll be missing the best aspect of these neighborhoods, which are primarily, expensively, residential. The sights along the way will probably detain you less than the shops; even though King's Road ain't what it used to be, it's still fruitful. In summer you'll want to spend time in the Physic Garden or around the Royal Hospital, so make sure you're heading out on one of the opening days. If you're dead set on the Physic Garden, that means Wednesday or Sunday afternoon, April to October.

HOW TO GET THERE

Chelsea is notoriously ill served by tube stops. The best, and really the only, way into the area is to get the District and Circle line to Sloane Square, then strike out by foot along the King's Road. Or catch a bus—Nos. 11, 19, 22, 137, or 211. Farther down toward the river, around World's End and Fulham, the 19, 49, 239, 249, 319, and 345 are the buses to look for. The edge of Belgravia farthest from Chelsea is accessible from Hyde Park Corner on the Piccadilly Line. Nos. 2, 8, 9, 10, 14, 16, 19, 22, 36, 38, 52, 73, 74, 82, and 137 buses also stop there. Choose a bus that appears on both lists for travel between the two neighborhoods.

Sights to See

❼ **Belgrave Place.** One of the main arteries of Belgravia—London's swankiest neighborhood—Belgrave Place is lined with grand, imposing Regency-era mansions (now mostly embassies). Walk down this street toward Eaton Place to pass two of Belgravia's most beautiful mews—Eaton Mews North and Eccleston Mews, both fronted by grand Westminster-white rusticated entrances right out of a 19th-century engraving: There are few other places where London is both so picturesque and elegant.

❷ **Carlyle's House.** Carlyle's house was a thriving salon of 19th-century authors attracted by the fame of Thomas Carlyle (who wrote a then-blockbuster, since all-but-forgotten history of the French Revolution, and founded the London Library), and by the wit of his wife, the poet Jane Carlyle. Dickens, Thackeray, Tennyson, and Browning were regular visitors, and you can see the second-floor drawing room where they met just as they saw it, complete with leather armchair, decoupage screen, fireplace, and oil lamps, all in ruddy Victorian hues. ⊠ *24 Cheyne Row,* ☎ *0171/352–7087.* 🎟 *£3.* ☉ *Apr.–Oct., Wed.–Sun. 11–5 (last admission 4:30). Tube: Sloane Square, then walk down King's Rd., or take Bus 11, 19, 22, 49, 219, or 249.*

❸ **Chelsea Physic Garden.** First planted by the Society of Apothecaries in 1673 for the study of medicinal plants, these gardens are still in use for the same purpose today. The herbs and shrubs and flowers, planted to a strict plan but tumbling rurally over the paths nevertheless, are interspersed with woodland areas, England's first rock garden, and an-

Chelsea and Belgravia

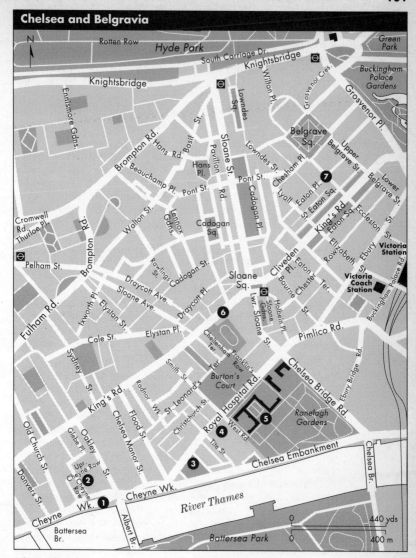

Belgrave Place, **7**
Carlyle's House, **2**
Chelsea Physic
Garden, **3**
Cheyne Walk, **1**
King's Road, **6**
National Army
Museum, **4**
Royal Hospital, **5**

cient trees, some of which were tragically uprooted in a 1987 hurricane. In the middle stands a statue of Sir Hans Sloane, physician to Queen Anne and George II, whose collection formed the basis of the British Museum, and who saved the garden from closure in 1722, making sure nobody would ever be allowed to build over it. ⊠ *Swan Walk, 66 Royal Hospital Rd.,* ☎ *0171/352–5646.* ▣ *£3.50.* ☉ *Apr.–Oct., Sun. and Wed. 2–5; daily noon–5 during Chelsea Flower Show (3rd wk of May). Tube: Sloane Square, then walk down King's Rd., or take Bus 11, 19, 22, 49, 219, or 249.*

★ ❶ **Cheyne Walk.** Rhyming with "rainy," this street features some beautiful Queen Anne houses (particularly Norman Shaw's ornamental 1876 Cheyne House, to the right off Albert Bridge) and a storm of Blue Plaques marking famous ex-residents' abodes. George Eliot died at No. 4 in 1880; Dante Gabriel Rossetti annoyed the neighbors of No. 16 with his peacock collection (there's still a clause in the lease banning the birds); at Carlyle Mansions (after the King's Head and Eight Bells pub), Henry James died, and T. S. Eliot and Ian Fleming lived. The western reaches was painters' territory, most notably James McNeill Whistler, who lived at No. 96 and then No. 101, and J. M. W. Turner, who used No. 119 as a retreat, shielding his identity behind the name Admiral "Puggy" Booth. Also toward the western end, outside the Church of All Saints, is a golden-faced statue of **Thomas More** (who wouldn't sign the Oath of Supremacy at Lambeth Palace in 1534 and was executed as a traitor), looking pensive and beatific on a throne facing the river, in a 1969 addition to the Walk.

❻ **King's Road.** This was where the miniskirt strutted its stuff in the '60s and where Vivienne Westwood and Malcolm McLaren clothed the Sex Pistols in bondage trousers from their shop, Sex, in 1975, thus spawning punk rock. Westwood, one of Britain's most innovative fashion stars, still has her shop at No. 430, where the road kinks. Both boutique and neighborhood are called **World's End,** possibly because Chelsea-ites believe that's what it does here. The Fulham district begins around this stretch, full of yuppie singles, and ever more shopping opportunities. The other end of King's Road, leading into Sloane Square, has various fashion stores (no longer style-setters, on the whole) and some rather good antiques shops and markets along the way. The **Pheasantry** at No. 152 is recognizable by some over-the-top Grecian statuary in a fancy portico. Named in its mid-19th-century pheasant-breeding days, it had a phase from 1916 to 1934 as a ballet school where Margot Fonteyn and Alicia Markova learned first position. Now it's a club-restaurant haunted by the braying breed of Chelsea yuppie, dubbed "Sloane Rangers" by '80s style-watchers. The Peter Jones department store marks the exit from the north of Chelsea and the beginning of Belgravia: Sloane Square.

❹ **National Army Museum.** This museum covers the history of British land forces from the Yeoman of the Guard (the first professional army, founded 1485 and ancestors of the Tower's Beefeaters) to the present. It is best explained in its newest exhibit, entitled The Rise of the Redcoat, which takes you from Henry V (1413–1422) all the way to George III (1760–1820). A great deal of effort is made to convey the experience of those who lived through the wars, and a visit should enhance anyone's grasp of London's history and its personages. ⊠ *Royal Hospital Rd.,* ☎ *0171/730–0717.* ▣ *Free.* ☉ *Mon.–Sat. 10–5:30, Sun. 2–5:30. Tube: Sloane Square.*

❺ **Royal Hospital.** The hospice for elderly and infirm soldiers was founded by Charles II in 1682—some say after a badgering from his soft-hearted, high-profile mistress, Nell Gwynn, but more probably as an act of expedience—his troops had hitherto enjoyed not so much as a meager pension and were growing restive after the civil wars of 1642–46 and 1648. Charles wisely appointed the great architect of burned-out City churches, Sir Christopher Wren, to design this small village of redbrick and Portland stone, set in manicured gardens (which you can visit) surrounding the "Figure Court"—named after the 1692 bronze figure of Charles II dressed up as a Roman soldier—and the Great Hall (dining room) and chapel. The latter is enhanced by the choir stalls of Grinling Gibbons (who did the bronze of Charles, too), the former by a vast oil of Charles on horseback by Antonio Verrio, and both are open to inspection.

No doubt you will run into some of the 400-odd residents. Despite their advancing years, these "Chelsea Pensioners" are no shrinking violets. In summer and for special occasions they sport dandy scarlet frock coats with gold buttons, breastfuls of medals, and natty tricorne hats, and, being of proven good character (a condition of entry, along with old age and loyal service), might offer to show you around—in which case you may wish to supplement their daily beer and tobacco allowance with a tip.

May is the big month at the Royal Hospital. The 29th is Oak Apple Day, when the pensioners celebrate Charles II's birthday by draping oak leaves on his statue and parading around it in memory of a hollow oak tree that expedited the king's miraculous escape from the 1651 Battle of Worcester. In the same month the Chelsea Flower Show, the year's highlight for thousands of garden-obsessed Brits, is also held here. ⊠ *Royal Hospital Rd.*, ☎ *0171/730–0161.* ☞ *Free.* ☉ *Apr.–Sept., Mon.–Sat. 10–noon and 2–4, Sun. 2–4; Oct.–Mar., Mon.–Sat. 10–noon and 2–4. Tube: Sloane Square.*

KNIGHTSBRIDGE, KENSINGTON, AND HOLLAND PARK

Princess Diana may have been "Throne Out" of the Windsor family, but she still lives here in Kensington Palace, an abode that is still stuffed with some favorite real royals. South and west of this historic edifice, you'll find this to be the stamping grounds of the Sloane Rangers—a quintessentially London type of gilded youth who have upper-class accents that make English sound like a foreign language. The most common example is "yah" said with a drawl, and meaning "yes." They tend to haunt salubrious Knightsbridge, east of Belgravia and north of Chelsea, offering as it does about equal doses of elite residential streets and ultra-shopping opportunities. To *its* east is one of the highest concentrations of important artifacts anywhere, the "museum mile" of South Kensington, with the rest of Kensington offering peaceful strolls and a noisy main street. The Holland Park neighborhood is worth visiting for its big, fancy, tree-shaded houses and its exquisite and unexpected park.

Kensington first became the *Royal* Borough of Kensington (and Chelsea) by virtue of a king's asthma. William III, who suffered terribly from the Thames mists over Whitehall, decided in 1689 to buy Nottingham House in the rural village of Kensington so that he could breathe more easily; besides, his wife and co-monarch, Mary II, felt confined by water and wall at Whitehall. Courtiers and functionaries and society folk soon followed where the crowns led, and by the time Queen Anne was on the throne (1702–14), Kensington was overflowing. In a way, it still is, because most of its grand houses, and the later, Victorian ones of

Holland Park, have been divided into apartments, or else are serving as foreign embassies.

Numbers in the text correspond to numbers in the margin and on the Knightsbridge, Kensington, and Holland Park map.

A Good Walk

This is an all-weather walk—museums and shops for rainy days, grass and strolls for sunshine. When you surface from the Knightsbridge tube station—one of London's deepest—you are immediately engulfed by the manic drivers, professional shoppers, and ladies-who-lunch who comprise the local population. If you're in a shopping mood, start with Harvey Nichols—right at the tube—and its six floors of total fashion. Sloane Street, leading south, is strung with the boutiques of big-name European designers, while **Harrods** ① is found to the west down Brompton Road—then continue west down this road, pausing at Beauchamp ("Bee-chum") Place and Walton Street if shopping is your intention. Presently, at the junction of Brompton and Cromwell roads, you'll come to the pale, Italianate **Brompton Oratory** ②, which marks the beginning of museum territory, with the **Victoria and Albert** ③ first, at the start of Cromwell Road, the **Natural History Museum** ④ next, and the **Science Museum** ⑤ behind it. (The neighborhood's three large museums, incidentally, can also be reached via a long underground passage from the South Kensington tube.) Turn left to continue north up Exhibition Road, a kind of unfinished cultural main drag that was Prince Albert's conception (the **National Sound Archive** ⑥ is here, among others), toward the road after which British moviemakers named their fake blood, Kensington Gore, to reach the giant, round Wedgwood china–box of the **Royal Albert Hall** ⑦, the scaffolding-shrouded **Albert Memorial** ⑧ opposite, and the **Royal College of Art** ⑨ next door.

Now follow **Kensington Gardens** (which is what this western neighbor of Hyde Park is called) west to its end, and a little farther, perhaps detouring into the Park to see **Kensington Palace** ⑩ and, behind it, one of London's rare private roads, "Millionaires' Row," **Kensington Palace Gardens** ⑪. Turn off Kensington High Street down little Derry Street, with the offices of London's local paper, the *Evening Standard*, on the left, and what was once Derry and Tom's department store—it closed down in the '70s—on the right. (The best feature of the store was its magical roof garden, complete with palm trees, ponds, and flamingoes; it's still there, now part of a nightclub owned by Richard Branson, the high-profile London figure also responsible for the Virgin Megastores, Virgin Atlantic Airways, etc.) Take a turn around peaceful **Kensington Square** ⑫, then, returning to the High Street, either follow Kensington Church Street up to Notting Hill Gate—with the little 1870 St. Mary Abbots Church on its southwest corner and a cornucopia of expensive antiques in its shops all along the way—or take the longer, scenic route.

Turn left off Kensington Church Street into Holland Street, admiring the sweet 18th-century houses (Nos. 10, 12–13, and 18–26 remain). As you cross Hornton Street you'll see to your left an orange-brick 1970s building, the Kensington Civic Centre (donor of parking permits, home of the local council), and Holland Street becomes the leafy Duchess of Bedford's Walk, with Queen Elizabeth College, part of London University, on the right. Turn left before Holland Park into Phillimore Gardens (perhaps detouring east into Phillimore Place to see No. 44, where Kenneth Grahame, author of *The Wind in the Willows*, lived from 1901 to 1908), then left again into Stafford Terrace to reach **Linley Sambourne House** ⑬. Step back to the High Street, and turn right. Past the gates of the park is the **Commonwealth Institute** ⑭, which you could explore before entering **Holland Park** ⑮. Exit the park at the gate by the tennis courts (near the Orangery) onto Ilchester Place, follow Melbury Road a few yards, and turn right onto Holland Park Road to reach **Leighton House** ⑯. Late last century, Melbury Road was a veritable colony of artists, though the Victorian muse they followed failed to appeal to later sensibilities, and they're now an obscure bunch—excepting Dickens's illustrator, Marcus Stone, who had No. 8 built in 1876. From here you could turn right onto Addison Road to see the Technicolor tiles rioting over Sir Ernest Debenham's "Peacock House" at No. 8 (he founded the eponymous Oxford Street department store). If you continue north, you reach the plane tree–lined Holland Park Avenue, main thoroughfare of an expensive residential neighborhood which provides more pleasant strolling territory, if you feel you haven't walked enough.

TIMING

This walk is at least 4 mi long, and is almost impossible to achieve without going inside somewhere. The best way to approach these neighborhoods is to treat Knightsbridge shopping and the South Kensington museums as separate days out—though you may find all three of the museums too much to take in at once. The rest of the tour works as a scenic walk on a fine day, because the places to see—Leighton and Linley Sambourne houses, the Commonwealth Institute, and Kensington Palace—are less time-consuming than the V&A, Natural History, and Science museums. During "term time," those are populated by more or less orderly school parties during the week, while weekends and school vacations see them fill up with more random arrangements of children. The parks are best in the growing seasons—from the crocuses and daffodils of early spring through the tulips to the roses—and during fall, when the foliage show easily rivals New England's. Kensington Gardens closes its gates at sundown, though you can get into Holland Park later during the summer, thanks to the restaurant, and the Open Air Theatre.

HOW TO GET THERE

There are many tubes here, but which you choose will depend on which part you want. As a rule of thumb, the eponymous tube stop will be your best bet—Knightsbridge on the Piccadilly Line, Kensington High Street on District and Circle, and Holland Park on the Central Line. The best buses between Kensington High Street and Knightsbridge are Nos. 9, 10, and 52. From Kensington to Holland Park, get the 9, or the 27, 28, or 31.

Sights to See

❽ Albert Memorial. Seemingly permanently shrouded in the world's tallest free-standing web of scaffolding, the intricate structure housing this 14-foot bronze statue of Albert is undergoing a £14-million renovation (including a pure gold-leaf coat donated by an anonymous benefactor). The work is not due to be finished until the year 2000. Albert's grieving widow, Queen Victoria, had this elaborate confection erected on the spot where his Great Exhibition had stood a mere decade before his early death from typhoid fever in 1861.

❷ Brompton Oratory. This is a product of the English Roman Catholic revival of the late 19th century led by John Henry Cardinal Newman (1801–1890), who established this oratory in 1884 and whose statue you see outside. A then-unknown 29-year-old architect, Herbert Gribble, won the competition to design the place, an honor that you may assume went to his head when you see the vast, incredibly ornate interior. It is punctuated by treasures far older than the church itself, like the giant Twelve Apostles in the nave, carved from Carrara marble by

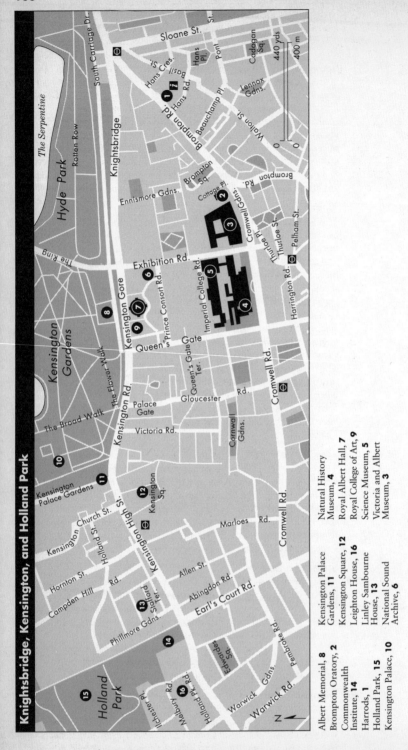

Knightsbridge, Kensington, and Holland Park

Albert Memorial, **8**
Brompton Oratory, **2**
Commonwealth
Institute, **14**
Harrods, **1**
Holland Park, **15**
Kensington Palace, **10**

Kensington Palace
Gardens, **11**
Kensington Square, **12**
Leighton House, **16**
Linley Sambourne
House, **13**
National Sound
Archive, **6**

Natural History
Museum, **4**
Royal Albert Hall, **7**
Royal College of Art, **9**
Science Museum, **5**
Victoria and Albert
Museum, **3**

Giuseppe Mazzuoli during the 1680s and brought here from Siena's cathedral.

🕒 ⑭ **Commonwealth Institute.** With its swimming-pool-blue walls and asymmetric copper tent roof, this museum is one of London's more eccentric structures. A tour of the interior is like a trip around the world, or at least around the 50 Commonwealth nations, with lifestyles and histories of other continents displayed. Education is an important part of the work done at this vibrant institute, which hosts a lot of music, art, and film events and the Disneyland-like simulator ride called "Wonders of the World." At press time, opening hours and admission charges were being revised. ✉ *230 Kensington High St.,* ☎ *0171/603–4535. Tube: High Street Kensington.*

🕒 ❶ **Harrods.** In case you didn't notice it, this well-known shopping mecca has its domed terra-cotta Edwardian bulk outlined in thousands of white lights by night. The 15-acre Egyptian-owned store's sales weeks are world-class, and the environment is as frenetic as a stock market floor; its motto, *Omnia, omnibus, ubique* ("everything, for everyone, everywhere") is not too far from the truth. Visit the pet department, a highlight for children, and don't miss the extravagant Food Hall, with its stunning Art Nouveau tiling in the neighborhood of meat and poultry and continuing on in the fishmongers' territory, where its glory is rivaled by displays of the sea produce itself. This is the place to acquire your green-and-gold souvenir Harrods bag, as food prices are surprisingly competitive.

NEED A
BREAK?
Patisserie Valerie (✉ 215 Brompton Rd., ☎ 0171/832–9971), just down the road from Harrods, offers light meals and a gorgeous array of pastries. It's perfect for breakfast, lunch, or tea.

🕒 ⑮ **Holland Park.** The former grounds of the Jacobean Holland House opened to the public only in 1952. Since then, many treats have been laid on within its 22 hectares. Holland House itself was nearly flattened by World War II bombs, but the east wing remains, now incorporated into a youth hostel and providing a fantastical stage for the April–September Open Air Theatre (box office, ☎ 0171/602–7856). The glass-walled Orangery also survived to host art exhibitions and wedding receptions, while next door, the former Garden Ballroom has become the Belvedere restaurant; nearby is a lovely café. From the Belvedere's terrace you see the formal Dutch Garden, planted by Lady Holland in the 1790s with the first English dahlias. North of that are woodland walks, lawns populated by peacocks and guinea fowl and the odd, awkward emu, a fragrant rose garden, great banks of rhododendrons and azaleas (which bloom profusely in May), a well-supervised children's Adventure Playground, and even a Japanese water garden, legacy of the 1991 London Festival of Japan. If that's not enough, you can watch cricket on the Cricket Lawn on the south side, or tennis on the several courts.

OFF THE
BEATEN PATH
KENSAL GREEN CEMETERY – Heralding itself as "London's first Necropolis," this west London cemetery was established in 1832 and beats the more famous Highgate for atmosphere, if only because it is less populous with the living. Within its 77 acres are more freestanding mausolea than in any other cemetery in Britain, some of them almost the size of small churches, and most of them constructed while their future occupants were still alive. Those who balked at burial but couldn't afford a mausoleum of their own could opt for a position in the catacombs, and these, with their stacks of moldering caskets, are a definite highlight for seekers of the macabre, though they can only be seen as part of a tour.

In the cemetery you will find the final resting places of the novelists Trollope, Thackeray, and Wilkie Collins; of the great engineer Isambard Kingdom Brunel (1806–1859); and of Decimus Burton, Victorian architect of the Athenaeum Club, the Wellington Arch, the Kew Gardens greenhouses, and many other bits of London you'll have just seen. ⊠ *Harrow Rd. W10,* ☎ *0181/969-0152.* 🖾 *Suggested donation £2.* ⊘ *Mon.–Sat. 9–5:30, Sun. 10–5:30 (times may vary Nov.–Feb., so call first); 2-hr guided tour (including catacombs) Mar.–Oct., weekends at 2:30, and Oct.–Feb., Sun. at 2; catacomb tour 1st Sun. of month (call for times). Tube: Kensal Green.*

🔟 **Kensington Palace.** This royal palace stands close to the western edge of Kensington Gardens. It did not enjoy a smooth passage as royal residence. Twelve years of renovation were needed before William and Mary could move in; it continued to undergo all manner of refurbishment during the next three monarchs' times. By coincidence, these monarchs happened to suffer rather ignominious deaths. First, William III fell off his horse when it stumbled on a molehill, and succumbed to pleurisy in 1702. Then, in 1714, Queen Anne (who, you may recall, was fond of brandy) suffered an apoplectic fit brought on by overeating. Next, George I, the first of the Hanoverian Georges, had a stroke as a result of "a surfeit of melons"—admittedly not at Kensington, but in a coach to Hanover, in 1727. Worst of all, in 1760, poor George II burst a blood vessel while on the toilet (the official line was, presumably, that he was on the throne).

The best-known royal Kensington story, though, concerns the 18-year-old Princess Victoria of Kent, who was called from her bed in June 1837, by the Archbishop of Canterbury and the Lord Chamberlain. Her uncle, William IV, was dead, they told her, and she was to be queen. The state rooms where Victoria had her ultrastrict upbringing have recently been renovated, a process which still continues, gradually restoring more of the fabulous Court Dress Collection to our sight. Meantime, the King's Apartments are the best part of the (compulsory) guided tour. Look out for Tintorettos and Van Dykes among the canvases; see the Mortlake tapestries commissioned by Charles I, and look at that ceiling in the cupola room: It appears domed but is actually as flat as a, well, ceiling. This palace is an essential stop for royalty vultures, because it's the only one where you may actually catch a glimpse of the real thing. Diana has an apartment here (watch for the white Audi), as well as Princess Margaret, the Duke and Duchess of Gloucester, and Prince and Princess Michael of Kent. Console yourself after striking out on the live princess count with tea in the Orangery—surely one of London's most civilized settings. ⊠ *Kensington Gardens,* ☎ *0171/937-9561.* 🖾 *£5.50.* ⊘ *May–Dec., daily 10–3:30. Tube: High Street Kensington.*

⓫ **Kensington Palace Gardens.** Starting behind Kensington Palace, this is one of London's rare private roads, guarded and gated both here and at the Notting Hill Gate end. If you walk it, you will see why it earned the nickname "Millionaires' Row"—it is lined with palatial whitestucco houses designed by a selection of the best architects of the mid-19th century. The novelist William Makepeace Thackeray, author of *Vanity Fair,* died in 1863 at No. 2—a building that now houses an embassy (Israeli), as do most of the others.

⓬ **Kensington Square.** Having been laid out around the time William moved to Kensington Palace up the road, this is one of London's most venerable squares. A few early 18th-century houses remain, with Nos. 11 and 12 the oldest.

NEED A
BREAK?

In Wright's Lane you'll find **The Muffin Man,** a cozy anachronism of a tea shop. Here waitresses in floral aprons serve toasted sandwiches, cream teas, and, yes, English muffins.

⓰ **Leighton House.** This was the home of Frederic Leighton—painter, sculptor, president of the Royal Academy. Endowed with a peerage by Queen Victoria, he unfortunately expired a month later. The prize room here is the incredible Arab Hall. George Aitchison designed this Moorish fantasy in 1879 to show off Leighton's valuable 13th- to 17th-century Islamic tile collection, and, adorned with marble columns, dome, and fountain, it is exotic beyond belief. The rest of the rooms are more conventionally, stuffily Victorian, but they do feature many paintings by Leighton, plus Edward Burne-Jones, John Millais, and other leading Pre-Raphaelites. ⊠ *12 Holland Park Rd.,* ☎ *0171/602–3316.* 🎫 *Free.* ⊙ *Mon.–Sat. 11–5. Tube: Holland Park.*

★ ⓭ **Linley Sambourne House.** During the 1870s, this was home to the political cartoonist Edward Linley Sambourne. It has been renovated by the Victorian Society to look as it did then, complete with William Morris wallpapers and illustrations from the (recently deceased) satirical magazine *Punch,* including many of Sambourne's own, adorning the walls. ⊠ *18 Stafford Terr.,* ☎ *0181/994–1019.* 🎫 *£3.* ⊙ *Mar.–Oct., Wed. 10–4, Sun. 2–5. Tube: High Street Kensington.*

☾ **London Toy & Model Museum.** Here are five floors of—yes—toys and models of all vintages from practically prehistoric (okay, AD Year One) to not yet born, in the case of the Whatever Next? gallery's displays. Two highlights are the minutely detailed working coal mine and cityscape with moving parts. ⊠ *21–23 Craven Hill,* ☎ *0171/262–9450.* 🎫 *£4.95.* ⊙ *Tues.–Sat. 10–5:30, Sun. 11–5:30.*

❻ **National Sound Archive.** In this aural outpost of the British Library, you may listen to the queen who made this neighborhood possible: The million recordings held here include one of Victoria speaking sometime in the 1880s, but you have to book in advance to hear her or anyone else. There's a small exhibit of early recording equipment and ephemera, too. ⊠ *29 Exhibition Rd.,* ☎ *0171/589–6603.* 🎫 *Free.* ⊙ *Weekdays 10–5 (Thurs. 10–9). Tube: South Kensington.*

☾ ❹ **Natural History Museum.** Architect Alfred Waterhouse had relief panels scattered across the outrageously ornate French Romanesque–style terra-cotta facade of this museum, depicting extant creatures to the left of the entrance, extinct ones to the right. Inside, that categorization is sort of continued in reverse, with Dinosaurs on the left and the Ecology Gallery on the right. Both these newly renovated exhibits (the former with life-size moving dinosaurs, the latter complete with moonlit "rain forest") make essential viewing in a museum that, realizing it was becoming crusty, has subsequently invested millions overhauling itself in recent years.

The Creepy Crawlies Gallery features a nightmarish superenlarged scorpion, yet ends up making tarantulas cute (8 out of 10 animal species, one learns here, are arthropods). Other wonderful bits include the Human Biology Hall, which you arrive at through a birth-simulation chamber; the full-size blue whale; and the moving dinosaur diorama (which is a bit too bloody for toddlers). The Earth Galleries are also unmissable, with ambitious exhibits about the structure of our planet: "The Power Within," "Restless Surface," and "Visions of the Earth." Understandably, this place usually resembles grade-school recess. The White Card is accepted. ⊠ *Cromwell Rd.,* ☎ *0171/938–9123.* 🎫 *£5.50, free weekdays 4:30–5:50 and weekends*

5–5:50. ⊙ Mon.–Sat. 10–5:50, Sun. 11–5:50. Tube: South Kensington.

❼ Royal Albert Hall. This domed, circular 8,000-seat auditorium (as well as the Albert Memorial, opposite) was made possible by the Victorian public, who donated funds for it. More money was raised, however, by selling 1,300 future seats at £100 apiece—not for the first night, but for every night for 999 years. (Some descendants of purchasers still use the seats.) The Albert Hall is best-known and best-loved for its annual July–September Henry Wood Promenade Concerts (the "Proms"), with bargain-price standing (or promenading, or sitting-on-the-floor) tickets sold on the night of the world-class classical concerts. London also enjoys the "Erics," when the rock guitarist Eric Clapton services adoring fans for 10 days here every February. ⊠ *Kensington Gore,* ☏ *0171/589–3203.* ▣ *Fee varies according to event. Tube: South Kensington.*

❾ Royal College of Art. Housed in a glass-dominated building designed by Sir Hugh Casson in 1973, the RCA provides great contrast with the Victoriana surrounding it, including the Albert Hall next door. Famous in the '50s and '60s for processing David Hockney, Peter Blake, and Eduardo Paolozzi, the college is still one of the country's foremost art schools, and there's usually an exhibition, lecture, or event here open to the public. ⊠ *Kensington Gore,* ☏ *0171/584–5020.* ▣ *Free.* ⊙ *Weekdays 10–6 (call to check times). Tube: South Kensington.*

☾ ❺ Science Museum. This, the third of the great South Kensington museums stands behind the Natural History Museum in a far plainer building. It features loads of hands-on exhibits, with entire schools of children apparently decanted inside to interact with them; but it is, after all, painlessly educational. Highlights include the Launch Pad gallery, which demonstrates basic scientific principles (try the beautiful plasma ball, where your hands attract "lightning"—if you can get them on it); the Computing Then and Now show, which gets the most crowded of all; *Puffing Billy,* the oldest train in the world; and the actual *Apollo 10* capsule. The White Card is accepted. ⊠ *Exhibition Rd.,* ☏ *0171/938–8000.* ▣ *£5.* ⊙ *Mon.–Sat. 10–6, Sun. 11–6. Tube: South Kensington.*

★ ❸ Victoria and Albert Museum. Recognizable by the copy of Victoria's Imperial Crown it wears on the lantern above the central cupola, this institution is always referred to as the V&A. It is a huge museum, showcasing the applied arts of all disciplines, all periods, all nationalities, and all tastes, and is a wonderful, generous place to get lost in, full of innovation and completely devoid of pretension. The collections are *so* catholic that confusion is a hazard—one minute you're gazing on the Jacobean oak 12-foot-square four-poster Great Bed of Ware (one of the V&A's most prized possessions, given that Shakespeare immortalized it in *Twelfth Night*); the next, you're in the 20th-century end of the equally celebrated Dress Collection, coveting a Jean Muir frock you could actually buy at nearby Harrods.

Prince Albert, Victoria's adored consort, was responsible for the genesis of this permanent version of the 1851 Great Exhibition, and his queen laid its foundation stone in her final public London appearance in 1899. From the start, the V&A had an important role as a research institution, and that role continues today, with many resources available to scholars, designers, artists, and conservators. Two of the latest are the Textiles and Dress 20th Century Reference Centre, with ingenious space-saving storage systems for thousands of bolts of cloth, and the Textile Study Galleries, which perform the same function for 2,000 years' worth of the past.

Follow your own whims around the 7 mi of gallery space, but try to reach the new and spectacular Glass Gallery, where a collection spanning four millennia is reflected between room-size mirrors, under young designer Danny Lane's breathtaking glass balustrade. The latest additions are the Raphael Galleries, where seven massive cartoons the painter completed in 1516 for his Sistine Chapel tapestries are housed, and the Silver Galleries, displaying six centuries of English silver. On Wednesdays, Late View continues—a kind of museum salon, with lectures and a wine bar. The White Card is accepted. ✉ *Cromwell Rd.,* ☎ *0171/938–8500.* ✇ *£5, free Thurs.–Tues. after 4:30.* ☉ *Mon. noon–5:50, Tues.–Sun. 10–5:50; call for Late View time. Tube: South Kensington.*

NEED A BREAK?	Rest your overstimulated eyes in the brick-walled **V&A café,** where full meals and small snacks are available, and where the Sunday Jazz Brunch (11–5), accompanied by live music and Sunday papers, is fast becoming a London institution.

HYDE PARK, KENSINGTON GARDENS, BAYSWATER, AND NOTTING HILL

The Royal Parks of Hyde Park and Kensington Gardens are among London's unique features: Great swathes of green in the middle of the city, where it really is possible to escape from London's fast-lane. The description "royal" is somewhat paradoxical, for today, these are the most democratic of places, where Londoners from all walks of life come to relax (and let off steam as soapbox orators). Although it's probably been centuries since any major royal had a casual stroll here, these parks remain the property of the Crown, and it was the Crown that saved them from being devoured by the city's late-18th-century growth spurt. North of the parks—which are separate entities, although the boundary is virtually invisible—lies Bayswater. The main drag, Queensway, expresses Bayswater's nature quite aptly: This is a neighborhood that looks fancy, with its grand white-stucco terraced houses and leafy squares, but is somewhat disreputable, as demonstrated by the 1963 Profumo sex scandal—involving a government minister, a teenage showgirl, and a Soviet naval attaché—which unfurled behind closed Bayswater doors and toppled a government (see the movie *Scandal* for the whole story). Farther northwest lies Notting Hill, a trendsetting square mile of multi-ethnicity, music, and markets, with lots of see-and-be-seen-in restaurants and the younger, more egalitarian, and adventurous versions of the Cork Street commercial modern-art galleries. The style-watching media dub the musician/novelist/filmbiz/drugdealer/fashion-victim local residents and hangers-out Notting Hillbillies. The whole thing has mushroomed around one of the world's great antiques markets, the Portobello Road.

Numbers in the text correspond to numbers in the margin and on the Hyde Park, Kensington, and Notting Hill map.

A Good Walk

Where else would you enter Hyde Park but at **Hyde Park Corner.** The most impressive of the many entrances is the Hyde Park Screen by Apsley House, usually called **Decimus Burton's Gateway** because it was he who designed this triple-arched monument in 1828. The next gate along to the north, a gaudy unicorns-and-lions-rampant number wrought in scarlet-, cobalt-white-, and gold-painted metal was a 90th-birthday gift to Elizabeth the Queen Mother (who is as old as the century), and is therefore the **Queen Mother's Gate.** Follow the southern perimeter along the sand track called **Rotten Row,** now used by the House-hold Cavalry, who live at the **Knightsbridge Barracks** to the left.

Follow Rotten Row west to the **Serpentine.** When you pass its **Bridge,** you leave Hyde Park, enter **Kensington Gardens,** and come to the **Serpentine Gallery.** En route to the formal garden at the end of the Long Water, **The Fountains,** you pass the statues of **Peter Pan,** and the horse and rider called **Physical Energy,** then continuing westward you reach the **Round Pond,** and **Kensington Palace.** Follow the Broad Walk north past the playground on the left, to the Bayswater Road leaving the park by Black Lion Gate, and you are almost opposite Queensway, a rather peculiar, cosmopolitan street of ethnic confusion, late-night cafés and restaurants, a skating rink, and the Whiteleys shopping-and-movie mall. Turn left at the end into Westbourne Grove, however, and you've entered Notting Hill, and will reach the famous **Portobello Road** after a few blocks. Turn left for the Saturday antiques market and shops; right to reach the Westway, and the flea market.

TIMING

This is a route that changes vastly on weekends. Saturday is Portobello Road's most fun day, so you may prefer to start at the end and work backward, using the parks as r&r from your shopping exertions. Ditto Fridays, if you're a flea market fan. Sundays, the Hyde Park and Kensington Gardens railings all along the Bayswater Road are hung with very bad art, which may slow your progress; also this is prime per-ambulation day for locals. Whatever your priorities, this is a long walk if you explore every corner, with the perimeter of the two parks alone covering a good 4 mi, and about half as far again around the re-mainder of the route. You could cut out a lot of park without missing out on essential sights, and walk the whole thing in a brisk three hours.

HOW TO GET THERE

For Hyde Park and Kensington Gardens, get off the Central Line at Queensway or Lancaster Gate, or enter the park from Hyde Park Cor-ner on the Piccadilly Line. If you want Portobello Market and envi-rons, the best tube stops are Ladbroke Grove or Westbourne Park (Hammersmith and City lines), then ask directions; the Notting Hill stop on the District, Circle, and Central lines is also an option. Buses for the area include Nos. 12, 70, and 94 for anything off the Bayswa-ter Road, or Nos. 27, 28, 31, and 52 for penetrating the depths of Not-ting Hill.

Sights to See

☙ **Hyde Park.** Along with the smaller St. James's and Green Parks to the east, Hyde Park started as Henry VIII's hunting grounds. He had no altruistic intent but more or less stole the land, for his pleasure, from the monks at Westminster at the 1536 Dissolution of the Monaster-ies. James I was more generous and allowed the public in at the be-ginning of the 17th century, as long as they were "respectably dressed." Nowadays, as summer visitors can see, you may wear whatever you like—a bathing suit will do. Along its south side runs **Rotten Row.** It was Henry VIII's royal path to the hunt—hence the name, a corrup-tion of *route du roi.* It's still used by the Household Cavalry, who live at the **Knightsbridge Barracks**—a high-rise and a long, low, ugly red block—to the left. This is the brigade that mounts the guard at the palace, and you can see them leave to perform this duty, in full regalia, plumed helmet and all, at around 10:30, or await the return of the exhausted ex-guard about noon.

☙ **Kensington Gardens.** More formal than neighboring Hyde Park, Ken-sington Gardens was first laid out as palace grounds. The paved Ital-

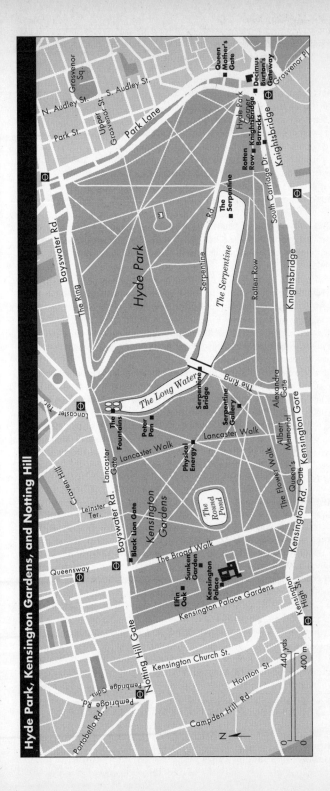

Hyde Park, Kensington Gardens, and Notting Hill

ian garden at the top of the Long Water, **The Fountains** is a reminder of this, though, of course **Kensington Palace** itself is the main clue to its royal status, with its early 19th-century Sunken Garden north of it, complete with a living tunnel of lime trees and golden laburnum. Several statues are worth looking out for: George Frampton's 1912 *Peter Pan* is a bronze of the boy who lived on an island in the Serpentine and never grew up, and whose creator, J. M. Barrie, lived at 100 Bayswater Road, not 500 yards from here. Southwest of Peter at the intersection of several paths is George Frederick Watts's 1904 bronze of a muscle-bound horse and rider, entitled *Physical Energy*. By the playground close to the Round Pond is the remains of a tree carved with scores of tiny woodland creatures, Ivor Innes's *Elfin Oak*. The **Round Pond** is a magnet for model-boat enthusiasts and duck feeders.

NEED A BREAK?	About halfway down Queensway (No. 127), **Maison Pechon** is a patisserie, but one that serves full English breakfasts, omelets, jacket potatoes, and salads alongside its French tarts, brioches, cream cakes, and cookies.

Portobello Road. Famous for its Saturday antiques market, this street begins at Notting Hill Gate, though the stalls start a couple of blocks north, around Chepstow Villas. They continue for about three blocks before giving way to fruit and vegetable stalls. Lining the sloping street are also dozens of antiques shops and indoor markets, open most days. Where the road levels off, around Elgin Crescent, youth culture and a vibrant neighborhood life kicks in, with all manner of interesting small stores and restaurants interspersed with the fruit and vegetable market. This continues to the Westway overpass ("flyover" in British), where London's best flea market (high-class, vintage, antique, and second-hand clothing; jewelry; and junk) happens Friday and Saturday, then on up to Goldbourne Road. There's a strong West Indian flavor to Notting Hill, with a Trinidad-style Carnival centered along Portobello Road on the August bank-holiday weekend. *Tube: Notting Hill Gate, Ladbroke Grove.*

Serpentine Gallery. A gallery influential on the trendy art circuit, this hangs several exhibitions of modern work a year, often very avant-garde indeed, and always worth a look. It overlooks the west bank of the **Serpentine**, a beloved lake, much frequented in summer, when the south shore Lido resembles a beach and the water is dotted with hired rowboats. Walk the bank and you will soon reach the picturesque, stone **Serpentine Bridge** built in 1826 by George Rennie, which marks the boundary between Hyde Park and Kensington Gardens. ✉ *Kensington Gardens,* ☎ *0171/402–6075.* 🎟 *Free.* ☉ *Daily 10–6. Closed Christmas wk. Tube: Lancaster Gate.*

NEED A BREAK?	The **tearoom** on the Serpentine is constantly changing hands, and always seems rather overpriced, but it does offer tea, coffee, and snacks in an overwhelming green setting.

REGENT'S PARK AND HAMPSTEAD

Regent's Park and Hampstead in north London contain some of the prettiest and most rural parts of the city, as well as fine architecture and some important historical sights. For the sheer pleasure of idle exploring they are hard to beat. All told, this section covers a large area. It starts from the Georgian houses superimposed on medieval Maryburne, continues around John Nash's Regency facades, and his park, stretches on into North London's canalside youth center, climbs up the hill to the city's prettiest, most expensive "village," and finishes, fittingly, at its most famous cemetery.

Marylebone Road (pronounced "Marra-le-bun") these days is remarkable mostly for its permanent traffic jam, some of it heading to Madame Tussaud's. At the east end is the first part of John Nash's impressive Regent's Park scheme, the elegantly curvaceous Park Crescent (1812–1818), which Nash planned as a full circus at the northern end of his ceremonial route from St. James's. Like most of the Nash houses around the park, it was wrecked during World War II, reconstructed, and rebuilt behind the repaired facade in the 1960s. Northeast of the park, Camden Town is the neighborhood that houses London's highest concentration of single people in their twenties.

The cliché about Hampstead is that it is just like a pretty little village—albeit one with designer shops, expensive French delicatessens, restaurants, cafés, cinemas, and so on. In fact, like so many London neighborhoods, Hampstead did start as a separate village, when plague-bedeviled medieval Londoners fled the city to this clean hilltop 4 mi away. By the 18th century its reputation for cleanliness had spread so far that its water was being bottled and sold to the hoi polloi down the hill as the Perrier of its day. That was the beginning of Hampstead's heyday as an artistic and literary retreat attracting many famous writers, painters, and musicians to its leafy lanes—as it still does today. Just strolling around here is rewarding: Not only are the streets incredibly picturesque, they also harbor some of London's best Georgian buildings.

Numbers in the text correspond to numbers in the margin and on the Regent's Park and Hampstead map.

A Good Walk

Begin at the tube station whose name will thrill the Sherlock Holmes fan: Baker Street—the **Sherlock Holmes Museum** ① is at 221B, of course. Turn left and follow the line of tour buses past **Madame Tussaud's** ② and the **London Planetarium,** then the end of Harley Street—an English synonym for private (as opposed to state-funded) medicine, because it is lined with the consulting rooms of the country's top specialist doctors—to Park Crescent and, across the street, **Regent's Park** ③. Enter along the Outer Circle, and turn left on Chester Road. Straight ahead are Queen Mary's Gardens, the Lake, and the **Regent's Park Open-Air Theatre** ④. Turn left onto the Broad Walk from Chester Road, look west past the mock-Tudor prefab tearoom for one of London's rare uninterrupted open vistas toward the London Central Mosque, then continue on to the **London Zoo** ⑤. From here, you can take a round-trip detour on the water bus and spy on the back gardens along the **Grand Union Canal** (which everyone calls the Regent's Canal) to Little Venice. Don't get *too* excited—the canal you're on (constructed 1812–1820) is the only one there is, but this peaceful little bit of London does have an atmosphere unique to it, with enormous white wedding-cake houses set back from the banks, and it's a good strolling location.

North of the zoo, cross Prince Albert Road to Primrose Hill, a high point (literally, at 206 feet), and the best place to be on the night of November 5, when London's biggest bonfire burns a Guy Fawkes effigy, and there's a spectacular fireworks display. Heading east from here (the easiest route is Regent's Park Rd.), then left down Parkway, past the **Jewish Museum** ⑥ brings you to the center of Camden Town. Turn left at the foot of Parkway, and battle your way north along Camden High Street (actually, the crowds are unbearably dense only on the weekend), to **Camden Lock** ⑦. From here you can keep going east, although it's less scenic, to King's Cross, site of one of London's main train stations, of the new British Library building, of the city's highest concentration of for-hire streetwalkers, and the **London Canal Museum** ⑧.

Back at the Lock, you could walk up Haverstock Hill, or travel three stops on the Northern Line from Camden Town tube (make sure you take the Edgware branch) to Hampstead (or 181 feet below it, in London's deepest tube station). Cross the High Street to Heath Street and turn right to Church Row, said to be London's most complete Georgian street. At the west end is the 1745 "village" church of St. John's, where the painter John Constable is buried. Just south of the tube, Flask Walk is another pretty street, narrow and shop-lined at the High Street end, then widening after you pass The Flask—the pub it is named for, which in turn is named for the flasks that contained that therapeutically clean Hampstead spa water. The pub has a pretty courtyard, by the way. Nearby Well Walk was where the spring surfaced, its place now marked by a dried-up fountain. John Constable lived here, as well as John Keats (in, of course, **Keats House** ⑨) and, later, D. H. Lawrence. You now have two choices: If you've had enough fresh air, walk down Fitzjohn's Avenue and visit the **Freud Museum** ⑩ and then continue down Finchley Road to the impressive **Saatchi Collection** ⑪; Beatles aficionados will head post haste, instead, to the fabled **Abbey Road Studios** ⑫. If you've been blessed by a clear London day, take advantage and take the long walk northeast up Spaniards Road, traversing **Hampstead Heath,** to Hampstead Lane, to the bucolic oasis of **Kenwood House** ⑬, well worth a visit for its setting alone. To the east of Hampstead, and also topping a hill, is the former village of Highgate, which has some fine houses, especially along its Georgian High Street, and retains a peaceful period atmosphere. But it is most famous for **Highgate Cemetery** ⑭.

TIMING

You may well want to divide this tour into segments, using the (notoriously inefficient) Northern Line of the tube to jump between the Regent's Park and Hampstead neighborhoods. It will take you at least three hours to cover on foot the full length of this walk.

There are several approaches, of course. In summer, with children, you might center a north London jaunt around Regent's Park, the Zoo, Camden Lock, and a canal trip, a day's worth of sightseeing. If you wanted to add Madame Tussaud's and the Planetarium, you'd have a frenetic day, especially in summer, because you may be in line for an hour. A summer's day without children might start at the other end, with Hampstead Heath, Kenwood House, a stroll around Hampstead and a pub or two on the agenda—plenty for one day. Teenagers and youth will spend all day and night in Camden Town, and may as well admit it. They, and anyone else who wants the whole Camden Lock spectacle, should go north on a weekend; those who prefer quiet should do the opposite. Neither Camden nor Hampstead are completely dead during the week, though, because both have residents who tend to go out a lot. Bear in mind that much of this itinerary is washed out by rain, not only because there's a lot of ground to cover, but because many of the pleasures are to be had from strolling.

HOW TO GET THERE

For Regent's Park, Regent's Park tube (on the Bakerloo Line) is obviously an option, though Camden Town on the Northern Line, then a walk up Parkway is almost as close. Hampstead is best accessed from, yes, Hampstead tube. Make sure you get on the right "branch" of the Northern Line—you want the train to Edgware. Buses for Regent's Park include Nos. 18, 27, and 30 along the Marylebone Road or Nos. 13, 82, 113, 139, and 274 to Lord's Cricket Ground. The 274 is the bus for the Zoo. For Hampstead, catch the 268.

Sights to See

★ ⑫ **Abbey Road Studios.** The most famous Beatles site in London, this is the fabled studio where the Fab Four recorded their entire output. The studios themselves are closed to the public, but many travelers journey here to see the famous traffic crossing used by the group on the cover of their *Abbey Road* album (☞ Close-Up section "Strawberry Beatles Forever: A Trip to Abbey Road"). ⊠ *3 Abbey Rd. Tube: St. John's Wood.*

☝ ❼ **Camden Lock.** What was once just a pair of locks on the Grand Union Canal has now developed into London's third most-visited tourist attraction. It's a vast honeycomb of markets that sell just about everything, but mostly crafts, clothing (vintage, ethnic, and young designer), and antiques, and is a virtual caricature of its neighborhood, Camden Town. Here, especially on a weekend, the crowds are dense, young, and relentless, and you may tire of the identical T-shirts, pants, boots, vintage wear, and cheap leathers on their backs and in the shops. Camden definitely has its charms, though. Gentrification has been layered over a once overwhelmingly Irish neighborhood, vestiges of which coexist with the youth culture: Inverness Street fruit-and-vegetable market alongside the Arlington House homeless shelter, architects' offices, and antiques stores. ⊠ *Camden Lock, Camden High St. NW1, no phone.* ☉ *Markets weekends. Tube: Camden Town or Chalk Farm.*

NEED A BREAK?	You will not go hungry in Camden Town. Among the countless cafés, bars, pubs, and restaurants, the following stand out for good value and good food: **Marine Ices** (⊠ 8 Haverstock Hill, past lock) has a window dispensing ice cream to strollers, or pasta, pizza, and sundaes inside. **Bar Gansa** (⊠ 2 Inverness St., near Tube) offers Spanish *tapas*—small dishes for sharing. **Cottons Rhum Shop, Bar and Restaurant** (⊠ 55 Chalk Farm Rd., past lock) is a Caribbean island in miniature, with great rum cocktails and jerk chicken.

❿ **Freud Museum.** The father of psychoanalysis lived here for only a few months, between his escape from Nazi persecution in his native Vienna in 1938 and his death in 1939. Many of his possessions emigrated with him and were set up by his daughter, Anna (herself a pioneer of child psychoanalysis), as a shrine to her father's life and work. Four years after Anna's death in 1982, the house was opened as a museum. It replicates the atmosphere of Freud's famous consulting rooms, particularly through the presence of The Couch. You'll find Freud-related books, lectures, and study groups here, too. ⊠ *20 Maresfield Gardens,* ☏ *0171/435–2002.* 🎟 *£3.* ☉ *Wed.–Sun. noon–5. Tube: Swiss Cottage, Finchley Road.*

☝ **Hampstead Heath.** However pretty the houses may be, this wild park, which spreads for miles to the north, is quite the nicest thing about Hampstead. On the southwest corner stands the rebuilt version of a famous inn, **Jack Straw's Castle**. It is named after the Peasant Revolt leader who hid out and was captured here in 1381 after destroying Sir Robert Hales's residence and Priory, the Prior of St. John. Hales was hated for enforcing the poll tax, which led to the uprising—and which, when reintroduced in 1990, proved as unpopular the second time around. Another historic pub stands off the northwest edge, on Hampstead Lane. The **Spaniard's Inn,** in contrast to the above, is little changed since the early 18th century, when (they say) the notorious

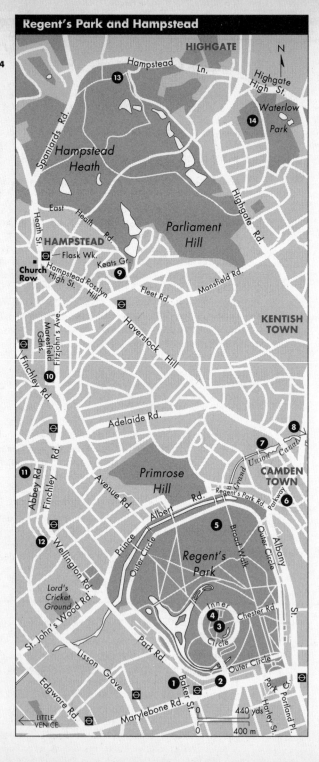

Regent's Park and Hampstead

STRAWBERRY BEATLES FOREVER

A TRIP TO ABBEY ROAD

FOR COUNTLESS Beatlemaniacs and baby boomers, No. 3 Abbey Road is an especially beloved spot in London. Here, outside the legendary Abbey Road Studios is the most famous zebra crossing in the world. Immortalized on the Beatles's *Abbey Road* 1969 album, this footpath became a Mod monument when, on August 8 of that year, John, Paul, George, and Ringo posed—walking symbolically *away* from the recording facility, incidentally—for photographer Iain Macmillan for the famous album shot.

Today, many fans venture to Abbey Road to leave their signature on the white stucco fence that fronts the studio facility. "All You Need is Beatles!", "God is a Beatle!", "Imagine— John coming back!", "John is Gone— What a price to pay for being a genius!", "Why don't you do it in the road?" and "Strawberry Beatles Forever" are a few of the flourishes left (note that these are whitewashed out every three months, by agreement with the neighborhood community, to make room for new grafitti).

The recording facility's Studio 2 is where the Beatles recorded their entire output, from "Love Me Do" onward, including, most momentously, *Sgt. Pepper's Lonely Hearts Club Band* (early 1967). Today, tourists like to Beatle-ize themselves by taking the same sort of photo, but be careful: Rushing cars make Abbey Road a dangerous intersection. Currently, there are few places in London that commemorate the Fab Four (wouldn't it be wonderful if Abbey Road Studios, now closed to the public, could become a Beatles museum one day?), so the best way Beatle-lovers can enjoy the history of the group is to take one of the smashing walking tours offered by The Original London Walks, including "The Beatles In-My-Life Walk" (11 AM at the Baker St. Underground on Saturdays and Tuesdays) and "The Beatles Magical Mystery Tour" (11 AM at Dominion Theater Exit, Tottenham Court Road, on Sundays and Thursdays; call ☎ 0171/624– 3978).

Abbey Road is in the elegant neighborhood of St. John's Wood, just a ten-minute ride on the tube from central London; Take the Jubilee subway line to the St. John's Wood tube stop, head southwest three blocks down Grove End Road, and—especially if you were one of the 63 million people that tuned in to the *Ed Sullivan Show* February 8, 1964 and grew up with the Beatles—be prepared for a heart-stopping vista right out of Memory Lane.

highwayman Dick Turpin hung out here. Keats also drank here, as did Shelley and Byron—but not Dickens; when his eternal pub crawl brought him up to Hampstead, he preferred Jack Straw's Castle. ✉ *Jack Straw's Castle, North End Way NW3,* ☎ *0171/435–8885.* ✉ *Spaniard's Inn, Spaniard's Rd., NW3,* ☎ *0181/455–3276. Tube: Hampstead.*

⑭ Highgate Cemetery. The older, west side of this sprawling early Victorian graveyard, featuring many an overwrought stone memorial, can be visited only by a tour given by the Friends of Highgate Cemetery—a group of volunteers who virtually saved the place from ruin. The shady streets of the dead, Egyptian Avenue and the Circle of Lebanon, are particularly Poe-like, but the famous graves are mostly on the newer, less atmospheric east side, which is still in use and may be wandered freely. No tour is required to explore the newer, east side of Highgate Cemetery, home to some famous permanent residents: Karl Marx's enormous black bust is probably the most visited site, but George Eliot is also buried here. This is not London's oldest cemetery—that distinction belongs to Kensal Green, with its spine-chilling catacombs and Gothic mausolea. ✉ *Swains La., Highgate,* ☎ *0181/340–1834.* ✉ *East side £1, west side tour £2.* ☉ *East side Apr.–Oct., daily 10–4:45, and Oct.–Mar., daily 10–3:45; west side tour Apr.–Oct., weekdays at 2 and 4, weekends periodically 11–4, and Nov.–Mar., weekdays at noon, 2, and 3, weekends periodically 11–3. Tube: Archway.*

NEED A BREAK?   **Lauderdale House** in Waterlow Park, across Swain's Lane from Highgate Cemetery, was built during the 16th century by a master of the Royal Mint and is now a community and arts center, with a great café serving homemade hot meals as well as snacks.

---

⑥ Jewish Museum. This newly located museum tells a potted history of the Jews in London from Norman times, though the bulk of the exhibits date from the end of the 17th century (when Cromwell repealed the laws against Jewish settlement) and later. ✉ *Raymond Burton House, 129 Albert St., NW1,* ☎ *0171/284–1997.* ✉ *£3.* ☉ *Sun.–Thurs. 10–4.*

⑨ Keats House. Here you can see the plum tree under which the young Romantic poet composed "Ode to a Nightingale," many of his original manuscripts, his library, and other possessions he managed to acquire in his short life. He died in Rome of consumption, aged 25, two years after taking up residence here, in 1818. ✉ *Keats House, Wentworth Pl., Keats Grove,* ☎ *0171/435–2062.* ✉ *Free.* ☉ *Apr.–Oct., weekdays 10–6, Sat. 10–5, Sun. 2–5; Nov.–Mar., weekdays 1–5, Sat. 10–5, Sun. 2–5. Closed 1 hr for lunch. Tube: Hampstead.*

NEED A BREAK?   Hampstead is full of eating places, including a few that have been here forever. Try **The Coffee Cup** (✉ 74 Hampstead High St.), serving all-day English breakfasts, pastries, and things-on-toast; or the **Hampstead Tea Rooms** (✉ 9 South End Rd.) for its sandwiches, pies, and its great windowful of pastries and cream cakes.

---

⑬ Kenwood House. This Palladian and proper mansion was first built in 1616 and remodeled by Robert Adam in 1764. Adam refaced most of the exterior and added the gaudy library, which, with its curved, painted ceiling, rather garish coloring, and gilded detailing, is the sole highlight of the house for decor-buffs. What is unmissable here is the **Iveagh Bequest**—a collection of paintings the Earl of Iveagh gave the nation in 1927, starring a very great Rembrandt self-portrait and works by Reynolds, Van Dyck, Hals, Gainsborough, and Turner. Top billing goes to Vermeer's *Guitar Player*—one of the most beautiful paintings anywhere. In front of the house, a graceful lawn slopes down to a little lake crossed by a dinky bridge—all in perfect 18th-century upper-class taste. Nowadays the lake is dominated by its concert bowl, which stages a popular summer series of orchestral concerts, including at least one performance of Handel's *Music for the Royal Fireworks,* complete with fireworks. There's a handy café in the former stables. ⊠ *Hampstead La.,* ☎ *0181/348–1286.* ☞ *Free.* ☉ *Easter–Sept., daily 10–6; Oct.–Easter, daily 10–4. Tube: Golder's Green, then Bus 210.*

8 **London Canal Museum.** Here, in a former ice storage house, you can learn about the rise and fall of London's once extensive canal network. Outside, on the Battlebridge Basin, float the gaily painted narrow boats of modern canal dwellers—a few steps and a world away from King's Cross, which remains one of London's least salubrious neighborhoods. The quirky little museum is accessible from Camden Lock if you take the towpath. ⊠ *12–13 New Wharf Rd., N1,* ☎ *0171/713–0836.* ☞ *£2.50.* ☉ *Apr.–Sept., Tues.–Sun. 10–4; call for winter hrs. Tube: King's Cross.*

London Planetarium. This domed building stands right next to Madame Tussaud's (☞ *below*), but could hardly provide greater contrast with the waxworks (though you can save a bit of cash by combining them in a single visit). Inside the dome, exact simulations of the night sky are projected by the Digistar Mark 2 projector and accompanied by gosh-wow-fancy-that narration. The shows, which change daily, are good enough to addict children to astronomy. There are regular laser shows and rock music extravaganzas. ⊠ *Marylebone Rd.,* ☎ *0171/935–6861.* ☞ *£5.45, joint ticket with Madame Tussaud's (☞ below) £10.95; show every 40 min weekdays 12:20–5, weekends 10:20–5. Tube: Baker Street.*

5 **London Zoo.** The Zoo opened in 1828, peaked in popularity during the 1950s (when more than 3 million visitors passed through its turnstiles every year), but recently faced the prospect of closing its gates forever. Its problems started when animal-crazy Brits, apparently anxious about the morality of caging wild beasts, simply stopped visiting. But the zoo fought back, pulling heartstrings with a *Save Our Zoo* campaign and tragic predictions of mass euthanasia for homeless polar bears, and, at the 11th hour, found commercial sponsorship that was generous enough not only to keep the wolves from the door (or the wolves indoors) but also to fund a great big modernization program.

Zoo highlights that will not change include the Elephant and Rhino Pavilion, which closely resembles the South Bank Arts Complex; the graceful Snowdon Aviary, spacious enough to allow its tenants free flight; and the 1936 Penguin Pool, where feeding time sends small children into raptures. New thrills will include the construction of a desert swarming with locusts; a rainforest alive with butterflies, bats, and hummingbirds; and a cave lighted by fireflies. This being the headquarters of the Zoological Society of London, much work is done here in wildlife conservation, education, and the breeding of endangered species, and emphasis is being shifted onto these aspects in the exhibits, with more displays to help explain them to visitors. The first step along this road was the Children's Zoo, which shows how people and animals live together, and features domestic animals from around the world. ⊠ *Regent's Park,* ☎ *0171/722–3333.* ☞ *£7.80.* ☉ *Summer, daily 9–6; winter, daily 10–4; penguin feed daily 2:30; aquarium feed daily 2:30; reptile feed Fri. 2:30; elephant bath daily 3:45. Tube: Camden Town, and bus 74.*

🐚 ❷ **Madame Tussaud's.** This—one of London's busiest sights—is nothing more, nothing less, than the world's premier exhibition of lifelike wax-work models of celebrities. Madame T. learned her craft while making death masks of French Revolutionary victims and in 1835 set up her first show of the famous ones near this spot. Nowadays, "Super Stars" of entertainment, in their own hall of the same name, outrank any aristo in popularity, along with the newest segment, "The Spirit of London," a "time taxi ride" that visits every notable Londoner from Shakespeare to Benny Hill. But top billing still goes to the murderers in the Chamber of Horrors, who stare glassy-eyed at you—this one from the electric chair, that one next to the tin bath where he dissolved several wives in quicklime. What, aside from ghoulish prurience, makes people stand in line to invest in London's most expensive museum ticket? It must be the thrill of rubbing shoulders with Shakespeare, Martin Luther King, Jr., the queen, and the Beatles—most of them dressed in their own clothes—in a single day. ✉ *Marylebone Rd.,* ☎ *0171/935–6861.* 💷 *£8.75, joint ticket with planetarium (☞ above) £10.95.* ⊙ *Sept.–June, weekdays 10–5:30, weekends 9:30–5:30; July and Aug., daily 9:30–5:30. Tube: Baker Street.*

❸ **Regent's Park.** This, the youngest of London's great parks, was laid out in 1812 by John Nash, working, as ever, for his patron, the Prince Regent (hence the name), who was crowned George IV in 1820. The idea was to re-create the feel of a grand country residence close to the center of town, with all those magnificent white-stucco terraces facing in on the park. As you walk the Outer Circle, you'll see how successfully Nash's plans were carried out, although the center of it all, a palace for the prince, was never built—George was too busy fiddling with the one he already had, Buckingham Palace. The most famous and impressive of Nash's terraces would have been in the prince's line of vision from the planned palace, so was extra-ornamental. **Cumberland Terrace** has a central block of Ionic columns surmounted by a triangular Wedgwood-blue pediment that is like a giant cameo. Snow-white statuary personifying Britannia and her empire (the work of the on-site architect, James Thomson) further single it out from the pack.

As in all London parks, planting here is planned with the aim of having something in bloom in all seasons, but if you hit the park in May, June, or July, head first to the Inner Circle. Your nostrils should lead you to **Queen Mary's Gardens,** a fragrant 17-acre circle that riots with roses in summer, and heather, azaleas, and evergreens in other seasons. The **Broad Walk** is a good vantage point to glimpse the minaret and golden dome of the **London Central Mosque** on the far west side of the park, or—if it's a summer evening or a Sunday afternoon—witness a remarkable recent phenomenon. Wherever you look, the sport being enthusiastically played (subject to the ritual annual banning by the park authorities) is not cricket but softball, now Britain's fastest-growing participant sport (bring your mitt). Actually, you're likely to see cricket, too.

❹ **Regent's Park Open-Air Theatre.** This has been mounting mostly Shakespeare productions every summer since 1932. *A Midsummer Night's Dream* is the one to catch—never is that enchanted Greek wood more lifelike than it is here, augmented by genuine bird squawks and a rising moon. The park can get chilly, so bring a blanket—and rain stops the play only when heavy, so an umbrella may be wise, too. ✉ *Open-Air Theatre, Regent's Park,* ☎ *0171/486–2431.* ⊙ *June–Aug. Tube: Baker Street, Regent's Park.*

⓫ **Saatchi Collection.** This blinding white space is all crisp lines and quietness, the better to contemplate the front lines of contemporary paintings, installations, and sculpture—by the likes of Lucian Freud, Paula Rego, Damian Hirst, Rachel Whiteread, Janine Antoni—collected by the advertising mogul. ⊠ *98a Boundary Rd., NW8,* ☎ *0171/624–8299.* ◪ *Free.* ☉ *Fri. and Sat. noon–6. Tube: Swiss Cottage.*

❶ Sherlock Holmes Museum. You can tell you've reached this museum when you see the actor dressed as a Victorian policeman outside, and the sign that claims this as 221B Baker Street, the address of Conan Doyle's fictional detective. Inside, "Holmes's housekeeper" conducts you into a series of Victorian rooms, full of Sherlockabilia. The 221B, if it existed, would be down the block in the Abbey National Building Society's head office at Abbey House, 215–229 Baker Street, by the way. ⊠ *"221B" Baker St.,* ☎ *0171/935–8866.* ◪ *£5.* ☉ *Daily 10–6. Tube: Baker Street.*

2 Willow Road. Moderne Movement master Erno Goldfinger put this up in the 1930s, and the National Trust has now kindly restored it, filled it with important (and currently very trendy) Modernist furniture and art. Note that there are limited visitor hours with timed tickets, because the house is small, and these had not been set at press time. ⊠ *2 Willow Rd.,* ☎ *0171/435–6166.* ◪ *£3.60.* ☉ *Spring–fall (call for times). Tube: Hampstead.*

GREENWICH

About 8 mi downstream—which means seaward, to the east—from central London lies a neighborhood you'd think had been conceived to provide the perfect day out. Greenwich is another of London's self-contained "villages," only one with unique sights surrounding the residential portion. The buildings of Greenwich are among the most splendid in Britain: Spreading both grandly and elegantly beside the river, the colonnades and pediments of Sir Christopher Wren's Royal Naval College and Inigo Jones's Queen's House seem to be part of a complex of Grecian temples, transported to the Thames. Here, too, is the Old Royal Observatory, which measures time for our entire planet, and the Greenwich Meridian, which divides the world in two—you can stand astride it with one foot in either hemisphere. The National Maritime Museum and the proud clipper ship *Cutty Sark* are thrilling to seafaring types, and landlubbers can stroll the green acres of parkland that surround the buildings, the quaint 19th-century houses, and the weekend crafts and antiques markets.

Numbers in the text correspond to numbers in the margin and on the Greenwich map.

A Good Walk

Before you start to walk, bear in mind that the journey to Greenwich is fun in itself, especially if you approach by river, arriving at the best possible vista of the **Royal Naval College,** with the **Queen's House** behind. On the way, the boat glides past famous sights on the London skyline (there's a guaranteed spine chill on passing the Tower) and ever-changing docklands, and there's always a cockney navigator enhancing the views with wiseguy commentary. You could also take the Docklands Light Railway (DLR), a high-speed elevated track, which opened in 1987. It connects with the tube network at Bank, and brings you to Island Gardens, exactly opposite the Royal Naval College, with the finest possible view, of course. You can't miss the squat little circular brick building with its glass-domed roof; this is the entrance to the Greenwich Foot Tunnel, where an ancient elevator takes you down to a walkway under the Thames that brings you up very close to the *Cutty Sark* ① and the *Gipsy Moth IV* ②.

By continuing along King William Walk, you come to the wrought-iron gates of the **Royal Naval College** ③, from the south end of which you approach the building that Wren's majestic quadrangles frame, the **Queen's House** ④ followed by the **National Maritime Museum** ⑤. Now head up the hill in Greenwich Park overlooking the Naval College and Maritime Museum to the **Old Royal Observatory** ⑥ and the **Ranger's House** ⑦. Walking back through the park toward the river, you'll enter the pretty streets of Greenwich Village to the west. There are plenty of bookstores and antiques shops for browsing, and, at the foot of Crooms Hill, the modern **Greenwich Theatre** ⑧—a West End theater, despite its location, which mounts well-regarded, often star-spangled productions—and the **Fan Museum** ⑨ opposite. Finish up at the excellent **Greenwich Antique Market** ⑩ (on Burney St. near the museum and theater), and the Victorian **Covered Crafts Market** ⑪ by the *Cutty Sark*, on College Approach. An additional 25-minute boat-ride away is the **Thames Barrier** ⑫, which helps keep London dry—at least from the ground up.

TIMING

First of all, the boat trip takes about an hour from Westminster Pier (next to Big Ben), or 25 minutes from the Tower of London, so figure in enough time for the round-trip, unless the weather's really awful, or it's winter and the boats have stopped. Aim for an early start. Although the distance covered in this walk is barely a mile, Greenwich can't be "done" in a day. There are such riches here, especially if the maritime theme is your thing, that whatever time you allow will seem halved. If the weather's good, you'll be tempted to stroll aimlessly around the quaint villagelike streets, too, and maybe take a turn in the park. If you want to take in the markets, you'll need to come on a weekend. The antiques market is open 8–4; the crafts market, 9–5.

HOW TO GET THERE

See information in the chapter for details. Buses 188 and 286 are alternatives.

Sights to See

⑪ *Covered Crafts Market.* You'll find this Victorian market by the *Cutty Sark*, on College Approach. As you'd expect, this one features crafts, but there are more of the sort of ceramics, jewelry, knitwear, and leather goods that you might actually want to own than is common in such places, and you get to buy them from the people who made them. ⊙ *Weekends 9–5.*

⑥ ① *Cutty Sark.* This romantic tea clipper was built in 1869, one of fleets and fleets of similar wooden tall-masted clippers which during the 19th century plied the seven seas trading in exotic commodities—tea, in this case. The *Cutty Sark,* the last to survive, was also the fastest, sailing the China–London route in 1871 in only 107 days. Now the photogenic vessel lies in dry dock, a museum of one kind of seafaring life—and not a comfortable kind for the 28-strong crew, as you'll see. The collection of figureheads is amusing, too. ⊠ *King William Walk,* ☎ *0181/858–3445.* ☞ *£3.50.* ⊙ *Apr.–Sept., Mon.–Sat. 10–6, Sun. noon–6; Oct.–Mar., Mon.–Sat. 10–5, Sun. noon–5; last admission 30 min before closing.*

⑨ *Fan Museum.* In two newly restored houses dating from the 1820s opposite the Greenwich Theatre is this highly unusual museum. The 2,000 fans here, which date from the 17th century onward, comprise the world's only such collection, and the history and purpose of these often exquisitely crafted objects are explained satisfyingly. It was the personal vision—and fan collection—of Helene Alexander that brought

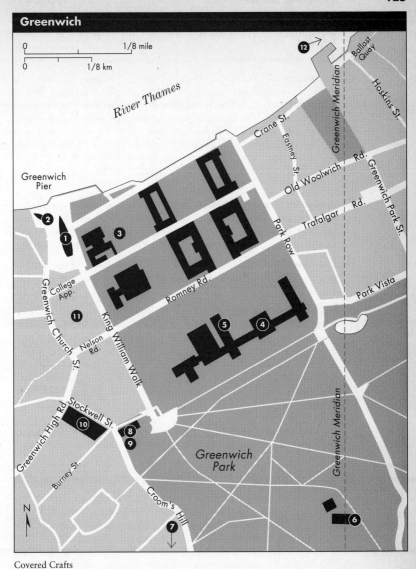

Greenwich

Covered Crafts
Market, **11**
Cutty Sark, **1**
Fan Museum, **9**
Gipsy Moth IV, **2**
Greenwich Antique
Market, **10**
Greenwich Theatre, **8**
National Maritime
Museum, **5**
Old Royal
Observatory, **6**
Queen's House, **4**
Ranger's House, **7**
Royal Naval College, **3**
Thames Barrier, **12**

it into being in 1991, and the workshop and conservation and study center that she has also set up ensure that this anachronistic art has a future. ✉ *10–12 Croom's Hill,* ☎ *0181/858–7879.* ▣ *£3.* ☉ *Tues.–Sat. 11–4:30, Sun. noon–4:30.*

② Gipsy Moth IV. The boat in which Sir Francis Chichester achieved the first single-handed circumnavigation of the globe in 1966 is dry-docked beside the *Cutty Sark.* Inside you'll see the tiny space the sailor endured for 226 days, and the ingenious way everything he needed was installed. The queen knighted him on board here, using the same sword with which the previous Elizabeth had knighted that other seagoing Francis, Sir Francis Drake, three centuries before. ✉ *King William Walk,* ☎ *0181/858–3445.* ▣ *50p.* ☉ *Apr.–Oct., Mon.–Sat. 10–6, Sun. noon–6.*

➓ Greenwich Antique Market. If you're visiting on the weekend, this market on Burney Street near the Fan Museum and Greenwich Theatre is open for business. It has a lot of bric-a-brac and books, too, and is well known among the cognoscenti as a good source for vintage clothing.

➑ Greenwich Theatre. Officially a West End theater, despite its location, this modern venue mounts well-regarded, often star-spangled productions. ☎ *0181/858–7755.*

➎ National Maritime Museum. Greenwich's star attraction contains everything to do with the British at sea, in the form of paintings, models, maps, globes, sextants, uniforms (including the one Nelson died in at Trafalgar, complete with bloodstained bullet hole), and—best of all—actual boats, including a collection of ornate, gilded royal barges. ✉ *Romney Rd.,* ☎ *0181/858–4422.* ▣ *£5.50, including Queen's House and Old Royal Observatory (☞ below).* ☉ *Mon.–Sat. 10–6, Sun. noon–6.*

NEED A BREAK?	The **Dolphin Coffee Shop** on the National Maritime Museum grounds is a good place to recuperate after the rigors of the museum; non-museum visitors are also welcome.

➏ Old Royal Observatory. Founded in 1675 by Charles II and designed the same year by Christopher Wren for John Flamsteed, the first Astronomer Royal. The red ball you see on its roof has been there only since 1833. It drops every day at 1 PM, and you can set your watch by it, as the sailors on the Thames always have. In fact, nearly everyone sets their watch by it: This "Greenwich Timeball," along with the Gate Clock inside the observatory, are the most visible manifestations of Greenwich Mean Time, and since 1884, the ultimate standard for time around the world. Also here is the **Prime Meridian,** a brass line laid on the cobblestones at 0° longitude, one side being the eastern, one the western hemisphere. In 1948, the Old Royal Observatory lost its official status: London's glow had grown too intense, and the astronomers moved to Sussex, while the Astronomer Royal decamped to Cambridge. They left various telescopes, chronometers, and clocks for you to view in their absence. ✉ *Greenwich Park,* ☎ *0181/858–4422.* ▣ *Joint admission with National Maritime Museum (☞ above).* ☉ *Mon.–Sat. 10–6, Sun. noon–6.*

★ ➍ Queen's House. The queen for whom Inigo Jones began designing it in 1616 was James I's Anne of Denmark, but she died three years later, and it was Charles I's French wife, Henrietta Maria, who inherited the building when it was completed in 1635. It is no less than Britain's first Classical building—the first, that is, to use the lessons of Italian Renaissance architecture—and is therefore of enormous importance in the history of English architecture. Inside, the Tulip Stair, named for the fleur-de-lys–style pattern on the balustrade, is especially fine, spiraling up, without a central support, to the Great Hall. The Great Hall itself is a perfect cube, exactly 40 feet in all three directions, and decorated with paintings of the Muses, the Virtues, and the Liberal Arts. The White Card is accepted. ☎ *0181/858–4422.* ⊡ *£5.50, including National Maritime Museum and Old Royal Observatory (☞ above).* ⊙ *Mon.–Sat. 10–6, Sun. noon–6.*

⑦ Ranger's House. This handsome early 18th-century mansion, which was the Greenwich Park Ranger's official residence during the 19th century, now houses collections of Jacobean portraits and early musical instruments. Concerts are regularly given here, too. It stands just outside the park boundaries, on the southwest side of **Greenwich Park,** which is one of London's oldest royal parks. It had been in existence for more than 200 years before Charles II commissioned the French landscape artist Le Nôtre (who was responsible for Versailles and for St. James's Park) to redesign it in what was, in the 1660s, the latest French fashion. The Flower Garden on the southeast side and the deer enclosure nearby are particularly pleasant. Look also for Queen Elizabeth's Oak on the east side, around which Henry VIII and his second queen, Anne Boleyn, Elizabeth I's mother, are said to have danced. ⊠ *Chesterfield Walk, Blackheath,* ☎ *0181/853–0035.* ⊡ *Free.* ⊙ *Apr.–Sept., daily 10–6; Oct.–Mar., daily 10–4; closed 1 hr for lunch.*

③ Royal Naval College. Begun by Christopher Wren in 1694 as a home, or hospital (as in the Chelsea Royal Hospital; not Charing Cross Hospital), for ancient mariners, it became instead a school for young ones in 1873. You'll notice how the blocks part to reveal the Queen's House across the central lawns. Wren, with the help of his assistant, Hawksmoor, was at pains to preserve the river vista from the house, and there are few more majestic views in London than the awe-inspiring symmetry he achieved. Behind the college are two buildings you can visit. The **Painted Hall,** the college's dining hall, derives its name from the baroque murals of William and Mary (reigned 1689–95; William alone 1695–1702) and assorted allegorical figures, the whole supported by trompe l'oeil pillars that Sir James Thornhill (who decorated the inside of St. Paul's dome, too) painted between 1707 and 1717. In the opposite block stands the **College Chapel,** which was rebuilt after a fire in 1779 and is altogether lighter, in a more restrained, neo-Grecian style. At Christmas 1805, Admiral Nelson's body was brought from the battle of Trafalgar to lie in state here. ⊠ *Royal Naval College, King William Walk,* ☎ *0181/858–2154.* ⊡ *Free.* ⊙ *Daily 2:30–4:45.*

⑫ Thames Barrier. This mammoth piece of civil engineering will come in handy if the water table ever again rises as high as it did in 1928 and 1953 and London is threatened with another flood. This curiously haunting ¼-mi barrier, with its 10 upstanding steel gates, contains enough concrete to build 10 mi of six-lane freeway, and looks like a cross between the Sydney Opera House and a line of submerged alien beings. You can visit an exhibition and also take in **Hallett's Panorama,** an incongruous re-creation, with oils and sculpture, of the city of Bath. Everything lies a few miles farther downstream from Greenwich—another 25-minute boat ride away (though you can also get here by Network SouthEast trains from Greenwich or Charing Cross to Charlton). ⊠ *Unity Way, off Woolwich Rd.,* ☎ *0181/854–1373.* ⊡ *£3.40, including Hallett's Panorama.* ⊙ *Weekdays 10:30–5, weekends 10:30–5:30.*

UPSTREAM FROM LONDON

The Thames is Britain's longest river. It winds its way through the Cotswolds, beyond the "dreaming spires" of Oxford and past majestic Windsor Castle—far more the lazy, leafy country river than the dark gray urban waterway you see in London. Once you leave the city center, going west, or upstream, you reach a series of former villages—Chiswick, Kew, Richmond, Putney—that, apart from the roar of aircraft coming in to land at Heathrow a few miles farther west, still retain a peaceful, almost rural atmosphere, especially in places where parkland rolls down to the riverbank. In fact, it was really only at the beginning of this century that these villages expanded into London proper. The royal palaces and grand houses that dot the area were built not as town houses but as country residences with easy access to London by river.

TIMING

Each of the places we list here could easily absorb a whole day of your time, and Hampton Court is especially huge. Access is fairly easy: The District Line of the Underground runs out to Kew and Richmond, as does Network SouthEast from Waterloo, which also serves Twickenham and Hampton Court. Chiswick House can be reached by tube to Turnham Green, then the E3 bus; or by tube to Hammersmith and Bus 290. A pleasant, if slow, way to go is by river. Boats depart Westminster Pier (just by Big Ben) for Kew (1½ hours), Richmond (2–3 hours), and Hampton Court (4 hours) several times a day in summer, less frequently from October through March. As you can tell from those sailing times, the boat trip is worth taking only if you make it an integral part of your day out, and even then, be aware that it can get very breezy on the water and that the scenery going upstream is by no means constantly fascinating. ⊠ *Westminster Pier*, ☎ *0171/930–4097.*

Chiswick and Kew

Chiswick is the nearest Thames-side destination to London, with Kew just a mile or so beyond it. Much of Chiswick today is a nondescript suburb developed at the beginning of this century. But, incongruously stranded among the terraced houses, a number of fine 18th-century houses and a charming little village survive. The village atmosphere of Kew is still distinct, making this one of the most desirable areas of outer London. What makes Kew famous, though, are the Royal Botanic Gardens.

A Good Walk

Chiswick's **Church Street** (reached by an underpass from Hogarth's House) is the nearest thing to a sleepy country village street in all of London, despite its proximity to the Great West Road. Follow it down to the Thames and turn left at its foot to reach the sturdy 18th-century riverfront houses of **Chiswick Mall.** The ½-mi walk along here takes you far away from London and into a world of elegance and calm. You will pass several riverside pubs as you head along this stretch of the Thames toward Hammersmith Bridge. The **Dove** is the prettiest, if the most crowded, with its terrace hanging over the water, though the food is better at the **Blue Anchor,** which you reach first.

There's a similarly peaceful walk to be had about 1 mi to the west, along the 18th-century river frontage of **Strand-on-the-Green**, whose houses look over the narrow towpath to the river, their tidy brick facades covered with wisteria and roses in summer. Strand-on-the-Green ends at Kew Bridge, opposite which is **Kew Green,** where local teams play cricket on summer Sundays. All around it are fine 18th-century houses, and, in the center, a church in which the painters Gainsborough and John Zoffany (1733–1810) are buried.

Sights to See

★ **Chiswick House.** Built circa 1725 by the Earl of Burlington as a country residence in which to entertain friends, and as a kind of temple to the arts, this is the very model of a Palladian villa, inspired by the Villa Capra near Vicenza in northeastern Italy. The house fans out from a central octagonal room in perfect symmetry, guarded by statues of Burlington's heroes, Palladio himself and his disciple Inigo Jones. Burlington's friends—Pope, Swift, Gay, and Handel among them—were well qualified to adorn a temple to the arts. This is the Lord Burlington of Burlington House, Piccadilly, home of the Royal Academy and, of course, Burlington Arcade. It goes without saying that he was a great connoisseur, and an important patron, of the arts, but he was also an accomplished architect in his own right, fascinated—obsessed even— by the architecture and art of the Italian Renaissance and ancient Rome, with which he'd fallen in love during his Italian grand tour (every well-bred boy's rite of passage). Along with William Kent (1685–1748), who designed the interiors and the rambling gardens here, Burlington did an awful lot to disseminate the Palladian ideals around Britain: Chiswick House sparked enormous interest, and you'll see these forms reflected in hundreds of subsequent English stately homes both small and large. ⊠ *Burlington La.,* ☎ *0181/995–0508.* ☜ *£2.50.* ☉ *Apr.–Sept., daily 10–6; Oct.–Mar., daily 10–4; closed 1 hr for lunch. Tube: Turnham Green.*

Hogarth's House. This is where the painter lived from 1749 until his death in 1764. Unprotected from the six-lane Great West Road, which remains a main route to the West Country, the poor house is besieged by the surrounding traffic, but is worth visiting for its little museum consisting mostly of the amusingly moralistic engravings for which Hogarth is best known, including the most famous one of all, *The Rake's Progress* series of 1735. ⊠ *Hogarth La.,* ☎ *0181/994–6757.* ☜ *Free.* ☉ *Apr.–Sept., Mon.–Sat. 11–6, Sun. 2–6; Oct.–Mar., Mon.–Sat. 11–4, Sun. 2–4. Closed 1st 3 wks of Sept. and last 3 wks of Dec. Tube: Turnham Green.*

★ **Kew Gardens.** The Royal Botanic Gardens at Kew are a spectacular 300 acres of public gardens, containing more than 60,000 species of plants. In addition, this is the country's leading botanical institute, with strong royal associations. Until 1840, when Kew Gardens was handed over to the nation, it had been the grounds of two royal residences: the White House (formerly Kew House), and Richmond Lodge, or the Dutch House. George II and Queen Caroline lived at Richmond Lodge in the 1720s, while their eldest son, Frederick, Prince of Wales, and his wife, Princess Augusta, came to the White House during the 1730s. The royal wives were keen gardeners. Queen Caroline got to work on her grounds, while next door Frederick's pleasure garden was developed as a botanic garden by his widow after his death. She introduced all kinds of "exotics," foreign plants brought back to England by botanists. Caroline was aided by a skilled head gardener and by the architect Sir William Chambers, who built a series of temples and follies, of which the crazy 10-story **Pagoda** (1762), visible for miles around, is the star turn. The celebrated botanist Sir Joseph Banks (1743–1820) then took charge of Kew, which developed rapidly in both its roles—as a beautiful landscaped garden, and as a center of study and research.

The highlights of a visit to Kew are the two great 19th-century greenhouses filled with tropical plants, many of which have been there as long as their housing. Both the **Palm House** and the **Temperate House** were designed by Sir Decimus Burton, the first opening in 1848, the second in 1899 (though it had been begun 40 years earlier); the latter was the biggest greenhouse in the world and today contains the biggest greenhouse plant in the world, a Chilean wine palm rooted in 1846. You can climb the spiral staircase almost to the roof and look down on this and the dense tropical profusion from the walkway. The **Princess of Wales Conservatory**, the latest and the largest plant house at Kew, was opened in 1987 by Princess Diana. Under its bold glass roofs, designed to maximize energy conservation, there are no less than 10 climatic zones, their temperatures all precisely controlled by computer.

The **Centre for Economic Botany** is housed in the newly constructed Joseph Banks Building, the majority of which is devoted to Kew's research collection on economic botany and to its library. But the public can enjoy exhibitions here on the theme of plants in everyday life. (There is no admission charge, and the center is open Monday–Saturday 9:10–4:30 and Sunday 9:30–5:30.) The plant houses make Kew worth visiting even in the depths of winter, but in spring and summer the gardens come into their own. In late spring, the woodland nature reserve of Queen Charlotte's Cottage Gardens is carpeted in bluebells; a little later, the Rhododendron Dell and the Azalea Garden become swathed in brilliant color. High summer features glorious displays of roses and water lilies, while fall is the time to see the heather garden, near the pagoda. Whatever time of year you visit, something is in bloom, and your journey is never wasted. ⊠ *Royal Botanic Gardens,* ☎ *0181/940–1171.* 🖅 *£5, including Queen Charlotte's Cottage Apr.–Sept.* ☉ *Gardens daily 9:30–sunset, greenhouses daily at 10–sunset. Tube: Kew Gardens.*

Kew Palace. Kew Palace remains to this day quietly domestic and the smallest royal palace in the land. Through spring 1999, the palace is closed for refurbishment, but you can glimpse the little formal gardens to its rear, redeveloped in 1969 as a 17th-century garden. ⊠ *Kew Gardens,* ☎ *0181/940–3321.*

NEED A BREAK? | **Maids of Honour** (⊠ 288 Kew Rd.), the most traditional of Olde Worlde English tearooms, is named for the famous tarts invented here and still baked by hand on the premises. It's only open for tea from Tuesday through Saturday, 2:45–5:30.

Richmond

Named after the palace Henry VII built here in 1500, Richmond is still a welcoming and extremely pretty riverside "village" with many handsome (and mountainously expensive) houses, many antiques shops, a Victorian theater, and, best of all, the biggest of London's royal parks.

Sights to See

★ **Ham House.** Ham House stands to the west of Richmond Park, overlooking the Thames and nearly opposite the oddly named Eel Pie Island. The house was built in 1610 by Sir Thomas Vavasour, knight marshal to James I, then refurbished later the same century by the Duke and Duchess of Lauderdale, who, although not particularly nice (a contemporary called the duchess "the coldest friend and the most violent enemy that ever was known"), managed to produce one of the finest houses in Britain at the time. Now that £2 million has been sunk into restoring Ham House—a project overseen by the National Trust—its splendor can be appreciated afresh. The formerly empty library has been

We'll give you a $20 tip for driving.

See the real Europe with Hertz.

It's time to see Europe from a new perspective. From behind the wheel of a Hertz car. And we'd like to save you $20 on your prepaid Affordable Europe Weekly Rental. Our low rates are guaranteed in U.S. dollars and English is spoken at all of our European locations. Computerized driving directions are available at many locations, and Free Unlimited Mileage and 24-Hour Emergency Roadside Assistance are standard in our European packages. For complete details call 1-800-654-3001. Mention PC #95384 So, discover Europe with Hertz.

Offer is valid at participating airport locations in Europe from Jan.1 – Dec.15, 1998, on Economy through Full size cars. Reservations must be made at least 8 hours prior to departure. $20 will be deducted at time of booking. Standard rental qualifications, significant restrictions and blackout periods apply.

Pick up
the phone.

Pick up
the miles.

MCI   **Calling Card**

415 555 1234 2244
J.D. SMITH

WorldPhone

Use your MCI Card® to make an international call from virtually anywhere in the world and earn frequent flyer miles on one of seven major airlines.

Enroll in an MCI Airline Partner Program today. In the U.S., call **1-800-FLY-FREE.** Overseas, call MCI collect at **1-916-567-5151.**

1. To use your MCI Card, just dial the WorldPhone access number of the country you're calling from.
   (For a complete listing of codes, visit www.mci.com.)
2. Dial or give the operator your MCI Card number.
3. Dial or give the number you're calling.

# Austria (CC) ♦	022-903-012	# Netherlands (CC) ♦	0800-022-91-22
# Belarus (CC)		# Norway (CC) ♦	800-19912
From Brest, Vitebsk, Grodno, Minsk	8-800-103	# Poland (CC) ⊹	00-800-111-21-22
From Gomel and Mogilev regions	8-10-800-103	# Portugal (CC) ⊹	05-017-1234
# Belgium (CC) ♦	0800-10012	Romania (CC) ⊹	01-800-1800
# Bulgaria	00800-0001	# Russia (CC) ⊹ ♦	
# Croatia (CC) ★	99-385-0112	To call using ROSTELCOM ■	747-3322
# Czech Republic (CC) ♦	00-42-000112	For a Russian-speaking operator	747-3320
# Denmark (CC) ♦	8001-0022	To call using SOVINTEL ■	960-2222
# Finland (CC) ♦	08001-102-80	# San Marino (CC) ♦	172-1022
# France (CC) ♦	0-800-99-0019	# Slovak Republic (CC)	00-421-00112
# Germany (CC)	0130-0012	# Slovenia	080-8808
# Greece (CC) ♦	00-800-1211	# Spain (CC)	900-99-0014
# Hungary (CC) ♦	00▼800-01411	# Sweden (CC) ♦	020-795-922
# Iceland (CC) ♦	800-9002	# Switzerland (CC) ♦	0800-89-0222
# Ireland (CC)	1-800-55-1001	# Turkey (CC) ♦	00-8001-1177
# Italy (CC) ♦	172-1022	# Ukraine (CC) ⊹	8▼10-013
# Kazakhstan (CC)	8-800-131-4321	# United Kingdom (CC)	
# Liechtenstein (CC) ♦	0800-89-0222	To call using BT ■	0800-89-0222
# Luxembourg	0800-0112	To call using MERCURY ■	0500-89-0222
# Monaco (CC) ♦	800-90-019	# Vatican City (CC)	172-1022

Is this a great time, or what? :-)

Automation available from most locations. (CC) Country-to-country calling available to/from most international locations. ♦ Public phones may require deposit of coin or phone card for dial tone. ★ Not available from public pay phone. ▼ Wait for second dial tone. ⊹ Limited availability. ■ International communications carrier. Limit one bonus program per MCI account. Terms and conditions apply. All airline program rules and conditions apply. ©1997 MCI Telecommunications Corporation. All rights reserved. Is this a great time or what? is a service mark of MCI.

filled with 17th- and 18th-century volumes; the original decorations in the Great Hall, Round Gallery, and Great Staircase have been replicated; and all the furniture and fittings, on permanent loan from the V&A, have been cleaned and restored. The 17th-century gardens, too, merit a visit in their own right. You can reach Ham from Richmond on Bus 65 or 371, or by one of Greater London's most pleasant rural walks, along the eastern riverbank south from Richmond Bridge, of half an hour or so. ⊠ *Ham St., Richmond,* ☏ *0181/940–1950.* ☏ *£4.50, gardens free.* ☉ *Mar.–Oct., Sat.–Wed. 1–5; Nov.–Dec., weekends 1–5. Tube: Richmond.*

Marble Hill House. On the northern bank of the Thames, almost opposite Ham House, stands another mansion, this one a near-perfect example of a Palladian villa. Marble Hill House was built during the 1720s by George II for his mistress, the "exceedingly respectable and respected" Henrietta Howard. Later the house was occupied by Mrs. Fitzherbert, who was secretly married to the Prince Regent (later George IV) in 1785. Marble Hill House was restored in 1901 and opened to the public two years later, looking very much like it did in Georgian times. A ferry service operates during the summer from Ham House across the river; access by foot is via a half-hour walk south along the west bank from Richmond Bridge. ⊠ *Richmond Rd., Twickenham,* ☏ *0181/892–5115.* ☏ *Free.* ☉ *Easter–Sept., daily 10–6; Oct.–Easter, daily 10–4. Tube: Richmond.*

🦢 **Richmond Park.** Charles I enclosed this one in 1637 for hunting purposes, as with practically all the parks. Unlike the others, however, Richmond Park still has wild red and fallow deer roaming its 2,470 acres of grassland and heath and among the oldest oaks you're likely to see— vestiges of the medieval forests that once encroached on London from all sides. White Lodge, inside the park, was built for George II in 1729. Edward VIII was born here; now it houses the Royal Ballet School. You can walk from the park past the fine 18th-century houses in and around Richmond Hill to the river, admiring first the view from the top. At the Thames, you may notice Quinlan Terry's recent Richmond Riverside development, which met with the approval of England's architectural advisor, Prince Charles, for its classical facades, and was vilified by many others for playing it safe. *Tube: Richmond.*

NEED A BREAK? | The **Cricketers** on Richmond Green serves a good pub lunch. The modern, partially glass-roofed **Caffé Mamma,** on Hill Street, serves inexpensive Italian food. **Beeton's,** on Hill Rise, offers a good, traditional English breakfast, lunch, and afternoon tea, as well as proper dinners.

Hampton Court Palace

★ **Hampton Court.** Some 20 mi from central London, on a loop of the Thames upstream from Richmond, lies one of London's oldest royal palaces, more like a small town in size, and requiring a day of your time to do it justice. The magnificent Tudor brick house was begun in 1514 by Cardinal Wolsey, the ambitious and worldly lord chancellor (roughly, prime minister) of England and archbishop of York. He wanted it to be the absolute best palace in the land, and in this he succeeded so effectively that Henry VIII grew deeply envious, whereupon Wolsey felt obliged to give Hampton Court to the king. Henry moved in in 1525, adding a great hall and chapel, and proceeded to live much of his rumbustious life here. James I made further improvements at the beginning of the 17th century, but by the end of the century the palace was getting rather run-down. Plans were drawn up by the joint monarchs William III and Mary II to demolish the building and replace it

132

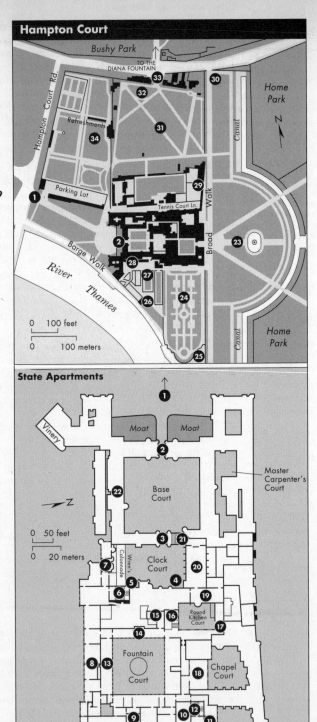

with a still larger and more splendid structure in conscious emulation of the great palace of Versailles outside of Paris. However, the royal purse wouldn't stretch quite that far. It was decided to keep the original buildings but add a new complex adjoining them at the rear, for which Wren was commissioned, and his graceful South Wing is one of the highlights of the whole palace. (A serious fire badly damaged some of Wren's chambers in 1986, but they were restored and opened again in 1992, with some of the Tudor features he had covered up uncovered again.) William and, especially, Mary loved Hampton Court and left their mark on the place—see their fine collections of Delftware and other porcelain.

The site beside the slow-moving Thames is perfect. The palace itself, steeped in history, hung with priceless paintings, full of echoing cobbled courtyards and cavernous Tudor kitchens, complete with deer pies and cooking pots—not to mention the ghost of Catherine Howard, who is still abroad, screaming her innocence (of adultery) to an unheeding Henry VIII—is set in a fantastic array of ornamental gardens, lakes, and ponds. Among the horticultural highlights are an Elizabethan Knot Garden, Henry VIII's Pond Garden, the enormous conical yews around the Fountain Garden, and the Great Vine near the Banqueting House, planted in 1768 and still producing Black Hamburg grapes, which you can buy in season. Best of all is the celebrated maze, which you enter to the north of the palace. It was planted in 1714 and is truly fiendish.

Royalty ceased living here with George III; poor George preferred the seclusion of Kew, where he was finally confined in his madness. The private apartments that range down one side of the palace are now occupied by pensioners of the Crown. Known as "grace and favor" apartments, they are among the most coveted homes in the country, with a surfeit of peace and history on their doorsteps. ⊠ *East Molesey,* ☎ *0181/977–8441.* ⌨ *Apartments and maze £8, maze alone £1.70, grounds free.* ☺ *State apartments Apr.–Oct., Tues.–Sun. 9:30–6, Mon. 10:15–6; Nov.–Mar., Tues.–Sun. 9:30–4:30, Mon. 10:15–4:30; grounds daily 8–dusk.*

3 Dining

No longer would Somerset Maugham be justified in saying, "If you want to eat well in England, have breakfast three times a day." London is in the midst of a restaurant revolution. Nearly everyone has become a foodie—even Sir Andrew Lloyd Webber, composer of Cats and Phantom, who has taken on a second career as dining critic. For a nightcap, take in London's fabulous pubs—more than a few are Victorian-era mini-theme parks. Hit the right one on the right night and watch that legendary British reserve melt away.

AS ANYONE KNOWS WHO READS the Sunday paper's travel section, London has had a restaurant boom, or rather, a restaurant atomic bomb explosion. The city has fallen head-over-heels in love with its restaurants—all 5,000 of them—from its vast, glamorous feederies to its tiny neighborhood joints, from pubs where young foodniks find their feet to swank boîtes where celebrity chefs launch their ego flights. You, too, must also be smitten, since you're spending, on average, 25% of your travel budget on eating out.

To appreciate London's rise in the culinary firmament, it helps to recall that at one time it was understood the British ate to live while the French lived to eat. Change was slow in coming after the Second World War, when steamed puddings and overboiled Brussels sprouts were still consumed on a daily basis by tweed-and-flannel-wrapped Brits. When people thought of British cuisine, fish 'n' chips came to mind. The latter was a grab-and-gulp dish that seemed to taste best wrapped in newspaper (a spoil-sport bureaucracy decreed that this wasn't sanitary, so the days of peeping at the latest murder news through a coating of tasty oil came to an end). Then there was always shepherd's pie, ubiquitously available in pubs—though not made according to the song from *Sweeney Todd,* "with real shepherd in it."

Today, nearly everything on the culinary front has changed. London's restaurant renaissance is credited to the new wave of cutting-edge chefs and inspired entrepreneurs. Sir Terence Conran, inventor of Habitat (British precursor to IKEA), began it all with Quaglino's, the first of the mega-restaurants that now decorate every corner of town. His 700-seater Mezzo became the biggest restaurant in Europe when it opened in 1995, though his Bluebird, opening in the King's Road mid-1997 will give it a run for its money, as will his City place, No. 1 Poultry, due out at press time. Antony Worrall Thompson's several places—Bistro 190, dell'Ugo, The Atrium, and a '60s revival, Drones—consistently please the dining public, while the biggest ego belongs to Marco Pierre White, the first British chef to earn three Michelin stars for his eponymous restaurant in the Hyde Park Hotel. Now, he's taking over everywhere: the Criterion, Les Saveurs, Mirabelle, and—in tandem with Damien Hirst, the award-winnning artist—Quo Vadis. The only thing that could top all this is his latest and vastest project—the 400-seat hubristically named Titanic.

The young Turk of the restaurateurs' club is Oliver Peyton, who unearthed a loophole in England's egregious alcohol licensing laws that enabled him to keep the once-trendissimo Atlantic Bar and Grill open (nearly) all hours. Next he pioneered the brash New York–style of see-and-be-seen place at Mayfair's Coast, and by now his huge Knightsbridge Italian concept will have joined his pack. Lunching ladies, models, and other assorted glitterati are catered to by gossip column regular, Mogens Tholstrup, at his South Kensington eaterie, Daphne, and at The Collection, in well-heeled Brompton Cross, while media darlings, actors, and novelists prefer the two perfect restaurants owned by Christopher Corbin and Jeremy King: Le Caprice and The Ivy. There are, of course, many more stars of this new celebrity category (Restaurateurs and Chefs), but you'll have to read about them when you get here—which you can easily do by picking up any newspaper. To keep up with the onslaught, they have about 15 restaurant reviewers apiece.

Luckily, London also does a good job of catering to people more interested in satisfying their appetites without breaking the bank than

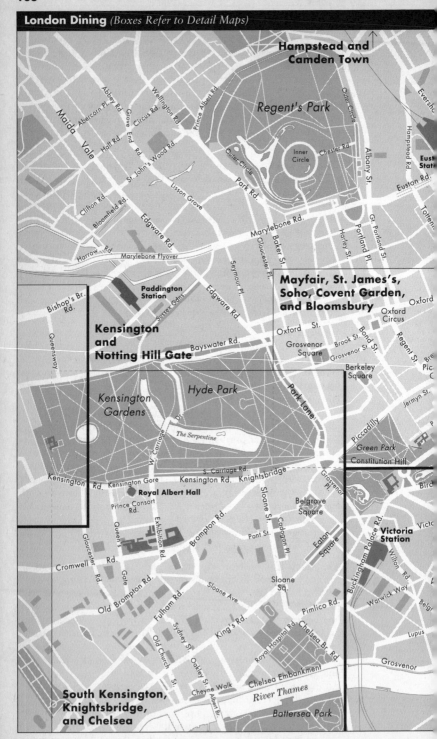

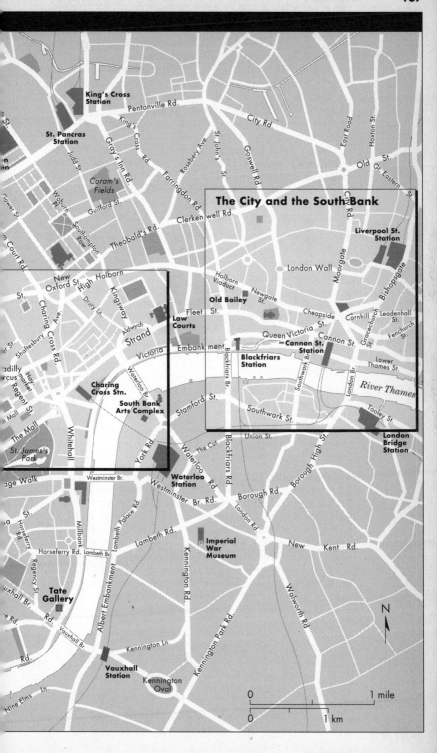

The City and the South Bank

King's Cross Station

St. Pancras Station

Pentonville Rd.

City Rd.

Coram's Fields

Guilford St.

Clerkenwell Rd.

Liverpool St. Station

London Wall

Moorgate

New Oxford St.

High Holborn

Holborn Viaduct

Old Bailey

Newgate St.

Law Courts

Fleet St.

Cheapside

Cornhill

Leadenhall St.

Charing Cross Rd.

Strand

Victoria

Embankment

Queen Victoria St.

Cannon St.

Cannon St. Station

Charing Cross Stn.

South Bank Arts Complex

Blackfriars Station

Southwark

London Br.

River Thames

Lower Thames St.

Stamford St.

Southwark St.

Tooley St.

London Bridge Station

Union St.

Waterloo Station

The Cut

Blackfriars Rd.

Borough Rd.

Borough High St.

Westminster Br.

Westminster Br. Rd.

London Rd.

New Kent Rd.

Lambeth Rd.

Imperial War Museum

Horseferry Rd.

Lambeth Br.

Kennington Rd.

Tate Gallery

Albert Embankment

Kennington Park Rd.

Walworth Rd.

N

Vauxhall Br.

Kennington Ln.

Vauxhall Station

Kennington Oval

Nine Elms Ln.

| 0 | | | | 1 mile |

| 0 | | | 1 km |

in the latest food fashions. We have tried to strike a balance in our list-ings between these extremes, and have included hip and happening places, neighborhood places, ethnic alternatives, and old favorites, plus some completely undemanding burger joints and regular restaurants for when you merely want to be fed. There are about 50 different cuisines on offer in London, and ethnic restaurants have always been a good bet here, especially the thousands of Indian restaurants, since Londoners see a good tandoori as their birthright (don't worry if they've changed from tandoori places to balti houses since you last looked—balti is only a name for a gloopily sauced curry that you scoop up with nan bread). Londoners are busy enlarging their purview to encompass most of the world. You'll see Malaysian, Spanish, and Turkish places, a drove of Thai restaurants, and a new wave of Japanese places, including the soba noodle cafés that are emulating the wonderful and popular Wagamama. With all this going on, traditional British food, when you track it down, appears as one more exotic cuisine in the pantheon.

As for cost, the democratization of restaurants does not necessarily mean smaller checks, and London is still not an inexpensive city. Damage-control methods include making lunch your main meal—the very top places often have bargain lunch menus, halving the price of evening à la carte—and ordering a second appetizer instead of an entrée, to which few places should object. (Note that an appetizer, usually known as a "starter," or "first course," is sometimes called an "entrée," as it is in France, and an entrée in England is dubbed "the main course," or simply "mains.") Seek out fixed-price menus, and watch for hid-den extras on the check: "cover," bread, and vegetables charged sep-arately, and service.

Many restaurants exclude service charges from the menu (which the law obliges them to display outside), then add 10%–15% to the check or else stamp SERVICE NOT INCLUDED along the bottom, in which case you should add the 10%–15% yourself. Don't pay twice for service—unscrupulous restaurateurs may add service, then leave the total in the credit card slip blank, hoping for more.

Two final caveats: First, is the roast beef of old England going to give you mad cow disease? If you recall, in 1996, there was a major cull of English oxen infected with feed gone bad. Now, most restaurants still have some form of disclaimer for the purity of their beef, and you can bet they're not lying if they say it's safe. Second, beware of Sundays. Many restaurants are closed on this day, especially in the evening; like-wise public holidays. Over the Christmas period, London shuts down completely—only hotels will be prepared to feed you. When in doubt, call ahead. It's as well to book a table anyway—one to four weeks ahead in some places. In 1996, Britons spent $33.6 billion on eating out, so you see, you'll have some competition for those tables.

CATEGORY	COST*
££££	over £45
£££	£30–£45
££	£15–£30
£	under £15

per person for a three-course meal, excluding drinks, service, and VAT

Mayfair

AMERICAN

££   ✕ **Smollensky's Balloon.** This American-style bar-restaurant is useful for those with children in tow, especially on weekends, when the young are fed burgers, fish sticks, and "Kids' Koktails," and taken off your hands by sundry clowns and magicians. The grown-ups' menu is absolutely committed to (fresh, additive-free) red meat, with several cuts of steak the specialty, all served with fries and a choice of sauces. There are also a handful of weekly specials, some fish dishes, and a couple of vegetarian choices, like Sicilian pasta shells, though you should not travel far for these. ⊠ *1 Dover St., W1, ☎ 0171/491–1199. AE, DC, MC, V. Tube: Green Park.*

£ ✕ **Gourmet Pizza Company.** Some of the wackier toppings at this California-style über-pizza joint don't hit the spot when you're dying for a Sicilian White, but there's always the "Plain and Simple" with fresh tomatoes and mozzarella, or the "Italian Sausage" if you can't face Chinese duck with Hoisin Sauce or Thai Chicken pies, and dinner salads are good and fresh. ⊠ *7–9 Swallow St. ☎ 0171/734–5182. Tube: Piccadilly Circus.*

BRITISH

£££ ✕ **The Greenhouse.** Tucked away behind the Mayfair mansions in a cute, cobbled mews is this elegant salon for people who like their food big and strong. You sit among extravagant topiary and men in ties to partake of British menus in the style of the now-departed, famous-from-TV-chef, Gary Rhodes: faggots (a type of meatball, once reviled) and braised oxtails; smoked eel risotto, venison and bacon stewed in red wine; stodgy, sticky English desserts like bread-and-butter pudding and steamed syrup sponge. Mr. Rhodes was also consultant chef at the People's Palace (☞ *below*). ⊠ *27A Hay's Mews, W1, ☎ 0171/499–3331. Reservations essential. AE, DC, MC, V. No lunch Sat. or dinner Sun. Tube: Green Park.*

£££ ✕ **The Square.** Young chef Philip Howard's sophisticated menu
★ changes every five minutes, but features a lot from the sea, and game fowl, all with its soul mate on the side: sweet and sour scallops and spiced squid; saddle of rabbit and *tarte fine* of onions; roast Tuscan pigeon paired with trompettes and balsamic vinegar; roasted salmon with asparagus risotto. Desserts are subtle—vanilla cream with red fruit compote, or a pile of crème brûlée with its sugar crust balanced on top, in a perfect square. Worldwide wines are grouped by grape and are not overpriced; waitstaff is knowledgeable, likeable, and efficient. We can't tell you about the decor, because the place moved after press time, but it used to be as subtle, sophisticated, and soaring as the food. ⊠ *Bruton St., ☎ 0171/495–7100. Reservations essential. AE, MC, V. No lunch weekends. Tube: Green Park.*

£–££ ✕ **Browns.** Unpretentious, crowd-pleasing, child-friendly English feeding is accomplished here at the former establishment of the bespoke tailors, Messrs. Cooling and Wells, now converted in Edwardian style by the owner of the very successful regional Browns eateries (the Oxford and Cambridge ones have put generations of students through school). Eat an all-day English breakfast, or steak and Guinness pie or salmon cakes, then sticky toffee pudding or sherry trifle. ⊠ *47 Maddox St., ☎ 0171/491–4565. Tube: Oxford Circus.*

FRENCH

££££ ✕ **Chez Nico at Ninety Park Lane.** Those with refined palates and very deep pockets would be well advised not to miss Nico Ladenis's exquisite cuisine, served in this suitably hushed and plush Louis XV dining room next to the Grosvenor House Hotel. Autodidact Nico is one of the world's great chefs, and he's famous for knowing it. The menu is in French and untranslated; vegetarians and children are not welcome. There is no salt on the table—ask for some at your peril. It's all more affordable in daylight, proffering set menus from £29 for three courses. ⊠ *90 Park La., W1, ☎ 0171/409–1290. Reservations essential. Jacket*

Dining in Mayfair, St. James's, Soho, Covent Garden, and Bloomsbury

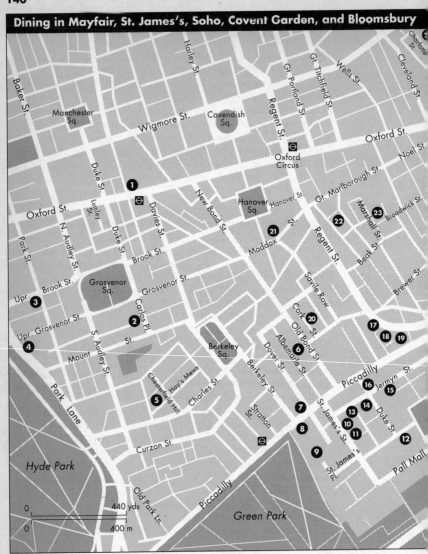

Alastair Little, **32**
The Avenue, **11**
Bahn Thai, **35**
Belgo Centraal, **42**
Bertorelli's, **46**
Browns, **21**
Bruno Soho, **36**
Café Fish, **39**
Café Flo, **44**
Chez Gerard, **25**
Chez Nico at Ninety
Park Lane, **4**
Coast, **6**
The Connaught, **2**

Crank's, **23**
Criterion, **38**
Deal's West, **22**
dell'Ugo, **31**
Down Mexico Way, **18**
Elena's L'Etoile, **24**
Fatboy's Diner, **50**
Food for Thought, **41**
The Fountain, **16**
Fung Shing, **37**
Gourmet Pizza
Company, **17**
The Greenhouse, **5**
Green's Restaurant
and Oyster Bar, **14**
The Ivy, **40**

Joe Allen's, **51**
Le Caprice, **9**
Le Gavroche, **3**
Le Palais du
Jardin, **43**
L' Escargot, **34**
L'Odéon, **19**
L'Oranger, **10**
Mandeer, **27**
Maxwell's, **47**
Mezzo, **30**
Mulligans, **20**
Museum Street Café, **29**
North Sea Fish
Restaurant, **53**
Orso, **48**

Pret a Manger, **45**
Quaglino's, **13**
The Ritz, **8**
Rules, **49**
Savoy Grill, **52**
Smollensky's
Balloon, **7**
Soho Soho, **33**
The Square, **12**
Wagamama, **28**
White Tower, **26**
Wilton's, **15**
Zoe, **1**

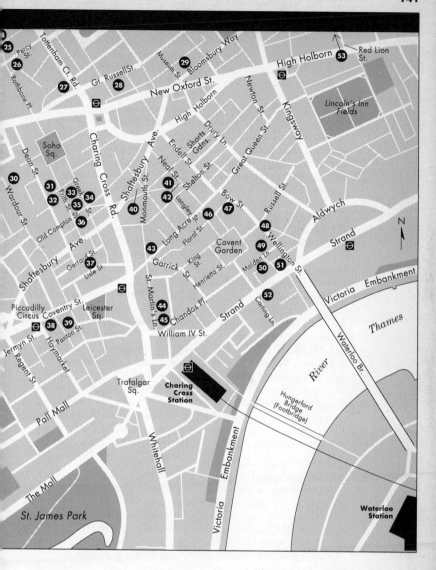

and tie. AE, DC, MC, V. Closed weekends and 3 wks in Aug. Tube: Marble Arch.

££££ ✕ **Le Gavroche.** Albert Roux has handed the toque to his son, Michel,
★ who retains many of his father's capital-C-Classical dishes under the heading *"Hommage à mon père,"* and who has added his own style to the place that was once considered London's finest restaurant. The basement dining room is comfortable and sedate, pleasing only if you like low-ceilinged rooms that are accented with potted plants and modern paintings. Yet again, the set lunch is relatively affordable at £38 (for canapés and three courses, plus mineral water, a half-bottle of wine, coffee, and petit fours, service *compris*). In fact, it's the only way to eat here if you don't have a generous expense account at your disposal—which most patrons do. You must reserve at least one week in advance. ✉ *43 Upper Brook St., W1,* ☎ *0171/408–0881. Reservations essential. Jacket and tie. AE, DC, MC, V. Closed weekends and 10 days at Christmas. Tube: Marble Arch.*

£££ ✕ **Criterion.** This spectacular neo-Byzantine mirrored marble hall, which first opened in 1874, is firmly back on the map, with the arrival of a new regime led by the somewhat self-promoting but super-talented Marco Pierre White. He doesn't cook here, but some of his well-known and often copied dishes appear on a menu whose divisions include one headed "Farinaceous Dishes"–where you'll find his black, buttery risotto of squid ink, for instance. The glamour of the soaring golden ceiling, peacock blue theater-size drapes, oil paintings, and attentive Gallic service adds up to an elegant night out. ✉ *Piccadilly Circus, W1,* ☎ *0171/930–0488. AE, DC, MC, V. Tube: Piccadilly Circus.*

££–£££ ✕ **L'Odéon.** This contribution to London's mania for giant restaurants overlooks Regent Street in a former airline office, its long, low dimensions peculiarly reminiscent of an aircraft, despite the gauzy partitions throughout. Bruno Loubet's French terroir/modern Brit food is startling and satisfying—invention without pretension. Tables by the huge arched windows are fun for people-watching. ✉ *65 Regent St., W1,* ☎ *0171/287–1400. AE, MC, V. Tube: Piccadilly Circus.*

FRENCH/TRADITIONAL BRITISH

££££ ✕ **The Connaught.** This charming and very grand mahogany-paneled,
★ velvet-upholstered, and crystal-chandeliered dining room belongs to the absolutely exclusive eponymous hotel (☞ Chapter 4). Waiters wear tails, tables must be booked far in advance, and prices are fearsome; but the restaurant remains London's most respected traditional dining room, with famed French chef Michel Bourdin still in charge of the kitchens after many years. This is the place for game—venison, guinea fowl, pigeon (not local birds)—presented with traditional trimmings or perhaps with some confection of wild mushrooms. "Luncheon dishes" change according to the day of the week (if this is Friday, it must be oxtail) and are not as exorbitant as they seem at first, because the price includes a starter and dessert. The Connaught is by no means a fashionable place, but it is never out of fashion. ✉ *Carlos Pl., W1,* ☎ *0171/499–7070. Reservations essential. Jacket and tie. MC. Closed weekends. Tube: Bond Street.*

INTERNATIONAL

£££ ✕ **Coast.** This former car showroom is now a posing palace of cool white curves, a piece of art that also draws a mini-version of itself (via a computer) on your check. It features a *slightly* pretentious menu that careens all over the world ("sauté of scallops, lettuce hearts with a creamed lemon and vanilla dressing," "roast sea bass, croûte of herb risotto, grilled *ventreche* and piquant *velouté*"—please don't ask for translations), ending with the signature dessert of tomato jam on vanilla cream. Avoid downstairs, which is like the set of Kubrick's film,

2001. ⊠ *26B Albermarle St., W1,* ☎ *0171/495–5999. AE, MC, V. Tube: Green Park.*

££ ✗ **Mulligans.** Mulligans is straight out of Dublin, down to the draught Guinness and copies of *The Irish Times* in the upstairs bar. Downstairs in the upscale restaurant department, order traditional dishes like steak, Guinness and oyster pie, and Irish stew with homey accompaniments like *colcannon* (buttery mashed potatoes with cabbage), then a big, Irish pudding. ⊠ *13–14 Cork St., W1,* ☎ *0171/409–1370. AE, MC, V. No lunch Sat. or dinner Sun. Tube: Green Park.*

££ ✗ **Zoe.** Handy for West End shopping, this two-level place serves two-level food—proper dinners downstairs in a sunlit basement of jazzy colors; and posh cocktails, coffee, and sandwiches ("hot spicy pork with prunes and crispy bacon" is typical) upstairs. It's another Antony Worrall Thompson place (☞ Bistrot 190 *in* South Kensington, *below*) and so features the trademark heartiness and 10,000 ingredients per dish (poached ham, parsley sauce, pease pudding, and hot potato salad; steak, spicy pumpkin and amaretto tortellini, spinach terrine, *Madeira jus*). ⊠ *St. Christopher's Pl., W1,* ☎ *0171/224–1122. AE, DC, MC, V. Closed Sun. No lunch Sat. Tube: Bond Street.*

£ ✗ **Down Mexico Way.** London is not known for its fine Tex-Mex, but here among the usual tortillas and burritos are a few adventurous numbers like fish in almond-chili sauce, with sides of cheese and jalapeño muffins or spiced spinach. Look for the beautiful Spanish ceramic tiles. Avoid evenings here if you want a quiet night out—the place is often taken over by party animals. ⊠ *25 Swallow St., W1,* ☎ *0171/437–9895. AE, MC, V. Tube: Piccadilly Circus.*

St. James's

£££ ✗ **L'Oranger.** Reserve weeks in advance, because this 1996 offshoot
★ of the impossible-to-get-into Aubergine in Chelsea just gets better and better, and everyone wants in. Marcus Wareing is the chef, and he cooks with gobsmacking precision and perfection: a tartare of mixed fish; a little cylinder of brill on a raft of crisped potato; the perfect plum *tarte fine* (brandied plum tart). The conservatory room with its train of tables up the middle is not the prettiest in town, but there's a little courtyard where the last duel in London was fought, and the all-French waiters are courteous and unsnobby. ⊠ *5 St. James's St.,* ☎ *0171/839–3774. AE, DC, MC, V. No lunch Sun. Tube: Green Park.*

££ ✗ **Café Fish.** Just to the east of St. James's proper, this cheerful, bustling restaurant has an encyclopedic selection of fish (shark and turbot join the trout, halibut, salmon, and monkfish, some brought daily from Normandy), arranged on the menu according to cooking method: chargrilled, steamed, meunière; smoked fish pâté is brought with the bread to get you in the mood as you choose your main selection. Downstairs there's an informal wine bar with a smaller selection of dishes. ⊠ *39 Panton St., SW1,* ☎ *0171/930–3999. AE, DC, MC, V. No lunch Sat. Tube: Piccadilly Circus.*

££££ ✗ **The Ritz.** Constantly accused of being London's prettiest dining room, this Belle Epoque palace of marble, gilt, and trompe l'oeil would moisten even Marie Antoinette's eye; add the view over Green Park and the Ritz's secret sunken garden, and it seems obsolete to consider eating. But David Nicholls' British/French cuisine stands up to the visual onslaught with costly morsels (foie gras, lobster, truffles, caviar, etc.), super-rich, all served with a flourish. Old retainers take great pride in this smooth operation, and are still here, despite the hotel's change of ownership. Englishness is wrested from Louis XVI by a daily roast "from the trolley," and a "British speciality" like Irish stew or braised oxtail. A three-course prix fixe lunch at £23 and a dinner at £29 make the check more bearable, but the wine list is pricey. A Friday and Saturday dinner dance sweetly maintains a dying tradition. ⊠ *Piccadilly, W1,* ☎ *0171/493–8181. Reservations essential. Jacket and tie. AE, DC, MC, V. Tube: Green Park.*

MODERN BRITISH

£££   ✕ **The Avenue.** Huge and loud, especially since it got permission to ply its City-glitzy clientele with beverages way beyond their bedtime (here that's until midnight Monday–Thursday; 12:30 AM Friday–Saturday), this was London's first restaurant to be owned by committee. Unlike the horse designed by committee (a camel), it's worked out OK, emulating New York/singles-heavy/dining-as-theater glamour, with a long, acid-yellow uplit glass bar and a very '80s bank of blinking TV screens at the entrance. The food is pretty good generic Euro-Brit (endive *tarte Tatin*; crab and crispy pork salad with chili dressing; chicken *pot au feu*), though the Baked Alaska could feed 10, and tastes like a s'more with a cocktail cherry. ⊠ *7–9 St. James's St.,* ☎ *0171/321–2111. AE, DC, MC, V. Tube: Green Park.*

£££   ✕ **Le Caprice.** Secreted in a small street behind the Ritz, Caprice may
★   command the deepest loyalty of any restaurant in London because it gets everything right: the glamorous, glossy black Eva Jiricna interior, the perfect pitch of the informal but respectful service, the food, halfway between Euro-peasant and fashion plate. This food—crispy duck and watercress salad; seared scallops with bacon and sorrel; risotto nero; Lincolnshire sausage with bubble-and-squeak (potato-and-cabbage hash); grilled rabbit with black olive polenta; and divine desserts, too—it has no business being so good, because the other reason everyone comes here is that everyone else does, which leads to the best people-watching in town. (Also try its sister restaurant, The Ivy; ☞ Covent Garden, *below.*) ⊠ *Arlington House, Arlington St., SW1,* ☎ *0171/629–2239. Reservations essential. AE, DC, MC, V. No lunch Sat. Tube: Green Park.*

£££   ✕ **Quaglino's.** Sir Terence Conran—of Bibendum, Mezzo, and Pont de la Tour fame—lavished £2.5 million doing up this famous pre–World War II haunt of the rich, bored, and well connected. Now past its fifth birthday, "Quags" is *the* out-of-towners' post-theater or celebration destination, while Londoners like its late hours. The gigantic sunken restaurant boasts a glamorous staircase, "Crustacea Altar," large bar, and live jazz music. The food is fashionably pan-European with some Asian trimmings—crab with mirin and soy; noodles with ginger, chili and cilantro; rabbit with prosciutto and herbs; roast crayfish; plateaux de fruits de mer. Desserts come from somewhere between the Paris bistro and the English nursery (raspberry sablé, parkin pudding with butterscotch sauce), and wine from the Old World and the New, some bottles at modest prices. ⊠ *16 Bury St., SW1,* ☎ *0171/930–6767. Reservations essential. AE, DC, MC, V. Tube: Green Park.*

TRADITIONAL BRITISH

££££ ✕ **Green's Restaurant and Oyster Bar.** The oyster side of things and the comfy-wood-paneled-restaurant angle are in equal balance at this reliable purveyor of the British dining experience, complete with the whiff of public (meaning private and exclusive) school, and its former inmates. Oysters, of course, are served (and not only whenever there's an "R" in the month), in two varieties, "small" or "large," alongside smoked fish, lobster cocktail, grilled sole, fish cakes, and so on, but there are comforting non-fishy English dishes, like shepherd's pie, too, and—the proper ending to a nanny-sanctioned meal—warm and fattening "nursery puddings," like steamed sponge with custard, and treacle tart. The wine list is notable, especially from the Champagne region. ⊠ *36 Duke St., St. James's, SW1,* ☏ *0171/930–4566. Reservations essential. Jacket and tie. AE, DC, MC, V. No dinner Sun. Tube: Green Park.*

££££ ✕ **Wilton's.** The search for the British Establishment stops here, among Edwardian booths full of politicians in a restaurant that traces its pedigree back to 1742 and offers a taste of the adjacent gentlemen's clubs—for which you pay through the nose. Fish is the mainstay of a plainspeaking menu, from which grilled Dover sole is probably ordered most often, with sherry trifle for afters, and an old-fashioned savory like angels-on-horseback (crisp bacon wrapped around oysters) with the port. Service is buttoned to the neck; one feels one ought to ask permission to use the bathroom. ⊠ *55 Jermyn St., SW1,* ☏ *0171/629–9955. Jacket and tie. AE, DC, MC, V. Closed Sat., last wk in July, 1st 2 wks in Aug., and 10 days at Christmas. Tube: Green Park.*

£ ✕ **The Fountain.** At the back of Fortnum and Mason's is this old-fash-
★ ioned restaurant, as frumpy and as popular as a boarding school matron, serving delicious light meals, toasted snacks, sandwiches, and ice-cream sodas. During the day, go for the Welsh rarebit or cold game pie; in the evening, a no-frills fillet steak is a typical option. Just the place for afternoon tea and ice-cream sundaes after the Royal Academy or Bond Street shopping, and for pre-theater meals. ⊠ *181 Piccadilly, W1,* ☏ *0171/734–4938. AE, DC, MC, V. Closed Sun. Tube: Green Park.*

Soho

CHINESE

££ ✕ **Fung Shing.** This comfortable, cool-green restaurant is a cut above
★ the Lisle/Wardour Street crowd in both service and ambience, as well as food. The usual Chinatown options are supplemented by some exciting dishes. Salt-baked chicken, served on or off the bone with an accompanying bowl of intense broth, is essential, and the adventurous might try intestines—deep-fried cigarette-shape morsels, far more delicious than you'd expect. ⊠ *15 Lisle St., WC2,* ☏ *0171/437–1539. AE, DC, MC, V. Tube: Leicester Square.*

FRENCH

££ ✕ **Bruno Soho.** Bruno is Bruno Loubet, who earned three Michelin stars at the Four Seasons, and is now at L'Odéon. Here, at the former Bistrot Bruno (are you following this?), his protégé, Pierre Khodja cooks a Middle Eastern/Moroccan/Mediterranean hybrid cuisine, with a separate mezze menu available: Typical offerings are marinated feta with nuts and raisins; lamb tajine with prunes and cinnamon; grilled sea bream (1997's trendiest fish) with cherimoya; and, for dessert, fried semolina with caramelized quince or frozen yogurt with lime, honey, and candied pumpkin. ⊠ *63 Frith St., W1,* ☏ *0171/734–4545. AE, DC, MC, V. Closed Sun. No lunch Sat. Tube: Leicester Square.*

£–£££ ✕ **Mezzo.** What does one do after opening London's biggest glamour restaurant? Open an even bigger one, of course. This is what Sir Terence Conran did after Quaglino's (☞ *above*); in fact, the 700-seater Mezzo isn't only London's biggest; it's the most gigantic restaurant in all of Europe. Downstairs is the restaurant proper, with its huge glass-walled kitchen, its Allen Jones murals, its grand piano and dance floor, and its typically Conran-French menu of things like seafood, rabbit stew, steak-frites, fig tart. Upstairs, the bar overlooks a canteen-style operation called Mezzonine, where bowls of coconut-galangal fish soup and grilled squid salad and red duck curry are Asian style. Finally, a late-night café/patisserie/newsstand has a separate entrance next door. The place was a London landmark from day one, with a see-and-be-seen bustle, despite its low celebrity count. ⊠ *100 Wardour St., W1,* ☎ *0171/314–4000. AE, DC, MC, V. Tube: Leicester Square.*

MEDITERRANEAN

££ ✗ **dell'Ugo.** At this three-floor Mediterranean café-restaurant from the stable of Antony Worrall Thompson (☞ Bistrot 190 *in* South Kensington, *below*) you can choose light fare—bruschetta loaded with marinated vegetables, mozzarella, Parmesan, etc., Tuscan soups, and country bread—or feast on wintry, warming one-pot ensembles and large plate-fuls of such sunny dishes as spicy sausage and white bean casserole with onion confit. The place gets overrun with hormone-swapping youth some weekends, but trendiness, on the whole, doesn't mar pleasure. ⊠ *56 Frith St., W1,* ☎ *0171/734–8300. Reservations essential for restaurant, not accepted for café. AE, MC, V. Closed Sun. Tube: Leicester Square.*

££ ✗ **Soho Soho.** The ground floor is a lively café bar with a (no booking) rotisserie, while upstairs is a more formal and expensive restaurant. Inspiration comes from Provence, both in the olive-oil cooking style and the decor, with its murals, primary colors, and pale-ocher terracotta floor tiles. The rotisserie serves omelets, salads, charcuterie, and cheeses, plus a handful of such bistro dishes as Toulouse sausages with fries; herbed, grilled poussin fish; and tarte Tatin. Or you can stay in the café-bar and have just a kir or a beer. ⊠ *11–13 Frith St., W1,* ☎ *0171/494–3491. AE, DC, MC, V. Closed Sun. Tube: Leicester Square.*

MODERN BRITISH

£££ ✗ **Alastair Little.** Little is one of London's most original—and most imitated—chefs, drawing inspiration from practically everywhere—Thailand, Japan, Scandinavia, France—and bringing it off brilliantly. His restaurant is starkly modern, so all attention focuses on the menu, which changes not once but twice daily in order to take advantage of the best ingredients. There will certainly be fish, but other than that it's hard to predict. Anyone truly interested in food will not be disappointed. Look out also for his newer, smaller, cheaper version—but with the same name—just by Ladbroke Grove tube. ⊠ *49 Frith St., W1,* ☎ *0171/734–5183. No credit cards. Closed weekends, 2 wks at Christmas, and 3 wks in Aug. Tube: Leicester Square.*

££ ✗ **L'Escargot.** This ever-popular media haunt serves Anglo-French food in its ground floor brasserie and its more formal upstairs restaurant. A comprehensive, reasonably priced wine list sets off a robust ragout of spiced lamb or a simple, fresh poached or grilled fish. This place is reliable and relaxed. ⊠ *48 Greek St., W1,* ☎ *0171/437–2679. AE, DC, MC, V. Closed Sun. Tube: Leicester Square.*

THAI

££ ✗ **Bahn Thai.** Many people find this the best of London's many Thai restaurants (you can see at least four others from the door), better still now that its ancient, gloomy decor has been excised. An immensely long menu features little chili symbols for the nervous of palate, plus easy options like char-grilled poussin marinated in honey and spices with a plum dipping sauce. Other Thai dishes are well explained. ⊠ *21A Frith St., W1,* ☎ *0171/437–8504. AE, MC, V. Tube: Leicester Square.*

THAI/AMERICAN

££ ✗ **Deals West.** Viscount Linley, Princess Margaret's son, and his two partners have hit on a winning formula here (and in the two other Dealses, at Chelsea Harbour and Hammersmith): an unlikely sounding merger between America and Thailand. Off Carnaby Street in a relaxed, barnlike diner with exposed brick walls, wooden floors, and beams, loudish music accompanies ribs, salads, and burgers—as well as Thai curries. Cocktails, extended hours, and live soul and funk on weekends make this popular with a young, after-work crowd. ⊠ *14– 16 Fouberts Pl., W1,* ☎ *0171/287–1001. AE, DC, MC, V. No dinner Sun. Tube: Oxford Circus.*

VEGETARIAN

£ ✗ **Crank's.** This is a popular vegetarian chain (there are other branches at Covent Garden, Great Newport Street, Adelaide Street, Tottenham Street, and Barrett Street), bought out by the management in 1992, and still serving meatless meals similar to the '60s menu that made their name. They are always crowded and, irritatingly, insist on closing at 8. ⊠ *8 Marshall St., W1,* ☎ *0171/437–9431. Reservations not accepted. AE, DC, MC, V. Closed Sun. Tube: Leicester Square.*

Covent Garden

AMERICAN

££ ✗ **Joe Allen's.** Long hours (thespians flock here after the curtain falls
★ in theaterland) and a welcoming, if loud, brick-walled interior mean New York Joe's London branch is still swinging after two decades. The fun, California-inflected menu helps: roast, stuffed poblano chili, or black bean soup are typical starters; entrées feature barbecue ribs with black-eyed peas and London's only available corn muffins, or roast monkfish with sun-dried-tomato salsa. There are the perennial egg dishes and huge salads, too, and Yankee desserts like grilled banana bread with ice cream and hot caramel sauce. It can get chaotic, with long waits for the cute waiters, but at least there'll be famous faces to ogle in the meantime. ⊠ *13 Exeter St., WC2,* ☎ *0171/836–0651. Reservations essential. No credit cards. Tube: Covent Garden.*

£ ✗ **Fatboy's Diner.** One for the kids, this is a 1941 chrome trailer transplanted from the banks of the Susquehanna in Pennsylvania and now secreted, unexpectedly, in a back street, complete with Astroturf "garden." A '50s jukebox accompanies the dogs, burgers, and fries. ⊠ *21 Maiden La., WC2,* ☎ *0171/240–1902. Reservations not accepted. No credit cards. Tube: Covent Garden.*

£ ✗ **Maxwell's.** London's first-ever burger joint, which turned 21 in '93, cloned itself and then grew up. Here's the result, a happy place under the Opera House serving the kind of food you're homesick for: quesadillas and nachos, Buffalo chicken wings, barbecue ribs, Cajun chicken, chef's salad, a real NYC Reuben, and a burger to die for. ⊠ *8–9 James St., WC2,* ☎ *0171/836–0303. AE, DC, V. Tube: Covent Garden.*

BELGIAN

£–££ ✗ **Belgo Centraal.** The wackiest dining concept in town started in Camden (☞ *below*), and was so adored, it was cloned uptown in a big basement space you have to enter by elevator. Have mussels and fries in vast quantities, served with your choice of 100 Belgian beers (fruit-flavored, Trappist-brewed, white, or light) by people dressed as monks in a hall like a refectory in a Martian monastery. Also eat *stoemp* (mashed potato and cabbage) with steak; wild boar sausages; lobster or roast chicken. The luxury index is low, but so is the check. ⊠ *50 Earlham St., WC2,* ☎ *0171/813–2233. AE, DC, MC, V. Tube: Covent Garden.*

FRENCH

££ ✗ **Le Palais du Jardin.** This does a fair imitation of a Parisian brasserie, complete with a seafood bar offering lobsters for a tenner, though there's plenty else—duck confit with apples and prunes; coq au vin; tuna with a black olive-potato cake. It's not quite as chic as it looks, but neither is it as expensive, which accounts for why it is always busy. ✉ *136 Long Acre, WC2,* ☎ *0171/379–5353. AE, DC, MC, V. Tube: Covent Garden.*

£ ✗ **Café Flo.** This useful brasserie serves the bargain "Idée Flo"—soup or salad, *steak-frites* or *poisson-frites,* and coffee—a wide range of French café food, breakfast, wines, *tartes,* espresso, fresh orange juice, simple set-price weekend menus . . . everything for the Francophile on a budget. There are branches in Hampstead, Islington, Fulham, and Kensington. ✉ *51 St. Martin's La., WC2,* ☎ *0171/836–8289. MC, V. Tube: Covent Garden.*

FRENCH/TRADITIONAL BRITISH

££££ ✗ **Savoy Grill.** The grill continues in the first rank of power dining locations. Politicians, newspaper barons, and tycoons like the comforting food and impeccably discreet and attentive service in the low-key, yew-paneled salon. On the menu, an omelet Arnold Bennett (with cheese and smoked fish) is perennial, as is beef Wellington on Tuesday and roast Norfolk duck on Friday. Playgoers can split their theater menu, eating part of their meal before the show, the rest after. ✉ *Strand, WC2,* ☎ *0171/836–4343. Reservations essential. Jacket and tie. AE, DC, MC, V. Closed Sun. No lunch Sat. Tube: Aldwych.*

INTERNATIONAL

£££ ✗ **The Ivy.** This seems to be everybody's favorite restaurant—every-
★ body who works in the media or the arts, that is. In a deco dining room with blinding white tablecloths, and Hodgkins and Paolozzis on the walls, the celebrated and the wannabes eat Caesar salad, roast grouse, shrimp gumbo, braised oxtail, and rice pudding with Armagnac prunes or sticky toffee pudding. For star-trekking ("Don't look now, dear, but there's Ralph Fiennes."), this is probably the top place in London. ✉ *1 West St., WC2,* ☎ *0171/836–4751. AE, DC, MC, V. Tube: Covent Garden.*

£ ✗ **Pret a Manger.** You'll fall over this 10-year-old sandwich chain's cafés wherever you go, and, sooner or later, you'll be grateful, because the quality and freshness of the chicken breast and avocado on walnut bread, or the lox and cream cheese bagel, or the spinach quiche, lemon cake, banana bread, almond croissant, etc., are tops. There's even sushi. ✉ *78 St. Martin's La.,* ☎ *0171/379–5335. No credit cards. Tube: Covent Garden.*

ITALIAN

£££ ✗ **Orso.** The Italian brother of Joe Allen's (☞ *below*), this basement restaurant has the same snappy staff and a glitzy clientele of showbiz types and hacks. The Tuscan-style menu changes every day, but always includes excellent pizza and pasta dishes, plus entrées based perhaps on grilled rabbit or roast sea bass and first courses of roquette (arugula) with shaved Parmesan or deep-fried zucchini flowers stuffed with ricotta. Food here is never boring, much like the place itself. ✉ *27 Wellington St., WC2,* ☎ *0171/240–5269. Reservations essential. No credit cards. Tube: Covent Garden.*

££–£££ ✗ **Bertorelli's.** Right across from the stage door of the Royal Opera House, Bertorelli's is quietly chic, the food is tempting, and the menu is just innovative enough: poached *cotechino* (highly spiced) sausage with lentils and monkfish ragout with fennel, tomato, and olives are two typical dishes. A top-to-toe refurbishment recently rearranged the casual vs. formal options, with a big café-bar downstairs and a smaller restaurant upstairs. ⊠ *44A Floral St., WC2, ☎ 0171/836–3969. AE, DC, MC, V. Tube: Covent Garden.*

TRADITIONAL BRITISH

£££ ✗ **Rules.** Come, escape from the 20th century. Almost 200 years old,
★ this gorgeous London institution has welcomed everyone from Dickens to Charlie Chaplin to Lillie Langtry and the Prince of Wales. The menu is historic and good, even if some food critics feel it's "theme-park-y"; try the noted Steak and Kidney and Mushroom Pudding for a virtual taste of the 18th century. Happily, the decor is even more delicious: With plush red banquettes and lacquered Regency-yellow walls (which are festively adorned with 19th-century oil paintings and dozens of framed engravings), this is probably the most marvelous dining salon in London. For a main dish, try the seasonal entrées on the list of daily specials, which will, in season, include game from Rules's own Scottish estate (venison is disconcertingly called "deer"). Rules is more than a little touristy, but that's because it's so timelessly quaint. ⊠ *35 Maiden La., WC2, ☎ 0171/836–5314. AE, DC, MC, V. Tube: Covent Garden.*

VEGETARIAN

£ ✗ **Food for Thought.** This simple basement restaurant (no liquor license) seats only 50 and is extremely popular, so you'll almost always find a line of people down the stairs. The menu—stir-fries, casseroles, salads, and desserts—changes every day, and each dish is freshly made; there's no microwave. ⊠ *31 Neal St., WC2, ☎ 0171/836–0239. Reservations not accepted. No credit cards. Closed 2 wks at Christmas. Tube: Covent Garden.*

Bloomsbury

FRENCH

££–£££ ✗ **Elena's L'Etoile.** Elena Salvoni presided for years and years over
★ L'Escargot in Soho, where she made so many friends among happy customers she was rewarded with her name in lights—at 75 years old. This understated century-old place, whose only concession to trendiness of decor is a row of bentwood chairs unaccountably roped to the top of one wall, is one of London's few remaining unreconstructed French bistro restaurants. There's duck braised with red cabbage in an individual casserole, there's sole meunière, and poulet rôti, terrines, salade frisée, crème caramel, tarte au citron, and a warm smile from Elena, whether you're one of the politician/journalist/actor regulars, or just you. Upstairs is a table for sharing—useful for single travelers or business trippers. ⊠ *30 Charlotte St., W1, ☎ 0171/636–7189. AE, DC, MC, V. Closed Sun. No lunch Sat. Tube: Goodge Street.*

££ ✗ **Chez Gerard.** One of an excellent chain of steak-frites restaurants, this one has widened the choice on the utterly Gallic menu to include more for non–red meat eaters: new options now include brioche filled with wild mushrooms and artichoke hearts, for instance, plus fish dishes and even something for vegetarians, such as stuffed roast onion. Steak, served with shoestring fries and béarnaise sauce, remains the reason to visit, though. ⊠ *8 Charlotte St., W1, ☎ 0171/636–4975. AE, DC, MC, V. Tube: Goodge Street.*

GREEK

£££ ✗ **White Tower.** The White Tower is quite different from the average London Greek restaurant: its three Georgian stories are lined with antique pistols and prints (and a portrait of that most famous Hellenist, Lord Byron), and its menu lists many unusual dishes, like the cracked wheat, fruit, and nut-stuffed duck you must order in advance, or the chicken Paxinou, served with fried banana and aubergine (eggplant). The *taramasalata* (cod's roe dip) is the best in town, was the first in town, and is always ordered by the many establishment types who love this place. ✉ *1 Percy St., W1,* ☎ *0171/636–8141. Reservations essential. Jacket and tie. AE, DC, MC, V. Closed weekends, 3 wks in Aug., and 1 wk at Christmas. Tube: Goodge Street.*

INDIAN VEGETARIAN

£ ✗ **Mandeer.** Buried in a basement, with tile floors, brick walls, and temple lamps, the Mandeer is useful for being central (off Tottenham Court Road, where there's nothing much else), and extremely cheap at lunchtime, when you help yourself to the buffet. ✉ *21 Hanway Pl., W1,* ☎ *0171/580–3470. Reservations not accepted for lunch. AE, DC, MC, V. Closed Sun. and 2 wks at New Year'. Tube: Tottenham Court Road.*

JAPANESE

£ ✗ **Wagamama.** London is wild for Japanese noodles in this big base-
★ ment. It's high-tech (your order is taken on a hand-held computer), high-volume—there are always crowds, with which you share wooden refectory tables—and high-turnover, with a fast-moving line always at the door. You can choose ramen in or out of soup, topped with sliced meats or tempura; or "raw energy" dishes—rice, curries, tofu, and so on—all at give-away prices and doggy-bag sizes. So successful has this formula proved, there is now an entire range of clothing, so that grateful diners can *wear* Wagamama. Many of them alternate this Wagamama experience with the newer one at 10a Lexington Street (☎ 0171/292–0990), near Oxford Circus. ✉ *4 Streatham St., WC1,* ☎ *0171/323–9223. Reservations not accepted. No credit cards. Tube: Tottenham Court Road.*

MODERN BRITISH

££ ✗ **Museum Street Café.** This useful and reliable restaurant near the British Museum serves a limited selection of impeccably fresh dishes, intelligently and plainly cooked by the two young owners, and charged prix fixe. The evening menu might feature char-grilled, maize-fed chicken with pesto, followed by a rich chocolate cake; at lunchtime you might choose a sandwich of Stilton on walnut bread and a big bowl of soup. Repeat customers, be prepared for a shock—the place has doubled in size, and you no longer have to bring your own wine, but there's still an atypical (for London) ban on smoking. ✉ *47 Museum St., WC1,* ☎ *0171/405–3211. Reservations essential. MC, V. Closed weekends. Tube: Tottenham Court Road.*

SEAFOOD

£ ✗ **North Sea Fish Restaurant.** This is the place for the British national
★ dish of fish-and-chips—battered and deep-fried whitefish with thick fries shaken with salt and vinegar. It's a bit tricky to find—three blocks south of St. Pancras station, down Judd Street. Only freshly caught fish is served, and you can order it grilled—though that would defeat the object. You can take out or eat in. ✉ *7–8 Leigh St., WC1,* ☎ *0171/387–5892. AE, DC, MC, V. Closed Sun. Tube: Russell Square.*

South Kensington

FRENCH

££££ ✗ **Bibendum.** When it opened a decade ago, this reconverted Miche-
★ lin showroom, adorned with art deco decorations and brilliant stained glass, became one of London's dining showplaces; today, with the Princess of Wales sometimes in attendance, it's still a major lure. You can come here for the Conran Shop (☞ Chapter 7) or Oyster Bar, but

most arrive to enjoy the kitchen's offerings, superlatively created for the past several years by Simon Hopkinson. He is famous for preparing simple dishes perfectly, whose preparation he now details in various magazines, while still keeping an eye on this restaurant, of which he is part-owner. Current chef, Matthew Harris, continues in a similar vein. Thus you can order herring with sour cream, a risotto, leeks vinaigrette followed by steak au poivre or the perfect boeuf bourgignon, or you might try brains or tripe as they ought to be cooked. The £27 set-price menu at lunchtime is money well spent. ⊠ *Michelin House, 81 Fulham Rd., SW3,* ☎ *0171/581–5817. Reservations essential. MC, V. Closed Sun. Tube: South Kensington.*

££ ✕ **Lou Pescadou.** This place is like a little *tranche* of the South of France,
★ with the sea-theme decor and emphatically French staff. The menu changes often and is based on fish—don't miss the *soupe de poisson* with croutons and *rouille* (rose-color, garlicky mayonnaise) if it's on—but there are other dishes, too, from steak-frites to, perhaps, delicate braised *cervelles* (brains). ⊠ *241 Old Brompton Rd., SW5,* ☎ *0171/370–1057. Reservations not accepted. AE, DC, MC, V. Closed Aug. Tube: Earl's Court.*

MEDITERRANEAN

£££ ✕ **The Collection.** Enter the former Katherine Hamnett shop through the spotlighted tunnel over the glass drawbridge, and immediately get engulfed in one of the most fashionable crowds in London. A huge warehouse setting—adorned with industrial wooden beams and steel cables, a vast bar, and suspended gallery—makes a great theater for people-watching. Around you are well-dressed nobs gawping at the neighboring tables for an Amber Valletta sighting, or hoping owner-*doré* Mogens Tholstrup will table-hop to theirs, while they pick at Med food seasoned with Japanese and Thai bits and bobs (seared tuna with sesame, soy, and shiitake mushrooms, or sea bream with cilantro. Ah, fashion, fashion, fashion! ⊠ *264 Brompton Rd.,* ☎ *0171/225–1212. AE, DC, MC, V. No dinner Sun. Tube: South Kensington.*

££ ✕ **Bistrot 190.** Chef-restaurateur Antony Worrall Thompson (☞ dell'Ugo, *above*) specializes in happy, hearty food from Southern Europe and around the Mediterranean rim in raucous hardwood-floor-and-art settings. The identifiable feature of an AWT menu is its lists of about 100 loosely related ingredients (pork chop with rhubarb compote, cheese, and mustard mash, for instance), which when read all at once, cause you to salivate (or occasionally gag). Country bread with tapenade and smoked haddock butter are brought first to the table; char-grilled squid with red and green salsa, and a great lemon tart are always in favor. This place, which was Thompson's first, is handy to museum or Albert Hall excursions. ⊠ *190 Queen's Gate, SW7,* ☎ *0171/581–5666. Reservations not accepted. AE, DC, MC, V. No lunch Sat. Tube: Gloucester Road.*

££ ✕ **Downstairs at 190.** This is a Worrall Thompson creation—this time a good-value fish restaurant (☞ Bistrot 190, *above*). You can choose appetizers, like grilled mussels and clams with garlic crumbs or smoked haddock and salmon carpaccio with anchovy ice cream, then go for lobster ravioli or a cassoulet of fish, and attempt whisky fudge cake with caramelized oranges. ⊠ *190 Queen's Gate, SW7,* ☎ *0171/581–5666. AE, DC, MC, V. Closed Sun. Tube: Gloucester Road.*

POLISH

£ ✕ **Daquise.** This venerable and well-loved Polish café by the tube station is incongruous in this neighborhood, as it is neither style-conscious nor expensive. Fill your stomach without emptying your pocketbook (or, it must be said, overstimulating your taste buds) on *bigos* (sauerkraut with garlic sausage and mushrooms), stuffed cabbage, cucumber salad,

Dining in South Kensington, Knightsbridge, and Chelsea

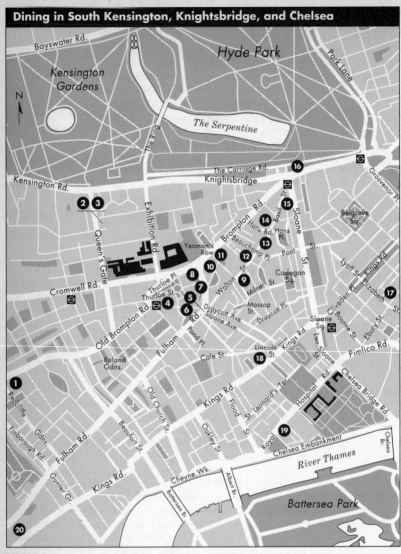

or just coffee and cake. ✉ *20 Thurloe St., SW7,* ☎ *0171/589–6117. No credit cards. Tube: South Kensington.*

Knightsbridge

FRENCH

££££ ✗ **The Capital.** This elegant, clublike dining room has chandeliers and greige rag-rolled walls, a grown-up atmosphere, and formal service. Chef Philip Britten keeps his star bright with perhaps a subtle baked mousse of haddock and ginger, an *emincé* of chicken with olives, or pot-roasted pigeon with Armagnac, then a perfect caramel soufflé with butterscotch sauce. Set-price menus both at lunch (£25) and in the evening (£40—for *six* courses) make it somewhat more affordable, although the best dishes are found à la carte. ✉ *22–24 Basil St., SW3,* ☎ *0171/589–5171. Reservations essential. Jacket and tie. AE, DC, MC, V. Tube: Knightsbridge.*

££ ✗ **St. Quentin.** A very popular slice of Paris, this restaurant is frequented by French expatriates and locals alike. Every inch of the Gallic menu is explored—Gruyère quiche, escargots, cassoulet, lemon tart—in the bourgeois provincial comfort so many London chains (the Dômes, the Cafés Rouges) try for yet fail to achieve. ✉ *243 Brompton Rd., SW3,* ☎ *0171/589–8005. AE, DC, MC, V. Tube: South Kensington.*

INTERNATIONAL

£ ✗ **Stockpot.** You'll find speedy service in this large, jolly restaurant, often packed to the brim with young people and shoppers. The food is filling and wholesome: try the Lancashire hot pot, for example, and the apple crumble. ✉ *6 Basil St., SW3,* ☎ *0171/589–8627. No credit cards. Tube: Knightsbridge.* ✉ *40 Panton St., off Leicester Sq.,* ☎ *0171/839–5142;* ✉ *18 Old Compton St., Soho,* ☎ *0171/287–1066;* ✉ *273 King's Rd., Chelsea,* ☎ *0171/823–3175.*

ITALIAN

££££ ✗ **Marco Pierre White: The Restaurant.** One fears one ought to have read The Book and seen The Movie before patronizing The Restaurant. Actually, if one is from London, one has. Bad boy Marco enjoys Jagger-like fame from his TV appearances and gossip column reports of his complicated love life and random eruptions of fury. He should stick to his pans, say superchef critics, meaning it literally in some cases. But, hype aside, Marco is a great chef and now gets to show off in his most serious setting yet—all valuable oils, crisp napery, and batteries of flatware. If you invest in an evening here, know that he will despise you for ordering his Assiette of Chocolate, which he considers low-class. ✉ *Hyde Park Hotel, Knightsbridge, SW3,* ☎ *0171/259–5380. Reservations essential. Jacket and tie. AE, DC, MC, V. Tube: Knightsbridge.*

£££ ✗ **San Lorenzo.** This well-established, well-heeled trattoria has unexceptional decor and is nothing special foodwise, but it's just the ticket if you're keen to spot celebrities or the very occasional royal, or to gaze into the world of ladies-who-lunch. The usual upscale Italian dishes are here, but they nod to fashion—try wood pigeon with polenta, or any of the veal dishes. ✉ *22 Beauchamp Pl., SW3,* ☎ *0171/584–1074. AE, DC, MC, V. Closed Sun. Tube: South Kensington.*

PORTUGUESE

££ ✗ **Caravela.** This narrow lower-ground-floor place is one of London's few Portuguese restaurants. You can get *Caldo verde* (cabbage soup), *bacalhau* (salt-cured cod), and other typical dishes while listening (on Friday or Saturday) to the national music, fado—desperately sad songs belted out at thrash-metal volume. ⊠ *39 Beauchamp Pl., SW3, ☎ 0171/581–2366. AE, DC, MC, V. No lunch Sun. Tube: South Kensington.*

RUSSIAN

£ ✗ **Luba's Bistro.** Popular for decades: long wooden tables, plain decor, and authentic Russian cooking—chicken Kiev, beef Stroganoff, etc. Bring your own wine. ⊠ *6 Yeoman's Row, SW3, ☎ 0171/589–2950. Reservations essential. MC, V. Closed Sun. Tube: South Kensington.*

TRADITIONAL BRITISH

££££ ✗ **Waltons.** Popular with Americans, this formal, sumptuous, pampering restaurant has strong color schemes, acres of rich fabrics, and flowers. The cuisine is as rich as the surroundings and, though billed as British, is not so easy to categorize—ravioli stuffed with lobster or steamed red mullet in a fondue of tomatoes and fresh basil are as likely as roast lamb. Finish with a "mess" of berries, cream, and meringue. ⊠ *121 Walton St., SW3, ☎ 0171/584–0204. Jacket and tie. AE, DC, MC, V. Tube: South Kensington.*

Chelsea

AMERICAN

££ ✗ **PJ's.** The decor here evokes the Bulldog Drummond lifestyle, with wooden floors and stained glass, a vast, slowly revolving propeller from a 1940s Curtis flying boat, and polo memorabilia. A menu of all-American staples (soft-shell crab, chowder, gumbo, steaks, smoked ribs), big salads, pecan pie, brownies, and Häagen-Dazs should please all but vegetarians, and portions are big, but this place is more remarkable for ambience than for food—it's open late, it's relaxed, friendly, and efficient, and it has bartenders who can mix anything. The sister PJ's in Covent Garden (⊠ 30 Wellington St., ☎ 0171/240–7529) is worth remembering for its excellent weekend "Fun Club" for kids. ⊠ *52 Fulham Rd., SW3, ☎ 0171/581–0025. AE, DC, MC, V. Tube: South Kensington.*

ANGLO-INDIAN

£££ ✗ **Chutney Mary.** London's first-and-only Anglo-Indian restaurant provides a fantasy version of the British Raj, all giant wicker armchairs and palms. Dishes like Masala roast lamb (practically a whole leg, marinated and spiced) and "Country Captain" (braised chicken with almonds, raisins, chilies, and spices) alternate with the more familiar North Indian dishes such as *roghan josh* (lamb curry). The best choices are certainly the dishes re-created from the kitchens of Indian chefs cooking for English palates back in the old Raj days. For this reason, the all-you-can-eat Sunday buffet is not such a great idea, because it leaves those out. Service is deferential, and desserts, unheard of in tandoori places, are usually worth leaving room for. ⊠ *535 King's Rd., SW10, ☎ 0171/351–3113. Reservations essential. AE, DC, MC, V. Tube: Fulham Broadway.*D /rd

FRENCH

££££ ✗ **La Tante Claire.** Justly famous, this is probably the best restaurant
★ in London now. The decor is light and sophisticated, the service impeccable, the French wine list impressive, but the food is the point. From the *carte,* you might choose hot pâté de foie gras on shredded potatoes with a sweet wine and shallot sauce, roast spiced pigeon, or Pierre Koffmann's famous signature dish of pig's feet stuffed with mousse of white meat with sweetbreads and wild mushrooms. As every gourmet expense-accounter knows, the set lunch menu (£26) is a genuine bar-

gain. Lunch reservations must be made 2–3 days in advance, dinner reservations 3–4 weeks in advance. ⊠ *68 Royal Hospital Rd., SW3,* ☎ *0171/352–6045. Reservations essential. Jacket and tie. AE, DC, MC, V. Closed weekends, 2 wks at Christmas, 10 days at Easter, and 3 wks in Aug.–Sept. Tube: Sloane Square.*

£££ ✕ **Mijanou.** This is the leading haunt of politicians and Whitehall civil servants. Chef Sonia Blech claims on the menu that she "merely rearranges the natural ingredients which have always existed," but she's too modest, as such complicated dishes as her quail stuffed with wild rice and pecan nuts or lobster terrine with a mild saffron sauce will prove. Smoking is banned in the entire restaurant, which is just as well, because it's tiny. There is a small patio and a large, brilliant wine list drawn up by the chef's husband, Neville Blech. ⊠ *143 Ebury St., SW1,* ☎ *0171/730–4099. Reservations essential. Jacket and tie. AE, DC, MC. Closed weekends, 1 wk at Christmas, and most of Aug. Tube: Sloane Square.*

££ ✕ **La Brasserie.** This is a convenient spot for South Ken museum visits and has flexible and long opening hours, a menu of entirely French things—from fish soup to tarte tatin—and a good buzz on a Sunday morning when the entire well-heeled neighborhood sits around reading the papers and sipping cappuccino. No doing that at peak times, when you must eat, but the food's reliable, if a little overpriced. ⊠ *272 Brompton Rd., SW3,* ☎ *0171/584–1668. AE, DC, MC, V. Tube: South Kensington.*

INTERNATIONAL

£ ✕ **Chelsea Kitchen.** This café has been crowded since the '60s with hungry people after hot, filling, and inexpensive food. Expect nothing more fancy than pasta, omelets, salads, stews, and casseroles. The menu changes every day. ⊠ *98 King's Rd., SW3,* ☎ *0171/589–1330. Reservations not accepted. No credit cards. Tube: Sloane Square.*

Kensington and Notting Hill Gate

AMERICAN

£ ✕ **Tootsies.** A superior burger place, Tootsies is dark but cheerful, and decorated with vintage advertisements. Vintage rock plays in the background. Alternatives to the burgers, which come with great fries, are big salads, steak, BLTs, and several variations on chicken breast. The usual ices and pies do for dessert. There are branches in Fulham, Chiswick, and Notting Hill. ⊠ *120 Holland Park Ave., W11,* ☎ *0171/229–8567. Reservations not accepted. MC, V. Tube: Holland Park.*

FRENCH

£££ ✕ **Boyd's.** Boyd Gilmour was a professional percussionist who decided he'd rather rattle the pans, and so built this glass-roofed conservatory garden. It's a soothing, satisfying restaurant, the cooking unpretentious— crab ravioli with ginger and scallions; wood pigeon in a black-currant sauce; chocolate terrine—the atmosphere calmer than at near-neighbor Kensington Place (☞ *below*). A 100-bottle wine list includes about 10 to sample by the glass. ⊠ *135 Kensington Church St., W8,* ☎ *0171/727– 5452. Jacket and tie. AE, MC, V. Closed Sun., Mon., and 1 wk at Christmas. Tube: Notting Hill Gate.*

£££ ✕ **Chez Moi.** Sophisticated French food is served in a warm salmon-pink dining room, which, with the tables widely spaced and the lighting low, demands romantic behavior. There are dishes the menu admits are "traditional" that Chez Moi's fans have depended on for a quarter century—things like rack of lamb with garlic and mint, and beef tournedos with béarnaise—as well as more novel dishes such as the popular "Oursins Chez Moi," ersatz sea urchins made of shrimp and

156

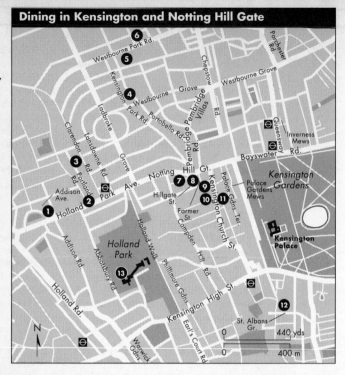

Dining in Kensington and Notting Hill Gate

scallop, with fried angel-hair pasta "spines." The desserts are hit-or-miss, but there are ample chocolates brought with the coffee. ✉ *1 Addison Ave., W11,* ☎ *0171/603–8267. Reservations essential. AE, DC, MC, V. Closed Sun., 2 wks at Christmas, and 2 wks in Aug. No lunch Sat. Tube: Shepherd's Bush.*

FRENCH/CALIFORNIAN

£££ ✗ **Clarke's.** There's no choice on the evening menu at Sally Clarke's award-winning restaurant; her dinners feature ultrafresh ingredients, plainly but perfectly cooked, accompanied by home-baked breads. The plant and art–speckled room is similarly home-style, if home is in the big white Kensington houses you see around here. ✉ *124 Kensington Church St., W8,* ☎ *0171/221–9225. Reservations essential. MC, V. Closed weekends and 2 wks in Aug. Tube: Notting Hill Gate.*

GREEK

£ ✗ **Costa's Grill.** Come for good value and such down-to-earth Greek food as grilled fish and *kleftiko* (roast lamb on the bone). The atmosphere is homey and happy, and there's a tiny garden open in summer. ✉ *14 Hillgate St., W8,* ☎ *0171/229–3794. No credit cards. Closed Sun. and 3 wks in summer. Tube: Notting Hill Gate.*

MEDITERRANEAN

££ ✗ **The Belvedere.** There can be no finer setting for a summer supper or a sunny Sunday brunch than a window table—or a balcony one if you luck out—at this stunning restaurant in the middle of Holland Park. The menu is big on shaved Parmesan, sun-dried tomatoes, and arugula, which suits the conservatorylike room, but both food and service do occasionally miss the target. Still, with a view like this, who cares about water glasses or bland chicken? ✉ *Holland Park, off Abbotsbury Rd., W8,* ☎ *0171/602–1238. Reservations essential. AE, DC, MC, V. No dinner Sun. Tube: Holland Park.*

MODERN BRITISH

£££ ✕ **First Floor.** A place for well-off but arty locals who know and watch each other, popular both for its inventive food and its ambience—it looks like a bombed church inhabited by distressed nobility. There's a great brunch on weekends; otherwise go for Thai fishcakes or Tuscan lamb stew; or grilled ostrich rump with mango salsa and potato pancake. Sides—coconut mashed potatoes or mustard apple puree—often hit the heights, as do desserts like pear and almond tart. ✉ 186 Portobello Rd., W11, ☎ 0171/243–0072. Reservations essential. AE, MC, V. Tube: Notting Hill Gate.

£££ ✕ **Kensington Place.** Being a favorite among the local glitterati keeps
★ this place packed and noisy. A huge plate-glass window and mural are backdrops to Rowley Leigh's fashionable food—grilled foie gras with sweet-corn pancake and baked tamarillo with vanilla ice are perennials—but it's the buzz that draws the crowds. ✉ 201 Kensington Church St., W8, ☎ 0171/727–3184. MC, V. Tube: Notting Hill Gate.

££ ✕ **192.** A noisy, buzzy wine bar/restaurant just off the Portobello
★ Road, this is as much a social hangout for the local media mafia as a restaurant, especially on weekends, when you'll feel like you've gate-crashed a party, if you manage to get a table, that is. Food likes to keep ahead of fashion, and is best on the appetizer list—many people order two of these instead of an entrée. Try the risottos, the seasonal salad (perhaps romanesco, broccoli, anchovy, and gremolata), the fish (sea bass with fennel, lemon, and rosemary; scallop, chickpea, chorizo, and clam casserole), or whatever sounds unusual. ✉ 192 Kensington Park Rd., W11, ☎ 0171/229–0482. AE, MC, V. Closed Mon. Tube: Notting Hill Gate.

£ ✕ **All Saints.** One warms to the wobbly kitchen chairs and spartan plaster walls here after a bottle or two of the inexpensive house wine, and an enormous portion of home-style cooking. Serial chefs alter the nature of the food, but not of the place, home-away-from-home for young and trendy Notting Hillbillies. Menu staples include roast vegetables with aioli, lamb brochette with tabbouleh and hummus, and a four-inch-high creamy lemon tart. Be warned that not so long ago this street was known as "the front line" in a neighborhood that mixes drug and antique deals on the same block. It's gentrified now, but the non-urban may still find it alarming. ✉ 12–14 All Saint's Rd., W11, ☎ 0171/243–2808. Reservations essential. MC, DC, V. No dinner Sun. Tube: Westbourne Park.

POLISH

££ ✕ **Wódka.** This smart, modern Polish restaurant is the only one in the
★ world, as far as we know, to serve smart, modern Polish food. It is popular with elegant locals plus a sprinkling of celebs and often has the atmosphere of a dinner party. Alongside the smoked salmon, herring, caviar, and eggplant *blinis,* you might also find venison sausages or roast duck with *krupnik* (honey-lemon vodka). Order from the separate menu a carafe of the purest vodka in London (and watch the check inflate); it's encased in a block of ice and hand-flavored (with bison grass, cherries, rowanberries) by the owner, who, being an actual Polish prince, is uniquely qualified to do this. ✉ 12 St. Albans Grove, W8, ☎ 0171/937–6513. Reservations essential. AE, DC, MC, V. No lunch weekends. Tube: High Street Kensington.

SEAFOOD

£ ✕ **Geales.** This is a cut above your typical fish-and-chips joint. The
★ decor is stark but the fish will have been swimming just hours beforehand, even the ones from the Caribbean (fried swordfish is a specialty). Geales is popular with the rich and famous, not just loyal locals. ✉ 2 Farmer St., W8, ☎ 0171/727–7969. Reservations not accepted. MC.

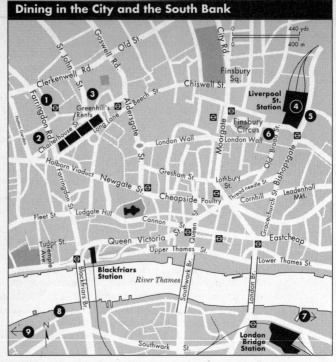

Dining in the City and the South Bank

Closed Sun., Mon., 3 wks in Aug., and 2 wks at Christmas. Tube: Notting Hill Gate.

TRADITIONAL BRITISH

£££ ✕ **Julie's.** This sweet '60s throwback has two parts: an upstairs wine bar and a basement restaurant, both decorated with Victorian ecclesiastical furniture. The cooking is sound, old-fashioned English (salmon-and-halibut terrine, roast pheasant with chestnut stuffing and wild rowan jelly). The traditional Sunday lunches are very popular, and in summer there's a garden for outside eating. ⊠ *135 Portland Rd., W11,* ☎ *0171/229–8331. MC, V. No lunch Sat. Tube: Holland Park.*

The City and the South Bank

FRENCH

£££ ✕ **Le Pont de la Tour.** Sir Terence Conran's place across the river, over-
★ looking the bridge that gives it its name, comes into its own in summer, when the outside tables are heaven. Inside the "Gastrodrome" (his word) there's a vintner and baker and deli, a seafood bar, a brasserie, and this '30s diner-style restaurant, smart as the captain's table. Fish and seafood (lobster salad; Baltic herrings in crème fraîche; roast halibut with aioli), meat and game (venison fillet, port and blueberry sauce; roast veal, caramelized endive) feature heavily—vegetarians are out of luck. Prune and Armagnac tart or chocolate terrine could finish a glamorous—and expensive—meal. By contrast, an impeccable salade niçoise in the brasserie is about £9. ⊠ *36D Shad Thames, Butler's Wharf, SE1,* ☎ *0171/403–8403. Reservations essential. MC, V. Tube: Tower Hill.*

ITALIAN

£ ✕ **The Eagle.** If the name makes it sound like a pub, that's because it
★ is a pub, albeit a superior one, with wooden floors, a few sofas, and art on the walls. It does, however, belong in the "Restaurants" section

by virtue of the amazingly good-value nouveau Tuscan food, which you choose from the blackboard menu (or by pointing) at the bar. There are about half a dozen dishes, a pasta and/or risotto always among them. There are currently quite a few places in London charging four times the price for remarkably similar food, as well as a welcome trend toward more and more pubs serving good meals—a trend which The Eagle all but started. ⊠ *159 Farringdon Rd., EC1,* ☎ *0171/837–1353. Reservations not accepted. No credit cards. No dinner weekends. Tube: Farringdon.*

JAPANESE

£ ✗ **Moshi Moshi Sushi.** London is taking to sushi like New Yorkers did a decade back, and this wacky glass-walled joint above Platform One in Liverpool Street Station set the ball rolling—or the fish train chugging, since the schtick here is that you pick *tekka* or *kappa maki* (tuna or cucumber seaweed rolls) or *maguro* (tuna), *sake* (salmon), *saba* (mackerel), etc.—in pairs off a conveyor belt that snakes around the counter. At the end, you count up your color-coded plates to pay. Great sushi, but not the place to go for a sophisticated evening. ⊠ *Unit 24 Liverpool St. Station, EC2,* ☎ *0171/247–3227. Reservations not accepted. No credit cards. Closed weekends. Tube: Liverpool Street.*

MODERN BRITISH

££–£££ ✗ **OXO Tower Brasserie and Restaurant.** How delightful it is for London finally to get a room with a view, *such* a view. On the eighth floor of the beautifully revived OXO Tower Wharf building near to the South Bank Centre is this elegant space, run by the same people who put the chic Fifth Floor at Harvey Nichols on the map, and featuring Euro food with this year's trendy ingredients (acorn-fed black pig charcuterie with tomato and pear chutney; calves kidneys with persillade and beetroot jus; Dover sole with sea urchin butter). The ceiling slats turn and change from white to midnight blue, but who on earth notices, with St. Paul's dazzling you across the water? The Brasserie is slighly less expensive than the restaurant but both have great river views. For food with a view, the terrace tables in summertime are probably the best places in London. ⊠ *Bankside, SE1,* ☎ *0171/803–3888. AE, MC, V. Tube: Waterloo.*

££ ✗ **People's Palace.** Thank goodness for this place. Now you can finally have a civilized meal during your South Bank arts encounter. With menus by trendy chef Gary Rhodes, of Greenhouse fame (☞ *above*), and run independently (from the Royal Festival Hall et al) by the same owners, this has remarkably low prices considering it has the greatest river view in town. As the baying critics noted around opening time, there are occasional mistakes here, but the more British the dish, the more reliable it proves—roast beef, potted duck, suckling pig sandwich on granary bread, marmalade sponge, sticky toffee pudding—all these are fine. Service is a bit flaky, but the soaring space with its giant windows makes up for everything. ⊠ *Royal Festival Hall, Level 3, South Bank, SE1,* ☎ *0171/928–9999. AE, DC, MC, V. Tube: Waterloo.*

££ ✗ **Quality Chop House.** This was converted from one of the most gorgeous "greasy spoon" caffs in town, retaining the solid Victorian fittings (including pewlike seats, which you often have to share). It is not luxurious, but the food is a glorious parody of caff food—bangers and mash turns out to be home-made herbed veal sausage with rich gravy, light, fluffy, potato, and vegetables *à point*; egg and chips (fries) are not remotely greasy. There are also such posh things as salmon fishcakes and steak, and desserts that change with the seasons. ⊠ *94 Farringdon Rd., EC1,* ☎ *0171/837–5093. Reservations essential. No credit cards. No lunch Sat. or dinner Sun. Tube: Farringdon.*

££ ✕ **St. John.** This former smokehouse (ham, not cigars), converted by
★   erstwhile architect owner/chef, Fergus Henderson, wowed the town when
it opened, with its soaring white walls, schoolroom lamps, stone floors,
iron railings, and plain wooden chairs, and its uncompromising fod-
der. Some find Henderson's chutzpah scary: One infamous appetizer
is carrots and egg (a bunch of carrots with green tops intact, and a boiled
egg), although the imaginativeness of others—roast bone marrow and
parsley salad; smoked eel, beetroot, and horseradish—excuses this
silliness. Entrées (roast lamb and parsnip; smoked haddock and fennel; deviled crab) can appear shockingly nude and lumpen on the
plate. There are failures, but they're heroic failures. An all-French
wine list has plenty of affordable bottles, plus lots of Malmseys and
ports. Service is efficiently matey, and the pastry chef's chocolate slice
belongs in the brownie hall of fame. ⊠ *26 St. John St., EC1,* ☎
*0171/251–0848. Reservations essential. AE, MC, V. No dinner Sun.
Tube: Farringdon.*

SEAFOOD

££ ✕ **Bill Bentley's.** You can see from the bare walls and the arched ceiling that this was once a wine merchant's vaults. There are four other
branches in London, all equally old-fashioned in feel, and all serving
old-fashioned boarding-school–like fish dishes and seafood platters. ⊠
Swedeland Ct., 202 Bishopsgate, EC2, ☎ *0171/283–1763. Reservations essential. Jacket and tie. MC, V. Closed weekends. No dinner. Tube:
Liverpool Street.*

THAI

££ ✕ **Sri Siam City.** The easterly cousin of this well-liked Soho Thai place
turns down the chili fire a little, perhaps. The Thai staples—green or
red chicken curry, *pad* Thai (noodles stir fried with vegetables and
shrimp)—are good, or try an easygoing squid salad with lemongrass,
lime, and chili. ⊠ *85 London Wall, EC2,* ☎ *0171/628–5772. Reservations advised. AE, DC, MC, V. Closed weekends. Tube: Moorgate.*

Camden Town and Hampstead

ANGLO-FRENCH

££ ✕ **Camden Brasserie.** The perfect neighborhood restaurant, this mel-
low, brick-walled, wood-floored haven makes its charcoal grill work
hard (barbecued corn-fed chicken, salmon fillet, steak, which come with
piles of matchstick fries, etc.) and offers a daily fish, pasta, soup, and
salad. Convenient for market, Canal, and Zoo excursions. ⊠ *216
Camden High St., NW1,* ☎ *0171/482–2114. MC, V. Tube: Camden
Town.*

BELGIAN

££ ✕ **Belgo Noord.** To enter what must be London's least normal restau-
★   rant, you pass the wavy concrete facade and cross the spotlit "drawbridge" over the brushed-steel open kitchen. Inside, waitstaff in maroon
monks' habits sweep over to your refectorylike table to take your
order of *moules-frites* (steamed mussels in various sauces with fries),
waterzooi (a whitefish stew), wild boar sausages, and other authentic
Belgian dishes. Try the Kriek, cherry beer brewed by Trappist monks.
Of course, this is the older, more handsome brother of the Covent Garden Belgo Centraal (☞ *above*). ⊠ *72 Chalk Farm Rd., NW1,* ☎
*0171/267–0718. Reservations essential. AE, MC, V. Tube: Chalk
Farm.*

BRITISH

£   ✕ **Coffee Cup.** A Hampstead landmark for just about as long as anyone can remember, this smoky, dingy, uncomfortable café is lovable,
very cheap, and therefore always packed. You can get anything (beans,

eggs, kippers, mushrooms) on toast, grills, sandwiches, cakes, fry-ups, etc.—nothing healthy or fashionable whatsoever. There are tables outside in the summer, but no liquor license. ⊠ *74 Hampstead High St., NW3,* ☎ *0171/435–7565. Reservations not accepted. No credit cards. Tube: Hampstead.*

GREEK

£ ✕ **Lemonia.** On a very pleasant street near Regent's Park is this superior version of London Greek—large and light, friendly, and packed every evening. Besides the usual *mezedes* (appetizers), *souvlakia* (kebabs), *stifado* (beef stewed in wine), and so on, there are interesting specials: quail, perhaps, or *gemista* (stuffed vegetables). ⊠ *89 Regent's Park Rd., NW1,* ☎ *0171/586–7454. Reservations essential. No credit cards. No lunch Sat. or dinner Sun. Tube: Chalk Farm.*

Brunch and Afternoon Tea

It is sometimes suggested that among Londoners, brunch is catching on while the afternoon ritual (often mistakenly referred to as "high tea") is dying out. Tea, the drink, however, is so ingrained in the national character, that tea, the meal, will always have a place in the capital, if only as an occasional celebration, a children's treat, or something you do when your American ¡friends are in town. Reserve for all these, unless otherwise noted.

Brunch

The Belvedere (☞ *above*) in bucolic Holland Park wins hands down for the setting, especially if you bag a rare terrace table on a rare sunny day. There is, admittedly no official brunch, but you can fake one from the regular menu. ⊠ *Holland Park, off Abbotsbury Rd., W8,* ☎ *0171/602–1238. Reservations essential. AE, DC, MC, V. Lunch served weekends noon–3.*

Butler's Wharf Chop House. At this—yet another Terence Conran (Quaglino's, Pont de la Tour, Bibendum . . .) venture—brunch (£13.50 for two courses) is as British as brunch ever gets, with Dublin Bay prawns, Stilton and celery soup and such, and a fabulous Thames-side setting. ⊠ *36E Shad Thames, SE1,* ☎ *0171/403–3403. AE, DC, MC, V. Brunch served Sun. noon–3.*

Christopher's. Imagine you're in Manhattan at this superior Covent Garden purveyor of American food, from pancakes to steak, eggs and fries, via salmon fishcakes and a Caesar salad. Two courses are £12. ⊠ *18 Wellington St., WC2,* ☎ *0171/240–4222. AE, DC, MC, V. Brunch served Sun. noon–3:30.*

Joe Allen (☞ *above*) is where to take refuge from the lovely British weather, down some bloody Marys, and maybe a grilled chicken sandwich with Swiss, or a salad of spicy sausage, shrimp, and new potato. ⊠ *13 Exeter St., WC2,* ☎ *0171/836–0651. Reservations essential. No credit cards. Brunch served Sun. noon–4.*

Room at the Halcyon. The Halcyon is favored by stars of Hollywood and rock, and is secreted in the leafy neighborhood of Holland Park. An excellent modern British kitchen. ⊠ *129 Holland Park Ave., W11,* ☎ *0171/221–5411. AE, DC, MC, V. Brunch served Sun. noon–3:30.*

Afternoon Tea

Note that Claridge's, the Ritz, and the Savoy all require jacket and tie.

Brown's Hotel does rest on its laurels somewhat, with a packaged aura and nobody around but fellow tourists who believe this the most famous. For £16 you get sandwiches, a scone with cream and jam (jelly), and two cream cakes. ⊠ *33 Albermarle St., W1,* ☎ *0171/493–6020. AE, MC, V. Tea served daily 3–6.*

Claridge's is the real McCoy, with liveried footmen proffering sandwiches, scones, and superior patisseries (£16.50) in the palatial yet genteel Foyer, to the sound of the resident "Hungarian orchestra" (actually a string quartet). ⊠ *Brook St., W1,* ☎ *0171/629–8860. AE, DC, MC, V. Tea served daily 3–5.*

Fortnum & Mason's. Upstairs at the queen's grocers, three set teas are ceremoniously offered: standard Afternoon Tea (sandwiches, scone, cakes, £10.50), old-fashioned High Tea (the traditional nursery meal, adding something more robust and savoury, £12.25), and Champagne Tea (£15.75). ⊠ *St. James's Restaurant, 4th floor, 181 Piccadilly, W1,* ☎ *0171/734–8040. AE, DC, MC, V. Tea served Mon.–Sat. 3–5:20.*

Harrods. For sweet-toothed people, the Georgian Room at this ridiculously well-known department store has a serve-it-yourself afternoon tea *buffet* that'll give you a sugar rush for a week. ⊠ *Brompton Rd., SW3,* ☎ *0171/730–1234. AE, DC, MC, V. Tea served Mon.–Sat. 3–5:30.*

The Ritz. The Ritz's new owners have put the once-peerless Palm Court tea back on the map, with proper, tiered, cake stands and silver pots, a harpist, and Louis XVI chaises, plus a leisurely four-hour time slot, all for £18.50. A good excuse for a glass of champagne. Reservations are taken only to 50% capacity. ⊠ *Piccadilly, W1,* ☎ *0171/493–8181. AE, DC, MC, V. Tea served daily 2–6.*

The Savoy. The glamorous Thames-side hotel does one of the most pleasant teas (£16.50), its triple-tiered cake stands packed with goodies, its tailcoated waiters thrillingly polite. ⊠ *The Strand, WC2,* ☎ *0171/836–4343. AE, DC, MC, V. Tea served daily 3–5:30.*

Pubs

Even today, when television keeps so many people glued to their own hearth and home, the public house, the pub, the "local"—it has many aliases—is still a vital part of British life. It also should be a part of the tourist experience, as there are few better places to meet the natives in their local habitat. There are hundreds of pubs in London, but the best—often swimming in Victorian etched glass, Edwardian panels, and Art Nouveau carvings—are listed below.

Along with pub-grub—and today, there is a full-scale pub-food renaissance underway—you'll want to order a pint. What Americans call beer, Brits call lager. However, the main Brit pub drink is "bitter"—usually drunk warm. Today, there is a flourishing movement to bring back the traditionally prepared ale that is much less gassy. There's also a vast range of bitters, ale, and other brews. Discuss your choices and other arcane details of drink with the barman, turn to your neighbor, raise the glass, and utter that most pleasant of toasts, "Cheers."

Arcane licensing laws forbid the serving of alcohol after 11 PM (10:30 on Sunday; different rules for restaurants) and have created, some argue, a nation of alcoholics, driven to down more pints than is decent in a limited time—a circumstance you see in action at 10 minutes to 11, when the "last orders" bell signals a stampede to the bar. The list below offers a few pubs selected for central location, historical interest, a pleasant garden, music, or good food, but you might just as happily adopt your own temporary local.

Black Friar. A step from Blackfriars tube, this pub has an arts-and-crafts interior that is entertainingly, satirically ecclesiastical, with inlaid mother-of-pearl, wood carvings, stained glass, and marble pillars all over the place, and reliefs of monks and friars poised above finely lettered temperance tracts, regardless of which there are six beers on tap. ⊠ *174 Queen Victoria St., EC4,* ☎ *0171/236–5650.*

Bunch of Grapes. A traditional (which means smoky, noisy, and anti-chic) pub, popular since Victoria was on the throne, in the heart of Shepherd Market, the village-within-Mayfair, and still featuring a full deck of London characters. ⊠ *16 Shepherd Market, W1,* ☎ *0171/629–4989.*

The Cow. Oh, not *another* Conran. Yes, this place belongs to Tom, son of Sir Terence, though it's a million miles from Quag's and Mezzo. A faux-Dublin back-room bar serves oysters, crab salad, and pasta with the wine and Guinness to hordes of the local fabulous people, with a proper restaurant upstairs. ⊠ *89 Westbourne Park Rd., W2,* ☎ *0171/221–0021.*

Crown and Goose. A sky-blue-wall, art-bedecked Camden Town local, where armchairs augment the tables, coffee and herb tea the beers, and good food (steak in baguettes, smoked chicken salad with honey vinaigrette, baked and stuffed mushrooms) is served to the crowds. ⊠ *100 Arlington Rd., NW1,* ☎ *0171/485–2342.*

Dove Inn. Read the list of famous ex-regulars, from Charles II and Nell Gwynn (mere rumor, but a likely one) to Ernest Hemingway, as you queue ages for a beer at this very popular, very comely 16th-century riverside pub by Hammersmith Bridge. If it's *too* full, stroll upstream to the Old Ship or the Blue Anchor. ⊠ *19 Upper Mall, W6,* ☎ *0181/748–5405.*

Freemason's Arms. This place is supposed to have the largest pub garden in London, with two terraces, a summerhouse, country-style furniture, and roses everywhere. Try your hand at the 17th-century game of pell mell—a kind of croquet—or at skittles. It's a favorite Hampstead pub, and popular with young locals. ⊠ *32 Downshire Hill, NW3,* ☎ *0171/435–2127.*

French House. In the pub where the French Resistance convened during World War II, Soho hipsters and eccentrics rub shoulders now. More than shoulders, actually, because this tiny, tricolore-waving, photograph-lined pub is always filled to bursting. ⊠ *49 Dean St., W1,* ☎ *0171/437–2799.*

George Inn. The inn sits in a courtyard where Shakespeare's plays were once performed. The present building dates from the late 17th century and is central London's last remaining galleried inn. Dickens was a regular—the inn is featured in *Little Dorrit.* Entertainments include Shakespeare performances, medieval jousts, and morris dancing. ⊠ *77 Borough High St., SE1,* ☎ *0171/407–2056.*

Island Queen. Gigantic caricature pirates leer down at you from the ceiling in this sociable Islington (☞ Minogues, *below*) pub, which offers superior home-cooked food (better still in Mojees, the upstairs restaurant), and a fab jukebox. The playwright Joe Orton frequented the place; he lived—and died—next door, murdered by his lover. ⊠ *87 Noel Rd., N1,* ☎ *0171/226–0307.*

Jack Straw's Castle. Straw was one of the leaders of the Peasant's Revolt of 1381, and was hanged nearby. In Tudor times it was a favorite hangout for highwaymen, but by the 19th century it had become picturesque and respectable; artists painted charming views from it and Dickens (inevitably) stayed here. Sadly, it was blitzed during World War II, and rebuilt in the 1960s. You can admire the views over Hampstead Heath and drink (weather permitting) in the large and lovely outside courtyard. ⊠ *North End Way, NW3,* ☎ *0171/435–8885.*

The Lamb. Another of Dickens's locals is now a picturesque place for a pint in summer, when you can drink on the patio. ⊠ *94 Lamb's Conduit St., WC1,* ☎ *0171/405–0713.*

Lamb and Flag. This 17th-century pub was once known as "The Bucket of Blood," because the upstairs room was used as a ring for bare-knuckle boxing. Now, it's a trendy, friendly, and entirely bloodless pub, serving food (at lunchtime only) and real ale. It's on the edge of Covent Garden, off Garrick Street. ⊠ *33 Rose St., WC2,* ☎ *0171/836–4108.*

Mayflower. An atmospheric 17th-century riverside inn, with exposed beams and a terrace, this is practically the very place from which the Pilgrims set sail for Plymouth Rock. The inn is licensed to sell American postage stamps. ⊠ *117 Rotherhithe St., SE16,* ☎ *0171/237–4088.*

Minogues. A little out of the way in Islington (but perfect for the Almeida theater or Camden Passage antiquing expeditions), this is a friendly, gentrified version of an Irish pub, with Guinness on tap, excellent live traditional folk music (Thur.–Sat. when it's open till midnight), and equally excellent Irish food in the adjoining brasserie. ⊠ *80 Liverpool Rd., N1,* ☎ *0171/354–4440.*

Museum Tavern. Across the street from the British Museum, this gloriously Victorian pub makes an ideal resting place after the rigors of the culture trail. With lots of fancy glass—etched mirrors and stained glass panels—gilded pillars, and carvings, the heavily restored hostelry once helped Karl Marx to unwind after a hard day in the Library. He could have spent his kapital on any one of six beers available on tap. ⊠ *49 Great Russell St., WC1,* ☎ *0171/242–8987.*

Pheasant and Firkin. David Bruce single-handedly revived the practice of serving beer that's been brewed on the premises (then sold the thriving business), and this is one of his jolly microbrewery/pubs, all named the something and Firkin (a small barrel), serving beers called "dog-bolter" or "rail ale," and selling T-shirts printed with bon mots like "I had a Pheasant time at the Firkin pub." Students like this a lot. ⊠ *166 Goswell Rd., EC1,* ☎ *0171/235–7429.*

Prospect of Whitby. Named after a ship, this is London's oldest riverside pub, dating back to 1520. Once upon a time it was called "The Devil's Tavern," because of the low-life criminals—thieves and smugglers—who congregated here. It's ornamented with pewter ware and nautical memorabilia. ⊠ *57 Wapping Wall, E1,* ☎ *0171/481–1095.*

St. James Tavern. Featured on this book's cover, this pub is steps away from Piccadilly Circus and five major West End theaters. The decor includes lovely hand-painted Doulton tiles depicting Shakespearean scenes. The kitchen is proud of its fish and chips. ⊠ *45 Great Windmill St., W1V,* ☎ *0171/437–5009.*

Sherlock Holmes. This pub used to be known as the Northumberland Arms, and Arthur Conan Doyle popped in regularly for a pint. It figures in *The Hound of the Baskervilles,* and you can see the hound's head and plaster casts of its huge paws among other Holmes memorabilia in the bar. ⊠ *10 Northumberland St., WC2,* ☎ *0171/930–2644.*

Spaniards Inn. This is another historic, oak-beamed pub on Hampstead Heath, boasting a gorgeous rose garden, scene of the tea party in Dickens's *Pickwick Papers.* Dick Turpin, the highwayman, used to frequent the inn; you can see his pistols on display. Romantic poets—Shelley, Keats, Byron—hung out here, and so, of course, did Dickens. It's extremely popular, especially on Sundays when Londoners take to the Heath in search of fresh air. ⊠ *Spaniards Rd., NW3,* ☎ *0171/455–3276.*

Star Tavern. In the heart of elegant Belgravia, this pub features a postcard-perfect Georgian-era facade. The inside is charming as all get out; Victorian decor and two roaring fireplaces make this a delightful spot. ⊠ *6 Belgrave Mews West, SW1,* ☎ *0171/235–3019.*

Three Greyhounds. Usefully Soho-central, this welcoming, reconditioned mock-Tudor pub serves a great bar meal—homemade Scotch eggs (hard boiled, wrapped in sausage meat, and deep fried in bread crumbs), matzo-coated Southern fried chicken, sandwiches of home-cured ham or herring, oysters by the half dozen. Its other claim to fame is its youth-

ful landlady's name—say hi to Roxy Beaujolais. ⊠ *25 Greek St., W1,*
☎ *0171/734–8799.*

Windsor Castle. This is one to rest at on a Kensington jaunt, saving a
large appetite for the food, especially on Sunday, when they do a traditional roast; other days there are oysters and salads, fishcakes and
steak sandwiches. In winter there are blazing fires; in summer, an
exquisite walled patio garden. ⊠ *114 Campden Hill Rd., W8,* ☎
0171/727–8491.

Ye Olde Cheshire Cheese. Yes, it is a tourist trap, but this most historic
of all London pubs (it dates from 1667) deserves a visit anyway, for
its sawdust-covered floors, low wood-beamed ceilings, the 14th-cen-
tury crypt of Whitefriars' monastery under the cellar bar, and the set
of 17th-century pornographic tiles upstairs. This was the most regular of Dr. Johnson's and Dickens's *many* locals. ⊠ *145 Fleet St., EC4,*
☎ *0171/353–6170.*

4 Lodging

Queen Elizabeth hasn't invited you this time? No matter. Staying at one of London's grand-dame hotels is the next best thing to being a guest at the palace. Royally resplendent decor abounds, and armies of staff are stuck in the pampering mode—the Windsors should have it so good. Even in more affordable, less grand, choices, rooms are swathed in Queen Mother pastels. Regal, stylish, or just plain down-home, most accommodations are kick-off-your-shoes comfy, with beds ever primed for late-afternoon slumber.

STANDING IN THE PARLORLIKE atmosphere of your lobby—burnished oak paneling, time-stained antiques, frock-coated staff, the distant tinkle of teacups in the air—a century seems to slip away. The concierge whispers that Queen Victoria used to visit—she, too, probably got willingly lost in the corridors and crannies. In the grand salon sit ancient Chippendale desks that once bore the concentrated energy of the empire's Kiplings and Hardys. Set near a crackling fire, a roomy leather Chesterfield beckons one to approach its quilted field. No, this harmonious picture is not a Christmas card illustration, and yes, there are hotels in London offering such civilized surroundings. Of course, the entire hotel landscape ranges from such undeniably traditional places to future-forward spots. Some hotels are heavy with style, others with history, but all offer uniquely individual reflections of their host city.

Two types of hotels typify the diversity and contrast found in ancient yet modern London. One is typified by the Connaught, a hotel whose guests wouldn't *dream* of staying anywhere else. Its Edwardian lobby, created in 1897, is unadulterated by things modern; grand and faded, it is filled with oil paintings and antiques in a way interior designers envy but can't really duplicate. In contrast to this dowager aunt–type are hotels such as the Pelham—most of them renovated town houses, aglitter with sensationally atmospheric Regency-style interiors and richly endowed with stunning furnishings and guests. Designed to be the very epitome of English country housedom, these newer boutique hotels appeal to clientele bent on revisiting the landed gentry culture. Waving the banner "Small is Beautiful," they have stolen a march on the genteel sleeping beauties—the Claridges, the Savoys, and the Dorchesters—who, recently awakened, have launched a broad counterattack. The Sultan of Brunei sunk tens of millions into refurbishing the Dorchester; a Hunt heiress sponsored a complete makeover of the Lanesborough, while the Connaught, Savoy, and Claridge's are each being renovated to the tune of a mint. At Claridge's alone, $60 million is being spent to install such things as 3-inch-thick doors in the guest rooms and TVs in the bathrooms; better, the Queen's nephew, Viscount Linley, is redesigning the lobby's woodwork. Beyond such top-draw (and top-price) places, London offers oodles of options. Happily, these include many hotels that place friendliness ahead of luxury. In between are establishments like Hazlitt's and the Gore, which are more affordable than they look.

As the city is the opposite of compact, where you stay can affect your experience significantly. For instance, the West End is equivalent to downtown, but it covers a lot of ground. There's a great deal of difference between, say, posh Park Lane and bustling, touristy Leicester Square, yet both are in the West End. Hotels in Mayfair and St. James's are central, but distant in both mileage and atmosphere from funky, youthful neighborhoods like Notting Hill and Camden Town, and from major tourist sights like the Tower of London, St. Paul's Cathedral, and the large Kensington museums. On the edges of the West End, Soho and Covent Garden have more urbanity, with lots of restaurants and more doings at night.

South Kensington, Kensington, Chelsea, and Knightsbridge are all patrician and peaceful, which will give you a more homey feeling than anything in the West End, while Belgravia is super-elegant, geographically and atmospherically about halfway between the extremes. From Bloomsbury it's a short stroll to the shops and restaurants of Covent Garden, to Theatreland, and to the British Museum. From here, it's a

London Lodging *(Boxes Refer to Detail Maps)*

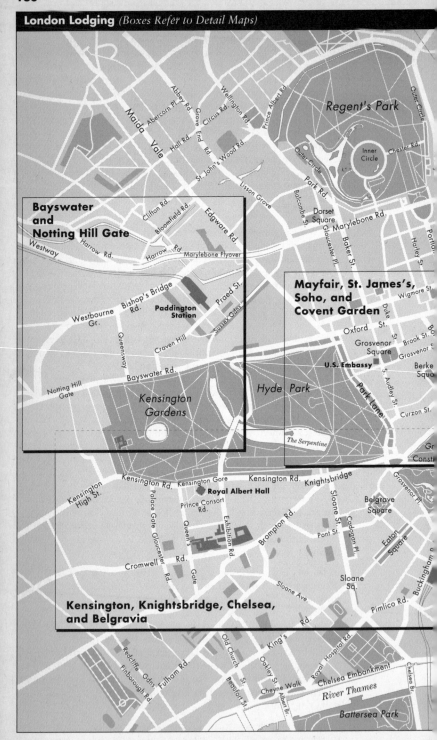

Regent's Park

Maida Vale

Abbey Rd.

Abercorn Pl.

Grove End Rd.

Hall Rd.

Circus Rd.

St. John's Wood Rd.

Wellington Rd.

Prince Albert Rd.

Lisson Grove

Park Rd.

Outer Circle

Inner Circle

Chester Rd.

Balcombe St.

Dorset Square

Gloucester Pl.

Baker St.

Marylebone Rd.

Harley St.

Portlan.

Bayswater and Notting Hill Gate

Westway

Harrow Rd.

Clifton Rd.

Bloomfield Rd.

Harrow Rd.

Edgware Rd.

Marylebone Flyover

Bishop's Bridge Rd.

Paddington Station

Praed St.

Sussex Gdns.

Mayfair, St. James's, Soho, and Covent Garden

Wigmore St.

Duke St.

Oxford St.

Grosvenor Square

Brook St.

Grosvenor.

Bo.

Westbourne Gr.

Queensway

Craven Hill

U.S. Embassy

Berke. Squa.

Notting Hill Gate

Bayswater Rd.

S. Audley St.

Park Lane

Curzon St.

Kensington Gardens

Hyde Park

The Serpentine

Gr. Const.

Kensington Rd.

Kensington Gore

Kensington Rd.

Knightsbridge

Grosvenor Pl.

Kensington High St.

Palace Gate

Royal Albert Hall

Prince Consort Rd.

Queen's Gate

Exhibition Rd.

Brampton Rd.

Sloane St.

Cadogan Pl.

Belgrave Square

Gloucester Rd.

Cromwell Rd.

Pont St.

Cadogan Pl.

Eaton Square

Buckingham.

Sloane Ave.

Sloane Sq.

Pimlico Rd.

Kensington, Knightsbridge, Chelsea, and Belgravia

Redcliffe Gdns.

Finborough Rd.

Fulham Rd.

Old Church St.

Oakley St.

Beaufort St.

King's Rd.

Cheyne Walk

Albert Br.

Royal Hospital Rd.

Chelsea Embankment

River Thames

Chelsea Br.

Battersea Park

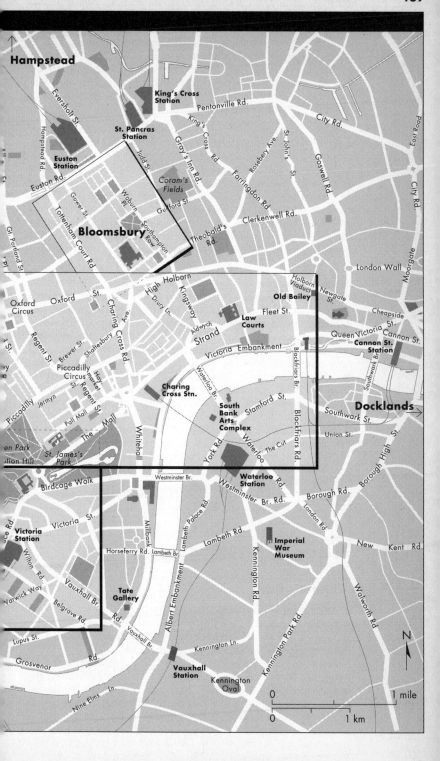

short bus ride to Camden and Regent's Park, too, and Hampstead and Islington are close enough to explore easily. Bayswater is a particularly affordable haven. It's barely considered a real neighborhood by Londoners, but everywhere is accessible from here, and Hyde Park is your backyard. Notting Hill and Holland Park are worth considering as a base if you want something more down-home, plus the antiques of Portobello Road, and its surrounding cutting-edge shops and restaurants on your doorstep.

The general custom these days in all but the bottom end of the scale is for rates to be quoted for the room alone (which unless otherwise noted is with bath); breakfast, whether Continental or "Full English," comes at extra cost. VAT is usually included, and service, too, in nearly all cases. All the hotels listed here are graded according to their spring 1997 rates, but it's best to check on these figures, which are spiraling ever-upward. Remember, too, that there can be a significant difference off-season. Like hotels in most other European countries, British hotels are obliged by law to display a tariff at the reception desk. If you have not booked ahead, you are strongly advised to study this carefully.

Be sure to make reservations well in advance, as seasonal events, trade shows, or royal occasions can fill hotel rooms for sudden brief periods, and, of course, during highly touristed July and August, too. Thinking ahead also allows you to investigate the various U.S.-based membership programs that offer discount travel in Europe, including on London hotel rooms at a savings of up to 50%. Try **Privilege Card International** (☎ 800/236–9732), Entertainment Publications' **Europe Hotel Directory** (☎ 800/445–4137), or **RMC Travel Centre** (☎ 800/782–2674). If you do manage to arrive in the capital without a room, the **London Tourist Board Information Centres** at Heathrow and Victoria Station Forecourt can help, and the Visitor Call service provides general advice, ☎ 0891/505–487 (calls cost 49p per minute, or 39p cheap rate); or call the **LTB Accommodation Sales Service** (☎ 0171/824–8844) weekdays 9:30–5:30 for prepaid credit-card bookings (MC, V).

CATEGORY	COST*
££££	over £180
£££	£120–£180
££	£70–£120
£	under £70

All prices are for a double room, VAT included.

Mayfair to Regent's Park

££££ 🏨 **Athenaeum.** This well-loved baby-grand hotel opposite Green Park received a new lease on life when it was sold to independent owners about five years ago. The welcome here is in the details: from Donald, the super-concierge at his doorside desk, to the disposable camera and Japanese rice crackers in the minibar, to the compact Health Spa. Rooms retain the distinctive custom-made leather-topped mahogany and yew furniture, now set against navy-and-cream drapes, Wedgwood green walls, and ultra-thick cream carpets. Without getting out of bed, you can control lighting and temperature, order free videos and CDs, and listen to your voice mail from your two phone lines. In glittering gray marble bathrooms are power showers, mirrors angled to get the back of your head, old-fashioned Bronnley toiletries, and—hallelujah— a real hair dryer; downstairs, there's the cozy Whisky Bar and the not-too-formal Bullochs restaurant. Rooms 201–205 face Green Park;

others have a bay that affords a partial, angled view. ⊠ *116 Piccadilly, W1V 0BJ,* ☎ *0171/499–3464,* FAX *0171/493–1860. 123 rooms. Restaurant, bar, in-room VCR and CD players, health club (no pool). AE, DC, MC, V. Tube: Green Park.*

££££ 🏠 **Brown's.** Founded in 1837 by Lord Byron's "gentleman's gentleman," James Brown, this Victorian country house in central Mayfair comprises 11 Georgian houses and is occupied by many Anglophile Americans—a habit that was established by the two Roosevelts (Teddy while on honeymoon). Bedrooms feature thick carpets, soft armchairs, brass chandeliers, and brocade wallpapers, as well as, in the newly refitted ones, air-conditioning, while the public rooms retain their cozy oak-paneled, chintz-laden, grandfather-clock-ticking-in-the-parlor ambience. Right outside the door are the boutiques and art galleries of Bond and Cork streets, while in the lounge, one of London's best-known afternoon teas is served from 3 to 6. ⊠ *34 Albemarle St., W1A 4SW,* ☎ *0171/493–6020,* FAX *0171/493–9381. 132 rooms. Restaurant, bar. AE, DC, MC, V. Tube: Green Park.*

££££ 🏠 **Claridge's.** Stay here, and you're staying at a hotel legend, with one
★ of the world's classiest guest lists. The liveried staff is friendly and not in the least condescending, and the rooms are never less than luxurious. Thanks to an ongoing $60 millon refurbishment (check when you book to make sure the dust has cleared), they will be even more so, with TVs in many bathrooms and 3-inch-thick doors. Claridge's was founded in 1812, but present decor is either 1930s art deco or country-house traditional, a note continued in the lobby's new woodwork furnishings, which were designed by Viscount Linley, the working royal. Have a drink in the Foyer lounge (24 hours a day) with its Hungarian mini-orchestra, or retreat to the reading room for perfect quiet interrupted only by the sound of pages turning. The bedrooms are spacious, as are the bathrooms, with their enormous shower heads and bells (which still work) to summon either "maid" or "valet" from their station on each floor. Beds are handmade and supremely comfortable—the King of Morocco once brought his own, couldn't sleep, and ended up ordering 30 from Claridge's to take home. The grand staircase and magnificent elevator are equally impressive. ⊠ *Brook St., W1A 2JQ,* ☎ *0171/629–8860 or 800/223–6800,* FAX *0171/499–2210. 200 rooms. 2 restaurants, beauty salon. AE, DC, MC, V. Tube: Bond Street.*

££££ 🏠 **Connaught.** Make reservations well in advance for this *very* exclu-
★ sive, small hotel just off Grosvenor Square—the most understated of any of London's grand hostelries. The bar and lounges have the air of an ambassadorial residence, an impression reinforced by the imposing oak staircase and dignified staff. Each bedroom has a foyer, antique furniture (if you don't like the desk, they'll change it), and fresh flowers, and the management is above such vulgarities as brochure and tariff—which would be extraneous for guests who inherited the Connaught habit from their great-grandfathers, anyway. If you value privacy, discretion, and the kind of luxury that eschews labels, then you have met your match here. For a preview of the hotel's style, lunch at its famous Grill or Restaurant (book well ahead), where waiters speak only when spoken to (☞ Chapter 3). ⊠ *Carlos Pl., W1Y 6AL,* ☎ *0171/499–7070,* FAX *0171/495–3262. 90 rooms. Restaurant, bar. MC. Tube: Bond Street.*

££££ 🏠 **The Dorchester.** A London institution since its 1931 inception, the
★ Dorchester appears on every "World's Best" list. The glamour level is off the scale: 1,500 square meters of gold leaf and 1,100 of marble gild this lily, and bedrooms (some not as spacious as you might imagine) feature Irish linen sheets on canopied beds, brocades and velvets, individual climate control, dual voltage outlets, and Italian marble and

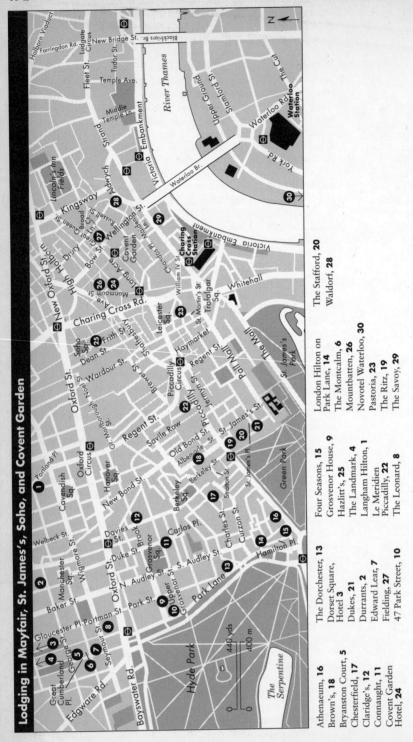

Lodging in Mayfair, St. James's, Soho, and Covent Garden

172

Athenaeum, **16**
Brown's, **18**
Bryanston Court, **5**
Chesterfield, **17**
Claridge's, **12**
Connaught, **11**
Covent Garden Hotel, **24**

The Dorchester, **13**
Dorset Square, Hotel **3**
Dukes, **21**
Durrants, **2**
Edward Lear, **7**
Fielding, **27**
47 Park Street, **10**

Four Seasons, **15**
Grosvenor House, **9**
Hazlitt's, **25**
The Landmark, **4**
Langham Hilton, **1**
Le Meridien Piccadilly, **22**
The Leonard, **8**

London Hilton on Park Lane, **14**
The Montcalm, **6**
Mountbatten, **26**
Novotel Waterloo, **30**
Pastoria, **23**
The Ritz, **19**
The Savoy, **29**

The Stafford, **20**
Waldorf, **28**

etched glass bathrooms with Floris goodies. Decor throughout is in opulent English country-house style, with more than a hint of art deco, in keeping with the original 1930s building. There's a beauty spa, run by Elizabeth Arden, a nightclub, a special theater-ticket concierge, the Oriental and Terrace restaurants, plus the well-known power-dining Grill Room, which has a magnificent gilt-edged decor. Afternoon tea, drinking, lounging, and posing are all accomplished in the catwalk-shape Promenade lounge, where you may spot one of the film-star types who will stay nowhere else (Elizabeth Taylor has been a habitué for decades—in fact, she was sitting in her tub here when that million-dollar offer to film *Cleopatra* came over the telephone). Probably no other hotel this opulent manages to be this charming. ⊠ *Park La., W1A 2HJ*, ☎ *0171/629–8888*, ⠵ *0171/409–0114. 197 rooms, 55 suites. 3 restaurants, bar, health club (no pool), nightclub, business services, meeting rooms, ballroom. AE, DC, MC, V. Tube: Marble Arch.*

££££ 🖪 **47 Park Street.** Secreted back to back with the grand hotels of Park
★ Lane, this dear (in every sense) little all-suite hotel has the best room service in town, with 24-hour food direct from the kitchen of Le Gavroche (☞ Chapter 3). The hotel shares its bar with that poshest-of-posh dining establishments, too, which means there's a jacket-and-tie requirement for your quiet nightcap. Bathrooms are on the small side, but no other drawbacks are apparent in this fabulously discreet, exquisitely decorated, quiet, relaxed, and homey haven, as long as you can afford it. One woman who could afford it liked it so much that she's still here—five years later. ⊠ *47 Park St., W1Y 4EB*, ☎ *0171/491–7282*, ⠵ *0171/491–7281. 52 suites with kitchen. Private dining room, bar (jacket and tie required), baby-sitting. AE, DC, MC, V. Tube: Marble Arch.*

££££ 🖪 **Four Seasons.** The discretion of this beautifully situated (opposite Hyde Park, off the end of Piccadilly, but tucked away), understated hotel inspires more-than-average loyalty in its guests, which have included Howard Hughes, but most of whom, these days, are business travelers. The bedrooms are extremely comfortable, with gigantic beds; the bathrooms have plenty of extras. Non-guests can also enjoy the Four Seasons restaurant, which has lost one star chef, Jean-Christophe Novelli, only to gain another—Sean Watling. ⊠ *Hamilton Pl., Park La., W1A 1AZ*, ☎ *0171/499–0888 or 800/223–6800*, ⠵ *0171/493–6629. 228 rooms. 2 restaurants, health club. AE, DC, MC, V. Tube: Hyde Park Corner.*

££££ 🖪 **Grosvenor House.** "The old lady of Park Lane" is in top-dowager
★ position again, having thrown off her creeping frumpiness during a complete overhaul, with the lobby, lounge, and facade the latest beneficiaries of the English Heritage–supervised work. It's still not the kind of place that encourages hushed whispers or that frowns on jeans, despite the marble floors and wood-paneled "library," open fires, oils, and fine antiques, all inspired by the Earl of Grosvenor's residence, which occupied the site during the 18th century. The hotel health club is just about the best around, especially since the gym part was completely redone in 1995 (the pool didn't need any help). Bedrooms are spacious, and most of the freshly glamorized spacious marble bathrooms have natural light. A handy theater-ticket service is on the premises. ⊠ *Park La., W1A 3AA*, ☎ *0171/499–6363*, ⠵ *0171/493–3341. 360 rooms, 70 suites. 3 restaurants, bar, indoor pool, health club. AE, DC, MC, V. Tube: Marble Arch.*

££££ 🖪 **The Landmark.** A year older than the century, the one-time Great Central Hotel and former BritRail HQ is London's newest luxury hotel—and a most elegantly understated place it is, too. A palm-filled, eight-story glazed atrium "Winter Garden" forms the core, and odd-numbered rooms overlook this. If size matters to you, note that even standard rooms here are among the largest in London and with their glamorous bathrooms in marble and chrome are outfitted with robe and hair dryer. Despite appearances, this is one of the only London grand hotels that doesn't force you to dress up—even jeans are okay. The Landmark is very near Regent's Park; the West End is a 15-minute walk away. ⊠ *222 Marylebone Rd., NW1 6JQ,* ☎ *0171/631–8000,* ℻ *0171/631–8080. 309 rooms. Restaurant, 2 bars, indoor pool, health club, business services. AE, DC, MC, V. Tube: Marylebone.*

££££ 🏨 **Langham Hilton.** Opened in 1865 by the Prince of Wales and once London's center of Victorian chic—regular guests included Dvořák, Toscanini, Mark Twain, and Oscar Wilde—the Langham has recently been renovated to become the London flagship of the Hilton chain. All columns and porticoes, its exterior looks very Grand Hotel, especially at night with fairy-tale floodlighting. Inside, the lobby soars to Castle Howard–heights, and there are two theme restaurants (one Raj, one Czarist Russia) and the Chukka Bar (this stately-house salon, glowing with daffodil yellow walls, is one of the prettiest watering holes in London). Most of the guest rooms are done in soothing Queen Mother pastels and many have marble-bedecked and cosseting bathrooms, but only the more expensive, larger front ones have the good view over Portland Place to the park. The hotel is handily located several blocks away from the central Oxford Circus tube stop. ⊠ *1C Portland Pl., W1N 3AA,* ☎ *0171/636–1000,* ℻ *0171/323–2340. 410 rooms. 2 restaurants, bar. AE, DC, MC, V. Tube: Oxford Circus.*

££££ 🏨 **Le Meridien Piccadilly.** The massive, turn-of-the-century building is fin de siècle elegant, if slightly antiseptic in its white-marble-and-plush-carpet public areas. The vast Oak Room restaurant, however, is exquisite in limed oak paneling and gilt, and it is (yes, another) one of the best hotel restaurants in London. The hotel's second restaurant, far less formal, is a miniature Kew Gardens of arched glass, ferns, and palms. Bedrooms vary ridiculously in size; most are on the small side, though others are very large indeed, and a few seventh-floor ones have balconies overlooking Piccadilly. Decor is Edwardian-gent's-club with frills. The health club is the most luxurious and exclusive in London and boasts squash courts, saunas, and billiard tables, as well as a swimming pool. You can't be more central than here. ⊠ *Piccadilly, W1V 0BH,* ☎ *0171/734–8000,* ℻ *0171/437–3574. 284 rooms. 3 restaurants, bar, indoor pool, health club, library, business services. AE, DC, MC, V. Tube: Piccadilly Circus.*

££££ 🏨 **London Hilton on Park Lane.** London's only major skyscraper hotel offers views over Hyde Park and Buckingham Palace (to the Queen's chagrin) and an impressive array of facilities. Public areas are glitzy in white marble; suites have been recently redecorated to bring them out of *Dynasty* territory and into the '90s. Bedrooms are a fair size, but you may forget which city they're in—decor is uniform corporate Hiltonese. This is hardly surprising in a hostelry whose guest list is 70% business travelers, for whom there is now a business center that is the largest in London (modem jacks are in every bedroom, and you can even make free local calls from the Clubroom on the designated Executive Floor). Business folk find it a preferred home-away-from-home—after all, its St. George's Bar stocks more than 30 types of Cuban cigars. ⊠ *22 Park La., W1A 2HH,* ☎ *0171/493–8000,* ℻ *0171/493–4957. 448 rooms. 3 restaurants, 3 bars, no-smoking floors, beauty salon, health club, baby-sitting, laundry service, business services, travel services. AE, DC, MC, V. Tube: Hyde Park Corner.*

££££ 🏨 **The Montcalm.** Secreted behind Marble Arch in a peaceful Georgian crescent, the Montcalm has kept a low profile since its rock-star days (when the Jackson 5, Stevie Wonder, and Elton John favored it above all other London grands), but it is now back up there with the best of them, after a major, and ongoing, refurbishment by the Japanese owners, Nikko, who have made it an especially efficient, spotless, and calm hotel, with some unusual features. Here is London's only low-allergen bedroom, its only canopied waterbed (not in the same room), and one of its few Japanese breakfasts; here are toilets with electronic hair dryers and bidets in the bathrooms, and, by the conservatorylike Crescent restaurant, a CD-operated player piano serenading lunchers with a little Brahms. The duplex suites, with their cast iron spiral staircases, are especially winning. ⊠ *Great Cumberland Pl., W1A 2LF,* ☎ *0171/402–4288,* FAX *0171/724–9180. 116 rooms. Restaurant, bar, meeting rooms. AE, DC, MC, V. Tube: Marble Arch.*

£££–££££ 🏨 **The Leonard.** Four 17th-century buildings were combined to create this property, new in 1996 and one of the few town-house hotels outside Knightsbridge. Shoppers will particularly appreciate the Mayfair location, just around the corner from Oxford Street. If you stay in a two-bedroom superior suite, you can swing by Marks & Spencer's food halls for provisions, then whip up a dinner in your private kitchen—a plus for families and visitors on longer trips. All the suites have a remarkably residential feel, with sitting and bedroom areas set off by small foyers, and complemented by a judicious mix of lived-in antiques and comfortable reproductions. For more elbow room, try one of the aptly named grand suites, with their palatial sitting rooms and tall windows. The welcoming lobby area is stocked with complimentary newspapers to read by the fire. ⊠ *15 Seymour St., W1H 5AA,* ☎ *0171/935–2010,* FAX *0171/935–700. 20 suites (3 with kitchenette), 6 rooms. Dining room, bar, room service, exercise room, business services. AE, DC, MC, V.*

£££ 🏨 **Chesterfield.** This former town house of the Earl of Chesterfield is popular with American visitors, many of whom are repeat guests or have links with the English Speaking Union, which has its headquarters next door. It is deep in the heart of Mayfair and has welcoming, wood-and-leather public rooms and spacious bedrooms. The staff is outstandingly pleasant and helpful. ⊠ *35 Charles St., W1X 8LX,* ☎ *0171/491–2622,* FAX *0171/491–4793. 113 rooms. Restaurant. AE, DC, MC, V. Tube: Green Park.*

£££ 🏨 **Dorset Square Hotel.** A little more than a decade old, this special
★ small hotel off Baker Street was the first of four London addresses for husband and wife Tim and Kit Kemp, an architect and an interior designer. What they did was decant the English country look into a fine pair of Regency town houses, then they turned up the volume. Everywhere you look are covetable antiques, rich colors, and ideas *House Beautiful* subscribers will steal. Naturally, every room is different: The first-floor balconied "Coronet" ones are the largest (two have grand pianos), and a virtue is made of the smallness of the small ones. The marble and mahogany bathrooms have power showers; glossy magazines, a half-bottle of claret, and boxes of vitamin C are complimentary. There's a reason for the ubiquitous cricket memorabilia: Dorset Square was the first Lord's ground. ⊠ *39–40 Dorset Sq., NW1 6QN,* ☎ *0171/723–7874,* FAX *0171/724–3328. 37 rooms. Bar/restaurant, car rental (vintage Bentley limousine). AE, MC, V. Tube: Baker Street.*

££ 🏨 **Bryanston Court.** Three Georgian houses have been converted into a hotel in an historic conservation area, a couple of blocks north of Hyde Park and Park Lane. The style is traditional English—open fireplaces, comfortable leather armchairs, oil portraits—though the bedrooms are small and modern, with pink furnishings, creaky floors, and minute bathrooms. Rooms at the back are quieter and face east, so they're bright in the mornings; Room 77 is as big as a suite, but being on the lower ground floor typical of London houses, it's dark. This family-run hotel is excellent value for the area. ⊠ *56–60 Great Cumberland*

Pl., W1H 7FD, ☎ *0171/262–3141,* FAX *0171/262–7248. 56 rooms. Restaurant, bar. AE, DC, MC, V. Tube: Marble Arch.*

££   🏨 **Durrants.** A hotel since the late-18th century, Durrants occupies a quiet corner almost next to the Wallace Collection, a stone's throw from Oxford Street and the smaller, posher shops of Marylebone High Street. It's good value for the area, and if you like ye wood-paneled, leather-armchaired, dark-red-patterned-carpeted style of olde Englishness, this will suit you. Bedrooms, by way of contrast, are wan and motel-like but perfectly adequate—a few have no bathroom, though this disadvantage has the advantage of saving you £10 a night. Best give the baron of beef-type restaurant a wide-berth. ✉ *George St., W1H 6BH,* ☎ *0171/935–8131,* FAX *0171/487–3510. 96 rooms, 85 with bath. Restaurant, bar, dining rooms. AE, MC, V. Tube: Bond Street.*

££   🏨 **Novotel Waterloo.** One thing often asked about London hotels is: "Where's the room with a view of the Houses of Parliament?" Well—until the County Hall Marriott opens in 1998 next to Westminster Bridge—the answer has been: Nowhere. Not from the exorbitant Conrad in Chelsea Harbour, nor the Savoy's river rooms . . . until now. Sort of. Looking otherwise precisely like 280 other hotels in 44 countries, this French-owned, inexpensive, reliable chain hotel offers a fitness center and brasserie, conference facilities, in-room satellite TV, tea/coffee maker, direct dial phone and hair dryer in very compact rooms, plus—in 40 of them—*that* view. Actually, the view is more a flagrant grandstand spying over Lambeth Palace than a river vista, though you can see from Big Ben to St. Paul's for the £5 supplement the higher rooms command. Mind you, the romance rating does plummet when you can't fling open the window to catch the Thames breeze on account of the guest room climate-control system. ✉ *113–127 Lambeth Rd., SE1 7JL,* ☎ *0181/748–3433 (central reservations). 189 rooms. Restaurant, bar, health club, meeting rooms. AE, DC, MC, V. Tube: Waterloo.*

£   🏨 **Edward Lear.** This is a good-value, family-run hotel in a Georgian town house, a minute's walk from Oxford Street, formerly the home of writer/artist Edward Lear (famous for his nonsense verse). Rooms vary enormously in size, with some family rooms very spacious indeed and others barely big enough to get out of bed (avoid Room 14); rooms at the back are quieter. It's a friendly place, but there are no hotel-type facilities (although if you want a jacket pressed you're welcome to borrow the iron). The management is very proud of the English breakfasts—they use the same butcher as the queen. Recent letters from readers indicate the hotel has seen better days. ✉ *28–30 Seymour St., W1H 5WD,* ☎ *0171/402–5401,* FAX *0171/706–3766. 31 rooms, 15 with shower (no WC), 4 with full bath. Breakfast room. MC, V. Tube: Marble Arch.*

St. James's

££££   🏨 **The Ritz.** Management of the Ritz was assumed in 1994 by the enormously respected Mandarin Oriental Group, which had yet to break into Europe. Mandarin has not altered the palatial (as in Versailles) Belle Epoque decor: Not in the Palm Court, with its cranberry velvet chairs, statuary, fluted columns, and greenery, nor in the resplendent dining room which, with its frescoes, gilding, and Italian Garden, is generally thought the prettiest in town. Bedrooms, too, remain as César Ritz prescribed—white pilasters and moldings on sorbet paintwork; antique bureaus; specially commissioned brass beds (17 of these remain); reproduction bronze figurines on the mantel, huge mirrors above it; heavy brocades, and linens embroidered with "R"—but they are getting rigorous refreshment and new bathrooms. Major work started early in 1996, and included the addition of a much-needed health club. Don't forget to check out the cozy, tiny, secret Rivoli Lounge up the curved staircase off Reception. ☒ *Piccadilly, W1V 9DG,* ☎ *0171/493–8181,* 🖷 *0171/493–2687. 129 rooms. Restaurant, bar, baby-sitting. AE, DC, MC, V. Tube: Green Park.*

££££ 🖬 **The Stafford.** The unique features here in ascending order of importance: The American Bar, where a million ties, baseball caps, and toy planes depend from a ceiling modeled, presumably, on New York's "21" Club's, and where Charles (who claims the first dry martini: see the Savoy) has been mixing for 35 years; and the 12 Carriage House rooms, installed in the 18th-century stable block, with their own cobbled mews entrances. These 18th-century-ish havens are very cute and private, with their gas-log fires, black-stained exposed beams, floral-sprigged drapes, and extra 20th-century features, such as CD players, CNN, and safes. They're also relative bargains. The main hotel has had a recent complete overhaul, with navy-and-gold hallways, rooms with china in cabinets or French doors to the bathrooms, air-conditioning throughout, and a new star chef in the cozy restaurant. The gorgeous mews remains the Stafford's best profile. ☒ *St. James's Place, SW1A 1NJ,* ☎ *0171/493–0111,* 🖷 *0171/493–7121. 80 rooms. Restaurant, bar, dining rooms. AE, DC, MC, V. Tube: Green Park.*

£££ 🖬 **Dukes.** This small, exclusive, Edwardian-style hotel, with its lantern-lighted entrance, is central but still quiet as it is set in its own discreet cul-de-sac behind the Ritz, where the Stafford also lies. A small hotel of character, it's suitably filled with squashy sofas, oil paintings of assorted dukes, and muted, rich colors. Its trump cards are that, for such a central location, it offers immense peace and quiet and very reasonable rates, plus personal service (they greet you by name every time), and an especially sweet suite or two, on the top floor, with views over St. James's Park. ☒ *35 St. James's Pl., SW1A 1NY,* ☎ *0171/491–4840,* 🖷 *0171/493–1264. 62 rooms. Restaurant, dining room. AE, DC, MC, V. Tube: Green Park.*

Soho and Covent Garden

££££ 🖬 **Covent Garden Hotel.** You've been warned: Staying at this new, re-★ lentlessly chic, extra-stylish hotel can become an expensive addiction. After spending two years revamping an 1880s-vintage hospital located in the midst of the artsy Covent Garden district, Tim and Kit Kemp now welcome a melange of off-duty celebrities, actors, and style-mavens to their newest hotel creation. Theatrically baronial, the public rooms will keep even the most picky atmosphere-hunter happy: Wallowing in painted silks, *style anglais* ottomans, and 19th-century Romantick oils, they are more theaters than salons—perfect places for a Hollywood star to be interviewed over a glass of sherry. Guest rooms are *World-of-Interiors* chic, each showcasing matching-but-mixed couturier fabrics to stunning effect. Antique-style desks are vast, beds are gargantuan, and modern bathrooms feature everything from Philippe Starck bidets to they-*have*-thought-of-everything heated mirrors (steam doesn't stick). Off the lobby, nibble a nibble in the Brasserie and you'll agree: For taste, in every sense of the word, the Covent Garden is the top. ☒ *10 Monmouth St., WC2H 9HB,* ☎ *0171/806–1000,* 🖷 *0171/806–1100. 46 rooms, 4 suites. Restaurant, minibars, laundry service, room service, exercise room. AE, MC, V. Tube: Covent Garden.*

££££ 🖬 **The Savoy.** This historic, grand, late-Victorian hotel is beloved by ★ the international influential, now as ever. Its celebrated Grill (☞ Chapter 3) has the premier power-lunch tables; it hosted Elizabeth Taylor's first honeymoon in one of its famous river-view rooms; and it poured the world's first martini in its equally famous American Bar—haunted by Hemingway, Fitzgerald, Gershwin, et al. And does it measure up to this high profile? Absolutely. The impeccably maintained, spacious, elegant, bright, and comfortable rooms are furnished with antiques and serviced by valets. A room facing the Thames costs an arm and a leg and requires an early booking, but there are few better views in London. Bathrooms have original fittings, with the same sunflower-size shower heads as at Claridge's. A theater ticket service is on the premises. Though the Savoy is as grand as they come, the air is tinged with a certain naughtiness, which goes down well with Hollywood types. ⊠ *Strand, WC2R 0EU,* ☎ *0171/836–4343,* FAX *0171/240–6040. 202 rooms. 3 restaurants, 2 bars, indoor pool, fitness center, beauty salon. AE, DC, MC, V. Tube: Aldwych.*

££££ 🔲 **Waldorf.** Close to the Aldwych theaters and Covent Garden, the Waldorf gleams in luscious Edwardiana, with polished marble floors, chandeliers, and cozily comfortable period bedrooms. This is another booking challenge for the wealthy theatergoer (Waldorf or Savoy?) and a suitably glamorous setting for the famous Palm Court tea dances, still going strong every weekend after nearly 90 years. ⊠ *Aldwych, WC2B 4DD,* ☎ *0171/836–2400,* FAX *0171/836–7244. 292 rooms. Restaurant, brasserie, beauty salon. AE, DC, MC, V. Tube: Aldwych.*

£££ 🔲 **Hazlitt's.** The solo Soho hotel is in three connected early 18th-
★ century houses, one of which was the last home of essayist William Hazlitt (1778–1830). It's a disarmingly friendly place, full of personality, but devoid of such hotel features as elevators, room service (though if the staff isn't too busy, you can get ad-hoc take-outs), and porter service. Robust antiques are everywhere, assorted prints crowd every wall, plants and stone sculptures appear in odd corners, and every room has a Victorian claw-foot tub in its bathroom. There are tiny sitting rooms, wooden staircases, and more restaurants within strolling distance than you could patronize in a year. Book way ahead—this is the London address of media people, literary types, and antiques dealers everywhere. ⊠ *6 Frith St., W1V 5TZ,* ☎ *0171/434–1771,* FAX *0171/439–1524. 23 rooms. AE, DC, MC, V. Tube: Tottenham Court Road.*

£££ 🔲 **Mountbatten.** It may seem rather odd for one of London's newer hotels to be named after the late Lord Mountbatten, last viceroy of India and favorite uncle of Prince Charles. But the name is probably just an excuse to go overboard with the old British Raj theme. The decor reflects Mountbatten's life: photos of the estate where he lived, Indian furnishings, silks, inlaid tables, and screens. It has a good standard of service, bedrooms in various shades of red, with chintz drapes, and bathrooms of Italian marble. A harpist plays in the lounge and a pianist in the comfortable bar, and there are post-theater cabarets in the Centre Stage restaurant three times a week, featuring the very actors you may have just left in the West End theaters. A minute's walk brings you to the Royal Opera House or the Covent Garden Piazza. ⊠ *Seven Dials, Covent Garden. WC2H 9HD,* ☎ *0171/836–4300,* FAX *0171/340–3540. 127 rooms. Restaurant, bar. AE, DC, MC, V. Tube: Covent Garden.*

££ 🔲 **Fielding.** Tucked away in a quiet alley by the world's first police station (now Bow St. Magistrates' Court), and feeling far from the madding crowds of Covent Garden, this very small and pretty hotel is so adored by its regulars that you'd be wise to book well ahead. Cameron Mackintosh, the Broadway musical producer (who could no doubt afford Claridge's), stays here—presumably for the homey atmosphere; the old London Town character; the continuity of a loyal, friendly staff which maintains the place as the two founders, now retired, kept it for more than two decades; and, of course, for the convenience of having the Royal Opera House, every theater, and half of

London's restaurants within spitting distance. It is not uneccentric. The bedrooms are all different, shabby-homey rather than chic, and cozy rather than spacious, though you can have a suite here for the price of a chain-hotel double. There's no elevator; only one room comes with bath (most have showers); and only breakfast is served in the restaurant. Cute. ⊠ *4 Broad Ct., Bow St., WC2B 5QZ,* ☎ *0171/836–8305,* FAX *0171/497–0064. 26 rooms, 1 with bath, 23 with shower. Bar, breakfast room. AE, DC, MC, V. Tube: Covent Garden.*

££ 🖭 **Pastoria.** A less exorbitant choice for the theatergoer than the Waldorf (although rates are at the very top of this category), the Pastoria is handily situated just off Leicester Square. The building is about 70 years old, with a suitably modern decor, the bedrooms done in limed oak with light pink walls and navy blue carpets. There's a brasserie-style restaurant to dine in, but Soho, which is restaurant central, is only a few hundred yards away. ⊠ *3–6 St. Martin's St., WC2H 7HL,* ☎ *0171/930–8641,* FAX *0171/925–0551. 58 rooms. Restaurant, bar, coffee shop. AE, DC, MC, V. Tube: Leicester Square.*

Kensington

££££ 🖭 **Blakes.** Blakes is another world—some would say a '70s rock-star
★   era time-warp. It was designed by owner Anouska Hempel (also known as Lady Weinberg), and each room is a fantasy packed with precious Biedermeier, Murano glass, and modern pieces inside walls of red lacquer and black, or dove-gray moiré, or perhaps—like Room 007, the movie stars' favorite suite—pink. Cinematic mood lighting, featuring recessed halogen spots, compounds the impression that you, too, are a movie star living in a big-budget biopic. The foyer sets the tone with its piles of cushions, Phileas Fogg valises and trunks, black walls, rattan and bamboo, and a noisy parakeet under a gigantic Asian parasol. Downstairs is an equally dramatic, exotic black-and-white restaurant. Stay away if you don't like Hollywood or the music biz. ⊠ *33 Roland Gardens, SW7 3PF,* ☎ *0171/370–6701,* FAX *0171/373–0442. 52 rooms. Restaurant. AE, DC, MC, V. Tube: Gloucester Road.*

£££ 🖭 **The Cranley.** The pedigree of this small, young, Georgian town-house hotel is Ann Arbor, Michigan (where the owners hail from), out of South Ken (where it stands, near the big museums), and it looks the part. Anglo antiques, oils, and etchings are mixed with a lot of U.S.-style swagged drapery in assorted florals and vivid color schemes. Bedrooms have kitchenettes, and many are high-ceilinged and huge-windowed, while two of the apartments have Jacuzzis and patio gardens. The cheaper rooms here and at their nearby 10-room **One Cranley Place** (SW7 3AB, ☎ 0171/589–7944, FAX 0171/225–3931), which operates March to October, belong in the ££ category. ⊠ *10–12 Bina Gardens, SW5 0LA,* ☎ *0171/373–0123,* FAX *0171/373–9497. 26 rooms, 10 apartments. Breakfast room. AE, DC, MC, V. Tube: Gloucester Road.*

£££ 🖭 **The Gore.** Just down the road from the Albert Hall, this very friendly
★   hotel is run by the same people who run Hazlitt's (☞ *above*) and features a similar eclectic selection of prints, etchings, and antiques. Here, though, are spectacular follylike rooms—Room 101 is a Tudor fantasy with minstrel gallery, stained glass, and four-poster bed, and Room 211, done in over-the-top Hollywood style, has a tiled mural of Greek goddesses in the bathroom. Despite all that, the Gore manages to remain most elegant. Bistrot 190 and Downstairs at 190 (☞ Chapter 3) serve as dining rooms and bar. ⊠ *189 Queen's Gate, SW7 5EX,* ☎ *0171/584–6601,* FAX *0171/589–8127. 54 rooms. Brasserie. AE, DC, MC, V. Tube: Gloucester Road.*

£££ 🖭 **Number Sixteen.** A luxury bed-and-breakfast close to South Kensington tube and three blocks or so from the great museums, Number Sixteen stands in a white-porticoed row of Victorian houses, with not

Lodging in Kensington, Knightsbridge, Chelsea, and Belgravia

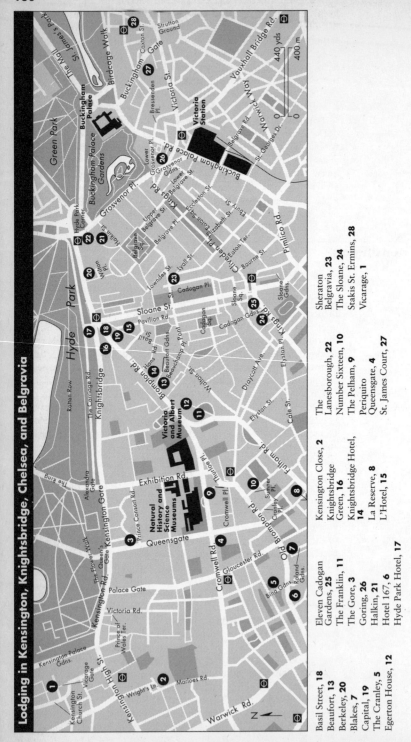

Basil Street, **18**
Beaufort, **13**
Berkeley, **20**
Blakes, **7**
Capital, **19**
The Cranley, **5**
Egerton House, **12**

Eleven Cadogan
Gardens, **25**
The Franklin, **11**
The Gore, **3**
Goring, **26**
Halkin, **21**
Hotel 167, **6**
Hyde Park Hotel, **17**

Kensington Close, **2**
Knightsbridge
Green, **16**
Knightsbridge Hotel,
14
La Reserve, **8**
L'Hotel, **15**

The
Lanesborough, **22**
Number Sixteen, **10**
The Pelham, **9**
Periquito
Queensgate, **4**
St. James Court, **27**

Sheraton
Belgravia, **23**
The Sloane, **24**
Stakis St. Ermins, **28**
Vicarage, **1**

a sign outside to indicate it. There's no uniformity to the bedrooms except for their spaciousness and recently refitted bathrooms, but the decor overall is not so much interior-designed as understated, with new furniture and modern prints juxtaposed with yellowed oils and antiques. There's an elevator, and an enticing garden complete with conservatory and fountain-ette. ⊠ *16 Sumner Pl., SW7 3EG,* ☎ *0171/589–5232,* FAX *0171/584–8615. 36 rooms. Bar. AE, DC, MC, V. Tube: South Kensington.*

££   ⊞ **Hotel 167.** This friendly little bed-and-breakfast is a two-minute walk from the V&A, in a grand white-stucco Victorian corner house. The lobby is immediately cheering, with its round marble tables, wrought-iron chairs, palms, and modern paintings; it also does duty as lounge and breakfast room. Bedrooms have a hybrid, Victoriana/IKEA decor with Venetian blinds over double-glazed windows (which you need on this noisy road), plus cable TV and minibars. ⊠ *167 Old Brompton Rd., SW5 0AN,* ☎ *0171/373–0672,* FAX *0171/373–3360. 19 rooms with bath or shower. Breakfast room. AE, DC, MC, V. Tube: Gloucester Road.*

££   ⊞ **Kensington Close.** This large, fairly utilitarian hotel feels like a smaller one and boasts a few extras you wouldn't expect for the reasonable rate and convenient location (in a quiet lane off Kensington High Street). The main attraction is the health club, with a sizeable pool, two squash courts, a steam room, and a beauty salon; there's also a secluded little water garden. Standard rooms are on the small side, with plain chain-hotel built-in furniture. Some "executive" rooms are twice the size and are a particularly good value. ⊠ *Wrights La., W8 5SP,* ☎ *0171/937–8170,* FAX *0171/937–8289. 530 rooms. 2 restaurants, 2 bars, indoor pool, health club, baby-sitting. AE, DC, MC, V. Tube: High Street Kensington.*

£   ⊞ **Periquito Queensgate.** When a hotel calls its own rooms "compact," you should imagine a double bed, then add a foot all around, and, yes, that is about the size of a room here. However, like in a cruise ship's stateroom, all you need is creatively secreted—there's a closet, mirror, satellite TV, tea/coffee maker, and a hair dryer. Rooms are double-glazed against noisy Cromwell Road, though earplugs are useful on account of LOUD color schemes, like purple, kingfisher, and canary, caused by this small chain's tropical parrot logo. The kids can share free—if you can fit a cot into these rooms—or else they get their own room at half price. The Natural History Museum is just across the street. ⊠ *68–69 Queensgate, London SW7 5JT,* ☎ *0171/370–6111,* FAX *0171/370–0932. 61 rooms. Bar. AE, MC, V. Tube: Gloucester Road.*

£   ⊞ **Vicarage.** A great deal of care goes into the running of this family-
★   owned hotel in a leaf-shaded, large white Victorian house just off Kensington Church Street (spend the cash you save here in its antiques shops). The decor is sweetly anachronistic, full of heavy, dark-stained wood furniture, patterned carpets, and brass pendant lights, and there's a little conservatory. Many of the spotless bedrooms now have TVs. ⊠ *10 Vicarage Gate, W8 4AG,* ☎ *0171/229–4030. 19 rooms. No credit cards. Tube: High Street Kensington.*

Knightsbridge, Chelsea, Belgravia, and Westminster

££££   ⊞ **Berkeley.** The Berkeley is a remarkably successful mixture of the
★   old and the new. It is a luxurious, air-conditioned, double-glazed modern building with a splendid penthouse swimming pool that opens to the sky when the weather's good. The bedrooms tend to be serious and opulent, some with swags of William Morris prints, others plain and masculine with little balconies overlooking the street. All have sitting areas and big, tiled bathrooms with bidets. For the ridiculously rich,

there are spectacular suites, one with its own conservatory terrace, another with a sauna, but—such is the elegance of this place—you'd feel almost as spoiled in a normal room. Its restaurant is Vong, the Thai/French hybrid cloned from New York; its expensive decor, work-of-art dishes, and exorbitant prices are going down very well with London's big spenders. The hotel is conveniently located for Knightsbridge shopping. ⊠ *Wilton Pl., SW1X 7RL,* ☎ *0171/235–6000,* ℻ *0171/235–4330. 160 rooms. 2 restaurants, indoor and outdoor pool, health club, beauty salon, cinema. AE, DC, MC, V. Tube: Knightsbridge.*

££££   🔟 **Capital.** Reserve well ahead if you want a room here—as you must for a table in the hotel's superb restaurant (☞ Chapter 3). This grand hotel decanted into a private house is the work of David and Margaret Levin, who also own L'Hôtel (☞ *below*), and it exudes their irre-proachable taste, with French floral fabrics, fine-grained woods, sober prints, and shelves of books. The 10 rooms of the Edwardian Wing, with its carved wooden staircase, enjoyed the attentions of superstar designer Nina Campbell and were already the height of fashion in the 1920s, when this was the Squires Hotel. ⊠ *22–24 Basil St., SW3 1AT,* ☎ *0171/589–5171,* ℻ *0171/225–0011. 48 rooms. Bar. AE, DC, MC, V. Tube: Knightsbridge.*

££££   🔟 **The Halkin.** If you can't take any more Regency stripes, English-
★   country florals, or Louis XV chaises, this luxurious little place is the antidote. You could say its slickness doesn't belong in the '90s, or you could just enjoy the Milanese design: the clean-cut white marble lobby with its royal-blue leather bucket chairs, the arresting, curved, char-coal-gray corridors, the "diseased mahogany" veneers, and the gray-on-gray bedrooms that light up when you insert your electronic key. Wealthy business and media types frequent the Halkin, and they can't breathe easy without a fax, Reuters, and two phone lines with con-ference-call. These are provided, along with two touch-control pads for all the gadgets, cable TV, and video. The bathrooms are palaces of shiny chrome. It might be like living in the Design Museum, except that this place employs some of the friendliest staff around—and they look pretty good in their white Armani uniforms, too. ⊠ *Halkin St., SW1X 7DJ,* ☎ *0171/333–1000,* ℻ *0171/333–1100. 41 rooms. Restaurant, business services. AE, DC, MC, V. Tube: Hyde Park Corner.*

££££   🔟 **Hyde Park Hotel.** For more than 100 years, the Hyde Park has en-
★   tertained lavishly, its banqueting rooms and ballroom regularly host-ing royalty—including the current batch, who still have a designated Royal Entrance—its bedrooms comforting assorted celebrities from Rudolph Valentino to Winston Churchill. Its halls boast eight kinds of marble and there are fine antiques and paintings strewn through-out. Bedrooms are large and hushed. Some have gentle windowfuls of treetop; from others, you can preview your Harvey Nichols purchases, as the building stands on the cusp of Knightsbridge shops and Hyde Park itself. The 1993 opening of Marco Pierre White: The Restaurant (☞ Chapter 3) did no harm to the Hyde Park's image, and continues to be a glamorous extra. The blinding white basement gym is also a plus. ⊠ *66 Knightsbridge, SW1Y 7LA,* ☎ *0171/235–2000,* ℻ *0171/235–2000. 160 rooms. 2 restaurants, bar, beauty salon, health club, theater ticket desk. AE, DC, MC, V. Tube: Knightsbridge.*

££££   🔟 **The Lanesborough.** This very grand hotel acts for all the world as though the Prince Regent took a ride through time and is about to re-sume residence. Royally proportioned public rooms (not lounges but "The Library" and "The Withdrawing Room") lead one off the other like an exquisite giant Chinese box in this multimillion-pound Amer-ican-run conversion of the old St. George's Hospital opposite Welling-ton's house. Everything undulates with richness—brocades and Regency stripes, moiré silks and fleurs-de-lys in the colors of precious stones, magnificent antiques and oil paintings, reproductions of more gilded splendor than the originals, handwoven £250-per-square-yard carpet, as if Liberace and Laura Ashley had collaborated on the design. All you do to register is sign the visitors book, then retire to your room, where you are waited on by a personal butler. Full-size Lanesborough toiletries, umbrellas (take them home), robes (don't), a drinks tray (pay by the inch), and even business cards with your temporary fax (in every room) and phone numbers (two lines) are waiting. If you yearn for a bygone age and are very rich, this is certainly for you. ⊠ *1 Lanesborough Pl., SW1X 7TA,* ☎ *0171/259–5599,* ⅋ʌx *0171/259– 5606. 95 rooms. 2 restaurants, bar. AE, DC, MC, V. Tube: Hyde Park Corner.*

££££ 🖬 **St. James Court.** You enter this Edwardian pile through a pair of enormous wrought-iron gates, which used to admit carriages into what is now the towering Reception. From here, you pass ranks of green leather sofas to reach the pièce de résistance, the landscaped courtyard with its fountain and ceramic frieze of scenes from Shakespeare. Some bedrooms are disproportionately large but cost the same as standards—the reverse is also true, so beware the expensive shoeboxes— and all are plainly decorated in pallid shades with a smattering of antiques and the odd (and some *are* very odd) painting. There are two good restaurants, a business center, and many apartments offer good deals for weekly and longer stays, but, unless you have business at Buckingham Palace or around Victoria, the location is a fraction uncentral for the rates. ⊠ *Buckingham Gate, SW1E 6AF,* ☎ *0171/834–6655,* ⅋ʌx *0171/630– 7587. 400 rooms. 2 restaurants, coffee shop, health club, business services. AE, DC, MC, V. Tube: St. James's Park.*

£££–££££ 🖬 **Sheraton Belgravia.** In the very heart of Belgravia, surrounded by chic 19th-century town houses and embassies, this Sheraton stands out— partly because it's nine stories tall and sheathed in glass and concrete, but mostly because its staff must be the most sensationally welcoming in all of London. Check-in comes with a glass of champagne, but also the kindest of smiles and the most charming of courtesies (perhaps the secret is that the major domo here used to be nanny to one of England's top royals). Rooms are cozily dimensioned and marvelously cheerful— a rainy day in London is no problem if your suite features daffodil-yellow walls. Serenely removed from the hurdy-gurdy of downtown London, this hotel is prized by those who want to enjoy the peace and beauty of London's most elegant neighborhood. The prime draw remains the staff: their grace and good cheer have to be experienced to be believed. ⊠ *20 Chesham Place, SW1 X8HQ,* ☎ *0171/235–6040,* ⅋ʌx *0171/259–6242. 89 rooms, 7 suites. Restaurant, bar, minibars, room service, laundry service, business services. AE, MC, V. Tube: Knightsbridge.*

£££ 🖬 **Basil Street.** This gracious Edwardian hotel is on a quiet street behind busy Brompton Road and off (rich) shoppers' heaven, Sloane Street. It's been family-run for three quarters of a century, and has always been popular with lone women travelers, who get automatic membership at the Parrot Club—an enormous lounge, with copies of *The Lady* and *Country Life* among the coffee cups. All the bedrooms are different; many are like grandma's guest room, with overstuffed counterpanes and a random selection of furniture. You can write letters home in the peaceful gallery, which has polished wooden floors and fine Turkish carpets underneath a higgledy-piggledy wealth of antiques. Americans with a taste for period charm favor this place; some come back often enough to merit the title "Basilite"—a privileged regular offered a 15% discount. ⊠ *Basil St., SW3 1AH,* ☎ *0171/581–3311,* ⅋ʌx *0171/581–3693. 92 rooms, 72 with bath. Restaurant, wine bar. AE, DC, MC, V. Tube: Knightsbridge.*

££££   🏨 **Beaufort.** You can practically hear the jingle of Harrods's cash reg-
★   isters from a room at the Beaufort, the brainchild of ex–TV announcer
        Diana Wallis, who employs an all-woman team to run the hotel. Ac-
        tually, "hotel" is a misnomer for this elegant pair of Victorian houses.
        There's a sitting room instead of Reception; guests have a front door
        key and the run of the drinks cabinet, and even their own phone num-
        ber, with the customary astronomical hotel surcharges waived. The high-
        ceilinged, generously proportioned rooms are decorated in muted,
        sophisticated shades to suit the muted, sophisticated atmosphere—but
        don't worry, you're encouraged by the incredibly sweet staff to feel at
        home. The rates are higher than the top range for this category but in-
        clude unlimited drinks, breakfast, plus membership at a local health
        club. ⊠ *33 Beaufort Gardens, SW3 1PP,* ☎ *0171/584–5252,* FAX
        0171/589–2834. 29 rooms. AE, DC, MC, V. Tube: Knightsbridge.

££££   🏨 **Egerton House.** This absolutely peaceful, private house–style small
        hotel was the first in the stable that includes the Franklin and Dukes,
        and remains many people's favorite, appealing especially, for some rea-
        son, to bankers. Many chintzy, floral, or Regency-stripe bedrooms over-
        look the gorgeous gardens in back; some have quirky shapes, others
        have four-poster beds, still others are extra–well endowed with closet
        space—in other words, all are different. The staff here is especially per-
        sonable—and the manager would love to know what you thought of
        the selections in his handwritten local restaurant guide. ⊠ *Egerton Ter-
        race, SW3 2BX,* ☎ *0171/589–2412,* FAX *0171/584–6540. 30 rooms.
        AE, DC, MC, V. Tube: Knightsbridge.*

££££   🏨 **Eleven Cadogan Gardens.** This aristocratic, late-Victorian gabled
        town house is the perfect spot for a pampered honeymoon, but very
        difficult to get into—and we're not referring to the lack of a sign or a
        reception desk. Fine period furniture and antiques, books and maga-
        zines on the tables, landscape paintings and portraits, coupled with some
        of that solid, no-nonsense furniture that *real* English country houses
        have in unaesthetic abundance make for a family-home ambience; you
        might be borrowing the house and servants of some wealthy friends
        while they're away. Take the elevator or walk up the fine oak staircase
        to your room, which will have mahogany furniture, a restful color
        scheme, and pretty bedspreads and drapes. The best rooms are at the
        back, overlooking a private garden. ⊠ *11 Cadogan Gardens, Sloane
        Sq., SW3 2RJ,* ☎ *0171/730–3426,* FAX *0171/730–5217. 62 rooms.
        Chauffeur-driven car. AE, MC, V. Tube: Sloane Square.*

££££   🏨 **The Franklin.** It's hard to imagine, while taking tea in this pretty hotel
        overlooking a quiet, grassy square, that you're an amble away from
        busy Brompton and Cromwell roads and the splendors of the V&A.
        A few of the rooms are small, but the marble bathrooms—in which
        Floris toiletries and heated towel racks are standard issue—are not; the
        large garden rooms and suites (which fall into the ££££ category) are
        romantic indeed. Tea is served daily in the lounge, and there's also a
        self-service bar. The staff is friendly and accommodating. ⊠ *28 Egerton
        Gardens, SW3 2DB,* ☎ *0171/584–5533,* FAX *0171/584–5449. 40
        rooms. Bar, parking (fee). AE, DC, MC, V. Tube: South Kensington.*

££££   🏨 **Goring.** This hotel is useful if you have to drop in at Buckingham
        Palace, just around the corner. In fact, visiting VIPs use it regularly as
        a conveniently close, and suitably dignified, base for royal occasions.
        The hotel was built by Mr. Goring in 1910 and is now run by third-
        generation Gorings. The atmosphere remains Edwardian: Bathrooms
        are marble-fitted, and some of the bedrooms have brass bedsteads and
        the original built-in closets; many have been opulently redecorated. The
        bar/lounge looks onto a well-tended garden. ⊠ *15 Beeston Pl.,
        Grosvenor Gardens, SW1W 0JW,* ☎ *0171/834–8211,* FAX *0171/834–
        8211. 87 rooms. Restaurant, bar. AE, DC, MC, V. Tube: Victoria.*

£££   ⊞ **L'Hotel.** An upscale bed-and-breakfast run by the same Levins who
★   own the Capital next door (and run the People's Palace on the South
Bank; ☞ Chapter 3), L'Hotel is a plainer alternative—less pampering,
unfussy decor. There's an air of provincial France, with white wrought-
iron bedsteads, pine furniture, and delicious breakfast croissants and
baguettes (included in the room rate) served on chunky dark green and
gold Parisian café china in Le Metro cellar wine bar (also open to non-
guests). This really is like a house—you're given your own front door
key, there's no elevator, and the staff leaves in the evening. Reserve
ahead—it's very popular. ⊠ *28 Basil St., SW3 1AT,* ☎ *0171/589–6286,*
FAX *0171/225–0011. 12 rooms. Restaurant, wine bar. AE, V. Tube:*
Knightsbridge.

£££   ⊞ **The Pelham.** The second of Tim and Kit Kemp's gorgeous hotels;
★   they opened it in 1989 and run it along exactly the same lines as the
Dorset Square (☞ Mayfair to Regent's Park, *above*), except that this
one looks more the country house to end all country houses. There's
18th-century pine paneling in the drawing room—one of the most rav-
ishingly elegant hotel salons anywhere—flowers galore, quite a bit of
glazed chintz and antique lace bed linen, and the odd four-poster and
bedroom fireplace. The first floor (American second floor) suites are
extra-spacious with their high ceilings and chandeliers, while some of
the top-floor rooms under the eaves have adorable sloping ceilings and
casement windows. The Pelham stands opposite the South Kensington tube stop, by the big museums, and close to the shops of Brompton Cross and Knightsbridge, with Kemps restaurant supplying an on-site
trendy menu. Little wonder Lauren Bacall deserted the Athenaeum for
this hotel. ⊠ *15 Cromwell Pl., SW7 2LA,* ☎ *0171/589–8288,* FAX
0171/584–8444. 37 rooms. Restaurant, outdoor pool. AE, MC, V. Tube:
South Kensington.

£££   ⊞ **Stakis St. Ermins.** Smack dab in the middle of Westminster, this hotel
is just a short stroll away from Westminster Abbey, and minutes from
Buckingham Palace and the Houses of Parliament. Within the shadow
of modern skyscrapers, the hotel is housed in a delightfully Edwardian
pile, set on a tiny cul-de-sac courtyard that's fronted with beasts-
rampant gates. The lobby is an extravaganza of Victorian Baroque—
all cake-frosting stucco work in shades of baby blue and creamy white.
The less costly of the two restaurants, the Cloisters, features one of the
most magnificent (and overlooked) dining decors in London: a 19th-
century Jacobethan-style salon. Guest rooms are tastefully decorated;
some have snug dimensions—but are all the cozier for it. ⊠ *Caxton*
St., SW1H 0QW, ☎ *0171/222–7888,* FAX *0171/222–6914. 290 rooms,*
7 suites. 2 restaurants, bar, room service, minibars, laundry service. AE,
DC, MC, V. Tube: St. James's Park.

££–£££   ⊞ **The Sloane.** Many hotels abuse the word "unique" to describe their
identical canopied beds or garden views, but the tiny Sloane really *is*
unique. It is the only hotel we know of in which you can lie in your
canopied bed, pick up the phone, and buy the bed. You could buy the
phone too, but it's the covetable, tasty antiques that you might actually be tempted to take home, and these are also for sale. Nothing so
tacky as a price tag besmirches the gorgeous decor—which doesn't stint
on strong hues to show off the ever-changing collection of Regency ar-
moires and occasional tables, Victorian desk lamps and crystal decanters,
Japanese screens and Edwardian oils, all collected by the antiques-
addicted owner—instead the sweet, young Euro staff harbor a book
of price lists at the desk. Room service is not 24-hour, but there's an
aerie of a secret roof terrace, with upholstered garden furniture and a
panorama over Chelsea, where lunch and dinner is served to guests.
⊠ *29 Draycott Pl., SW3 2SH,* ☎ *0171/581–5757,* FAX *0171/584–1348.*
12 rooms. AE, DC, MC, V. Tube: Sloane Square.

££ 🛏 **Knightsbridge Green.** There are more suites than bedrooms at this Georgian hotel that's a two-minute walk from Harrods. One floor is French-style, with white furniture, another English, in beech. Costing only £15 more than a double room, the suites are not overpriced, and all the rooms have trouser presses and tea/coffee makers. There's no restaurant, but there are plenty in the area; or if you ask they'll send the porter out to find you a sandwich. There's also coffee and cake left out in the lounge—a detail that exemplifies the friendliness of this place. ✉ *159 Knightsbridge, SW1X 7PD,* ☎ *0171/584–6274,* 🖷 *0171/225– 1635. 13 rooms, 12 suites. AE, MC, V. Closed 5 days over Christmas. Tube: Knightsbridge.*

££ 🛏 **Knightsbridge Hotel.** When it comes to measuring location versus value, this choice could be considered an ideal stopping place. Located on a tree-lined, quiet, stately square, the Knightsbridge is just a moment from Harrods and a few blocks from the chic boutiques and restaurants of Beauchamp Place. A family-run hotel, it's set in a townhouse built in the early 1800s. Guest rooms are unassuming yet well furnished, and there's even an exercise room on the premises. ✉ *12 Beaufort Gardens, SW3 1PT,* ☎ *0171/589–9271,* 🖷 *0171/823–9672. 40 rooms with bath. Exercise room. AE, MC, V. Tube: Knightsbridge.*

££ 🛏 **La Reserve.** You'll find this unusual small hotel in the lively, classy residential neighborhood of Fulham. The varnished floorboards, black Venetian blinds, works of art (for sale), and primary-color upholstery in the public areas are contemporary and sophisticated. Bedrooms are cluttered only with the minibars, hair dryers, trouser presses, and tea/coffee makers of more expensive places. Fulham is not within walking distance of central London, but it is two minutes from Fulham Broadway tube, near Chelsea Football (soccer) Grounds and plenty of restaurants; there's also a brasserie in-house. ✉ *422–428 Fulham Rd., SW6 1DU,* ☎ *0171/385–8561,* 🖷 *0171/385–7662. 37 rooms. Restaurant, bar. AE, DC, MC, V. Tube: Fulham Broadway.*

Bayswater and Notting Hill Gate

££££ 🛏 **Halcyon.** Discretion, decadent decor, and disco divas (everyone ★ from RuPaul and Simple Minds to Snoop Doggy Dogg) make this expensive, enormous, wedding cake Edwardian on Holland Park Avenue desperately desirable. You want film stars? They got Johnny Depp and William Hurt and Julia Roberts, and there are usually local residents like Sting, John Cleese, and *Absolutely Fabulous* Joanna Lumley haunting the absolutely excellent restaurant. But that's all by the by, because it's for perfect service and gorgeous rooms you'd follow them here. Many hotels lie when they claim "individual" room decor; not this one. The Blue Room has moons and stars, the famous Egyptian Suite is canopied like a bedouin tent, one room has heraldic motifs, and the Halcyon Suite has its own conservatory. All rooms are very large, with the high ceilings and big windows typical of the grand houses here—here being a 10-minute tube ride to the West End, and steps from London's most exquisite park. ✉ *81 Holland Park, W11 3RZ,* ☎ *0171/727–7288,* 🖷 *0171/229–8516. 44 rooms. Restaurant. AE, DC, MC, V. Tube: Holland Park.*

££££ 🛏 **The Hempel.** This is a prime contender for the Most Glamorous Hostelry in London prize (though at press time, we hadn't yet seen the new Metropolitan yet). Anouska Hempel attempted to get the name of the parklike square which this eponymously named hotel overlooks changed to Hempel Square, but you may forgive her this failure of modesty when you step inside these absolutely stunning, crisp, clean, white-on-white-on-white-on-white spaces—and we do mean spaces. There's nothing jarring, nothing extraneous, no visible means of sup-

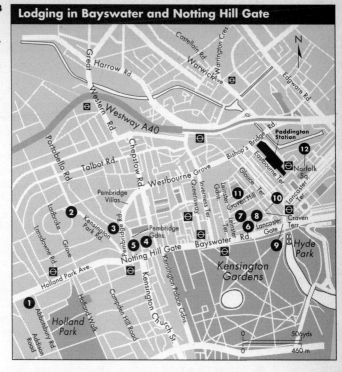

Lodging in Bayswater and Notting Hill Gate

port beneath the furniture, nothing like the over-the-top colors and mania for drapes and *objets* (and tiny rooms) of her other hotel, Blakes (☞ Kensington, *above*). Of course, the Hempel appeals greatly to showbizzy style hounds. Elton John (remember when he went Zen and sold all his gewgaws) was one of the first party-throwers in the restaurant here. But beware: the minimalist decor is not for everyone. ⊠ *31–35 Craven Hill Gdns., W2 3EA,* ☎ *0171/298–9000,* FAX *0171/472–4666. 43 rooms. Restaurant, bar. AE, DC, MC, V. Tube: Lancaster Gate.*

££££ 🏩 **Whites.** Ease into this cream-facaded Victorian "country mansion" with a white wrought-iron portico and a view of Kensington Gardens. Thick carpets, gilded glass, marble balustrades, swagged silk drapes, and Louis XV–style furniture all make this the most luxurious traditional hotel in the area. Some of the bedrooms have balconies (one also has a four-poster bed), and the colors are muted—powder blue, old rose, and lemon yellow—and prettiest when softly illuminated by the crystal wall-lights. The bathrooms are splendid. ⊠ *Lancaster Gate, W2 3NR,* ☎ *0171/262–2711,* FAX *0171/262–2147. 55 rooms. Restaurant. AE, DC, MC, V. Tube: Lancaster Gate.*

£££ 🏩 **Abbey Court.** This is a very elegant little hotel that is more like a private home—albeit one with a resident designer. It's in a gracious white Victorian mansion in a quiet streetlet off Notting Hill Gate, which gives easy access to most of London. Inside, the era of Victoria is reflected in deep-red wallpapers (downstairs), Murano glass and gilt-framed mirrors, framed prints, mahogany, and plenty of antiques. Bathrooms look the part but are entirely modern in gray Italian marble, with brass fittings and whirlpool baths. There's 24-hour room service instead of a restaurant (there are plenty around here, though), and guests can relax in the sitting room or the pretty conservatory. ⊠ *20 Pembridge Gardens, W2 4DU,* ☎ *0171/221–7518,* FAX *0171/792–0858. 22 rooms. AE, DC, MC, V. Tube: Notting Hill.*

££–£££ ⊡ **Pembridge Court.** A few doors down from the Abbey Court (☞ *above*), in a similar colonnaded white-stucco Victorian row house, is this sweet home-away-from-home of a hotel, cozy with scatter-cushions and books, quirky Victoriana, and framed fans from the neighboring Portobello Market. Bedrooms have a great deal of swagged floral drapery, direct-dial phones, and satellite TV, and there's an elevator to the upper floors. Rates include English breakfast—take that into account when doing your sums, since only the half-size small twin rooms fall into the ££ category; larger ones are £10–£30 more. ⊠ *34 Pembridge Gardens, W2 4DX,* ☎ *0171/229–9977,* FAX *0171/727–4982. 25 rooms. Restaurant. AE, DC, MC, V. Tube: Notting Hill.*

££–£££ ⊡ **Portobello.** This small, eccentric hotel consists of two adjoining Victorian houses that (as is common around here) back onto a beautiful large garden that is shared with the neighbors. It has long been a favorite of high-style mavens in the music and design worlds, and it must be said a tinge of the groovy early '70s still adheres to the corners, and also to the Victorian/Chinoiserie decor (which has turned a bit shabby in a few rooms, actually enhancing the overall effect for those who prefer to be somewhere louche and laid back). "Cabin Rooms" are minute, but have made a virtue of this fact, with everything you need accessible by reaching out your hand from bed, just like on board a ship. Many bigger rooms have free-standing Victorian claw-foot bathtubs, though the famous round-bedded suite has the *pièce de résistance* of the bath world—an Edwardian "bathing machine," all knobs and shiny brass pipes. Rates include breakfast, and there's a 24-hour bar/restaurant in the basement, though there are a hundred other options in this very happening area. ⊠ *22 Stanley Gardens, W11 2NG,* ☎ *0171/727–2777,* FAX *0171/792–9641. 25 rooms. Restaurant, bar. AE, DC, MC, V. Closed 10 days over Christmas. Tube: Ladbroke Grove.*

££ ⊡ **London Elizabeth.** Steps from Hyde Park, Lancaster Gate tube, and from rows of depressing, cheap hotels, is this family-owned gem. Foyer and lounge are crammed with coffee tables and chintz drapery, lace antimacassars, and little chandeliers, and this country sensibility persists through the bedrooms. All have been redone—in palest blue-striped walls, wooden picture rails and Welsh wool bedspreads, or in pink cabbage rose prints and mahogany furniture—and although they do vary in size, there's a thoughtful tendency here to make sure that what you lose on the swings (small wedge-shaped room), you gain on the roundabouts (bigger, brand-new bathroom, or a small balcony). Some rooms lack a full-length mirror, but they do have TV, direct-dial phone, and hair dryer, and they're serviced by an exceptionally charming Anglo-Irish staff, on call around the clock. ⊠ *Lancaster Terrace, W2 3PF,* ☎ *0171/402–6641,* FAX *0171/224–8900. 55 rooms. Restaurant, bar. AE, DC, MC, V. Tube: Lancaster Gate.*

£ ⊡ **Camelot.** This is an affordable hotel, just around the corner from Paddington Station, with bedrooms featuring utility pine furniture, TVs, tea/coffee makers, and attractive bathrooms. There's a sitting room, and a very pretty breakfast area. Everyone here is friendly beyond the call of duty. The few single rooms without baths are great bargains; the normal rate just busts the top of this category, but includes a breakfast of anything you want—full English or organic muesli, fruit, and herb tea. ⊠ *45–47 Norfolk Sq., W2 1RX,* ☎ *0171/723–9118,* FAX *0171/402–3412. 44 rooms, 36 with bath. MC, V. Tube: Paddington.*

£ ⊡ **Columbia.** If you're a sucker for '70s kitsch and like to stay out late, or alternatively, if you're a family on a tight budget, this unique paradox of a bargain hotel is worth a try. The public rooms in these five joined-up Victorians are as big as museum halls. During the day, at one end they contain the most hip band du jour drinking alcohol; at the other, there are sightseers sipping coffee. However, the place is big enough and the walls thick enough that you'd not even know they were shooting sleazy clubwear for *The Face* magazine in Room 100 while you sip tea (provided) in Room 101. Rooms are clean and some are very large, with park views and balconies. It's just a shame that teak veneer, khaki-beige-brown color schemes, and avocado bathroom suites haven't made it back into the style bible yet. ⊠ *95–99 Lancaster Gate, W2 3NS,* ☎ *0171/402–0021,* ℻ *0171/706–4691. 103 rooms. Restaurant, bar, meeting rooms. AE, MC, V. Tube: Lancaster Gate.*

£ ★ **Commodore.** This peaceful hotel of three converted Victorians is close to the Columbia, deeper in the big leafy square known as Lancaster Gate. It's another find of a very different stripe, as you'll notice on entering the cozy, carpeted lounge. Try your best to get one of the amazing rooms—as superior to the regular ones as Harrods is to Woolworth's, but priced the same. Twenty of these are split-level rooms, with sleeping gallery, all large, all different, all with something special—like a walk-in closet with its own stained-glass window. One (No. 11) is a duplex, entered through a secret mirrored door off a lemon-yellow hallway with palms and Greek statuary, with thick-carpeted *very* quiet bedroom upstairs and its toilet below. It's getting very popular here, so book ahead. ⊠ *50 Lancaster Gate, W2 3NA,* ☎ *0171/402–5291,* ℻ *0171/262–1088. 90 rooms. Bar, business services. AE, MC, V. Tube: Lancaster Gate.*

£ 🖭 **The Gate.** It's absolutely teeny, the Gate, just a normal house at the very top of Portobello Road, off Notting Hill Gate. The plain bedrooms have fridges, TVs, direct-dial phones, and tea/coffee facilities, plus bath (unless you opt for a smaller, £10 cheaper, shower-only room), and you can have the inclusive Continental breakfast brought up to you, or take it in the first-floor lounge. ⊠ *6 Portobello Rd., W11 3DG,* ☎ *0171/221–2403,* ℻ *0171/221–9128. 6 rooms. AE, MC, V. Tube: Notting Hill.*

£ 🖭 **Lancaster Hall Hotel.** This modest hotel is owned by the German YMCA, which guarantees efficiency and spotlessness. There's a bargain 20-room "youth annex" offering basic rooms with shared baths. ⊠ *35 Craven Terr., W2 3EL,* ☎ *0171/723–9276,* ℻ *0171/224–8343. 100 rooms, 80 with bath or shower. Restaurant, bar. MC, V. Tube: Lancaster Gate.*

Bloomsbury

££–£££ 🖭 **The Kingsley.** On the main street, steps from the British Museum, this is one Edwardian-style hotel that really does feel sweetly old-fashioned, while avoiding shabbiness or stuffiness. Flouncy, English country house–decor has the strong color schemes currently favored in hotel-land, and has been recently refreshed, with tea/coffee makers and free in-house movies among the facilities. The rooms in the turret on the southwest corner with their curved, six-window wall are worth asking for, being brighter than most, while executive suites have four-posters and Jacuzzis at a rate falling about halfway down the £££ category. ⊠ *Bloomsbury Way, WC1A 2SD,* ☎ *0171/242–5881,* ℻ *0171/831–0225. 145 rooms. Restaurant, bar, meeting rooms. AE, DC, MC, V. Tube: Holborn.*

££ 🖭 **Academy.** These three joined-up Georgian houses, boasting a little patio garden and a fashion-conscious mirrored and wood-floor basement bar/brasserie, supply the most sophisticated and hotel-like facilities in the Gower Street "hotel row." The comfortable bedrooms have TV (with no extra channels), direct-dial phones, and tea/coffee makers, and the two without en suite bathrooms are an entire £30/night cheaper. Like all the hotels in this section, the Academy neighbors the British Museum and University of London, a circumstance that appeals

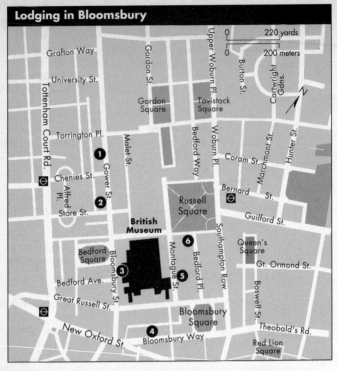

Lodging in Bloomsbury

to culture vultures on a budget and affluent students. ⊠ *17–21 Gower St., WC1E 6HG,* ☎ *0171/631–4115,* FAX *0171/636–3442. 33 rooms, 25 with bath/shower. Restaurant/bar. AE, DC, MC, V. Tube: Russell Square.*

£ ★ **Morgan.** This is a Georgian row-house hotel, family-run with charm and panache. Rooms are small and functionally furnished, yet friendly and cheerful overall, with phones and TVs. The five newish apartments are particularly pleasing: three times the size of normal rooms (and an extra £15/night, placing them in the ££ category), complete with eat-in kitchens (gourmet cooking sessions are discouraged) and private phone lines. The tiny, paneled breakfast room (rates include the meal) is straight out of a doll's house. The back rooms overlook the British Museum. ⊠ *24 Bloomsbury St., WC1B 3QJ,* ☎ *0171/636–3735. 15 rooms with bath or shower, 5 apartments. Breakfast room. No credit cards. Tube: Russell Square.*

£ **Ridgemount.** The kindly owners, Mr. and Mrs. Rees, make you feel at home. The public areas, especially the family-style breakfast room, have a friendly, cluttered Victorian feel. Some rooms overlook a leafy garden, and two now have an en suite bathroom, for an extra £9/night. ⊠ *65 Gower St., WC1E 6HJ,* ☎ *0171/636–1141. 34 rooms, 2 with bath. No credit cards. Tube: Russell Square.*

£ **Ruskin.** Immediately opposite the British Museum, the family-owned Ruskin is both pleasant and quiet—all front windows are double-glazed. The bedrooms are clean, though nondescript; the back ones overlook a pretty garden. Note the bucolic mural (c. 1808) in the sitting room. Well-run, the Ruskin remains a very popular option. ⊠ *23–24 Montague St., WC1B 5BN,* ☎ *0171/636–7388,* FAX *0171/323–1662. 35 rooms, 7 with shower. AE, DC, MC, V. Tube: Russell Square.*

£ **St. Margaret's.** This guest house on a tree-lined Georgian street has been run for many years by a friendly Italian family. You'll find spacious rooms and towering ceilings, and a wonderful location close to

Russell Square. The back rooms have a garden view. ⊠ *24 Bedford Pl., WC1B 5JL,* ☎ *0171/636–4277. 64 rooms, 10 with bath. No credit cards. Tube: Goodge Street.*

Docklands

££ ▦ **Scandic Crown.** This Swedish-owned place is Scandic by name and by nature, with efficiency and blond wood everywhere. It has its peculiarities, because it's split in two. Block 2 comprises a modern apartment building, while Block 1, containing all the bars and fun stuff, is a converted warehouse. Bedrooms in the latter (prefixed by a "1") are 10 times nicer than the new ones, with rich exposed-brick walls, recessed spotlights, and big windows, some overlooking the Thames. The dining options (you need them out here—the courtesy bus into town stops early) include the lower deck of a dry-docked three-masted bark and summertime riverside terrace barbecues. ⊠ *265 Rotherhithe St., SE16 1EJ,* ☎ *0171/231–1001,* ⅢX *0171/231–0599. 386 rooms. 2 restaurants, 2 bars, indoor pool, health club. AE, DC, MC, V.*

Hampstead

££ ▦ **Swiss Cottage Hotel.** It's a little out of the way on a peaceful street behind Swiss Cottage tube stop, but this charming, family-run hotel will suit those who like to stay in a residential district, save a little on the check, and still have their home comforts. The lounge, bar, and reception area are stuffed with antiques and reproductions, cheerfully lighted, and smilingly staffed. In summer, French windows open from the bar and the downstairs restaurant—which serves an old-fashioned Anglo-French menu—onto the garden. Bedrooms off the creaky, labyrinthine corridors are in Victorian style, and most are good-sized. (Note that the elevator doesn't reach the 4th floor.) ⊠ *4 Adamson Rd., NW3 3HP,* ☎ *0171/722–2281,* ⅢX *0171/483–4588. 80 rooms. Restaurant, bar. AE, DC, MC, V. Tube: Swiss Cottage.*

£ ▦ **La Gaffe.** Another find, a short walk from the Hampstead tube stop. Italian Bernardo Stella has been welcoming the same guests back to these early–18th-century shepherds' cottages for more than a decade. Make no mistake, rooms are tiny with showers only, and the predominantly pink and beige decor isn't luxurious, but the popular wine bar and restaurant, which (naturally) serve Italian food, are yours to lounge around in at all hours. Between the two "wings" is a raised patio for summer, and each room has TV and phone. You'll love the place if you're a fan of quaint. ⊠ *107–111 Heath St., NW3 6SS,* ☎ *0171/435–8965,* ⅢX *0171/794–7592. 14 rooms with shower. Restaurant, wine bar/café. AE, MC, V. Tube: Hampstead.*

Bed-and-Breakfast Agencies

££ ▦ **Uptown Reservations.** As the name implies, this B&B booking service accepts only the tonier addresses, and specializes in finding hosted apartments and homes for Americans, often executives of small corporations. Nearly all the 50 or so homes on their register are in Knightsbridge, Belgravia, Kensington, and Chelsea, with a few lying farther west in Holland Park and Maida Vale. The private homes vary, of course, but all are good-looking and have private en suite bathrooms for guests. ⊠ *50 Christchurch St., SW3 4AR,* ☎ *0171/351–3445,* ⅢX *0171/351–9383. Facilities vary. Payment by bank transfer or U.S. check; 20% deposit required. No credit cards.*

£ ▦ **Primrose Hill B&B.** A small, friendly bed-and-breakfast agency that's genuinely "committed to the idea traveling shouldn't be a rip-off." Expatriate American Gail O'Farrell has family homes (to which guests get their own latchkeys) in or near villagey Hampstead on her books, and all are comfortable or more than comfortable. So far this has been one of those word-of-mouth secrets, but now that everyone knows, book well ahead. ⊠ *14 Edis St., NW1 8LG,* ☎ *0171/722–6869. 15 rooms with varying facilities. No credit cards.*

5 Nightlife and the Arts

"Ladies and Gentlemen, the curtain is about to rise" on London's artful pleasures: Balanchine at the ballet, Pavarotti at the Royal Albert Hall, and the best theater in the world—Ralph Fiennes and Vanessa Redgrave doing star turns, Oliver! *in a West End revival, and unparalleled servings of Shakespeare. Now you can see, say,* The Winter's Tale *at the reconstructed Globe theater, where the interaction between player and audience often goes beyond polite applause. Finish off the night at a club sizzling with comedy, cabaret, or all that jazz.*

NIGHTLIFE

Nighttime London has rejuvenated itself in the past few years, with a tangible new spirit of fun abroad on the streets, and new hangouts opening at an unprecedented rate. Whatever your pleasure, there's somewhere to go. Are you a club animal? London's boîtes are famously hip, hot, and happening. Music? From indie bands to resident orchestras, free jazz to opera, it's everywhere. Cabaret of the traditional torch-song sort is undergoing a little revival, while comedy, which never slowed down in the first place, remains one of the city's favorite ways to wind down. The gay listing is small, but gives you all you need to find the scene, and there is a fabulous scene. All you need remember when you hit the town at night is that regular bars (those without special extended licenses) stop serving alcohol at 11 PM (10:30 on Sundays), and the tubes stop running around midnight.

Both those facts do inhibit the free flow of enjoyment, it has to be said. Although there's been a lot of hype about swinging London in recent years, it is no less depressing than it ever was to be thrown out of your warm and fuzzy pub corner at the sound of the bell to try to find a bar with a late license. On the whole, the club scene is for under-30s. If you don't have your ear to the ground in the youth culture department, you will feel out of place in nearly all venues listed under "Clubs" in *Time Out*, the weekly magazine that updates everything to do in London. But if you must put on the glad rags and boogie, we do list a couple of places for swingers nostalgic for that action. The jazz and world music (we used to call it folk) scenes are a different matter. Live music makes for a popular night out for all ages and types. A general rule of thumb: If you like the music, you'll like the crowd.

No doubt you've heard a lot about Britpop in the past couple of years. The bands that made it big are playing the stadium venues now, of course (Wembley, principally), but one of the joys of the London music scene is discovering your own "indie" bands (short for "independent" and refers to their record label, not their state of mind), and catching the latest hype before it's hyped. Again, read between the lines in the listings magazines to find your comfort level. Another, completely weird trend you may choose to follow has been for imitation, or "tribute," bands—Utter Madness, Björn Again, Abba Gold, Ludwig Beatles, YMCA Village People, Below Average White Band, and so on—which perform to party-animal crowds. On the opposite end of the authenticity scale, Latin and flamenco sounds are growing, and you can sometimes learn the dances in a free class before the band comes on.

Bars

The Atlantic. This vast, glamorous, wood-floored basement caused a revolution when, in early 1994, it became the first central London bar to be granted a late-late alcohol license. Although there are now others, it's still popular, so that the only way to get a table on a weekend night is to book it for dinner—luckily the food's fine. ⊠ *20 Glasshouse St., W1,* ☎ *0171/734–4888.* ☉ *Mon.–Sat. noon–3 AM, Sun. noon–11.* AE, MC, V. *Tube: Piccadilly Circus.*

Beach Blanket Babylon. In Notting Hill, close to Portobello market, this always packed singles bar is distinguishable by its fanciful decor—like a fairy-tale grotto, or a medieval dungeon, visited by the gargoyles of Notre Dame. ⊠ *45 Ledbury Rd., W11,* ☎ *0171/229–2907.* ☉ *Daily noon–11 PM.* AE, MC, V. *Tube: Notting Hill Gate.*

The Library. In this very comfortable, dress code–free but self-consciously "period" (doesn't matter which one as long as it looks old) bar at the swanky Lanesborough Hotel, Salvatore Calabrese offers his completely eccentric collection of ancient cognacs, made in years when something important happened. A shot of this "liquid history" can set you back £500. Don't ask for a brandy Alexander. ✉ *Hyde Park Corner, SW1,* ☎ *0171/259–5599.* ⊗ *Mon.–Sat. 11–11, Sun. noon–2:30 PM and 7–10:30. AE, DC, MC, V. Tube: Hyde Park Corner.*

Cabaret

Comedy Café. Talent nights, jazz, and video karaoke, but mostly stand-up comedy, take place at this popular dive in the City. Admission charges are occasionally waived. There's food available in the evening and usually a late license (for alcohol). ✉ *66 Rivington St., EC2,* ☎ *0171/739–5706.* ▣ *Free–£7.* ⊗ *Wed.– Thurs. 7:30–1, Fri. and Sat. 7:30–2. MC, V. Tube: Old Street.*

Comedy Store. This is the improv factory where the United Kingdom's funniest stand-ups cut their teeth, now relocated to a bigger and better place. The name performers and new talent you'll see may be strangers to you, but you're guaranteed to laugh. ✉ *Haymarket House, Oxendon St., SW1,* ☎ *0171/344–4444 or 01426/914433.* ▣ *£8–£10.* ⊗ *Shows Tues.–Thurs. and Sun. at 8, Fri. and Sat. at 8 and midnight. AE, MC, V. Tube: Piccadilly Circus.*

Casinos

The 1968 Gaming Act states that any person wishing to gamble *must* make a declaration of intent to gamble at the gaming house in question and *must* apply for membership in person. Membership usually takes about two days. In many cases, clubs prefer for the applicant's membership to be proposed by an existing member. Personal guests of existing members are, however, allowed to participate.

Crockford's. This is a civilized club, established 150 years ago, with none of the jostling for tables that mars many of the flashier clubs. It has attracted a large international clientele since its move from St. James's to Mayfair. The club offers American roulette, Punto Banco, and blackjack. ✉ *30 Curzon St., W1,* ☎ *0171/493–7771.* ▣ *Membership £150 per yr.* ⊗ *Daily 2 PM–4 AM. Jacket and tie. Tube: Green Park.*

Golden Nugget. This large casino just off Piccadilly has blackjack, roulette, and Punto Banco. ✉ *22 Shaftesbury Ave., W1,* ☎ *0171/439–0099.* ▣ *Membership £3.50 for life.* ⊗ *Daily 2 PM–4 AM. Jacket required. Tube: Piccadilly Circus.*

Palm Beach Casino. In what used to be the old ballroom of the Mayfair Hotel, this is a fast-moving and exciting club attracting a large international membership. It has a red-and-gold interior, with a plush restaurant and bar. You can choose from American roulette, blackjack, and Punto Banco. ✉ *30 Berkeley St., W1,* ☎ *0171/493–6585.* ▣ *Membership £10.* ⊗ *Daily 2 PM–4 AM. Jacket and tie. Tube: Green Park.*

Sportsman Club. This one has a dice table as well as Punto Banco, American roulette, and blackjack. ✉ *3 Tottenham Court Rd., W1,* ☎ *0171/637–5464.* ▣ *Membership £3.45 per yr.* ⊗ *Daily 2 PM–4 AM. Jacket and tie. Tube: Tottenham Court Road.*

Clubs

Always call ahead, especially to the dance and youth-oriented places, because the club scene is constantly changing.

Camden Palace. It would be difficult to find a facial wrinkle in this huge place, even if you could see through the laser lights and find your way around the three floors of bars. There's often a live band. ✉ *1A Camden High St., NW1,* ☎ *0171/387–0428.* ▣ *£3–£9.* ⊗ *Tues.–Sat. 9–3. No credit cards. Tube: Mornington Crescent or Camden Town.*

Gardening Club. Next door to the Rock Garden, but far hipper than that ancient dive, this club has different music, ambience, and groovers on different nights. There's also a much bigger Gardening Club 2 (☞ The Gay Scene, *below*). ⊠ *4 The Piazza, WC2,* ☎ *0171/497–3154.* ▨ *£4–£12.* ☉ *Mon.–Wed. 10–3, Fri. and Sat. 11–6. AE, DC, MC, V. Tube: Covent Garden.*

Heaven. London's premier (mainly) gay club is the best place for dancing wildly for hours. A state-of-the-art laser show and a large, throbbing dance floor complement a labyrinth of quieter bars and lounges and a snack bar (☞ The Gay Scene, *below*). ⊠ *Under the Arches, Villiers St., WC2,* ☎ *0171/930–2020.* ▨ *£4–£10.* ☉ *Usually Tues.–Sat. 10–3:30, but call ahead. AE, DC, MC, V. Tube: Charing Cross.*

Hippodrome. A neon horseman marks Peter Stringfellow's second-string club. Much like his first-string one (☞ *below*), this one has lots of sparkly black and silver, several tiers of expensive bars, a restaurant, and lots of enthusiastic lighting around a large dance floor. Very middle-of-the-road. ⊠ *Hippodrome Corner, Cranbourn St., WC2,* ☎ *0171/437–4311.* ▨ *Mon.–Thurs. £8, Fri. £10, Sat. £12 (£6 before 10:30).* ☉ *Mon.–Sat. 9–3:30. AE, DC, MC, V. Tube: Leicester Square.*

Ministry of Sound. This is more of an industry than a club, with its own record label, line of apparel, and, of course, DJs. Inside, there are chill-out rooms, dance floors, promotional Sony Playstations, Absolut shot bars—all the club kid's favorite things. ⊠ *103 Gaunt St., SE1,* ☎ *0171/378–6528.* ▨ *£10–£15.* ☉ *Wed.–Sat. 11–8. MC, V. Tube: Elephant & Castle.*

Salsa! Where to go for the Latin beat. If you're no good on your feet, get there early for the dance class, though this isn't on every night, so call. Cheap *caipirinhas* are poured on slow nights, too. ⊠ *96 Charing Cross Rd., W1,* ☎ *0171/379–3277.* ☉ *Mon.–Sat. 8–2. Tube: Leicester Square.*

Stringfellows. Peter Stringfellow's first London nightclub is not at all hip, but it *is* glitzy, with mirrored walls, the requisite dance-floor light show, and an expensive art deco–style restaurant. Suburbanites and middle-aged swingers frequent it. ⊠ *16–19 Upper St. Martin's La., WC2,* ☎ *0171/240–5534.* ▨ *Mon.–Wed. £8, Thurs. £10, Fri. and Sat. £15 (£10 before 10).* ☉ *Mon.–Sat. 8–3:30. AE, DC, MC, V. Tube: Charing Cross.*

The Wag. This tenacious representative of Soho's club circuit takes on a different character according to the night and which DJ is spinning. One extremely loud, sweaty level houses bars and dance spaces, and on a quieter, cooler one there's a restaurant serving dinner and breakfast. ⊠ *33–35 Wardour St., W1,* ☎ *0171/437–5534.* ▨ *£5–£10.* ☉ *Mon.–Thurs. 10:30–3, Fri. and Sat. 10:30–6. No credit cards. Tube: Piccadilly Circus.*

Jazz

Jazz Café. This palace of high-tech cool in a converted bank in bohemian Camden remains an essential hangout both for fans of the mainstream end of the repertoire and younger crossover performers. It's way north, but steps from Camden Town tube. ⊠ *5–7 Pkwy., NW1,* ☎ *0171/344–0044 or 0181/963–0940.* ▨ *£7–£12.* ☉ *Mon.–Sat. 7–late. AE, DC, MC, V. Tube: Camden Town.*

100 Club. The best for blues, trad, and Dixie, plus the occasional straight rock-and-roll, this Oxford Street subterranean has the correct paint-peeling, smoke-choked, dance-inducing atmosphere. There's a food counter most nights. ⊠ *100 Oxford St., W1,* ☎ *0171/636–0933.* ▨ *£4–£10.* ☉ *Mon.–Wed. 7:30–midnight, Thurs.–Sat. 8:30–1, Sun. 7:30–11:30. No credit cards. Tube: Oxford Circus.*

Pizza Express. It may seem strange, since Pizza Express is the capital's best-loved chain of pizza houses, but this is one of London's principal jazz venues, with music every night except Monday in the basement restaurant. The subterranean interior is darkly lighted, the lineups (often featuring visiting U.S. performers) are interesting, and the Italian-style thin-crust pizzas are great! ⊠ *10 Dean St., W1,* ☎ *0171/437–9595.* ⊡ *£8–£20.* ☺ *From noon for food, music Tues.–Sun. 9:30–1. AE, DC, MC, V. Tube: Tottenham Court Road.*

The Rhythmic. Another one that's a little out of the way, but certainly worth the trip, this civilized restaurant/club on an Islington street that's a produce market by day gets great lineups, from Jimmy Smith to the Master Musicians of Joujouka. ⊠ *89–91 Chapel Market, N1,* ☎ *0171/713–5859.* ⊡ *£7–£12 nonmembers.* ☺ *Mon.–Sat. 8:30–3. MC, V. Tube: Angel.*

Ronnie Scott's. The legendary Soho jazz club that, since opening in the early '60s, attracts all the big names. It's usually packed and hot, the food isn't great, service is slow—the staff can't move through the crowds, either—but the atmosphere can't be beat, and it's probably still London's best. ⊠ *47 Frith St., W1,* ☎ *0171/439–0747.* ⊡ *£10–£15 nonmembers.* ☺ *Mon.–Sat. 8:30–3, Sun. 8–11:30. Reservations essential. AE, DC, MC, V. Tube: Leicester Square.*

South Bank. A certain kind of really big name (such as Carla Bley, Jan Garbarek, Richard Thompson) ends up here, at the Royal Festival Hall, or the Queen Elizabeth Hall. What you lose in atmosphere, you gain in acoustical clarity, and you save wear and tear on the shoe leather. ⊠ *Waterloo,* ☎ *0171/928–8800.* ⊡ *£7.50–£24.* ☺ *Jazz concerts usually start at 7:30; call for information. Reservations essential. AE, MC, V. Tube: Waterloo.*

The Vortex. In the wilds of Stoke Newington, a very happening, liberal-arts neighborhood with tons of vegetarian/Asian restaurants, is this show-case venue for the healthy British jazz scene, with the emphasis on advanced, free, and improvised work. ⊠ *Stoke Newington Church St., N16,* ☎ *0171/254–6516.* ⊡ *£4–£7.* ☺ *Most nights 8–11. MC, V. British Rail: Stoke Newington.*

Rock

The Astoria. Very central, quite hip, this place hosts bands there's a buzz about, plus late club nights. ⊠ *157 Charing Cross Rd., W1,* ☎ *0171/434–0403.* ⊡ *£8–£12.* ☺ *Check listings. No credit cards. Tube: Tottenham Court Road.*

The Forum. This ex-ballroom with balcony and dance floor packs in the customers, and consistently attracts the best medium-to-big-name performers, too. ⊠ *9–17 Highgate Rd., NW5,* ☎ *0171/284–2200.* ⊡ *£8–£12.* ☺ *Most nights 7–11. AE, MC, V. Tube: Kentish Town.*

The Roadhouse. True to its name, this pays homage to the American dream of the open road, with a Harley behind the bar and much memorabilia. Music fits into the feel-good, tuneful, middle-of-the-road end of the R&B/blues/rock/soul spectrum. ⊠ *Jubilee Hall, Covent Garden, WC2,* ☎ *0171/240–6001.* ⊡ *£3–£6.* ☺ *Mon.–Wed. 5:30–1, Thurs.–Sat. 5:30–3, Sun. 12:30 PM–5:30 PM. AE, MC, V. Tube: Covent Garden.*

Shepherd's Bush Empire. Converted from the BBC TV theater, where Terry Wogan, the United Kingdom's Johnny Carson, recorded his show for years and years, this now hosts the same kind of medium-big names as the north London Forum. ⊠ *Shepherd's Bush Green, W12,* ☎ *0181/740–7474.* ⊡ *£8–£12.* ☺ *Most nights 7:30–11. AE, MC, V. Tube: Shepherd's Bush.*

Station Tavern. For a taste of local life, head into the wastelands for a (usually) completely unfamous R&B band in a lover'ly un-redone old-fashioned London pub. Bob's aptly named Goodtime Blues has been honking here forever. It's opposite the tube, luckily. ⊠ *41 Bramley Rd., W10,* ☎ *0171/727–4053.* ✆ *Free–£3.* ☉ *Most nights 8:30–11. Tube: Latimer Road.*

The Gay Scene

Since February 1994, with the long-overdue lowering of the age of consent from 21, 18-year-old gay men in Britain have had the blessing of the law in doing what they've always done. (Westminster mooted 16, the boys-and-girls age, but British MPs could not quite deal with that.) The change did not extend to lesbians, nor did it need to, because there has never been any legislation that so much as mentions gay women—a circumstance that, believe it or not, dates from Queen Victoria's point-blank refusal to believe that women did it with women. AIDS is, of course, a large issue, but the epidemic hasn't yet had quite as devastating an impact on the London scene as it has had in San Francisco and New York.

The whole of London has benefited hugely from the blossoming of gay nightlife. Soho, especially Old Compton Street, has something of a pre-AIDS Christopher Street atmosphere, with gay shops, bars, restaurants, and even beauty salons (get your chest waxed here) jostling for space. The lavender pound is a desirable pound. Though lesbians are included in the "Compton" scene (as are anyone's straight friends), it's predominantly men-for-men. The dyke scene certainly exists, and lesbian chic is as trendy in London as it is in New York or Los Angeles, but it has a lower profile, generally, than the male equivalent, and also tends to be more politically strident. Any women-only event in London attracts a large proportion of gay women.

Check the listings in *Time Out,* the weekly *MetroXtra* (MX), and the monthly *Gay Times* for events.

Bars, Cafés, and Pubs
Pub hours for the listings in this section are the same as for all London pubs, with drinks available up to 11 PM.

The Box. On two floors, one bright, one dark, there's good, light food and (at least at press time) the Sunday night Girl Bar, which wows all London dykes. ⊠ *Seven Dials, Monmouth St., WC2,* ☎ *0171/240–5828. Tube: Leicester Square.*

Drill Hall. A woman-centric arts center with a great program of theater/dance/art events and classes, plus a popular bar, which is women-only Monday. ⊠ *16 Chenies St., WC1,* ☎ *0171/637–8270. Tube: Goodge Street.*

The Edge. Poseurs are welcome at this hip Soho hangout, where straight groovers mix in, and there are sidewalk tables in summer. Risk the vodkas infused with candy. ⊠ *11 Soho Sq., W1,* ☎ *0171/439–1223. Tube: Oxford Circus.*

First Out. This relaxed, fairly long-established café/bar is in the shadow of Centrepoint. Fridays are women-only. ⊠ *52 St. Giles High St., WC2,* ☎ *0171/240–8042. Tube: Tottenham Court Road.*

Freedom. This is a popular café/bar central to the Soho scene. In addition it has a late-night club, Le Fumoir, downstairs for dancing; there's even a theater. ⊠ *60–66 Wardour St., W1,* ☎ *0171/734–0071. Tube: Piccadilly Circus.*

The Village. A cavern of a fashionable three-floored bar/restaurant/café/disco, this nightspot's name makes explicit the similarities between New York a decade ago and London now. ⊠ *81 Wardour St., W1,* ☎ *0171/434–2124. Tube: Piccadilly Circus.*

The Yard. This is Soho's best-looking and biggest bar/café, centered around the eponymous courtyard, and closely related to The Village (☞ *above*). Get a bottomless coffee, or a club sandwich, or an entire night out here. ✉ *57 Rupert St., W1,* ☎ *0171/437–2652. Tube: Piccadilly Circus.*

Cabaret

Madame Jo Jos. By no means devoid of straight spectators, this place has long been one of the most fun drag cabarets in town, with a civilized atmosphere (despite bare-chested bar boys). There are various club events too, including London's first drag king night, held on Mondays. ✉ *8 Brewer St.,* ☎ *0171/287–1414.* ☒ *Mon.–Thurs. £6, Fri. and Sat. £8.* ☉ *Doors open most nights at 10 PM, shows nightly at 12:15 and 1:15. Tube: Piccadilly Circus.*

Vauxhall Tavern. This venerable, curved pub had a drag cabaret before the Lady Bunny was born. Sometimes it's full of gay mafia, other times it's local media folk having a different night out, and Friday is the night for the lesbian cabaret, Vixens. ✉ *372 Kennington La., SE11,* ☎ *0171/582–0833.* ☒ *Free.* ☉ *Mon. 8–1, Tues., Thurs.–Sat. 8–2, Wed. 8–midnight, Sun. 7–10:30. Tube: Oval.*

Clubs

Heaven. Aptly named, it has by far the best light show on any London dance floor, is unpretentious, *loud*, and huge, with a labyrinth of quiet rooms, bars, and live-music parlors. If you go to just one club, this is the one to choose. Thursday is straight night. ✉ *The Arches, Villiers St., WC2,* ☎ *0171/839–2520.* ☒ *£4–£8.* ☉ *Tues.–Sat. 10:30–3:30. Tube: Charing Cross.*

One-Nighters

Some of the best gay dance clubs are held once a week in mixed clubs. The following are well established, and likely still to be going strong, but it's best to call first.

Jo's Original Tea Dance. A longtime fave with the girls, this is a very camp and very fun Sunday ballroom, line-dance, time-warp disco, now in a new home after many years. ✉ *BJ's White Swan, 556 Commercial Rd., E14,* ☎ *0171/780–9870.* ☒ *£4.* ☉ *Sun., 5–midnight. DLR: Limehouse.*

Love Muscle. A steaming mixed-gender Saturday-night party, with eight hours of dance classics at a big Brixton club. ✉ *The Fridge, Town Hall Parade, Brixton Hill, SW2,* ☎ *0171/326–5100.* ☒ *£10 before midnight with flyer, £12 midnight–3 AM, £8 after 3 AM.* ☉ *Sat., 10–6. Tube: Brixton.*

THE ARTS

There isn't *a* London arts scene—there are lots of them. As long as there are audiences for Feydeau revivals, drag queens, obscure teenaged rock bands, hit musicals, body-painted Parisian dancers, and improvised stand-up comedy, someone will stage them in London. Commercial sponsorship of the arts is in its infancy here compared to what it is in the United States, and most major arts companies, as well as those smaller ones lucky enough to be grant-aided, are dependent, to some extent, on (inadequate) government subsidy. This ought to mean low ticket prices, but it doesn't necessarily work that way. Even so, when you consider how much a London hotel room costs, the city's arts are a bargain.

We've attempted a representative selection in the following listings, but to find out what's showing now, the weekly magazine *Time Out*

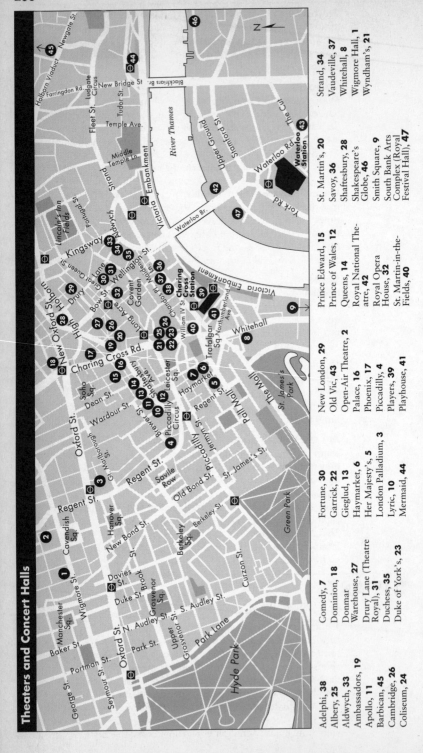

Theaters and Concert Halls

200

Adelphi, **38**
Albery, **25**
Aldwych, **33**
Ambassadors, **19**
Apollo, **11**
Barbican, **45**
Cambridge, **26**
Coliseum, **24**

Comedy, **7**
Dominion, **18**
Donmar
Warehouse, **27**
Drury Lane (Theatre
Royal), **31**
Duchess, **35**
Duke of York's, **23**

Fortune, **30**
Garrick, **22**
Gielgud, **13**
Haymarket, **6**
Her Majesty's, **5**
London Palladium, **3**
Lyric, **10**
Mermaid, **44**

New London, **29**
Old Vic, **43**
Open-Air Theatre, **2**
Palace, **16**
Phoenix, **17**
Piccadilly, **4**
Players, **39**
Playhouse, **41**

Prince Edward, **15**
Prince of Wales, **12**
Queens, **14**
Royal National The-
atre, **42**
Royal Opera
House, **32**
St. Martin-in-the-
Fields, **40**

St. Martin's, **20**
Savoy, **36**
Shaftesbury, **28**
Shakespeare's
Globe, **46**
Smith Square, **9**
South Bank Arts
Complex (Royal
Festival Hall), **47**

Strand, **34**
Vaudeville, **37**
Whitehall, **8**
Wigmore Hall, **1**
Wyndham's, **21**

(it's issued every Wednesday—Tuesday in central London) is invaluable. The *Evening Standard* also carries listings, especially in the supplement *Hot Tickets* that comes with the Thursday edition, as do the "quality" Sunday papers and the Saturday *Independent, Guardian,* and *Times.* You'll find leaflets and flyers in most cinema and theater foyers, too, and you can pick up the free fortnightly *London Theatre Guide* leaflet from hotels and tourist information centers.

Ballet

The Royal Opera House has been the traditional home of the world-famous **Royal Ballet,** but change is in the wind: The beloved opera house is now closed for a renovation that should take two years, and the multi-million pound rebuilding project includes, in fact, monies set aside for a completely new and separate theater for the ballet. During this time, the Royal Ballet will be performing at the Apollo Hammersmith Theatre and also the Royal Festival Hall. Prices are sure to be slightly more reasonable than they are for the opera, but bookings should be made well in advance, as tickets sell out fast. The **English National Ballet** and visiting international companies perform at the Coliseum—but that theater, too, is scheduled for a renovation program lasting several seasons and resident troupes will be performing elsewhere (call the Coliseum Box Office for further information). In addition, the **City Ballet of London** performs at the **Peacock Theatre. Sadler's Wells Theatre** also hosts various other ballet companies and regional and international modern dance troupes. Finally, that tear-jerking old Irish mass-jig, **Riverdance** is probably still clogging along at the **Apollo-Hammersmith.**

Ballet Box Office Information

Apollo Hammersmith, ⊠ *Hammersmith Broadway,* W6, ☎ *0171/416–6022. Tube: Hammersmith.*

Coliseum, ⊠ *St. Martin's La., WC2N 4ES,* ☎ *0171/632–8300. Tube: Leicester Square.*

Peacock Theatre, ⊠ *Portugal St., W1,* ☎ *0171/314–8800. Tube: Holborn.*

Royal Festival Hall, ⊠ *South Bank Arts Complex, SE1 8XX,* ☎ *0171/928–8800. Tube: Waterloo or Embankment Station.*

Royal Opera House, ⊠ *Covent Garden, WC2E 9DD,* ☎ *0171/304–4000. Tube: Covent Garden.*

Sadler's Wells, ⊠ *Rosebery Ave., EC1R 4TN,* ☎ *0171/713–6000. Tube: Angel.*

Concerts

The ticket prices to symphony-size orchestral concerts are fortunately still relatively moderately priced, usually ranging from £5 to £15. If you can't book in advance, then arrive at the hall an hour before the performance for a chance at returns.

The London Symphony Orchestra is in residence at the **Barbican Centre,** although other top orchestras—including the Philharmonia and the Royal Philharmonic—also perform here. The **South Bank Arts Complex,** which includes the **Royal Festival Hall,** the **Queen Elizabeth Hall,** and the small **Purcell Room,** forms another major venue; the Royal Festival Hall is one of the finest concert halls in Europe. Between the Barbican and South Bank, there are concert performances almost every night of the year. The Barbican also features chamber music concerts with such celebrated orchestras as the City of London Sinfonia.

For a different concert-going experience, as well as the chance to take part in a great British tradition, try the **Royal Albert Hall** during the Promenade Concert season: eight weeks lasting from July to September. Special "promenade" (standing) tickets usually cost half the price of normal tickets and are available at the hall on the night of the concert. Another summer pleasure is the outdoor concert series by the lake at **Kenwood** (⌧ Hampstead Heath, ☎ 0181/348–6684). Concerts are also part of the program at the open-air theater in **Holland Park** (☎ 0171/602–7856). Check the listings for details.

You should also look for the lunchtime concerts that take place all over the city in smaller concert halls, the big arts center foyers, and churches; they usually cost under £5 or are free and will feature string quartets, singers, jazz ensembles, or gospel choirs. **St. John's, Smith Square,** and **St. Martin-in-the-Fields** are two of the more popular locations. Performances usually begin about 1 PM and last an hour.

Concert Hall Box Office Information

Barbican Centre, ⌧ *Barbican, EC2Y 8DS,* ☎ *0171/638–8891 or 0171/638–4141. Tube: Moorgate.*

Royal Albert Hall, ⌧ *Kensington Gore, SW7 2AP,* ☎ *0171/589–8212. Tube: Gloucester Road.*

St. John's, Smith Square, ⌧ *SW1P 3HA,* ☎ *0171/222–1061. Tube: Westminster.*

St. Martin-in-the-Fields, ⌧ *Trafalgar Sq., WC2N 4JJ,* ☎ *0171/839–1930. Tube: Charing Cross.*

South Bank Arts Complex, ⌧ *South Bank, SE1 8XX,* ☎ *0171/928–8800 or 0171/928–3002. Tube: Waterloo.*

Wigmore Hall, ⌧ *36 Wigmore St., W1H 9DF,* ☎ *0171/935–2141. Tube: Bond Street.*

Modern Dance

Contemporary dance thrives in London, with innovative young choreographers and companies constantly emerging (and then, it often seems, moving to New York). Michael Clark was one of the first of the new wave; Yolanda Snaith, Bunty Matthias, and choreographer Lea Anderson's troupe, the Cholmondeleys (pronounced "Chumleys"), are more examples of home-grown talent. In addition to the many fringe theaters that produce the odd dance performance, the following theaters showcase contemporary dance:

The Place, ⌧ *17 Duke's Rd., WC1,* ☎ *0171/387–0031. Tube: Euston.*

Riverside Studios (☞ Fringe Theater, *below*).

Sadler's Wells (☞ Opera and Ballet, *below and above*).

Movies

Despite the video invasion, West End movie theaters continue to do good business. Most of the major houses (Odeon, MGM, etc.) are located in the Leicester Square/Piccadilly Circus area, where tickets average £7. Mondays and matinees are often cheaper at around £4, and there are also fewer crowds. Prices drop to around £5 as you get out of the West End, and are even lower in the suburbs, but unless you're staying there, any savings could be eaten up by transportation costs.

The few movie clubs and repertory cinemas that still exist screen a wider range of movies, including classic, Continental, and underground, as well as rare or underestimated masterpieces. Some charge a membership fee of under £1. The king is the **National Film Theatre** (⌧ South Bank Arts Complex, ☎ 0171/928–3232), where the London Film Festival is based in the fall; there are also lectures and presentations. Daily membership costs 40p. Also worth checking out are the **Everyman** (⊠ Hollybush Vale, Hampstead, ☎ 0171/435–1525; membership 60p/year), the **Rio** (⊠ Kingsland High St., Hackney E8, ☎ 0171/254–6677), though it's a bit of a trek, and the **Riverside** (☞ Fringe Theater, *below*).

Opera

The main venue for opera in London is the **Royal Opera House,** which ranks with the Metropolitan Opera House in New York—in every way, including expense. Beginning with the summer of 1997, however, the famous opera house will be closed for at least two years, due to a massive renovation program. For the 1997–98 season the opera will move full opera productions to the Barbican Theatre, the Shaftesbury Theater, and Royal Albert Hall, with concert versions given at Royal Festival Hall (South Bank Arts Complex), Barbican Hall, and Royal Albert Hall. For the 1998–99 season, most productions should be concentrated in the newly refurbished Sadler's Wells Theatre. In general, prices will probably have the same range—from £5 to more than £100 for the best seats, and performances will probably still be divided into booking periods and sell out early, although returns and standing spaces are sold on the day. (Conditions of purchase vary—call for information.)

English-language productions are staged at the **Coliseum** in St. Martin's Lane, home of the **English National Opera Company.** At it turns out, this theater will *also* be undergoing a renovation for the next few seasons. At press time, the temporary venue for the ENO had not been announced (inquire at the Coliseum Box Office for current information). Prices are lower than for the Royal Opera, ranging from £8 to £45, and productions are often innovative and exciting.

Opera Box Office Information
Barbican Centre, Royal Albert Hall, Royal Festival Hall (South Bank Arts Complex), ☞*Concert Hall Box Office Information, above.*
Coliseum, ⊠ *St. Martin's La., WC2N 4ES,* ☎ *0171/632–8300. Tube: Leicester Square.*
Royal Opera House, ⊠ *Covent Garden, WC2E 9DD,* ☎ *0171/304–4000. Tube: Covent Garden.*
Sadler's Wells, ⊠ *Rosebery Ave., EC1R 4TN,* ☎ *0171/713–6000. Tube: Angel.*
Shaftesbury, ⊠ *Shaftesbury Ave., WC2H 8DP,* ☎ *0171/379–5399. Tube: Holborn.*

Theater

Although the price of a seat rarely falls below a tenner, London's West End theaters still pull in enough punters to cause a mini traffic jam each night before the house lights dim and the curtain rises. From Shakespeare to the umpteenth year of *Les Misérables* (or *The Glums,* as it's affectionately known), the West End has what visitors think of as London's theater. But there's more to see in London than the offerings of Theatreland and the national companies.

Of the 100 or so legitimate theaters in the capital, 50 are officially "West End," while the remainder go under the blanket title of "Fringe." Much like New York's Off- and Off-Off Broadway, Fringe Theater encompasses everything from off-the-wall "physical theater" pieces to first runs of new plays and revivals of old ones. At press time, on the Fringe alone, you could catch two Strindbergs, a Sartre, a Kafka, an Anouilh, an Ionesco, and two Molière productions. There was a production of Sheridan's *School for Scandal* in far-off-off-off Ealing, and a feminist staging of *Ben Hur* in even farther-off Croydon. You could catch such diverse offerings as Fassbinder's *The Bitter Tears of Petra von Kant* in a pub in Camden, *The Complete History of America (abridged)* by the *other* RSC (the Reduced Shakespeare Company), an amateur production of *Godspell*, or a long-running show in which tube passengers are the unwitting actors, as the audience secretly follows a lone performer posing as a klutzy commuter. That's just the fringe.

For serious theatergoers, the top of the line is still the **Royal Shakespeare Company** and the **Royal National Theatre Company** which perform at London's two main arts complexes, the **Barbican Centre** and **The Royal National Theatre** respectively. Both companies mount consistently excellent productions and are usually a safe option for anyone having trouble choosing which play to see. In addition, the Bard is now served up at the spectacular new reconstruction of **Shakespeare's Globe Theatre,** which officially opened in June 1997 and offers summer season, open-air performances. For complete information ☞ Shakespeare's Globe *in* Chapter 2, *above.*

Most theaters have matinees twice a week (Wednesday or Thursday, and Saturday) and evening performances that begin at 7:30 or 8; performances on Sunday are rare, but not unknown. Prices vary, but in the West End you should expect to pay from £10 for a seat in the upper balcony to at least £20 for a good one in the stalls (orchestra) or dress circle (mezzanine). Tickets may be booked at the individual theater box offices or over the phone by credit card (some box offices or agents have special numbers for these marked "cc" in the phone book); most theaters still don't charge a fee for the latter. You can also book through ticket agents, such as **First Call** (☎ 0171/240–7941) or **Ticketmaster** (☎ 0171/413–3321 or 800/775–2525 in the U.S.), although these usually do charge a booking fee. **Keith Prowse** has a New York office (✉ 234 W. 44th St., Suite 1000, New York, NY 10036, ☎ 212/398–1430 or 800/669–8687), as does **Edwards & Edwards** (✉ 1 Times Sq. Plaza, 12th Floor, New York, NY 10036, ☎ 212/944–0290 or 800/223–6108). If you're a theater junkie, and want to put together a West End package, the *Complete Guide to London's West End Theatres* has seating plans and booking information for all the houses. It costs £9.95 (plus postage) from the Society of London Theatres (☞ *below*). Alternatively, the Half Price Ticket Booth (no phone) on the southwest corner of Leicester Square sells up to four half-price tickets per purchaser on the day of performance for about 25 theaters (subject to availability). It's open Monday–Saturday 1–6:30 and from noon for matinees; there is a £2 service charge, and only cash is accepted. All the larger hotels offer theater bookings, but as they tack on a hefty service charge, you would do better visiting the box offices yourself. You might, however, consider using one particular booking line that doubles the price of tickets: **West End Cares** (☎ 0171/976–8100) donates half of what it charges to AIDS charities.

Warning: Be *very* careful of scalpers outside theaters and working the line at the Half Price Ticket Booth; they have been known to charge £200 or more for a sought-after ticket. In recent years, there has been another problem: unscrupulous ticket agents, who sell tickets at four or five times their price from the ticket box offices. Although a service charge is legitimate, this type of scalping certainly isn't, especially because the vast majority of theaters have some tickets (returns and "house seats") available on the night of performance. If you have a bad experience with a scalper, contact the Development Officer at the **Society of London Theatres** (✉ Bedford Chambers, The Piazza, Covent Garden, WC2E 8HQ, ☎ 0171/836–3193). They probably can't get you a refund, but your letter will help stamp out scalpers in the future.

Theater Directory

The following is a list of West End theaters:

Adelphi, ✉ *Strand, WC2E 7NA,* ☎ *0171/379–8884 or 0171/344–0055. Tube: Charing Cross.*

Albery, ✉ *St. Martin's La., WC2N 4AH,* ☎ *0171/867–1115 or 0171/369–1730. Tube: Leicester Square.*

Aldwych, ✉ *Aldwych, WC2B 4DF,* ☎ *0171/836–6404 or 0171/416–6003. Tube: Covent Garden.*

Apollo, ✉ *Shaftesbury Ave., W1V 7HD,* ☎ *0171/494–5070. Tube: Piccadilly Circus.*

Apollo Victoria, ✉ *Wilton Rd., SW1V ILL,* ☎ *0171/416–6070. Tube: Victoria.*

Arts Theatre, ✉ *6–7 Great Newport St., WC2H 7JB,* ☎ *0171/836–2132. Tube: Leicester Square.*

Barbican, ✉ *Barbican, EC2Y 8DS,* ☎ *0171/638–8891 or 0171/628–2295. Tube: Moorgate.*

Cambridge, ✉ *Earlham St., WC2H 9HU,* ☎ *0171/379–5299 or 0171/494–5080. Tube: Covent Garden.*

Comedy, ✉ *Panton St., SW1Y 4DN,* ☎ *0171/494–5080 or 0171/369–1731. Tube: Piccadilly Circus.*

Dominion, ✉ *Tottenham Court Rd., W1 0AG,* ☎ *0171/416–6060. Tube: Tottenham Court Road.*

Donmar Warehouse, ✉ *41 Earlham St., WC2H 9LD,* ☎ *0171/867–1150 or 0171/369–1732. Tube: Covent Garden.*

Drury Lane (Theatre Royal), ✉ *Catherine St., WC2B 5JF,* ☎ *0171/494–5000. Tube: Covent Garden.*

Duchess, ✉ *Catherine St., WC2B 5LA,* ☎ *0171/494–5075. Tube: Covent Garden.*

Fortune, ✉ *Russell St., WC2B 5HH,* ☎ *0171/836–2238. Tube: Covent Garden.*

Garrick, ✉ *Charing Cross Rd., WC2H 0HH,* ☎ *0171/494–5085. Tube: Leicester Square.*

Gielgud, ✉ *Shaftesbury Ave., W1V 8AR,* ☎ *0171/494–5065. Tube: Piccadilly Circus.*

Globe (Shakespeare's Globe), ✉ *New Globe Walk, Bankside,* ☎ *0171/928–6406. Tube: Mansion House, they walk across Southwark Bride, or BlackFriars, then walk across BlackFriars Bridge.*

Haymarket Theatre Royal, ✉ *Haymarket, SW1Y 4HT,* ☎ *0171/930–8800. Tube: Piccadilly Circus.*

Her Majesty's, ✉ *Haymarket, SW1Y 4QR,* ☎ *0171/494–5400. Tube: Piccadilly Circus.*

London Palladium, ✉ *8 Argyll St., W1V 1AD,* ☎ *0171/494–5020. Tube: Oxford Circus.*

Lyceum, ✉ *Wellington St., WC2.* ☎ *0171/656–1803. Tube: Charing Cross.*

Lyric, ✉ *Shaftesbury Ave., W1V 7HA,* ☎ *0171/494–5045. Tube: Piccadilly Circus.*

Lyric Hammersmith, ✉ *King St., W6 0QL,* ☎ *0181/741–2311. Tube: Hammersmith.*

Mermaid, ✉ *Puddle Dock, EC4 3DB,* ☎ *0171/410–0000 or 0171/236–2211. Tube: Blackfriars.*

New London, ✉ *Drury La., WC2B 5PW,* ☎ *0171/405–0072. Tube: Covent Garden.*

Old Vic, ✉ *Waterloo Rd., SE1 8NB,* ☎ *0171/928–7616. Tube: Waterloo.*

Open-Air Theatre, ✉ *Inner Circle, Regent's Park, NW1 4NP,* ☎ *0171/935–5884. Tube: Regent's Park.*

Palace, ✉ *Shaftesbury Ave., W1V 8AY,* ☎ *0171/434–0909. Tube: Leicester Square.*

Phoenix, ✉ *Charing Cross Rd., WC2H 0JP,* ☎ *0171/867–1044 or 0171/369–1733. Tube: Leicester Square.*

Piccadilly, ✉ *Denman St., W1V 8DY,* ☎ *0171/867–1118 or 0171/369–1734. Tube: Piccadilly Circus.*

Players, ✉ *The Arches, Villiers St., WC2N 6NQ,* ☎ *0171/839–1134 or 0171/976–1307. Tube: Charing Cross.*

Playhouse, ✉ *Northumberland Ave., WC2N 6NN,* ☎ *0171/839–4401. Tube: Embankment.*

Prince Edward, ✉ *Old Compton St., W1V 8AH,* ☎ *0171/734–8951 or 0171/447–5400. Tube: Leicester Square.*

Prince of Wales, ✉ *31 Coventry St., W1V 8AS,* ☎ *0171/839–5972. Tube: Leicester Square.*

Queens, ✉ *51 Shaftesbury Ave., W1V 8BA,* ☎ *0171/494–5040. Tube: Leicester Square.*

Royal Court Downstairs at the Duke of York's, ✉ *St. Martin's Lane, WC2,* ☎ *0171/565–5000. Tube: Leicester Square.*

Royal Court Upstairs at the Ambassadors, ✉ *West St., WC2,* ☎ *0171/565–5000. Tube: Leicester Square.*

Royal National Theatre (Cottesloe, Lyttelton, and Olivier), ✉ *South Bank Arts Complex, SE1 9PX,* ☎ *0171/928–2252. Tube: Waterloo.*

St. Martin's, ✉ *West St., WC2H 9NH,* ☎ *0171/836–1443. Tube: Leicester Square.*

Savoy, ✉ *Strand, WC2R 0ET,* ☎ *0171/836–8888. Tube: Aldwych.*

Shaftesbury, ✉ *Shaftesbury Ave., WC2H 8DP,* ☎ *0171/379–5399. Tube: Holborn.*

Strand, ✉ *Aldwych, WC2B 5LD,* ☎ *0171/930–8800. Tube: Covent Garden.*

Vaudeville, ✉ *Strand, WC2R 0NH,* ☎ *0171/836–9987. Tube: Charing Cross.*

Victoria Palace, ✉ *Victoria St., SW1E 5EA,* ☎ *0171/834–1317. Tube: Victoria.*

Whitehall, ✉ *14 Whitehall, SW1A 2DY,* ☎ *0171/369–1735 or 0171/344–4444. Tube: Charing Cross.*

Wyndhams, ✉ *Charing Cross Rd., WC2H 0DA,* ☎ *0171/867–1116 or 0171/369–1736. Tube: Leicester Square.*

Fringe

Shows can be straight plays, circus, comedy, musicals, readings, or productions every bit as polished and impressive as those in the West End—except for their location and the price of the seat. Fringe tickets are always considerably less expensive than tickets for West End productions. The following theaters are among the better-known fringe venues:

Almeida, ✉ *Almeida St., N1 1AT,* ☎ *0171/359–4404. Tube: Angel.*

BAC, ✉ *176 Lavender Hill, Battersea SW11 1JX,* ☎ *0171/223–2223. BR: Clapham Junction.*

Bush, ✉ *Shepherds Bush Green, W12 8QD,* ☎ *0181/743–3388. Tube: Goldhawk Road.*

Canal Café Theatre, ✉ *Bridge House, Delamere Terr., W2,* ☎ *0171/289–6054. Tube: Warwick Avenue.*

Drill Hall, ✉ *16 Chenies St., WC1E 7EX,* ☎ *0171/637–8270. Tube: Goodge Street.*

The Gate, ✉ *The Prince Albert, 11 Pembridge Rd., W11 3HQ,* ☎ *0171/229–0706. Tube: Notting Hill Gate.*

Grace Theatre at the Latchmere, ✉ *503 Battersea Park Rd., SW11 3BW,* ☎ *0171/223–3549. BR: Clapham Junction.*

Hackney Empire, ✉ *291 Mare St., E8 1EJ,* ☎ *0181/985–2424. BR: Hackney Central.*

Hampstead, ✉ *Swiss Cottage, NW3 3EX,* ☎ *0171/722–9301. Tube: Swiss Cottage.*

ICA Theatre, ⊠ *The Mall, SW1Y 5AH,* ☏ *0171/930–3647. Tube: Charing Cross.*

Kings Head, ⊠ *115 Upper St., N1 1QN,* ☏ *0171/226–1916. Tube: Highbury & Islington.*

Lyric Studio, ⊠ *Lyric Theatre, King St., W6 9JT,* ☏ *0181/741–8701. Tube: Hammersmith.*

New End Theatre, ⊠ *27 New End, NW3 1JD,* ☏ *0171/794–0022. Tube: Hampstead.*

Orange Tree, ⊠ *1 Clarence St., Richmond, TW9 1SA,* ☏ *0181/940–3633. Tube: Richmond.*

Riverside Studios, ⊠ *Crisp Rd., W6 9RL,* ☏ *0181/748–3354. Tube: Hammersmith.*

Theatre Royal, ⊠ *Stratford East, E15 1BN,* ☏ *0181/534–0310. Tube: Stratford.*

Tricycle Theatre, ⊠ *269 Kilburn High Rd., NW6 7JR,* ☏ *0171/328–1000. Tube: Kilburn.*

Watermans Arts Centre, ⊠ *40 High St., Brentford, TW8 0DS,* ☏ *0181/568–1176. BR: Kew Bridge.*

Young Vic, ⊠ *66 The Cut, SE1 8LZ,* ☏ *0171/928–6363. Tube: Waterloo.*

6 Outdoor Activities and Sports

Some days you win, some you lose, and some you get rained out. But that never puts a damper on one of the liveliest sports calendars around. Tennis, of course, means Wimbledon (if center court is sold out, try for an outer-court game). In summer Her Majesty makes an appearance at Ascot, while the World Series of Cricket, the Tests, are played at the fields of Lord's. In cooler weather, football (also known as soccer) takes over, and in any season you can enjoy Pilates and yoga indoors and let it rain, rain, rain.

THERE ARE THE WIMBLEDON TENNIS CHAMPIONSHIPS, and there's cricket, and then there's soccer, and that's about it for the sports fan in London, right? Wrong. London is a great city for the weekend player of almost anything. It really comes into its own in summer, when the parks sprout nets and goals and painted white lines, outdoor swimming pools open, and a season of spectator events gets under way. The listings below concentrate on facilities available to the casual visitor in a whole range of sports and on the more accessible or well-known spectator events. Bring your gear, and branch out from that hotel gym.

PARTICIPANT SPORTS AND FITNESS

If your sport is missing from those listed below, or if you need additional information, **Sportsline** (☎ 0171/222–8000), staffed weekdays 10–6, supplies details about London's clubs, events, and facilities. It's a free service.

Aerobics

You don't need to buy a membership at any of the following studios, which offer a range of classes for all levels of fitness and are open daily. The average cost for an hour of sweating is £5.

Go West Studio. About seven daily classes are graded from beginner to pro, with step, yoga, circuit training, and aquaerobics included in the mix. ⊠ *Porchester Centre, Queensway, W2,* ☎ *0171/792–2919. Tube: Bayswater.*

Jubilee Hall. Many are addicted to Jamie Addicoat's "Fatbuster" classes, but there are plenty more, from body sculpting and step to Pilates and jazz dance. ⊠ *30 The Piazza, Covent Garden, WC2,* ☎ *0171/379–0008. Tube: Covent Garden.*

Portobello Green Fitness Centre. It's under the Westway overpass, and you'll have to battle through flea-market shoppers on weekends to reach the bargain (£4) classes. ⊠ *3–5 Thorpe Close, W10,* ☎ *0181/960– 2221. Tube: Ladbroke Grove.*

Seymour Leisure Centre. The best classes in the "Move It" program here fill to the brim, but the spacious studios can take the pressure. Arrive early for step; you'll need a ticket (classes cost around the £5 mark). ⊠ *Seymour Pl., W2,* ☎ *0171/402–5795. Tube: Marylebone.*

Bicycling

London is reasonably cycle-friendly for a big city, with special lanes marked for bicycles on some major roads, but it is never safe to ride without a helmet. **Bikepark** can rent anything you want—mountain, hybrid, or road bike—from £10/day, £30/weekend, or by the week, plus a deposit (MC, V) of 75%–100% of the bike's value. All machines are new models and are issued with locks; accessories are available, too. Reserve ahead in summer. ⊠ *14 Stukeley St., WC2,* ☎ *0171/430–0083. Tube: Covent Garden.*

Boxing

All Stars Gym. The "KO Circuit" at Isola Akay's friendly gym in a converted church is a two-hour intensive workout, with shadowboxing, heavy bags, pad work, rope jumping, weights, and a lengthy warm-up, cool-down, and stretch. It pulls in both serious fighters and dilettantes, and an average male-to-female ratio of 4 to 1. Total beginners are shown the ropes, too. ⊠ *576 Harrow Rd., W10,* ☎ *0181/960–7724.* ☉ *Weekdays at 7:30 PM, Sat. at 10 AM. Tube: Westbourne Park.*

Golf

Golf is as huge in England as it is in the States, but if you want to play a round in London, you'll have to tee off in the outer boroughs.

Regent's Park Golf and Tennis School. You don't have to travel far to get here—it's just by the zoo—but driving ranges and putting greens are all you'll get. The instructors have a good reputation. ⊠ *Outer Circle, Regent's Park, NW1,* ☎ *0171/724–0643. Tube: Regent's Park.*

Trent Park Golf Club. Here you do have to pay a modest fee to join, but it's worth considering for regular visitors; the setting of this countrified 18-hole course is beautiful, and it's easily reached on the Piccadilly line to Oakwood. ⊠ *Bramley Rd., Southgate N14,* ☎ *0181/366–7432. Tube: Oakwood.*

Horseback Riding

Hyde Park Riding Stables. One of the very few public stables left for riding in Hyde Park keeps a range of horses for hacking the sand tracks. ⊠ *63 Bathurst Mews, W2,* ☎ *0171/723–2813. Tube: Lancaster Gate.*

Ross Nye's. And here's the other one. About 16 horses and ponies are kept here for lessons as well as for hacking. ⊠ *8 Bathurst Mews, W2,* ☎ *0171/262–3791. Tube: Lancaster Gate.*

Rotten Row and the surrounding network of Hyde Park sand tracks make up the only place to ride in central London—better for posing in the saddle than serious maneuvers, and no galloping allowed. Outer London offers more scope, plus lessons.

Trent Park Stables. You'll think you've left London as you hack through 300 acres of near-rural Middlesex. You can't ride alone because of insurance restrictions, but all standards are accommodated, and indoor and outdoor lessons, from beginner to dressage and jumping, are available. ⊠ *East Pole Farm, Bramley Rd., N14,* ☎ *0181/363–9005. Tube: Oakwood.*

Ice Skating

Hockey is actually becoming pretty popular, but professional and leisure skating has a slight image problem in Britain, where it's perceived as downscale.

Broadgate Arena. It's a tiny circle, but it's outdoors—and therefore unique in London. Open from November to April, it's a fun place to skate because of the audience of city workers and the silly team games you can join. Skate rental is available. ⊠ *3 Broadgate, EC2,* ☎ *0171/588–6565. Tube: Liverpool Street.*

Queens Ice Skating Club. A figure-skating rink with disco tendencies, this is central London's only serious ice venue, and you can take a lesson should your outside edge be rusty. You can rent skates here, too. Queensway tube is next door. ⊠ *Queensway, W2,* ☎ *0171/229–0172. Tube: Queensway.*

Running

London is perfect for joggers. If you're after a crowd, the more popular routes include **Green Park,** which gets a stream of runners armed with maps from the Piccadilly hotels, and—to a lesser extent—adjacent **St. James's Park.** Both can get perilous with deck chairs on summer days. **Hyde Park** and **Kensington Gardens** together supply a 4-mi perimeter route, or you can do a 2½-mi run in Hyde Park alone if you start at Hyde Park Corner or Marble Arch and encircle the Serpentine. Most Park Lane hotels offer jogging maps for this, their local green space. **Regent's Park** has probably the most populated track because it's a sporting kind of place; the Outer Circle loop measures about 2½ mi.

Away from the center, there are longer, scenic runs over more varied terrain at **Hampstead Heath,** connecting with **Kenwood** and **Parliament Hill,** London's highest point, where you'll get a fabulous panoramic sweep over the entire city. **Richmond Park** is the biggest green space of all, but watch for deer during rutting season (Oct. and Nov.). Back in town, there's a rather traffic-heavy 1½-mi riverside run along **Victoria Embankment** from Westminster Bridge to Embankment at Blackfriars Bridge, or a beautiful mile among the rowing clubs and ducks along the Malls—Upper, Lower, and Chiswick—from **Hammersmith Bridge.**

GROUP RUNS

If you don't want to run alone, call the **London Hash House Harriers** (☎ 0181/995–7879). They organize noncompetitive hour-long runs around interesting bits of town, with loops and checkpoints built in. Cost: £1.

Softball

Control your mirth—the sport is huge here; in fact, it's the fastest-growing participatory sport in England. Pick up a game Sunday afternoon in **Regent's Park,** or on the south edge of **Hyde Park.**

Squash

Although squash is a popular English sport, its American cousin, raquetball, isn't played here. Most clubs restrict court use to club members, but the facilities listed are open to nonmembers as well.

Ironmonger Row. There are 10 squash courts in this popular city sports center. You can't book by phone without a membership, but you're likely to get a court if you show up to play during Londoners' regular office hours or possibly on weekends when courts are less busy. ⊠ *Ironmonger Row, EC1,* ☎ *0171/253–4011. Tube: Old Street.*

Portobello Green Fitness Centre. Only three courts here, but they're inexpensive. ⊠ *3–5 Thorpe Close, W10,* ☎ *0181/960–2221. Tube: Ladbroke Grove.*

Sobell Sports Centre. This is a popular place, but you can usually get court time. ⊠ *Hornsey Rd., N7,* ☎ *0171/609–2166. Tube: Finsbury Park.*

Swimming

London does not lack for public swimming pools—clean, lifeguard-attended, and usually open long hours.

BEACHES

Hampstead Ponds. These Elysian little lakes are surrounded by grassy lounging areas. The women's one is particularly secluded—and crowded in summer, though it's open all year. The "Mixed Pond" is open May through September. Both have murky-looking, but clean, fresh water. *Co-ed,* ⊠ *East Heath Rd., NW3,* ☎ *0171/435–2366. Women only,* ⊠ *Millfield La., N6,* ☎ *0171/348–1033. British Rail: Hampstead Heath.*

Serpentine Lido. Okay, so it's a beach on a lake, but a hot day in Hyde Park is surreally reminiscent of the seaside. There are changing facilities, and the swimming section is chlorinated. ⊠ *Hyde Park, W2,* ☎ *0171/262–5484.* ☉ *May–Sept. Tube: Knightsbridge.*

INDOOR POOLS

Chelsea. This renovated turn-of-the-century 27-by-10-yard pool is just off the King's Road, so it's usually busy, and packed with kids on weekends. ⊠ *Chelsea Manor St., SW3,* ☎ *0171/352–6985. Tube: South Kensington.*

Seymour Leisure Centre. There's usually a lane roped off for laps at this very central 44-by-20-yard pool, unless the aquaerobics class has taken over. ⊠ *Seymour Pl., W2,* ☎ *0171/402–5795. Tube: Marylebone.*

Swiss Cottage. A little out-of-the-way (but next to the Swiss Cottage tube), this is one of the largest (37 by 16 yards) pools and best for serious lap-swimmers. There's a shallow children's pool, too. ⊠ *Winchester Rd., NW3,* ☎ *0171/586–5989. Tube: Swiss Cottage.*

INDOOR/OUTDOOR POOLS

Oasis. And it is just that, with a heated pool (open May–Sept.) right in Covent Garden, and a 30-by-10-yard one indoors. Needless to say, they both get packed in summer. ⊠ *32 Endell St., WC2,* ☎ *0171/831–1804. Tube: Covent Garden.*

SPA POOLS

Ironmonger Row (☞ *above*). This 33-by-12-yard city pool is in a '30s complex that includes a Turkish bath, not quite as beautiful as Porchester's (☞ *below*). There are separate sessions for men and women.

Porchester Baths. Here there's a 33-by-11-yard pool for serious lap-swimmers, plus a 1920s Turkish bath, sauna, and spa of gorgeous, though slightly faded grandeur. It has separate sessions for men and women. ⊠ *Queensway, W2,* ☎ *0171/229–9950. Tube: Queensway.*

Tennis

Poor England never wins its own Grand Slam tournament. Some blame that circumstance on its being a nation of mere park players, which, for the visitor, has obvious benefits.

Holland Park. This is the prettiest place to play, with six hard courts available April through September. ⊠ *Kensington High St., W8,* ☎ *0171/602–2226. Tube: Holland Park.*

Islington Tennis Centre. It's about the only place where you don't need membership to play indoors (year-round), though you need it to reserve by phone. There are four outdoor courts, too, and coaching is available. ⊠ *Market Rd., N7,* ☎ *0171/700–1370. Tube: Caledonian Road.*

Paddington Sports Club. A surprisingly large and busy green space provides a set of eight hard courts where you compete for attention with track runners and soccer, cricket, and softball players. ⊠ *Castelain Rd., W9,* ☎ *0171/286–4515. Tube: Maida Vale.*

Weight Training

If your hotel lacks a gym, these are central and sell either daily or monthly temporary memberships.

Albany Fitness Centre. This is a deconsecrated church (buy a "Work Off Thy Last Supper" T-shirt), which means tons of space. There's Keiser equipment, free weights, cardio machines, and aerobics/sculpting classes. The cost is around £15/day, with lower weekly rates negotiable. ⊠ *St. Bede's Church, Albany St., NW1,* ☎ *0171/383–7131. Tube: Great Portland Street.*

Central YMCA. As you'd expect from the Y, this place boasts every facility and sport, including a great 25-meter pool and a very well-equipped gym. Weekly membership costs around £35. ⊠ *112 Great Russell St., WC1,* ☎ *0171/637–8131. Tube: Tottenham Court Road.*

Jubilee Hall. The day rate is £6, monthly £45 at this very crowded, but happening and super well-equipped central gym. ⊠ *30 The Piazza, Covent Garden, WC2,* ☎ *0171/379–0008. Tube: Covent Garden.*

The Peak. This hotel club is expensive (£30/day) but has top equipment, a brand-new pool, great ninth-floor views over Knightsbridge, and a sauna—with TV—in the full beauty spa. The 20-visit pass for £400 is fully transferrable, so a whole family could share one—almost a bargain. ⊠ *Hyatt Carlton Tower Hotel, 2 Cadogan Pl., SW1,* ☎ *0171/235–1234. Tube: Sloane Square.*

Seymour Leisure Centre. You must complete an hour-long introductory session to use the excellent gym and the cardio center overlooking a hall full of soccer, b-ball, or badminton players, but that and a full membership for a month costs a bargain £31. ⊠ *Seymour Pl., W2,* ☎ *0171/723–8019. Tube: Marylebone.*

Yoga

This discipline is becoming very popular in London, as it is in the United States.

Life Centre. London's newest, and without a doubt, best yoga school specializes in the dynamic, energetic Vinyasa technique. Beautiful premises enhance the experience. A huge range of holistic health therapies are available upstairs. ⊠ *15 Edge St., W8,* ☎ *0171/221–4602. Tube: Notting Hill Gate.*

SPECTATOR SPORTS

Boating

One of London's most beloved sporting events (since 1845) is also the easiest to see, and it's free. The only problem with the late-March **Oxford and Cambridge Boat Race** is securing a position among the crowds that line the Putney-to-Mortlake route (mostly at pubs along the Hammersmith Lower and Upper Malls, or on Putney Bridge). The Saturday start time varies from year to year according to the tides. The **Head of the River Race** is the professional version, only this time up to 420 crews of eight row the university course in the other direction. It usually happens the Saturday before the university race, or sometimes later the same day.

Cricket

Lord's (⊠ St. John's Wood, NW8, ☎ 0171/289–1611) has been hallowed turf for worshipers of England's summer game since 1811. The World Series of cricket, the Tests, are played here, but tickets are hard to procure. One-day internationals, though, can usually be seen by lining up on the day, and top-class county matches are similarly accessible—whether the rules are is quite another matter.
The Oval (⊠ Kennington Oval, SE11, ☎ 0171/582–6660) is a far easier place to witness the *thwack* of leather on willow. At London's seond string ground, you can see county games of very high standard.

Equestrian Events

It's one of those clichés based on truth that, from the queen down, the English are in love with the horse, as proved by the United Kingdom's Olympic medals. If you require further proof, attend one of the many parades, races, or show-jumping exhibitions.

PARADES

You can see all the city's working horses at the Easter Monday **London Harness Horse Parade** (⊠ Inner Circle, Regent's Pk., NW1), open 9:30–1. The show competitions have categories like "Heavy Horse" and "Single Horsed Commercial Van." Something similar happens to recreational equines at the **London Riding Horse Parade,** on the first Sunday in August in (where else?) Rotten Row.

RACING

The main events of "the Season," as much social as sporting, occur just outside the city. Her actual Majesty attends **Royal Ascot** (⊠ Grand Stand, Ascot, Berkshire, ☎ 01344/22211) in mid-June, driving from Windsor in an open carriage, and processing before the plebs daily at 2. For more information on this event, *see* the Close-Up box on Royalty-Watching *in* Chapter 2. **Derby Day** (⊠ The Grandstand,

Epsom Downs, Surrey, ☎ 01372/726311), usually held on the first Wednesday in June, is the other big one. One of the world's greatest races for three-year-olds, it kicks off at 3:45.

The **Horse of the Year Show** (✉ Wembley Arena, ☎ 0181/900–1234) in late October is the top international competition, with lots of fun events held alongside the serious. Best of all are the Pony Club Games, where child riders perform virtual gymnastics on horseback.

Marathon

Starting at 9 AM on the third Sunday in April, some 25,000 runners in the huge **London Marathon** (☎ 01891/234234) race from Blackheath or Greenwich to Westminster Bridge or the Mall. Entry forms for the following year are available starting in May.

Rugby

This is not a million miles different from gridiron, but team members play unpadded. It raises the British and (especially) Welsh blood pressure like no other sport, and has recently undergone a revolution, with the amateur Rugby Union, and the professional Rugby League, once distinct, more or less merging with the advent of major sponsorship of the amateur game. The **Rugby League Final** has always been played at Wembley Stadium (✉ Wembley, Middlesex, ☎ 0181/900–1234) on the last Saturday in April, while the Rugby Union **Pilkington Cup** is traditionally fought a week later at the Twickenham Rugby Football Ground (✉ Whitton Rd., Twickenham, Middlesex, ☎ 0181/892–8161). Tickets for both are more precious than gold. But you can see international matches at Twickenham during the September-to-April season or catch the home games of the London teams at the spectacular **Saracens** (✉ Dale Green Rd., N14, ☎ 0181/449–3770) and **Rosslyn Park** (✉ Priory La., Upper Richmond Rd., SW15, ☎ 0181/876–1879).

Soccer

To refer to the national winter sport as "soccer" is to blaspheme. It is football, and the British season culminates in the televised Wembley Stadium **FA Cup Final,** for which tickets are about as easy to get as they are for the Superbowl. International matches at Wembley (☎ 0181/900–1234) during the August-to-May season are easier to attend.

For a real taste of this British obsession, though, nothing beats a match at the home ground of one of the three London clubs competing in the Premier League. More than likely you won't see a hint of the infamous hooliganism but will be quite carried away by the electric atmosphere only a vast football crowd can generate. **Tottenham Hotspur,** or "Spurs" (✉ White Hart Lane, 748 High Rd., N17, ☎ 0181/808–3030), and **Arsenal** (✉ Avenell Rd., Highbury, N5, ☎ 0171/359–0131) have north Londoners' loyalties about equally divided, while **Chelsea** (✉ Stamford Bridge, Fulham Rd., SW6, ☎ 0171/385–5545) is adored by the slightly more genteel west London fan.

Tennis

The Wimbledon Lawn Tennis Championships—famous among fans for the green, green grass of Centre Court, for strawberries and cream, and for rain, which always falls, despite the last-week-of-June/first-week-of-July high-summer timing—comprise, of course, one of the top four Grand Slam events of the tennis year. Whether you can get tickets is literally down to the luck of the draw, because there's a ballot system for advance purchase. To apply, send a self-addressed, stamped envelope between October and December to the All England Lawn Tennis & Croquet Club (✉ Box 98, Church Rd., Wimbledon

SW19 5AE, ☎ 0181/946–2244), then fill in the application form, and hope.

But there are other ways to see the tennis. A block of Centre Court tickets is kept back to sell each day, but fanatics line up all night for these, especially in the second week. Each afternoon, though, tickets collected from early departing spectators are resold (profits go to charity). These can provide grandstand seats (with plenty to see—play continues till dusk), because those who can afford to care so little about tennis are often on expensive business freebies or company season tickets. You can also buy entry to the grounds to roam matches on the outer courts, where even the top-seeded players compete early in the fortnight. For up-to-date information, the London Tourist Board operates a **Wimbledon Information Line** (☎ 01839/123417), at a cost of 49p per minute (39p cheap rate) from the beginning of June.

7 Shopping

Napoléon must have known what he was talking about when he called Britain a nation of shopkeepers. The finest emporiums are in London, still. You can shop like royalty at Her Majesty's glove maker, run down a leather-bound copy of Wuthering Heights *at a Charing Cross bookseller, or find antique Toby jugs on Portobello Road. Whether you're out for fun— there's nothing like street markets to stimulate the acquisitive juices—or for fashion, London can be the most rewarding of hunting grounds. Little wonder Princess Di is a world-class shopper.*

AS BEFITS ONE OF THE GREAT trading capitals of the world, London's shops have been known to boast, "You name it, we sell it." Finding and buying "it" can be a delight (the craft shops at the new OXO Tower), or a trial (mobbed Oxford Street on a Saturday morning). No matter where you head in this city, you'll find you can melt as much plastic as your wallet can stand. Credit cards are accepted virtually everywhere, but do make sure that your Cirrus, Plus, or Amex card (to cite just three of the leading names) works in European ATMs, by having it reset to use a four-digit PIN number by your bank before your departure.

If you have a yen to keep up with the Windsors, head for stores proclaiming they are "By Appointment" to H.M. The Queen—or to the Queen Mother, Prince Philip, and the Prince of Wales. One such establishment is Brigg and Sons, which has crafted the great British "brolly" since Wellington reprimanded his officers for lugging umbrellas into battle. More fashion-forward Princess Di favors places like Harvey Nichols (shrine-of-all-shrines for *Absolutely Fabulous*'s Patsy and Edwina), but also delights in places like Frog Hollow—an enchanting spot for cuddlesome toys, especially frogs of every persuasion, including, naturally, one that turns into a prince.

If you have only limited time, zoom in on one or two of the West End's grand department stores where you'll find enough booty for your entire gift list. Marks & Spencer is one of Britain's largest, and most beloved, stores, legendary for the friendliness of its service. Selfridges, London's answer to Macy's in New York, is a splendid pile of '20s Ben Hur architecture, which dominates the whole of one block toward Marble Arch. Liberty is famous for its Liberty of London patterns, imprinted on everything from clothespin dolls to William Morris–inspired armchairs. Whether counting pennies or pounds, a visit to Harrods's Food Hall is not to be missed; apart from anything else, it's one of the best free shows in the city. And though Harrods trumpets that it can supply anything to anyone anywhere in the world (once, a baby elephant to Ronald Reagan) and boasts that the Queen sometimes does her Christmas shopping here, you can just pick up one of their distinctive green-and-gold logo'd totes—a perfect touch of class for your veggie marketing back home.

Apart from bankrupting yourself, the only problem you'll encounter is exhaustion, since London is a town of many far-flung shopping areas, each offering different kinds of merchandise. Below is a brief introduction to the major ones.

Shopping Districts

Camden Town
Crafts and vintage clothing markets and shops cluster in and around picturesque but over-renovated canalside buildings in this frenetic mecca for the world's youth. It's a good place for boots, T-shirts, inexpensive leather jackets, ethnic crafts, antiques, and recycled trendywear. Things are quieter midweek.

Chelsea
Chelsea centers on the King's Road, which is no longer synonymous with ultra-fashion but still harbors some designer boutiques, plus antiques and home furnishings emporia.

Covent Garden
A something-for-everyone neighborhood, the restored 19th-century market building features mainly high-class clothing chains, plus good-

218

Alfie's Antique Market, **1**
Aquascutum, **27**
Armoury of St. James's, **31**
Asprey's, **25**
Bell, Book and Radmell, **39**
Blazer, **51, 53**
Browns, **7**
Burberrys, **22, 37**
Butler and Wilson, **8**
Cartier, **24**
Christopher Gibbs, **28**
Contemporary Applied Arts, **57**

Contemporary Ceramics, **19**
Dance Books, **40**
Dillons, **65**
Droopie & Browns, **38**
Duffer of St. George, **58**
Favourbrook, **34**
Forbidden Planet, **64**
Fortnum & Mason, **33**
Foyles, **62**
Gabriel's Wharf, **67**
Garrard, **26**
Gray's Antique Market, **10**

Grosvenor Prints, **56**
Halcyon Days, **14**
Hamleys, **21**
Hatchards, **35**
The Hat Shop, **60**
Herbert Johnson, **29**
The Irish Linen Co., **30**
Jigsaw, **47**
John Lewis, **13**
Laura Ashley, **18**
Liberty, **20**
The Linen Cupboard, **15**
London Silver Vaults, **66**

Lush, **45**
Maison, **54**
Marchpane, **42**
Marks & Spencer, **2, 17**
Mulberry, **4**
Neal Street East, **52**
Nicole Farhi, **6**
The Outlaws Club, **59**
OXO Tower, **68**
Paddy Campbell, **5**
Paul Smith, **48**
Pellicano, **9**
Penhaligon's, **46**

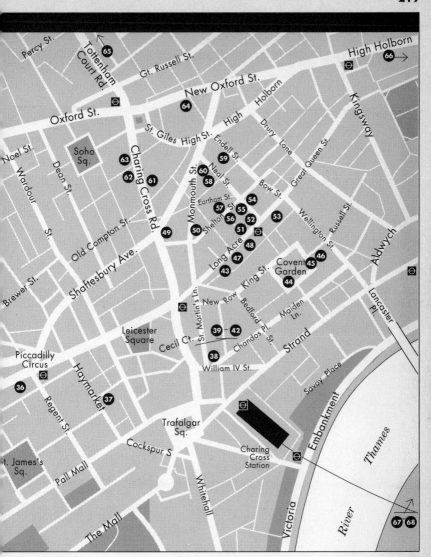

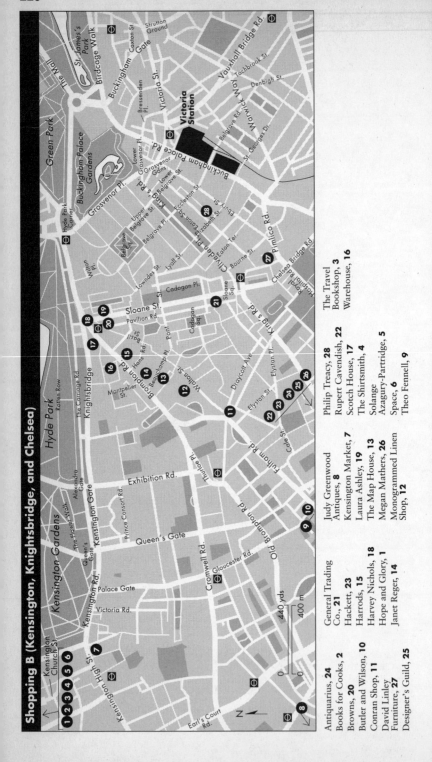

Shopping B (Kensington, Knightsbridge, and Chelsea)

220

Antiquarius, **24**
Books for Cooks, **2**
Browns, **20**
Butler and Wilson, **10**
Conran Shop, **11**
David Linley
Furniture, **27**
Designer's Guild, **25**

General Trading
Co., **21**
Hackett, **23**
Harrods, **15**
Harvey Nichols, **18**
Hope and Glory, **1**
Janet Reger, **14**

Judy Greenwood
Antiques, **8**
Kensington Market, **7**
Laura Ashley, **19**
The Map House, **13**
Megan Mathers, **26**
Monogrammed Linen
Shop, **12**

Philip Treacy, **28**
Rupert Cavendish, **22**
Scotch House, **17**
The Shirtsmith, **4**
Solange
Azagury-Partridge, **5**
Space, **6**
Theo Fennell, **9**

The Travel
Bookshop, **3**
Warehouse, **16**

quality crafts stalls and design shops, with additional stalls selling vintage, army-surplus, and ethnic clothing around it. Neal Street and the surrounding alleys offer amazing gifts of every type—bikes, kites, tea, herbs, beads, hats . . . you name it. Floral Street and Long Acre have designer and chain-store fashion in equal measure. It's good for people-watching, too.

Hampstead

For picturesque peace and quiet with your shopping, stroll around here midweek. Upscale clothing stores and representatives of the better chains share the half-dozen streets with cozy boutique-size shops for the home and stomach.

Kensington

Kensington Church Street features expensive antiques, plus a little fashion. The main drag, Kensington High Street, is a smaller, less crowded, and classier version of Oxford Street, with a selection of clothing chains and larger stores at the eastern end.

Knightsbridge

Harrods dominates Brompton Road, but there's plenty more, especially for the well-heeled and fashion-conscious. Harvey Nichols is the top clothes stop, with many expensive designers' *boîtes* along Sloane Street. Walton Street and narrow Beauchamp (pronounced "beecham") Place offer more of the same, plus home furnishings and knickknacks, and Brompton Cross, at the start of Fulham Road, is the most design-conscious corner of London, with the Conran Shop and Joseph leading the field.

Mayfair

Here is Bond Street, Old and New, with desirable dress designers, jewelers, plus fine art (old and new) on Old Bond Street and Cork Street. South Molton Street has high-priced, high-style fashion—especially at Browns—and the tailors of Savile Row are of worldwide renown.

Oxford Street

Overcrowded Oxford Street is past its prime and lined with tawdry discount shops. But many still flock here for some of London's great department stores—particularly Selfridges, John Lewis, and Marks & Spencer—and interesting boutiques secreted in little St. Christopher's Place and Gees Court.

Notting Hill

Branching off from the famous Portobello Road market are various enclaves of boutiques selling young designers' wares, antiques, and things for the home—now favored stops for the trendoisie. Explore the Ledbury Road/Westbourne Grove axis, Clarendon Cross, and Kensington Park Road, as well as Portobello Road itself.

Piccadilly

Though the actual number of shops is small for a street of its length (Green Park takes up a lot of space), Piccadilly manages to fit in several quintessential British emporia. Fortnum and Mason is its star, and the arcades are an elegant experience even for shop-phobics.

Regent Street

At right angles to Oxford Street, this wider, curvier version has another couple of department stores, including what is possibly London's most pleasant, Liberty. Hamleys is the capital's toy center; other shops tend to be chain stores, or airline offices, though there are also shops selling china and bolts of English tweed. "West Soho," around Carnaby Street, stocks designer youth paraphernalia.

St. James's

Where the English gentleman shops. Available are hats, handmade shirts and shoes, silver shaving kits and flasks, as well as the Prince of Wales's aftershave supplier and possibly the world's best cheese shop. Nothing is cheap, in any sense.

Department Stores

London's department stores range from Harrods—which every tourist is obliged to visit—through many serviceable middle-range stores, devoted to the middle-of-the-road tastes of the middle class, to a few cheap jack ones that sell merchandise you would find at a better rate back home. Most of the best and biggest department stores are grouped in the West End around Regent Street and Oxford Street, with two notable exceptions out in Knightsbridge.

Liberty (⊠ 200 Regent St., W1, ☎ 0171/734–1234) has one of London's most distinctive facades—a wonderful black-and-white mock-Tudor facade, making it a peacock among pigeons in humdrum Regent Street. Inside, it is a labyrinthine building, full of nooks and crannies, all stuffed with goodies like a dream of an eastern bazaar. Famous principally for its fabrics, it also has an Oriental department, rich with color; menswear that tends to the traditional; and women's wear that has lately been spiced up with extra designer ranges. It is a hard store to resist, where you may well find an original gift—especially one made from those classic Liberty prints (☞ Map A).

John Lewis (⊠ 278 Oxford St., W1, ☎ 0171/629–7711) is a short distance from Liberty, two blocks west on Oxford Street. This store's motto is "Never knowingly undersold," and for sensible goods at sensible prices John Lewis is hard to beat. For the visitor to London who's handy with the needle, John Lewis has a wonderful selection of dress and furnishing fabrics. Many's the American home with John Lewis drapes (☞ Map A).

Selfridges (⊠ 400 Oxford St., W1, ☎ 0171/629–1234) is near the Marble Arch end of Oxford Street, where blocks are crowded in the middle of the day and at sale time. This giant, bustling store was started early this century by an American, though it's now British-owned. If this all-rounder has an outstanding department, it has to be its Food Hall, or else its frenetic cosmetics department, which seems to perfume the air the whole length of Oxford Street. In recent years, Selfridges has made a specialty of high-profile popular designer fashions and has spent a lot of money sprucing up. There's also a branch of the London Tourist Board on the premises, a theater ticket counter, and a branch of Thomas Cook, the travel agent, in the basement (☞ Map A).

Harrods (⊠ 87 Brompton Rd., SW1, ☎ 0171/730–1234), being the only English department store classed among monuments and museums on every visitor's list, hardly needs an introduction. In fact, its Englishness is tentative, since it is owned by the Egyptian Al Fayed brothers—but who cares? It is swanky and plush and deep-carpeted as ever, its spectacular food halls are alone worth the trip, and it stands out from the pack for fashion, too. You can forgive the store its immodest motto, *Omnia, omnibus, ubique* ("everything, for everyone, everywhere"), because there are more than 230 departments, including a pet shop rumored to supply you with anything from aardvarks to zebras on request, and the toy department—sorry, *kingdom*—which does the same for its plush versions. During the pre-Christmas period and the sales, the entire store is a menagerie (☞ Map B).

Harvey Nichols (⊠ 109 Knightsbridge, SW1, ☎ 0171/235–5000) is just a few blocks from Harrods, but is not competing on the same turf, since its passion is fashion, all the way. There are six floors of it, including departments for dressing homes and men, but the woman who invests in her wardrobe is the main target. Accessories are strong suits, especially jewelry, scarves, and makeup—England's first MAC counter here was 10-deep for months. A reservation at the Fifth Floor restaurant is one of London's most coveted, too (☞ Map B).

Specialty Stores

Antiques

Investment quality or lovable junk, London has lots. Try markets first—even for pedigree silver, the dealers at these places often have the best wares and the knowledge to match. Camden Passage and Bermondsey (☞ Street Markets, *below*) are the best; the Portobello market has become a bit of a tourist trap, but its side streets are filled with interesting shops open outside market hours. Kensington Church Street is *the* antiques shopping street, with prices and quality both high. Out of the hundreds of stores, we list ten to whet your appetite.

Alfie's Antique Market (✉ 13-25 Church St., NW8, ☎ 0171/723–6066) is a huge and exciting labyrinth on several floors, with dealers specializing in anything and everything. You won't be deliberately stiffed, but it's a *caveat emptor* kind of place, thanks to the wide range of merchandise (☞ Map A).

Antiquarius (✉ 131–141 King's Rd., SW3, ☎ 0171/351–5353), at the Sloane Square end of the King's Road, is an indoor antiques market with more than 200 stalls offering a wide variety of collectibles, including things that won't bust your baggage allowance: Art Deco brooches, meerschaum pipes, silver salt cellars . . . (☞ Map B).

Christopher Gibbs (✉ 8 Vigo St., ☎ 0171/439–4557) attracts such leading London tastemakers as J. Paul Getty Jr. and Mick Jagger, who, the society columns note, will hardly make a move without the judgment of Mr. Gibbs's legendary eye. If you're in the market for *Louis Quatorzième* marble busts, priceless Elizabethan embroidery, and truly one-of-a-kind antiques from all ages, this is the place to go and dream (☞ Map A).

Gallery of Antique Costume and Textiles (✉ 2 Church St., NW8, ☎ 0171/723–9981) attracts numerous movie directors who come here to get the period just right, because everything on the premises, from bedspreads to bloomers, was stitched before 1930—except for the wonderful range of copycat brocade vests. Models and Hollywood actors find incredible (and expensive) clothes here, too. It lies off our maps, but is easily found three blocks north of the Edgware Road tube.

Gray's Antique Market (✉ 58 Davies St., W1, ☎ 0171/629–7034) and **Gray's Mews** (✉ 1–7 Davies Mews, W1, ☎ 0171/629–7034) around the corner are conveniently central. Both assemble dealers specializing in everything from Sheffield plate to Chippendale furniture all under one roof. Bargains are not impossible, and proper pedigrees are guaranteed (☞ Map A).

Hope and Glory (✉ 131a Kensington Church St., W8, ☎ 0171/727–8424) is one of the many specialist stores in the Kensington district with commemorative china and glass from 1887 to the present; there are also many affordable lesser pieces (☞ Map B).

Judy Greenwood Antiques (✉ 657 Fulham Rd., ☎ 0171/736–6037) beckons with its glowing red walls and a delightful selection of high-style antiques: Miss Havisham-y rattan settees, vintage fabrics and textiles, gilded mirrors, and side tables (☞ Map B).

London Silver Vaults (✉ Chancery House, 53–63 Chancery La., WC2, ☎ 0171/242–3844), a basement conglomeration of around 40 dealers, is a treasure trove for the average Joe. Some pieces are spectacular, of course, but you can pick up a set of Victorian cake forks or a dented candelabrum for under £50 (☞ Map A).

Megan Mathers (✉ 571 Kings Rd., ☎ 0171/371–7837) offers one of London's most delectable assortments of stylish antiques: decoupaged 19th-century table obelisks, mini-Nelson's Columns, Venetian blackamoor figures—perfect *touches finales* for any high-style room (☞ Map B).

Rupert Cavendish (✉ 610 King's Rd., SW6, ☎ 0171/731–7041), this most elevated of dealers, has the Biedermeier market cornered, with Empire and Deco bringing up the rear. The shop is a museum experience (☞ Map B).

Books

Charing Cross Road is London's booksville, with a couple of dozen stores here or hereabout. The many antiquarian booksellers tend to look daunting (deceptively, as Helene Hanff found by correspondence with No. 84), but there are many new bookshops, too.

Foyles (✉ 119 Charing Cross Rd, ☎ 0171/437–5660) is especially large—so vast it's almost challenging, but the place to come to find almost anything. **Waterstone's** (✉ 121–125 Charing Cross Rd., ☎ 0171/434–4291) is part of an admirable, and expanding, chain with long hours and a program of author readings and signings. **Hatchards** (✉ 187–188 Piccadilly, WC2, ☎ 0171/439–9921) is one of London's largest bookstores; oft favored by members of the royal family, it has a superb section on royalty. **Dillons** (✉ 82 Gower St., WC1, ☎ 0171/636–1577) has a huge stock and a well-informed staff to help you choose (☞ Map A).

Books for Cooks (✉ 4 Blenheim Cres., W11, ☎ 0171/221–1992) and its near neighbor, **The Travel Bookshop** (✉ No. 13, ☎ 0171/229–5260), are exactly what they say, and worth the trip for enthusiasts (☞ Map B). Travel books and maps are the specialty of **Stanfords** (✉ 12 Long Acre, WC2, ☎ 0171/836–1321). For art books, head for **Zwemmer** (✉ 24 Litchfield St., WC2, ☎ 0171/240–4158), just off Charing Cross Road. Sci-fi, fantasy, horror, and comic books are found by the mile at **Forbidden Planet** (✉ 71 New Oxford St., WC1, ☎ 0171/836–4179) (☞ Map A). On the Charing Cross Road, **Silver Moon** (✉ No. 64, ☎ 0171/836–7906) is an accessible and friendly women's bookshop.

Just off the south end of Charing Cross is Cecil Court—a pedestrians-only lane where every shop is a specialty bookstore. **Bell, Book and Radmell** (✉ 4 Cecil Court, ☎ 0171/240–2161), offers quality antiquarian volumes and modern first editions. **Marchpane** (✉ 16 Cecil Court, ☎ 0171/836–8661) stocks covetable rare and antique illustrated children's books. **Dance Books** (✉ 9 Cecil Court, ☎ 0171/836–2314) has—yes—dance books. **Pleasures of Times Past** (✉ 11 Cecil Court, ☎ 0171/836–1142) indulges the collective nostalgia for Victoriana (☞ Map A).

China and Glass

English Wedgwood and Minton china are as collectible as they ever were, and most large department stores carry a selection, alongside lesser varieties with smaller price tags. Regent Street has several off-price purveyors, and, if you're in search of a bargain, Harrods's sale can't be beat—but sharpen your elbows first. **Thomas Goode** (✉ 19 S. Audley St., W1, ☎ 0171/499–2823) is one of the world's top shops for formal china and leaded crystal (☞ Map A).

Clothing

London is one of the world's four fashion capitals (along with Paris, Milan, and New York), and every designer you've ever heard of is sold here somewhere. As well as the top names, though, London retains a reputation for quirky street style, and many an exciting young designer has cut his or her teeth selling early collections at a London street market. Don't just go by the label and you could be the first to wear clothes by a future star. Traditional British men's outfitters are also rather well known. From the Savile Row suit, handmade shirt, and custom shoes to the Harris-tweeds-and-Oxford-brogues English country look that Ralph Lauren purloined, England's indigenous garments make for real investment dressing.

GENERAL

Aquascutum (⊠ 100 Regent St., W1, ☎ 0171/734–6090) is known for its classic raincoats, but also stocks the garments to wear underneath, for both men and women. Style keeps up with the times but is firmly on the safe side, making this a good bet for solvent professionals with an anti-fashion attitude (☞ Map A).

Burberrys (⊠ 161–165 Regent St., W1, ☎ 0171/734–4060; ⊠ 18–22 The Haymarket, SW1, ☎ 0171/930–3343) tries to evoke an English Heritage ambience, with mahogany closets and stacks of neatly folded neckerchiefs alongside the trademark "Burberry Check" tartan, which adorns—in addition to those famous raincoat linings—scarves, umbrellas, and even pots of passion-fruit curd and tins of shortbread, in the British provisions line (☞ Map A).

Favourbrook (⊠ 19–21 Piccadilly Arcade, W1, ☎ 0171/491–2337) tailors exquisite, handmade vests and jackets, ties and cummerbunds out of silks and brocades, velvets and satins, embroidered linens and chenilles. There's a range made up for both men and women, or order your own *Four Weddings and a Funeral* outfit (☞ Map A).

Herbert Johnson (⊠ 30 New Bond St., W1, ☎ 0171/408–1174) is one of a handful of gentleman's hatters who still knows how to construct deerstalkers, bowlers, flat caps, and panamas—all the classic headgear, with some Ascot hats for women, too (☞ Map A).

Kensington Market (⊠ 49–53 Kensington High St., W8, ☎ 0171/938–4343) is the diametric opposite of British stiff-upper-lip anti-fashion. For more than two decades it has been a principal purveyor of the constantly changing, frivolous, hip London street style. Hundreds of stalls—some shop-size, others tiny—are crammed into this building, where you can get lost for hours trying to find the good bits (☞ Map B).

Marks & Spencer (main store, ⊠ 458 Oxford St., W1, ☎ 0171/935–7954) is a major chain of stores that's an integral part of the British way of life—sturdy practical clothes, good materials and workmanship, and basic accessories, all at moderate, though not bargain-basement, prices. "Marks and Sparks," as they are popularly known, have never been renowned for their high style, though that is changing as they continue to bring in (anonymously) big-name designers to spice up their ranges. What they *are* renowned for is underwear; all of England buys theirs here. This holds true for knitwear as well. This Marble Arch branch has the highest stock turnover of any shop in the land (☞ Map A).

Mulberry (⊠ 11–12 Gees Ct., W1, ☎ 0171/493–2546) outdoes Ralph Lauren in packaging the English look. Covetable, top-quality leather bags, belts, and cases, wool riding jackets, coats, sweaters, and corduroy and linen pants are the sorts of things found here—at a price (☞ Map A).

Scotch House (⊠ 2 Brompton Rd., SW3, ☎ 0171/581–2151), as you'd guess, is the place to buy your kilts, tartan scarves, and Argyll socks without going to Edinburgh. It's also well stocked with cashmere and accessories (☞ Map B).

Simpson (⊠ 203 Piccadilly, W1, ☎ 0171/734–2002) is a quiet, pleasant store with a well-thought-out variety of designer and leisure wear, luggage, and gifts. There are a barbershop, restaurant, and wine bar here, plus the most disturbing nonreflective glass in its windows on Piccadilly (☞ Map A).

HIGH STYLE

Philip Treacy (✉ 69 Elizabeth St., ☎ 0171/259–9605) is the name that tops every fashion maven's Santa Claus list. His magnificent hats regularly grace the pages of *Vogue* and *Harper's Bazaar*; one-half Mad Hatter, one-half Cecil Beaton, Treacy's creations always guarantee Making An Entrance. Only the most serious fashion plates should apply—literally: the atelier is open by appointment only (☞ Map B).

Solange Azagury-Partridge (✉ 171 Westbourne Grove, ☎ 0171/792–0197) is the most baubleicious shop in town, a bijou of a store that sells cutting-edge bangles and beads to the likes of Madonna, Elle MacPherson, Lady Forte, and Fiona Thyssen (☞ Map B).

Vivienne Westwood (✉ 6 Davies St., ☎ 0171/629–3757) is probably the greatest British designer today. If McQueen and Galliano have stolen a bit of her thunder recently, her Punk-Pompadour ball gowns, Lady Hamilton vest coats, and fopish getups still represent the apex of high-style British couture. Her boutique is as intoxicatingly glamorous as her creations (☞ Map A).

MENSWEAR

Most stores we list above under General Clothing stock excellent men's wear. Try Aquascutum, Burberrys, and Simpson. All the large department stores, too, carry a wide range of men's clothing, Selfridges and Harrods especially.

Blazer (✉ 36 Long Acre, ☎ 0171/379–6258; ✉ 117 Long Acre, WC2, ☎ 0171/379–0456) stocks medium-price formal wear at the first branch and a casual range at the second. Clothes tend toward the classic, but with style-conscious details and rich colors (☞ Map A).

Duffer of St. George (✉ 29 Shorts Gdns., ☎ 0171/379–4660) has a collection of hip designers of street style in several cities, as well as its own label of sporty and dress-up lines for clubbing and posing with attitude (☞ Map A).

Hackett (main store, ✉ 65B New King's Rd., SW6, ☎ 0171/371–7964) started as a posh thrift shop, recycling cricket flannels, hunting pinks, Oxford brogues, and similar Britishwear. Now they make their own, and they have become a genuine—and very good—gentlemen's outfitter (☞ Map B).

Paul Smith (✉ 41 Floral St., WC2, ☎ 0171/379–7133) is your man if you don't want to look outlandish but you're bored with plain pants and sober jackets. His well-tailored suits have a subtle quirkiness, his shirts and ties a sense of humor, and his jeans and sweats a good cut (☞ Map A).

Tom Gilbey (✉ 2 New Burlington Pl., W1, ☎ 0171/734–4877) is a custom tailor, but the exciting part of his shop is the Waistcoat Gallery, where exquisite vests, some in silk or brocade or embroidered by hand, others marginally plainer, are essential accessories for the dandy (☞ Map A).

Turnbull & Asser (✉ 70 Jermyn St., W1, ☎ 0171/930–0502) is *the* custom shirtmaker. Unfortunately for those of average means, the first order must be for a minimum of six shirts, from around £100 each. But there's a range of less expensive, still exquisitely made, ready-to-wear shirts, too (☞ Map A).

WOMEN'S WEAR

Browns (✉ 23–27 S. Molton St., W1, ☎ 0171/491–7833; ✉ 6C Sloane St., SW1, ☎ 0171/493–4232) was the first notable store to populate the South Molton Street pedestrian mall, and seems to sprout more offshoots every time you see it. Well-established, collectible designers (Donna Karan, Romeo Gigli, Jasper Conran, Jil Sander, Yohji Yamamoto) rub shoulder pads here with younger, funkier names (Dries Van Noten, Clements Ribiero, Anne Demeulemeester, Hussein Chalayan), and Browns also has its own label. Its July and January sales are famed (☞ Maps A and B).

Droopie & Browns (⊠ 99 St. Martin's La., WC2, ☎ 0171/379–4514) features beautifully constructed, extravagantly theatrical frocks and suits, made up in raw silks, fine linens, brocades, and velvets. Colors are strong, tailoring is unimpeachable, and kind salespeople don't turn up their noses at larger ladies (☞ Map A).

The Hat Shop (⊠ 58 Neal St., WC2, ☎ 0171/836–6718) is keeping the art of millinery alive and bringing it within reach of the average purse. The stock here ranges from classic trilbies, toppers, panamas, and matador hats to frivolous tulle-and-feather constructions, with scores of inexpensive, fun titfers in between. The shop is so tiny that only 10 people are allowed in at a time (☞ Map A).

Janet Reger (⊠ 2 Beauchamp Pl., SW3, ☎ 0171/584–9360) is still queen of the silk teddy, having become synonymous with the ultimate in luxurious negligees and lingerie many years ago (☞ Map B).

Jigsaw (main store, ⊠ 21 Long Acre, Covent Garden, WC2, ☎ 0171/240–3855) is popular for its separates that don't sacrifice quality to fashion, are reasonably priced, and suit women in their twenties to forties (☞ Map A).

Laura Ashley (main store, ⊠ 256–258 Regent St., W1, ☎ 0171/437–9760) offers design from the firm founded by the late high priestess of English traditional. Country dresses, blouses, skirts, plus wallpapers and fabrics in dateless patterns that rely heavily on flowers, fruit, leaves, or just plain stripes, have captured the nostalgic imagination of the world (☞ Map A).

Nicole Farhi (main stores, ⊠ 25–26 St. Christopher's Pl., W1, ☎ 0171/486–3416; ⊠ 27 Hampstead High St., NW3, ☎ 0171/435–0866) suits the career woman who requires quality, cut, *and* style in a suit, plus weekend wear in summer linens and silks, or winter handknitted woolens. Prices are on the high side, but there is some affordable wear as well, especially the sporty, casual Diversion label. Farhi offers an equally desirable men's line (☞ Map A).

Paddy Campbell (⊠ 8 Gees Ct., W1, ☎ 0171/493–5646) designs elegant matching separates in natural fabrics and subtle colors. Prices are reasonable for this level of workmanship, and the staff will alter garments for a perfect fit (☞ Map A).

Pellicano (⊠ 63 South Molton St., W1, ☎ 0171/629–2205) stocks only cutting-edge designers, like Brit phenoms Alexander McQueen, Bella Freud, and Sonnentag Mulligan, and the *Vogue*-ier of the internationals (Prada & co) in a salon that virtually opens onto the street. The sales staff can be unbelievably snotty (☞ Map A).

The Shirtsmith (⊠ 38A Ledbury Rd., W11, ☎ 0171/229–3090) does bespoke and ready-made shirts, suits, and jackets for women, using fine cottons and Indian silks. Some designs are classic and fitted, others slightly outrageous, like the Chatterton shirt, with more ruffles at the neck than a chrysanthemum has petals (☞ Map B).

Warehouse (main store, ⊠ 19 Argyll St., W1, ☎ 0171/437–7101) stocks practical, stylish, reasonably priced separates in easy fabrics and lots of fun colors. The finishing isn't so hot, but style, not substance, counts here, and the shop's youthful fans don't seem to mind. The stock changes very quickly, so it always presents a new face to the world (☞ Maps A and B).

Whistles (main stores, ⊠ The Market, Covent Garden, WC2, ☎ 0171/379–7401; also at Heath St., Hampstead, ☎ 0171/431–2395) is a small chain stocking its own high-fashion, mid-price label, plus several European (mostly French) designers. Clothes are hung color-coordinated in shops that resemble designers' ateliers (☞ Map A).

Design

There's been a tremendous resurgence of interest in objects not mass-produced, and London is currently breeding innovators in the field of design at the rate of knots. Forget the dirty word "crafts"—this work is more modern than modems.

Contemporary Applied Arts (✉ 43 Earlham St., WC2, ☎ 0171/836–6993) has a mixed bag of designers and craftspeople displaying their wares over two floors. Anything from glassware and jewelry to furniture and lighting can be found here (☞ Map A).

Contemporary Ceramics (✉ 7 Marshall St., W1, ☎ 0171/437–7605) was formed by some of the best British potters as a cooperative venture to market their wares. The result is a store that carries a wide spectrum of the potter's art, from thoroughly practical pitchers, plates, and bowls to ceramic sculptures. Prices range from the reasonable to way up (☞ Map A).

David Linley Furniture (✉ 60 Pimlico Rd., ☎ 0171/730–7300) is the outpost for Viscount Linley—the only gentleman in the kingdom who can call the Queen "Auntie" and, more importantly, one of the finest furniture designers of today. Heirlooms of the future, his desks and chairs have one foot in the 18th century, another in the 21st. The large pieces are suitably expensive, but small desk accessories and *objets d'art* are also available (☞ Map B).

Designer's Guild (✉ 227 King's Rd., SW3, ☎ 0171/351–5775) is where Tricia Guild shows her fabrics and accessories of fabulous, saturated colors. Inspirational, many designers vouch (☞ Map B).

Gabriel's Wharf (✉ Upper Ground, SE1, ☎ 0171/620–0544) consists of a collection of craftspeople who have set up a cute, brightly painted village near the South Bank Centre, selling porcelain, jewelry, mirrors, clothes, toys, papier mâché wares, and more. Off the map, but near the Thames on the South Bank.

The Glasshouse (✉ 21 St. Albans Pl., N1, ☎ 0171/359–8162) is off our map, but for indigenous glassware it's about the only place, and you could drop in while visiting nearby Camden Passage. See glass being blown, by several artists, then buy it. Tube: Angel.

OXO Tower (✉ Bargehouse St., ☎ 0171/401–3610) is one of London's newest shopping meccas. Many and varied designer/makers have to pass rigorous selection procedures to set up in prime riverside workshops to make, display, and sell their work. The workshops are glass-walled, and you're invited in, even if you're just browsing or chatting. You can commission, too—anything from a cushion cover to a steel hoverbed (☞ Map A). Tube: Blackfriars or Waterloo.

Space (✉ 28 All Saints Rd., W11, ☎ 0171/229–6533) is where star designer Tom Dixon sells his own work—mostly furniture—and also that of his favorite peers. A great place for lighting fixtures, it's off our map. Tube: Notting Hill Gate.

Gifts

Of course, virtually anything from any shop in this chapter has gift potential, but these selections lean toward stores with a lot of choice, both in merchandise and price. Chances are you'll be wanting the recipients of your generous bounty to know how far you traveled to procure it for them, so our suggestions tend toward identifiable Britishness. You should also investigate the possibilities in the shops attached to the major museums, most of which offer far more than racks of souvenir postcards these days. Some of the best are at the **British Museum,** the **V & A,** the **Royal Academy,** and the **London Transport Museum.**

The Armoury of St. James's (✉ 17 Piccadilly Arcade, SW1, ☎ 0171/493–5082) offers perfect playthings for overgrown schoolkids in the form of antique and new-painted lead soldiers (most wars with British involvement can be fought in miniature), plus medals, brass buttons, and military prints (☞ Map A).

Conran Shop (✉ Michelin House, 81 Fulham Rd., SW3, ☎ 0171/589–7401) is the domain of Sir Terence Conran, of course, who has been informing British middle-class taste since he opened Habitat in the '60s; this is the grown-up, upmarket version. Home enhancers from furniture to stemware, both handmade and mass-produced, famous name and young designer, are displayed in a suitably gorgeous building (☞ Map B).

Fortnum & Mason (✉ 181 Piccadilly, W1, ☎ 0171/734–8040), the Queen's grocer, is, paradoxically, the most egalitarian of gift stores, with plenty of irresistibly packaged luxury foods, stamped with the gold "by appointment" crest, for under £5. Try the teas, preserves, blocks of chocolate, tins of pâté, or a box of Duchy Originals oatcakes—like Paul Newman, the Prince of Wales has gone into the retail food business with these (☞ Map A).

General Trading Co. (✉ 144 Sloane St., SW1, ☎ 0171/730–0411) "does" just about every upper-class wedding gift list, from Charles and Diana's on down, but caters also to slimmer pockets with merchandise shipped from farther shores (as the name suggests), but moored securely to English taste (☞ Map B).

Halcyon Days (✉ 14 Brook St., W1, ☎ 0171/629–8811) specializes in enamelware. It's best known for its little pillboxes: These can be selected from a range of pastoral scenes or Regency dandies or even plain colors, and personalized with initials or messages, and will add mere ounces to your luggage weight (☞ Map A).

Hamleys (✉ 188–196 Regent St., W1, ☎ 0171/734–3161) has six floors of toys and games for children and adults. The huge stock ranges from traditional teddy bears to computer games and all the latest technological gimmickry. Try to avoid it at Christmas, when police have to rope off a section of Regent Street for Hamleys customers (☞ Map A).

Lush (✉ 7 The Piazza, Covent Garden, WC2, ☎ 01202/668545 mail order) is crammed with fresh, pure, very wacky, handmade cosmetics. "13 Rabbit" is chocolate and spice for the shower; "Angels on Bare Skin" is divine lavender cleansing mush; soaps ("Banana Moon," "Dirty Boy," "Pineapple Grunt") are sliced off huge slabs like cheese, and paper-wrapped like in an old-fashioned grocer; Bath Bombs fizz furiously, then leave the water scattered with rosebuds or scented with honey and vanilla. Quite irresistible (☞ Map A).

Maison (✉ 47–49 Neal St., WC2, ☎ 0171/240–2822) is a cool, spacious two floors of homage to design. Among the gorgeous goods displayed like museum pieces are lots of witty ideas for presents, from the sublime (Alvar Aalto vases) to the ridiculous (chocolate sardines) (☞ Map A).

Neal Street East (✉ 5 Neal St., WC2, ☎ 0171/240–0135) isn't big on British, no, but this importer of Oriental everything does carry stock with universal appeal. There are several floors of what you'd expect in the way of woks, chopsticks, bowls, books, kimonos, and toys, but also glorious lacquered boxes, woven baskets, amber and silver jewelry, silk flowers, Japanese kites, and loads of fun gifts for under a fiver (☞ Map A).

Penhaligon's (main stores, ✉ 41 Wellington St., WC2, ☎ 0171/836–2150; ✉ 16 Burlington Arcade, W1, ☎ 0171/629–1416) was established by William Penhaligon, court barber at the end of Queen Victoria's lengthy reign. He blended perfumes and toilet waters in the back of his shop, using essential oils and natural, often exotic ingredients, and you can buy the very same formulations today, along with soaps, talcs, bath oils, and accessories, with the strong whiff of Victoriana both inside and outside the pretty bottles and boxes (☞ Map A).

Ray Man (✉ 29 Monmouth St., WC2, ☎ 0171/240–1776), for "Eastern Musical Instruments," is probably the only place in Europe you can buy an *erhhu,* which is, of course, a two-stringed coconut fiddle. It's an amazing place, perfect for gifts for the weird. You can pick up a set of ankle bells or pan pipes for a song (☞ Map A).

The Tea House (✉ 15A Neal St., WC2, ☎ 0171/240–7539) purveys everything to do with the British national drink; you can dispatch your entire gift list here. Alongside every variety of tea—including strange or rare brews like orchid, banana, Japanese Rice, and Russian Caravan—are teapots in the shape of a British bobby or a London taxi, plus books, and what the shop terms "teaphernalia"—strainers, and trivets, and infusers, and some gadgets that need explaining (☞ Map A).

Jewelry

Jewelry—precious, semiprecious, and totally fake—can be had by just rubbing an Aladdin's lamp in London's West End. Of the department stores, Liberty and Harvey Nichols are particularly known for their fashion jewelry, but here are a few more suggestions for baubles, bangles, and beads.

Asprey's (✉ 165–169 New Bond St., W1, ☎ 0171/493–6767) has been described as the "classiest and most luxurious shop in the world." It offers a range of exquisite jewelry and gifts, both antique and modern. If you're in the market for a six-branched Georgian candelabrum or a six-carat emerald-and-diamond brooch, you won't be disappointed (☞ Map A).

Butler and Wilson (✉ 20 South Molton St., W1, ☎ 0171/409–2955; ✉ 189 Fulham Rd., SW3, ☎ 0171/352–8255) is designed to set off its irresistible costume jewelry to the very best advantage—against a dramatic black background. It has some of the best displays in town, and keeps very busy marketing silver, diamanté, French gilt, and pearls by the truckload (☞ Maps A and B).

Cartier (✉ 175 New Bond St., W1, ☎ 0171/493–6962) exudes an exclusivity that captures the very essence of Bond Street. It combines royal connections—Cartier's was granted its first royal warrant in 1902—with the last word in luxurious good taste. Many of the Duchess of Windsor's trinkets were wrought here. The store also sells glassware, leather goods, and stationery (☞ Map A).

Garrard (✉ 112 Regent St., W1, ☎ 0171/734–7020) has connections with the royal family going back to 1722 and is still in charge of the upkeep of the Crown Jewels. But they are also family jewelers, and offer an enormous range of items, from antique to modern (☞ Map A).

The Outlaws Club (✉ 49 Endell St., WC2, ☎ 0171/379–6940) stocks the work of around 100 designers, with prices ranging from a few pounds up to £200. The dominant style is avant-garde, meaning that this shop has been a favorite with fashion stylists for a decade (☞ Map A).

Theo Fennell (✉ 177 Fulham Rd., SW3, ☎ 0171/376–4855) designs pieces that are instantly recognizable—exquisitely detailed miniatures, and covetable jewelry (in gold studded with precious stones) that is reminiscent of the ecclesiastical (☞ Map B).

Linen

Among the traditional crafts that can still be bought in London, fine linen ranks high. Again, many of the department stores, Liberty and Harrods among them, carry a fair range of linen goods, but here are three specialty stores that you might want to try for more personal service.

The Irish Linen Co. (✉ 35–36 Burlington Arcade, W1, ☎ 0171/493–8949) is a tiny store bursting with crisp, embroidered linen for the table, the bed, and the nose. Their exquisite handkerchiefs should be within reach of everyone's pocket (☞ Map A).

The Linen Cupboard (✉ 21 Great Castle St., W1, ☎ 0171/629–4062) is stacked with piles of sheets and towels of all sorts and has by far the lowest-priced fine Irish linens and Egyptian cottons in town (☞ Map A).

The Monogrammed Linen Shop (✉ 168 Walton St., SW3, ☎ 0171/589–4033) has a range of fine Italian bed linen with matching towels, bathrobes, and nightshirts, as well as tablecloths, place mats, and napkins—all of which you can have monogrammed. Proud grandparents may want to buy a superbly embroidered christening gown here (☞ Map B).

Prints

London harbors trillions of prints, and they make great gifts—for yourself, perhaps. We list two West End stores, but try also street markets and Cecil Court (☞ Books, *above*), just north of Trafalgar Square.

Grosvenor Prints (✉ 28–32 Shelton St., WC2, ☎ 0171/836–1979) sells antiquarian prints, but with an emphasis on views and architecture of London—and dogs! It's an eccentric collection, and the prices range widely, but the stock is so odd that you are bound to find something interesting and unusual to meet both your budget and your taste (☞ Map A).

The Map House (✉ 54 Beauchamp Pl., SW3, ☎ 0171/589–4325) has antique maps that can run from a few pounds to several thousand, but the shop also has excellent reproductions of maps and prints, especially of botanical subjects and cityscapes (☞ Map B).

Street Markets

London is as rich in street markets as it is in parks, and they contribute as much to the city's thriving culture. Practically every neighborhood has its own cluster of fruit-and-vegetable stalls, but we list here the bigger, specialist sort of market, which provides not only (if you luck out) a bargain, but also a great day out. A Sunday morning strolling the stalls of Brick Lane and breakfasting on the native bagels (smaller than New York's, but just as good), or a Saturday antiquing in the Portobello Road are Londoners' pastimes as much as they are tourist activities, and markets are a great way to see the city from the inside out.

Bermondsey (✉ Tower Bridge Rd., SE1). Also known as the New Caledonian Market, this is London's best antiques market, one of the largest, and the one the dealers frequent. Due to their professional needs, the Fridays-only market starts at the unearthly hour of 4 AM, and it's then that the really great buys will be snapped up. You should still be able to find a bargain or two if you turn up a bit later. ✉ *Bus 15 or 25 to Aldgate, then Bus 42 over Tower Bridge to Bermondsey Sq.; or Tube to London Bridge and walk.* ✆ *Fri. 4 AM–1.*

Camden Lock Market (NW1). Visit the lock on a sunny August Sunday if you want your concept of a crowd redefined. Camden is actually several markets gathered around a pair of locks in the Regent's Canal, and was once very pretty. Now that further stalls and a new faux warehouse have been inserted into the surrounding brick railway buildings, the haphazard charm of the place is largely lost, although the variety of merchandise is mind-blowing—vintage and new clothes (design stars have been discovered here), antiques and junk, jewelry and scarves, candlesticks, ceramics, mirrors, toys . . . But underneath it's really a meat market for hip teens. The neighborhood is bursting with shops and cafés, and further markets, and is a whole lot calmer, if stall-free, midweek. ⊠ *Tube or Bus 24 or 29 to Camden Town.* ⊙ *Shops Tues.–Sun. 9:30–5:30, stalls weekends 8–6.*

Camden Passage (Islington, N1). Despite the name, this one is not in Camden but a couple of miles away in Islington, a neighborhood first gentrified by media hippies in the '60s. Around 350 antiques dealers set up stalls here Saturday and Wednesday, with a curtailed version on Thursday, and it remains a fruitful, fair-priced, and picturesque hunting ground. ⊠ *Bus 19 or 38 or Tube to Angel.* ⊙ *Wed. and Sat. 8:30–3.*

Greenwich Antiques Market (⊠ Greenwich High Rd., SE10). If you're planning to visit Greenwich, then combine your trip with a wander around this open-air market near St. Alfege Church. You'll find one of the best selections of secondhand and antique clothes in London— quality tweeds and overcoats can be had at amazing prices. The market for antiques is open on weekends only. ⊠ *British Rail to New Gate Cross, then Bus 117; or bus direct to Greenwich.* ⊙ *Antiques, crafts, and clothes weekends 9–5; fruit and vegetables weekdays 9–5.*

Leadenhall Market (EC3). The draw here is not so much what you can buy—plants and food, mainly—as the building itself. It's a handsome late-Victorian structure, ornate and elaborate, with plenty of atmosphere. ⊠ *Tube to Bank or Monument.* ⊙ *Weekdays 9–5.*

Petticoat Lane (⊠ Middlesex St., E1). Actually, Petticoat Lane doesn't exist, and this Sunday clothing and fashion market centers on Middlesex Street, then sprawls in several directions, including east to Brick Lane. Between them, the crammed streets turn up items of dubious parentage (CD players, bikes, car radios), alongside clothes (vintage, new, and just plain tired), jewelry, books, underwear, antiques, woodworking tools, bed linens, jars of pickles, and outright junk in one of London's most entertaining diversions. ⊙ *Sun. 9–2. Tube: Liverpool St., Aldgate, or Aldgate East.*

Portobello Market (⊠ Portobello Rd., W11). London's most famous market still wins the prize for the all-round best. It sits in a most lively and multicultural part of town, the 1,500-odd antiques dealers don't rip you off, and it stretches over a mile, changing character completely as it goes. The top end (Notting Hill Gate) is antiques-land (with shops midweek); the middle is where locals buy fruit and vegetables, and hang out in trendy restaurants; the section under the elevated highway called the Westway boasts the best flea market in town; and then it tails off into a giant rummage sale among record stores, vintage clothing boutiques, and art galleries. ⊠ *Bus 52 or Tube to Ladbroke Grove or Notting Hill Gate.* ⊙ *Fruit and vegetables Mon.–Wed. and Fri. 8–5, Thurs. 8–1; antiques Fri. 8–3; both food market and antiques Sat. 6–5.*

Spitalfields (⊠ Brushfield St., E1). Until it eventually becomes shops and offices, the developers of Camden Lock have got hold of the old 3-acre indoor fruit market near Petticoat Lane and have installed food, crafts, and clothes stalls, cafés, performance and sports facilities (including an opera house and a swimming pool), and a city farm. There's a different market every day; Saturday is antiques, Sunday a greenmarket. For directions, *see* Petticoat Lane, *above.* ⊙ *Weekdays 11–3, Sun. 9–3.*

VAT Refunds

To the eternal fury of Britain's storekeepers, who struggle under cataracts of paperwork, Britain is afflicted with a 17½% Value Added Tax. Foreign visitors, however, need not pay VAT if they take advantage of the Personal Export Scheme. Of the various ways to get a VAT refund, the most common are **Over the Counter** and **Direct Export.** Note that though practically all larger stores operate these schemes, information about them is not always readily forthcoming, so it is important to ask. Once you have gotten on the right track, you'll find that almost all of the larger stores have export departments that will be able to give you all the help you need.

The easiest and most usual way of getting your refund is the **Over the Counter** method. There is normally a minimum of £75, below which VAT cannot be refunded. You must also be able to supply proof of identity—your passport is best. The salesclerk will then fill out the necessary paperwork, Form 407 VAT. (Be sure to get an addressed envelope as well.) Keep the form and give it to customs when you leave the country. Lines at major airports are usually long, so allow plenty of time, and pack the goods you have purchased in your carry-on bags—you'll sometimes need to be able to produce them. The form will then be returned to the store and the refund forwarded to you, minus a small service charge, usually around $3. You can specify how you want the refund. Generally, the easiest way is to have it credited to your charge card. Alternatively, you can have it in the form of a sterling check, but your bank will charge a fee to convert it. Note also that it can take up to eight weeks to receive the refund.

The **Direct Export** method—whereby you have the store send the goods to your home—is more cumbersome. You must have the VAT Form 407 certified by customs, police, or a notary public when you get home and then send it back to the store. They, in turn, will refund your money.

If you are traveling to any other EC country from Britain, the same rules apply, except in France, where you can claim your refund as you leave the country.

However, in 1988 the **Tourist Tax-Free Shopping** service came into operation. This service, which uses special VAT refund vouchers, rather than Form 407, expedites your refund, provided that you make your purchases at a store (identified by the red, white, and blue Tax-Free for Tourists sign) offering the service. If you are going on from Britain to the Continent, you can even get cash refunds. Full details and a list of stores offering the Tax-Free service are available from the British Tourist Authority (⊠ 551 5th Ave., 7th floor, New York, NY 10176, ☎ 212/986–2200 or 800/462–2748) and the British Travel Centre (⊠ 12 Regent St., London SW1Y 4PQ).

Clothing Sizes

Men
Suit and shirt sizes in the United Kingdom and the Republic of Ireland are the same as U.S. sizes.

Women

DRESSES/COATS
U.S.	4	6	8	10	12	14	16
U.K./Ireland	6	8	10	12	14	16	18

BLOUSES/SWEATERS
U.S.	30	32	34	36	38	40	42
U.K./Ireland	32	34	36	38	40	42	44

SHOES
U.S.	4	5	6	7	8	9	10
U.K./Ireland	2	3	4	5	6	7	8

8 Side Trips from London

Sometimes you really need to get away from Old Smoke, and just because you only have two weeks doesn't mean you won't feel the urge to see trees and sky and stately homes. Take any of these side trips and you'll feel—such is the change of pace you'll experience—as though you added another week to your vacation. England is so much more than its capital—a fact that Londoners tend to forget.

LONDONERS ARE UNDENIABLY LUCKY. Few populaces enjoy such glorious—and easily accesible—options for day-tripping. This chapter presents five of the most popular destinations: Bath, Cambridge, Oxford, Stratford-upon-Avon, and Windsor. Each can easily be done as a day trip, but are also well worth considering for an overnight. Then you could add a glimpse of the English countryside to your repertoire, perhaps dropping into a stately home or two, visiting a garden, or embarking on a hike with the aid of an Ordnance Survey map—which reveals every feature of the landscape once you learn how to read it. These are high English pleasures, to be sure.

The fastest countryside fix out of the five can be had at royal Windsor, perhaps the Queen's most spectacular home, and situated less than an hour from London by train. The farthest is Stratford, birthplace of the Bard of Avon, old Will Shakespeare himself. Oxford and Cambridge, home to England's most celebrated, oldest, and finest pair of universities—the Ivy League equivalents—are also easily accessible; both are vibrant cities, best visited during term time. Bath is exquisite, and Jane Austen fans should have this Georgian city with its Roman baths at the very top of their must-do list—read the novels, or catch any of the numerous recent film versions for explication.

All five of these places are best reached by train; bus travel is a viable alternative to Oxford, Cambridge, and Windsor. Be sure to plan on an early start for all these side trips—if going by train or bus, it's a good idea to check schedules ahead of time. Below, the sights for each town are ordered in sequence to insure the most expedient walking tour of the varied attractions.

BATH

"I really believe I shall always be talking of Bath. . . . I do like it so very much. Oh! who can ever be tired of Bath," wrote Jane Austen in *Northanger Abbey* and, today, thousands of visitors heartily agree with the great 19th-century author. A remarkably unsullied Georgian city, Bath still looks as if John Wood, its chief architect, "Beau" Nash, its principal dandy, and Jane Austen might still be strolling on the promenade here. Stepping out of the train station plumps you right in the center, and Bath is compact enough to explore on foot. A single day is sufficient for you to take in the glorious yellow stone buildings, tour the Roman baths, and stop for tea, though it will give only a brief hint of the thriving cultural life that still goes on in this vibrant place.

Bath Spa is easily reached by hourly trains from Paddington Station (about 1 hour 25 minutes journey time), or by National Express coach (☎ 0171/730–0202) from Victoria Coach Station: journey time 3 hours (coaches run about every 2 hours). The Tourist Information Centre (☎ 01225/462–831) is on Bath Street in the Colonnades.

A Good Walk

The first sight you come to, having followed signs from the train station, is the **Pump Room and Roman Baths.** Built by the Romans when they settled here in AD 43, it became famous as the temple to Minerva, goddess of wisdom. Legend has it that the first taker of these sacred waters was King Lear's leprous father, Prince Bladud, in the 9th century BC. Yes, it was claimed he was cured. The waters can still be taken and anciently gush at a constant temperature of 46.5° C (116° F). Below the gorgeous and recently restored 18th-century Pump Room (as described in Austen's *Mansfield Park, Emma, Northhanger Abbey,* et al) is a museum of objects found during excavations. ⊠ *Abbey Church-yard,* ☎ *01225/461–111.*

Opposite the Pump Room and Roman Baths is **Bath Abbey.** This was commissioned by God. Really. The current design came to a bishop in a dream—although there's been an abbey on this site since the 8th cen-tury—and was built by the Vertue brothers during the 16th century. In the **Heritage Vaults** is a museum of archeological finds, including the preserved remains of an 800-year-old woman, and a scale model of 13th-century Bath. Look up at the fan-vaulted ceilings in the nave, and the carved angels on the newly restored West Front. ⊠ *Abbey,* ☎ *01225/446–300, 01225/422–462 Heritage Vaults.*

For the perfect Bath time-out, head for **Sally Lunn's** (⊠ North Parade Passage, ☎ 01225/461–634). A popular tourist trap, but one loved equally by locals, this is possibly the world's only tearoom with its own museum. A sally lunn is a sweet cross between an English muffin and a brioche measuring a foot in diameter, which is toasted, and plied with toppings like cinnamon butter, orange curd, coffee-walnut, or herbed goat's cheese.

Eastward of the Abbey, Bridge Street leads to one of the most famous landmarks of the city, **Pulteney Bridge.** This was the great Georgian architect Robert Adam's sole contribution to Bath, and is, in its way, as fine as the only other bridge in the world with shops lining either side: the Ponte Vecchio in Florence. Find it on the River Avon back down the hill, after wandering around up at the top, exploring the many nooks and crannies, the surprising secret passageways and cobbled streetlets.

North of Saw Close and the Theatre Royal is **The Circus.** You can also reach it from Bath Abbey by heading north up Union Passage, to Mil-som Street and Gay Street. This is a perfectly circular ring of Bath stone houses, designed by John Wood, and completed after his death by his son. On the east side of the Circus are the **Assembly Rooms.** Here are more thrills for Austen readers, her much-mentioned Assembly Rooms, now containing the self-explanatory Museum of Costume. ⊠ *Bennett St.,* ☎ *01225/461–111.*

West of the Circus is the most famous sight in Bath, the **Royal Cres-cent,** and you can't help but see why. Designed by John Wood the younger, it's perfectly proportioned and beautifully sited, with views sweeping over parkland. A marvelous museum at **Number 1 Royal Cres-cent** shows life as Beau Nash would have lived it circa 1765. ☎ *01225/428–126. Open Mar. 2–Dec. 11, Tues.–Sun.*

CAMBRIDGE

Having trouble distinguishing between the two Ivy League of England college towns, Oxford and Cambridge? That's not surprising because in the United Kingdom, these two important educational institutions are often elided into the term "Oxbridge," and British people them-selves—aside from Oxbridge graduates, of course—are hazy about the distinction. Cambridge lies in East Anglia, a quartet of counties con-sisting of Norfolk, Suffolk, Essex, and Cambridgeshire. It's a city of some 100,000 souls, dominated culturally and architecturally by its famous university, which is divided into Colleges, and beautified by parks and gardens, and the quietly flowing River Cam. Punting on the Cam is a quintessential Cambridge pursuit, followed by a stroll along the Backs, the quaintly entitled left bank of the Cam, to which Magdalen (say "maudlin"), St. John's, Trinity, Clare, King's, and Queen's Colleges show their beautiful backsides.

Need a key to the city? Think Rupert Brooke, the short-lived World War I–era poet ("There is some corner of a foreign field/ That is forever England"), a Cambridgeshire lad, who called his county "The shire for Men who Understand." Think Wordsworth and Thackeray, Byron and Tennyson, E.M. Forster and C.S. Lewis; and see *Chariots of Fire,* the film version of the true story of Harold Abrahams and Eric Liddell, who shone in the 1924 Olympic Games. Exquisite King's College Chapel's equally exquisite-sounding choir defines the season for an entire nation, when the *Festival of Nine Lessons and Carols* is broadcast live on Christmas Eve, December 24th.

Cambridge may be one of the most beautiful cities in Britain, but it is no museum. Even if the students are on vacation, there's a strong pulse here, and the city can trace its history back to the 1st century BC, when an Iron Age tribe settled on what's now Castle Hill. Still, a bucolic air persists, thanks largely to the green spaces and lovely "courts," or quadrangles, around which each college is built. Indeed, one of the special pleasures of Cambridge is that in just a few yards one can pass from the bustle of the shopping streets to the cloistered seclusion of the halls of academe. Cambridge became an academic center in 1284, when Peterhouse, the first of the colleges, was founded by the Bishop of Ely. By the end of the 16th century, there were sixteen colleges; there are now 31. Students apply not to the university of Cambridge, but to one of the individual Colleges, and inter-college rivalry is not unknown.

Trains to Cambridge leave King's Cross Station every hour, and take an hour. By National Express coach (☎ 0990/808080) from Victoria Coach Station, the journey takes 2 hours; coaches hourly. Cambridge Tourist Information Centre is in Wheeler Street, an extension of Benet Street, off King's Parade (☎ 01223/322–640).

VISITING THE COLLEGES

College visits are certainly a highlight of a Cambridge tour, but you must remember that these are private homes and workplaces, even out of termtime. Some are closed to the public, and access to others is restricted to the chapels and dining rooms (called halls) and sometimes the libraries, too (and you are politely requested to refrain from picnicking in the quadrangles). Some colleges charge a small fee for the privilege of nosing around. All are closed during exams, usually from Mid-April to late-June, when the May Balls are held, and everyone lets down their hair along with whatever else they can find. By far the best way to gain access without annoying anyone is to join a walking tour led by an official Blue Badge guide—in fact, many areas are off-limits unless you do. The two-hour tours leave up to five times daily from the Tourist Information Centre. Below is a walk that takes in most of the colleges, but it's best to set off with a map from the local tourist office and just tackle a portion of the city. Here's what to look out for in the halls of academe:

A Good Walk

On Trumpington Street is **Peterhouse,** the oldest college, founded in 1281 by the Bishop of Ely. Take a tranquil walk through its former deer park, by the river side of its ivy-clad buildings. Nearby is Cambridge's finest art gallery, the **Fitzwilliam Museum.** This contains outstanding collections of art, including several Constable paintings, and antiquities—starring some objects from ancient Egypt. ⊠ *Trumpington St.,* ☎ *01223/332–900.* 🖾 *Free.* ☉ *Tues.–Sat. 10–5, Sun. 2:15–5.*

Across from Peterhouse is Pembroke College (1347), with delightful gardens and bowling greens. Head down Pembroke Street to reach **Emmanuel College.** Harvard grads are especially obliged to make a pilgrimage to the Wren chapel here, to see the plaque to former student, John Harvard, who, fresh off the Mayflower, gave his name to that Boston institution. A number of the Pilgrims were Emmanuel alumni, and they remembered their alma mater by naming Cambridge, Massachusetts.

Westward from Jesus College, along Sidney Street, is **St. John's College.** The second-largest college in Cambridge, St. John's boasts noted alumni—Wordsworth had his rooms here—and two of the finest sights in town—the School of Pythagoras, the oldest house in Cambridge, and a copy of the Bridge of Sighs in Venice that reaches across the Cam to the mock-Gothic New Court (1825), whose white crenellations have earned it the nickname "the wedding cake." From here, it's most pleasant to head along the river and through the narrow lanes past Clare College and Trinity Hall to Trinity College.

Trinity College was founded by Henry VIII in 1546 and is the largest of all the colleges. Many of Trinity's features match its size, not least its 17th-century "great court" and the massive gate house that houses Great Tom, a giant clock that strikes each hour with high and low notes. Don't miss the wonderful library by Christopher Wren. Alumni include Sir Isaac Newton, Byron, Tennyson, and Thackeray, and the future King Charles III.

South of Trinity College is **King's College**, site of the world-famous Gothic-style (1446) **King's College Chapel,** with its great fan-vaulted roof supported by a delicate tracery of columns, is the final and, some would say, most glorious flowering of Perpendicular Gothic in Britain. "The noblest barn in Europe," it's truly a lovely sight and the home of the famous choristers. To cap it all, Rubens's *Adoration of the Magi* is secreted behind the altar.

Reached along the Backs and tucked away on Queens Lane, **Queens College** was built around 1446 and is one of Cambridge's most eye-catching colleges. The best way to enter it is over the **Mathematical Bridge.** Isaac Newton fashioned this arched wooden structure without benefit of any binding thing save gravity. Unfortunately, the curious scholars couldn't leave well enough alone, and dismantled it to find Newton's secret; they failed, and had to nail it back together like any other bridge. Be sure to take in the half-timbered President's Lodge. In from the river is **Peterhouse,** the oldest college. Along King's Parade is **Corpus Christi College.** If you see only one quadrangle, make it the medieval Old Court here.

OXFORD

To get Oxford fixed in your mind's eye, say the phrase "Dreaming Spires" over and over—all the tour guides do—and think *Brideshead Revisited,* Sebastian Flyte, and Evelyn Waugh, in general. Think Rhodes Scholar—President Clinton was one, of course—and think J.R.R. Tolkein and Percy Bysshe Shelley, and W.H. Auden and C.S. Lewis. (Wait—wasn't he in Cambridge? Yes, he *studied* here, and *taught* there.) Two more recent graduates were Margaret Thatcher and . . . Kris Kristofferson. Truly. The University of Oxford is older than Cambridge's, dating from the 11th century (only the Sorbonne in Paris is older), but once again, newcomers need to learn that the University is not one unified campus, but a collection of many colleges, scattered across the city.

Oxford is a bigger and much more cosmopolitan city than Cambridge, though here, too, there is no shortage of hushed quadrangles, chapels, and gardens. Bikes are propped, unlocked, against wrought-iron railings, and punting is popular along the Cherwell (rent one yourself from the foot of Magdalen Bridge), but Oxford is also quite a major industrial center, with large car and steel plants based in its suburbs. The same guidelines apply here as in Cambridge for visiting the colleges, with only the chapels and halls generally viewable.

Get here by hourly train from Paddington Station. The journey takes 55 minutes, or 1 hour 40 minutes by coach from Victoria Coach Station. Several companies operate services, so buses leave every 20 minutes or so. The Oxford Information Centre is in The Old School, Gloucester Green, ☎ 01865/726–871.

VISITING THE COLLEGES

See general information for Cambridge (☞ *above*). Guided city walking tours leave the Tourist Information center several times a day.

A Good Walk

This tour encompasses much of the city; for those with limited time, get a detailed map from the tourist office and focus on selected sights.

Any tour of Oxford should begin at its very center—actually a pleasant walk of ten minutes or so eastward of the train station—with the splendid university church of **St. Mary the Virgin,** located on High Street. From its 14th-century tower, you can get a Cinerama view of the entire city. The church's interior is crowded with 700 years' worth of funeral monuments. Just north of the church is one of Oxford's most famous sights, the **Radcliffe Camera,** which holds the august **Bodleian Library.** Don't get too excited, because not very much of this—one of the planet's best book collections—is on view to non-dons, but you can see part of the 2-million-volume library on a tour of the Camera—a magnificent building topped by one of Britain's biggest domes—and at the former Divinity School, where there's a changing exhibit of manuscripts and rare books, and a magnificent Gothic interior. ⊠ *Broad St.* ☎ *01865/277165.* ☜ *£3.50.* ☉ *Tour mid-Mar.–Oct., weekdays at 10:30, 11:30, 2, and 3; Nov.–mid-Mar., wekkdays at 2 and 3; occasional Sat.-morning tours (call for availability).*

A minute's stroll from the Radcliffe Camera is the **Sheldonian Theatre.** Built in 1663, the Sheldonian was Sir Christopher Wren's first work, modeled on a Roman amphitheater, in which students' graduation ceremonies are still held, entirely in Latin, as befits the building's spirit. Outside is one of Oxford's most striking sights—a metal fence topped with stone busts of 18 Roman emperors (modern reproductions of the originals, eaten away by pollution). ⊠ *Sheldonian Theatre, Broad St.,* ☎ *01865/277–299.* ☉ *Mon.–Sat. 10–3:30.*

Along Broad Street, you can stop in at **The Oxford Story.** Take your place at a medieval student's desk, as it trundles through 800 years of Oxford history. The multimedia ride concentrates on University life, visiting famous former students in dioramas of their workplaces. See Edmund Halley discover that comet! Watch the Scholastica's Day Riot of 1355! You can choose grown-up's or kid's commentary. ⊠ *6 Broad St.,* ☎ *01865/790–055.* ☜ *£4.50.* ☉ *Apr.– Oct., daily 9:30–5; July and Aug., daily 9–6; Nov.–Mar., daily 10–4:30.*

Broad Street leads into Giles Street and prestigious **Balliol College** (1263). The doors between the inner and outer quadrangles of Christ Church's neighbor still bear the scorch marks from the flames that roasted

Archbishop Cranmer and Bishops Latimer and Ridley in 1555, during Mary I's reign, for their Protestant beliefs.

Westward from Giles Street, Beaumont Street is the site of the **Ashmolean Museum,** Britain's oldest public museum, no less, in which some of the world's most precious things are stashed, all the property of the University. See Egyptian, Greek, and Roman artifacts, Michelangelo drawings, and European silverware and ceramics, Oriental paintings and more. In 1996, a new café opened, serving snacks and meals to the culturally replete. ⊠ *Beaumont St.,* ☎ *01865/278–000.* ☉ *Tues.–Sat. 10– 4, Sun. 2–4.*

North and across St. Giles Road from the Ashmolean Museum is **St. John's College.** This one was founded in 1555, and is worth visiting for its very large and lovely gardens.

The leading college of the southern half of Oxford is **Christ Church College,** found along the major road of St. Aldate's. Called "The House" by its modest members, Christ Church boasts the largest quadrangle in town, named **Tom Quad,** after the over-six-ton bell in the gate tower. This is where Charles Dodgson, better known as Lewis Carroll, was a math don; a shop opposite the meadows in St. Aldate's was the inspiration for the shop in *Through the Looking Glass.* Don't miss the 800-year-old chapel, nor the medieval dining hall, with its portraits of former students—John Wesley, William Penn, and 14 prime ministers. Also go to the **Canterbury Quadrangle,** whose gallery contains works by Leonardo, Michelangelo, and Rubens.

STRATFORD-UPON-AVON

Stratford-upon-Avon has become very adept at accommodating the hordes of visitors who come hoping for a taste of Shakespeare, and getting more than they bargained for. What we mean is that Stratford is a handsome town in its own right, punctuated with those distinctive black-and-white Tudor half-timbered buildings that survive from its 16th-century heyday as a crafts and trading center. Shakespeare's father participated in that boom—he was a glove maker and wool dealer who rose to the rank of town Bailiff. There are also fine shopping opportunities, including the Friday market, and various little side-sights, but what we're really all here for is Shakespeare.

It's difficult to avoid feeling like a herd animal, as you board the Shakespeare bus, but there is something to be said for taking advantage of packaged tours like **Stratford and the Shakespeare Story,** which allows you to come and go as you please around the five Shakespeare Properties, especially if your time is limited. If you can manage an overnight stay, taking in a production at one of the three Royal Shakespeare Company's Stratford theaters will satisfyingly deepen your immersion in the Bard's works.

Try to catch the direct train each morning from Paddington Station (☎ 0171/262–6767 for times), or else you'll be doomed to at least one change, at Leamington Spa. There are two direct trains back from Stratford each afternoon, too, and journey time is 2 hours 20 minutes. It takes no longer to go by National Express (☎ 0171/730– 0202) from Victoria Coach Station, and there are three coaches daily, though the fastest route is by train *and* bus: from Euston Station to Coventry, then switching to a Guide Friday bus. This trip takes 2 hours, and there are four departures daily (☎ 0171/387–7070). Stratford Tourist Information Centre is at Bridge Foot, by the bridge, (☎ 01789/293–127).

GUIDED TOURS

Many people like to see Stratford from the top of an open-top double-decker bus and the **Guide Friday's Stratford and Shakespeare Story Tour** is one of the better choices. It allows you to alight and reboard at any of the Bard sights on a ticket valid all day—a particularly handy mode of transport as two of the five sights are out of town. ✉ *14 Rother St.,* ☎ *01789/294466.* ☉ *Tour May–Sept., daily every 15 min; Oct.–Nov. and mid-Feb.–Apr., daily every 30 min; late Nov.–mid-Feb., daily hourly.*

A Good Walk

Most Stratford visitors begin at **Shakespeare's Birthplace.** With the Shakespeare Centre inside, this is the perfect place to start your Bard odyssey. The half-timbered building in which William grew has been a national memorial since 1847, and is now split in half: One part is a re-creation of a typical home of the time, while the other contains a new exhibit about the historical characters in the Shakespeare canon, plus a history of the house itself. ✉ *Henley St.,* ☎ *01789/204–016.* 🎟 *£3.50, combined admission for Shakespeare Birthplace Trust properties £9, 3 in-town properties £6.* ☉ *Mar.–Oct., Mon.–Sat. 9–5:30, Sun. 10–5:30; Nov.–Feb., Mon.–Sat. 9:30–4, Sun. 10:30–4.*

On High Street, the center road of Stratford, is **New Place.** What there is to see now, next to Nash's House—which belonged to Thomas Nash, first husband of Shakespeare's granddaughter, Elizabeth Hall—is an Elizabethan knot garden, planted over the foundations of the house where the Bard spent his last years, and died, in 1616. In Nash's House, see an exhibit about Stratford, and a Tudor decor job. ✉ *Chapel St.,* ☎ *01789/292325.* 🎟 *£2 or joint ticket (☞ above).* ☉ ☞ *Shakespeare's Birthplace, above.*

Along Chapel Street is one of the most picturesque set pieces of Stratford—the Guildhall buildings, comprising the Guildhall Chapel, the Almshouses, and **King Edward's Grammar School,** where Master Shakespeare learned "little Latin and less Greek." The chapel is open daily 9–5, but the schoolhouse is still used by students and can only be visited by prior arrangement (☎ 01789/293351) during after-school hours or vacation time.

On the venerable road called Old Town you'll find Stratford's most beautiful Tudor town house, **Hall's Croft.** This was—almost definitely—the home of Shakespeare's daughter, Susanna, and her husband, Dr. John Hall. It's rather charmingly outfitted, complete with furniture of the period and the doctor's dispensary, and the walled garden is delightful. ✉ *Old Town,* ☎ *01789/292–107.* 🎟 *£2 or joint ticket (☞ above).* ☉ *Mar.–Oct., Mon.–Sat. 9:30–5, Sun. 10:30–5; Nov.–Feb., Mon.–Sat. 10:30–4, Sun. 1:30–4.*

At the end of Old Town is "Shakespeare's Church," **Holy Trinity,** along the banks of the Avon, and fronted by a beautiful avenue of lime trees. Here, in the chancel, the Bard is buried, alongside his wife, his daughter, his son-in-law, and his granddaughter's husband. The bust of Shakespeare is thought to be an authentic likeness, executed a few years after his death. ✉ *Trinity St., Waterside.*

Perfectly positioned on the banks of the Avon not far from Holy Trinity Church, the **Royal Shakespeare Theatre** is where the Royal Shakespeare Company (known as the RSC) lives outside London, mounting several productions each season. The design of the smaller **Swan Theatre,** in the same building, is based on the original Elizabethan Globe. It's best to book well in advance, but day-of-performance tickets are nearly always available. ⊠ *Stratford-upon-Avon, CV37 6BB,* ☎ *01789/295–623.*

STRATFORD ENVIRONS

The two remaining stops on the Shakespeare trail are just outside Stratford. **Anne Hathaway's Cottage,** the early home of the playwright's wife, is possibly the most picturesque abode in Britain—a rather substantial thatched cottage, it has been restored to reflect the comfortable middle-class Hathaway life. You can walk—it's just over a mile from downtown Stratford in Shottery. **Mary Arden's House** is probably where Shakespeare's mother was raised, and if that doesn't get you interested, perhaps the farming exhibit in the **Shakespeare Countryside Museum,** or the unoccupied 600-bird dovecote will. There's also **Glebe Farm** to see, with a falconry (working), farm animals, and often a working blacksmith—it's just under 4 mi to Wilmcote. Farther afield, and not Shakespearean, are a few very worthwhile sights. **Warwick Castle**—only 8 mi away—will fulfill anyone's most clichéd Camelot daydreams, being a medieval, fortified, much-restored, castellated, moated, landscaped (by Capability Brown) castle, complete with dungeons and a torture chamber, State Rooms, and the occasional battle reenactment. ⊠ *Warwick,* ☎ *01926/495421.* ☞ *£8.75.* ۞ *Apr.–mid-Oct., daily 10–6; mid-Oct.–Mar., daily 10–5.*

WINDSOR

The star sight of this quiet Berkshire town is, without a shadow of a doubt, the largest inhabited castle in the world—Windsor Castle. Windsor Great Park, however, shouldn't be forgotten, and Eton College, England's most famous public school, is also here. There's also now a brand-new attraction to add to the Windsor value: the kid's paradise of Legoland.

Windsor Castle is the most impressive and the longest-serving of all England's royal palaces. It's the only royal residence to have been in continuous royal use since the days of William the Conqueror, who chose this site to build a timber stockade soon after his conquest of Britain in 1066. It was Edward III in the 1300s who really founded the castle, building the Norman gateway, the great round tower, and new state apartments, then subsequent monarchs added new buildings or improved existing ones according to their tastes and their finances. Charles II restored the state apartments during the 1600s, and during the 1820s George IV, that most extravagant of kings with a mania for building, converted what was still essentially a medieval castle into the royal palace you see today. The Queen uses Windsor a lot, spending most weekends here, often joined by family and friends. She's here when the Royal Standard is flown above the Round Tower, but not when you see the Union Jack.

Windsor is easy to reach by train, either from Waterloo direct to Windsor and Eton Riverside (50 minutes), or from Paddington to Windsor Central, changing at Reading (45 minutes); there are 2 trains per hour on each route. The Green Line bus (☎ 01737/242–411) leaves from Eccleston Bridge, behind Victoria train station, *not* from the Coach Station itself. Make sure you catch the fast direct service, which takes 45 minutes and runs hourly; the stopping services take up to 1 hour 15 minutes. Windsor's Tourist Information Centre (☎ 01753/852–010) is in Central Station.

WINDSOR CASTLE

The massive citadel occupies 13 acres, but the first part you notice on entering is the massive **Round Tower** on top of which the standard is flown, and at the base of which is the 11th-century Moat Garden, which you can occasionally visit in summer. Passing through the portcullised **Norman Gate,** you reach the **Upper Ward,** the quadrangle containing the State Apartments—which you may tour when the Queen is out— and the sovereign's Private Apartments, which you may not. Big ceremonies, like processions for foreign Heads of State, go on here, as does the Changing of the Guard, when the Queen is in. Next you reach the **Lower Ward,** where the star sight is the magnificent **St. George's Chapel,** symbolic and actual guardian of the Order of the Garter, the highest Chivalric Order in the land, founded in 1348 by Edward III. Ten sovereigns are buried in the Chapel—a fantastic Gothic Perpendicular vision, 230 feet long, complete with gargoyles, buttresses, banners, swords, choir stalls, and enameled plates displaying arms of the Knights of the Order of the Garter.

The **State Apartments** are grander than Buckingham Palace's, and have the added attraction of a few gems from the Queen's vast art collection: choice canvasses by Rubens, Rembrandt, Van Dyck, Gainsborough, Canaletto, and Holbein; da Vinci drawings; Gobelin tapestries, and limewood carvings by Grinling Gibbons. The views across to Windsor Great Park, the remains of a former royal hunting forest, are magnificent, too. One unmissable treat—and not only for children— is **Queen Mary's Dolls' House,** a 12:1 scale, seven-story palace, complete with electricity, running water, and working elevators, designed in 1924 by Sir Edwin Lutyens. The detail is literally incredible—for example, some of the miniature books in the library are by Kipling, Conan Doyle, Thomas Hardy, and G.K. Chesterton—written by the great authors in their own hand. The terrible fire of November 1992, which started in the Queen's private chapel, totally gutted some of the State Apartments. A swift rescue effort meant that, miraculously, hardly any works of art were lost. However, parts of the castle still remain closed while repairs and rebuilding are in progress—probably at least until the year 2000. ⊠ *Windsor Castle,* ☎ *01753/868–286. 01753/831–118 for opening times.* ✆ *£8.50.*

9 Portraits of London

London at a Glance: A Chronology

Theatreland: The True Heart of London

LONDON AT A GLANCE: A CHRONOLOGY

This date table parallels events in London's history with events in the world at large, especially in the Americas, to give a sense of perspective to the chronology of London. The dates of British kings and queens are those of their reigns, not of their lives.

c. 400 BC   Early Iron Age hamlet built at Heathrow (now London airport)

54 BC   Julius Caesar arrives with short-lived expedition

43   Romans conquer Britain, led by the emperor Claudius

60   Boudicca, queen of Iceni, razes the first Roman Londinium

c. 100   The Romans make Londinium center of their British activities, though not the capital

856   Alfred the Great (871–99), king of the West Saxons, "restored London and made it habitable"

1042   Edward the Confessor (1042–66) moves his court to Westminster and begins the reconstruction of the abbey and its monastic buildings

1066   William the Conqueror (1066–87), duke of Normandy, wins the battle of Hastings

1067   William grants London a charter confirming its rights and privileges

1078   The Tower of London begins with the building of the White Tower

1136   Fire destroys London Bridge (new one built 1176–1209)

1185   Knights Templar build the New Temple by the Thames

1191   First mayor of London elected

1265   First Parliament held in Westminster Abbey Chapter House

1314   Old St. Paul's Cathedral completed

1327   Incorporation of first trade guilds (which govern the City for centuries)

1348–58   The Black Death strikes London; one-third of the population dies

1382   The Peasants' Revolt destroys part of the city

1411   The Guildhall (already centuries on the same site) rebuilt

1476   William Caxton (1422–91) introduces printing to England in Westminster

1529   Hampton Court given by Cardinal Wolsey to Henry VIII; it becomes a favorite royal residence

1568   Royal Exchange founded

1588   Preparations at Tilbury to repel the Spanish invasion; the Armada defeated in the Channel

1599   Shakespeare's Globe Theatre built on the South Bank

1603   Population of London over 200,000

1605   Unsuccessful Gunpowder Plot to blow up the Houses of Parliament

1649   Charles I (1625–49) beheaded outside the Banqueting House on Whitehall

1658   Oliver Cromwell (Lord Protector) dies

1660 Charles II (1649–85) restored to the throne (the Restoration) after exile in Europe

1665 The Great Plague; deaths probably reach 100,000 (official figure for one week alone was 8,297)

1666 The Great Fire burns for three days; 89 churches, 13,200 houses destroyed over an area of 400 streets

1675 Sir Christopher Wren (1632–1723) begins work on the new St. Paul's Cathedral

1694 The Bank of England founded

1698 Whitehall Palace destroyed by fire

1732 Number 10 Downing Street becomes the prime minister's official residence

1739–53 Mansion House built

1755 Trooping the Colour first performed for George II

1762 George III (1760–1820) makes Buckingham Palace the royal residence

1802 First gaslights on the London streets

1817 First Waterloo Bridge built

1827 Marble Arch erected (in 1851 moved to the northeast corner of Hyde Park)

1829–41 Trafalgar Square laid out

1834 The Houses of Parliament gutted by fire; 1840–52 the present Westminster Palace built

1837 Victoria (1837–1901) comes to the throne

1838 National Gallery opens in Trafalgar Square

1845 British Museum completed

1851 The Great Exhibition, Prince Albert's brainchild, held in the Crystal Palace, Hyde Park

1863 Arrival of the Underground (the tube), first train on the Metropolitan Line

1869 Albert Embankment completed, first stage in containing the Thames's floodwaters

1897 Queen Victoria celebrates her Diamond Jubilee

1901 Victoria dies, marking the end of an era; London's population reaches about 4,500,000

1914–18 World War I—London bombed (1915) by German zeppelins (355 incendiaries, 567 explosives; 670 killed, 1,962 injured)

1939–45 World War II—air raids, between Sept. 1940 and July 1941, 45,000–50,000 bombs (including incendiaries) are dropped on London; 1944 Flying Bomb (Doodlebug) raids; 1945 V2 raids; during the latter two series of raids 8,938 killed, 24,504 injured. Total casualties for the whole war, about 30,000 killed, more than 50,000 injured

1946 Heathrow Airport opens

1951 The Festival of Britain spurs postwar uplift

1953 Coronation of Queen Elizabeth II (born 1926)

1956 Clean Air Act abolishes open fires and makes London's mists and fogs a romantic memory

1965 Sir Winston Churchill's funeral, a great public pageant

1974 Covent Garden fruit-and-vegetable market moves across the Thames; the original area is remodeled

1976 National Theatre opens on the South Bank

1977 Queen Elizabeth celebrates her Silver Jubilee

1979 Margaret Thatcher elected prime minister

1981 National Westminster Tower, Britain's tallest building, opens in the City; Prince Charles marries Lady Diana Spencer in St. Paul's Cathedral

1983 The first woman lord mayor takes office

1984 The Thames Barrier, designed to prevent flooding in central London, is inaugurated

1986 The Greater London Council (the city's centralized municipal government) is abolished by Parliament; London's population now stands at approximately 6,696,000

1990 Margaret Thatcher resigns as prime minister

1991 Cesar Pelli's Tower—1 Canada Square—opens at Canary Wharf and becomes Britain's tallest building

1994 The Channel Tunnel opens a direct rail link between Britain and Europe

1996 The Prince and Princess of Wales receive a precedent-breaking divorce. Diana retains many royal privileges as mother of the future King William.

THEATRELAND: THE TRUE HEART OF LONDON

MOST PEOPLE who become theatergoers in adult life have, I believe, a distinct memory of the first time they ever saw a live performance. And I suspect that many of those people, wherever they happen to have been born, will remember equally clearly the first time they went to the theater in London.

For myself, it was Christmas 1965, when my parents took me to see The Wind in the Willows in Her Majesty's Theatre. Five years old, I sat in wide-eyed wonder among a hushed, attentive audience, responding together to the enchantment of the bright lights and the strange costumes. Today, Her Majesty's Theatre houses *The Phantom of the Opera,* the most famous musical in the world; it has become a landmark among London sights for visitors from all over.

And yet Her Majesty's Theatre is only one of the 50-odd historic theaters in London's West End, with which the history of London has been bound up since Shakespeare gathered his company together at Bankside's Globe. London's theaters have always been at the center of its public life, and as a visitor to London, heading to the West End perhaps for that unforgettable first time, you join 11 million others who attend the city's theaters every year—without even counting the Fringe, London's equivalent of Off-Broadway. Of that 11 million, about a third come from abroad, theater high on their list of must-sees. So, welcome to the ranks of London theatergoers: You take your place in a noble tradition.

After the great age of Shakespeare and Jacobean drama came the 17th-century pleasure gardens, the theaters and bear pits of the South Bank; these in their turn gave way to the fiercely competitive Theatres Royal in 18th-century Covent Garden, dominated by the Theatre Royal, Drury Lane (home of *Miss Saigon* today), the Theatre Royal Covent Garden, and a frisky newcomer, the Little Theatre in the Haymarket. By virtue of an exclusive royal license to present plays for public entertainment, the mighty Theatre Royal, Drury Lane, had enjoyed a monopoly since the restoration of the monarchy in 1660; in 1729, the Little Theatre gained "royal" status, initiating a wave of competition that finally crested at the end of the 19th century—by which time central London was thoroughly alive with theaters.

In the latter part of Queen Victoria's reign, from the 1870s until her death in 1901, the theater district was thick with the dust, noise, and clatter of bizarrely ornate theaters going up as fast as audiences could fill them. Although it is now nearly 30 years since the last new theater went up in the commercial West End, we enjoy today the legacy of that extraordinary turn-of-the century outburst of building activity, which exchanged the debris of part of Victorian slum London for a gleaming new theater district.

A walk along Shaftesbury Avenue from Piccadilly Circus to Cambridge Circus provides a model education in fin de siècle British theater style. Seen during the daytime, when the avenue is bustling, or at night when the theaters light up, the theater district is as much the heart of London as the royal palaces, cathedrals, and parks for which the city is universally famous.

Shaftesbury Avenue begins on the north side of Piccadilly Circus, and its five theaters line its left side like sentinels. But before you set off along the avenue, seek out the Criterion, a tiny jewel box of a theater on the southern edge of Piccadilly Circus. Built in 1873 by Thomas Verity (who also built the Comedy Theatre in nearby Panton Street), the Criterion's Rococo entrance opens onto a dazzling staircase lined with mirrors and brightly colored ceramic tiles. This staircase takes you down to a pink-and-white auditorium, almost as far belowground as the tube trains that can be heard rumbling nearby during the quieter moments of a performance. When it first opened in 1874, the Criterion was considered a miracle of subterranean engineering—particularly for the system by which fresh air was pumped down into the auditorium to save the audience from asphyxiation. Nowadays the air-conditioning is more conventional, but the theater remains a must-see on your tour.

Back on Shaftesbury Avenue proper, the first theater is the oldest: the Lyric, built in 1888 by C. J. Phipps, a fine red stone building with a broad, handsome front. By contrast, the neighboring Apollo, opened in 1901, presents a creamy-white facade, with corner domes supported by graceful muses. If you look carefully to the right of the front entrance you can see the eccentric family crest of the first owner, Henry Lowenfield: a silver chain and buckle with a flying lizard, supported by lions.

Continue a few paces farther and you'll come to the Queen's and the Gielgud, built between 1906 and 1907 to balance the two corners of a block by prolific theater architect W.G.R. Sprague. Together they make one of London's trio of twin theaters. From the outside, the similarity between the Queen's and the Gielgud has been lost since the Queen's lost its facade to a bomb during the blitz. Inside, however, below street level, the auditorium still presents a perfect mirror image of its twin. Sprague was fond of this effect: You can see it again in the Aldwych and Strand theaters, which flank the Waldorf Hotel block in the Aldwych, and again at St. Martin's Court, near the southern end of Charing Cross Road, where the Albery and Wyndham's theaters stand back to back like friendly rivals.

Shaftesbury Avenue saves its greatest glory for last. As you walk from Queen's toward Cambridge Circus, you'll sense the shadow of a towering monolith rising on your left, the side wall of which takes up the whole block from Greek Street onward. Only when you cross to the other side of Cambridge Circus can you turn to take in the whole, magnificent view of the Palace Theatre, a flagship of Theatreland and a London landmark. The Palace was built in 1891 by architect G. H. Holloway for the great impresario Richard D'Oyly Carte, who intended it as a Royal Opera House for the presentation of British opera. Unfortunately D'Oyly Carte had overlooked the fact that, apart from his own favorites Gilbert and Sullivan, there were few British composers whose work could fill such a mighty edifice and attract the audiences to make it pay. Speedily renamed the Palace

Theatre of Varieties, it quickly became popular: a monument both to late–19th-century theater architecture and to the resourcefulness of a producer quick to get himself out of an unprofitable enterprise!

Indeed, it was variety theater, successor to the music-hall entertainment of the late 19th century, that proved the great money-maker of the early 1900s and the raison d'être of a number of the larger theaters that make their living today as venues for megamusicals or opera. One man, the architect Frank Matcham, was chiefly responsible for the gargantuan Empires, Hippodromes, and Coliseums that sprang up not only in London but across England between the 1890s and 1910s. Much of Matcham's work has been lost, but central London still boasts two of his masterpieces: the London Palladium, which you'll find tucked away in Argyll Street, an unlikely looking side street east of Oxford Circus, and the London Coliseum in St. Martin's Lane.

THE LONDON COLISEUM is one of the wonders of London. Its noteworthy features are many: a rosy-hued Italianate facade; a spacious foyer with a gloriously decorative mosaic domed ceiling; a well-proportioned 2,000-seat auditorium (the box office here can truthfully claim "there is no bad seat in the house"); one of the largest stages in the entire country; and the famous Coliseum lions leaping in gilded rampage from either side of the proscenium arch. The Coliseum was the first theater in the world to have a revolving stage, and royal guests in the early half of the century were transported from front door to royal box in a private curtained carriage that ran on rails still preserved beneath the foyer carpet! Anything was possible in this queen of theaters: ice shows, variety, musicals, pantomime, opera, or ballet. Today it makes a fitting home for the English National Opera, and at night its famous rooftop globe illuminates the sky and is visible from Covent Garden to Trafalgar Square. Its nearby friendly rival, the Royal Opera House in Covent Garden, may have a longer history, a royal pedigree, and a more classically beautiful interior, but the Coliseum remains uniquely impressive.

The history of theatreland is a history of people, too, and, as you wander the area's streets and alleyways, you'll learn about the men and women who have shaped commercial West End theater over the decades. It isn't hard to find the most famous among them. Noël Coward is honored with his very own bar at the Phoenix Theatre; composer and musical actor Ivor Novello is remembered with a sign on the wall outside the Strand Theatre; and a solemnly optimistic legend above the stage door of the Prince Edward Theatre in Soho's Greek Street observes that "the world's greatest artistes have passed, and will pass, through these doors." If you take a backstage tour of the Theatre Royal, Drury Lane, you'll be treated to the history behind many of London's most famous theatrical greats—from the leading Shakespearean actors of the 18th and 19th centuries, such as Garrick, Kean, and Mrs. Siddons, to the more recent roll call of 20th-century musicals to which Drury Lane has played host. Along the way, you will hear about some less-substantial personalities, among them the ghostly Man in Grey, who haunts the staircase above the Royal Circle.

SOME OF THE MOST famous names are honored in surprising places. The image of Sir Henry Irving, the first theatrical knight, hangs over the door to the Lyceum Public House, on the corner of The Strand and Wellington Street, just a few paces from the front steps of his own theater, the Lyceum. Irving, whose agent Bram Stoker wrote the horror classic *Dracula*, was the actor responsible for rescuing Shakespeare from the 19th-century rhetorical school of acting (better known as overacting).

Amid the serious lore of London theater life, you'll find some oddities, too: Did you know that the entrance that the Savoy Theatre shares with its neighbor, the Savoy Hotel, is the only piece of road in the United Kingdom where cars drive on the right? The Adelphi, whose severe black Art Deco facade now faces the Savoy across The Strand, stands on the site of a dairy that once supplied the royal household

with milk and butter. Dairy owner John Scott first built a theater here in 1806 to indulge the theatrical talents of his daughter Jane, and there has been a theater here ever since.

Today the West End is run by some 100 producers, theater owners, and managers. Some of them are newcomers, and some are themselves descendants of theatrical predecessors. It is here, perhaps, that the secrets of the West End's success lie: its continuity from one generation to the next, and its ability to reinvent itself along the way. From time to time, new technologies bring new competition—cinema, television, and multimedia home entertainment—but there is always an audience for live theater. It helps that the British have an uncanny capacity for producing an unending stream of gifted performers. But London also excels at large-scale musicals, à la Sir Andrew Lloyd Webber and Cameron Mackintosh, and at farces and thrillers, which are regularly exported to the United States. London theater is equally adept at reinterpretations of classic drama, and—although the cry goes up at regular intervals that the West End is dying, that new work by unheard-of writers is too risky—at theatrical analysis of contemporary social issues. Look around, and you'll find a half-dozen plays that have crossed into the commercial theater from the Fringe, nurtured by producers who believe that important new work should reach a wider audience. You'll also see an entirely new generation of directors, whose name on a bill guarantees a stimulating evening: Stephen Daldry, Nicholas Hytner, Phyllida Lloyd, Sam Mendes, Deborah Warner. Look out for these names, and strike out into new theatrical territory.

No other city in the world can offer you so stunning a variety. Whatever you choose, I can promise you won't forget it—as a child of five or as a seasoned adult culture addict. Welcome to the true heart of London.

— Jane Moss

Ms. Moss has contributed to many publications in London and the U.K. Since 1988, she has been Information Officer for the Society of the London Theatre and has a reputation as a walking encyclopedia on British theater, past and present.

INDEX

X = *restaurant*, ⌧ = *hotel*

WHEREVER YOU TRAVEL, *H*ELP IS NEVER FAR AWAY.

From planning your trip to providing travel assistance along the way, American Express® Travel Service Offices are always there to help.

London

American Express Travel Service
1 Savoy Court
0171/240-1521

American Express Travel Service
78 Brompton Road
0171/584-6182

American Express Travel Service
111 Cheapside
0171/600-5522

American Express Travel Service
6 Haymarket
0171/930-4411

American Express Travel Service
89 Mount Street Mayfair
0171/499-4436

American Express Travel Service
102 Victoria Steet
0171/828-7411

Travel

http://www.americanexpress.com/travel

American Express Travel Service Offices are found in central locations throughout the United Kingdom.